Paul Willetts made his literary debut in 2003 with *Fear and Loathing in Fitzrovia*, a biography of the bohemian writer and dandy, Julian Maclaren-Ross. His second book was *North Soho 999*, a narrative non-fiction police procedural set in late 1940s London. He is also the author of *Members Only*, which was adapted into the Soho movie, *The Look of Love*, starring Steve Coogan, Anna Friel and Stephen Fry.

He has written for the *Independent, Daily Telegraph, Guardian, Independent on Sunday, Spectator, The Times*, and *TLS*.

RENDEZVOUS
at the Russian Tea Rooms

Paul Willetts

Constable • London

First published in Great Britain in 2015 by Constable

This paperback edition published in 2016 by Constable

1 3 5 7 9 10 8 6 4 2

A CIP catalogue record for this book
is available from the British Library.

ISBN: 978-1-4721-1987-2

Typeset in Century Schoolbook by Saxon Graphics Ltd, Derby
Printed and bound in Great Britain by CPI Group (UK) Ltd,
Croydon CR0 4YY

Papers used by Constable are from well-managed forests and other responsible sources.

MIX
Paper from
responsible sources
FSC
www.fsc.org FSC® C104740

Constable
is an imprint of
Little, Brown Book Group
Carmelite House
50 Victoria Embankment
London EC4Y 0DZ

An Hachette UK Company
www.hachette.co.uk

www.littlebrown.co.uk

For David and Judy
with much love and gratitude

'He wasn't certain that he wasn't being watched at this moment;
he wasn't certain that it wasn't right for him to be watched ...
And the watcher, was he watched?
He was haunted for a moment by the vision of an endless distrust.'
(Graham Greene, *The Confidential Agent*)

Contents

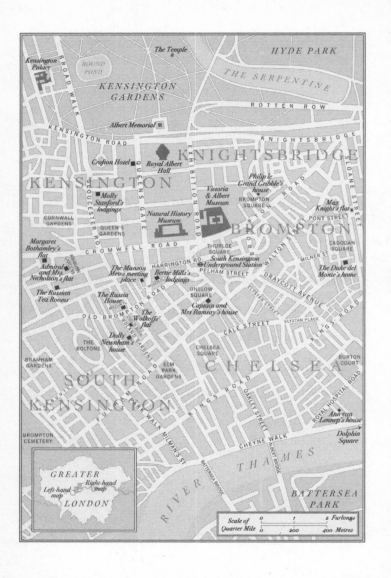

KENSINGTON PALACE

Kensington
Palace

BROAD
WALK

ROUND
POND

The Temple

KENSINGTON
GARDENS

HYDE PARK

THE SERPENTINE

ROTTEN ROW

KENSINGTON ROAD

Albert Memorial

KNIGHTSBRIDGE

Crofton Hotel

KENSINGTON

Royal Albert
Hall

QUEEN'S GATE

EXHIBITION ROAD

KNIGHTSBRIDGE

Philip le
Grand Gribble's
house

Molly
Stanford's
lodgings

GLOUCESTER RD.

Victoria
& Victoria
Museum

BROMPTON
SQUARE

SLOANE STREET

Max
Knight's flat

CORNWALL
GARDENS

QUEEN'S
GARDENS

Natural History
Museum

PONT STREET

BROMPTON

CADOGAN
SQUARE

Margaret
Bothamley's
flat

CROMWELL ROAD

THURLOE
SQUARE

WALTON STREET

MILNER ST

Admiral
and Mrs.
Nicholson's flat

HARRINGTON RD.

South Kensington
Underground Station

The Duke del
Monte's home

The Manson
Mews meeting
place

Bertie Mills's
lodgings

PELHAM STREET

DRAYCOTT AVENUE

The Russian
Tea Rooms

The Russia
House

ONSLOW
SQUARE

ELYSTAN STREET

The
Wolkoffs'
flat

Captain and
Mrs Ramsay's house

CALE STREET

ELYSTAN PLACE

KING'S ROAD

BRAMHAM
GARDENS

OLD BROMPTON ROAD

Dolly
Newnham's
house

THE
BOLTONS

CHELSEA
SQUARE

CHELSEA

BURTON
COURT

ELM
PARK
GARDENS

SOUTH

KENSINGTON

FULHAM ROAD

PARK WALK

MILMAN'S ST.

KING'S ROAD

OAKLEY STREET

ROYAL HOSPITAL ROAD

Ann van
Lennep's house

BROMPTON
CEMETERY

CHEYNE WALK

Dolphin
Square

BATTERSEA BRIDGE

ALBERT BRIDGE

RIVER

THAMES

BATTERSEA
PARK

GREATER

Left-hand
map

Right-hand
map

LONDON

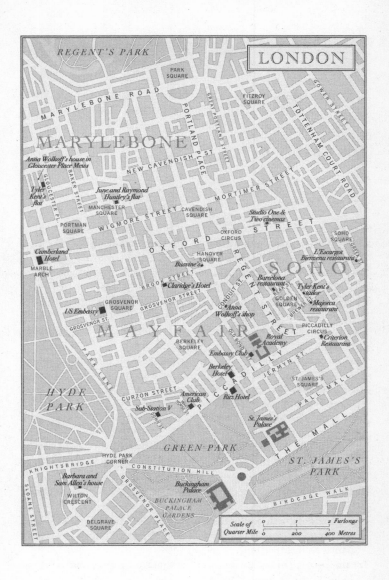

LONDON

REGENT'S PARK

PARK SQUARE

FITZROY SQUARE

MARYLEBONE ROAD

GOWER STREET

PORTLAND PLACE

GREAT PORTLAND STREET

TOTTENHAM COURT ROAD

MARYLEBONE

Anna Wolkoff's house in Gloucester Place Mews

NEW CAVENDISH ST

MORTIMER STREET

Tyler Kent's flat

June and Raymond Huntley's flat

MANCHESTER SQUARE

CAVENDISH SQUARE

GLOUCESTER PL

BAKER STREET

WIGMORE STREET

Studio One & Two cinemas

PORTMAN SQUARE

OXFORD CIRCUS

OXFORD STREET

SOHO SQUARE

Cumberland Hotel

HANOVER SQUARE

REGENT STREET

SOHO

L'Escargot Bienvenu restaurant

MARBLE ARCH

Busvine's

Barcelona restaurant

BEAK

GOLDEN SQUARE

Tyler Kent's tailor

BROOK STREET

Claridge's Hotel

GROSVENOR STREET

CONDUIT ST

BREWER

Majorca restaurant

GROSVENOR SQUARE

US Embassy

Anna Wolkoff's shop

PICCADILLY CIRCUS

GROSVENOR ST

MAYFAIR

OLD BOND ST

Criterion Restaurant

BERKELEY SQUARE

Royal Academy

PICCADILLY

JERMYN ST

PARK LANE

Embassy Club

Berkeley Hotel

ST. JAMES'S SQUARE

PALL MALL

HYDE PARK

CURZON STREET

American Club

Ritz Hotel

Sub-Station V

DOWN ST

St James's Palace

THE MALL

GREEN PARK

ST. JAMES'S PARK

HYDE PARK CORNER

KNIGHTSBRIDGE

CONSTITUTION HILL

Barbara and Sam Allen's house

WILTON CRESCENT

GROSVENOR PLACE

Buckingham Palace

BIRDCAGE WALK

SLOANE STREET

BELGRAVE SQUARE

BUCKINGHAM PALACE GARDENS

Scale of Quarter Mile

0   1   2 Furlongs

0   200   400 Metres

The Cast

Francis Aiken Sneath: MI5 colleague of Max Knight entrusted with supervising his investigation of Captain Ramsay and Anna Wolkoff.

Barbara Allen: wealthy, American-born friend of Anna Wolkoff and Tyler G. Kent.

Marjorie Amor: agent recruited by Max Knight to infiltrate Captain and Mrs Ramsay's fascist set.

Henry W. Antheil: friend of Tyler G. Kent at the US Embassy in Moscow.

Margaret Bothamley: one of Anna Wolkoff's fascist friends. During July 1939, Bothamley moved from London to Berlin.

Ambassador William C. Bullitt: Tyler G. Kent's first boss at the US Embassy in Moscow.

Louis-Ferdinand Céline: anti-Semitic French writer who became a friend of Anna Wolkoff.

Winston Churchill: British Cabinet minister. In May 1940 he was promoted to the role of Prime Minister in a coalition government.

Johnny Coast: young British fascist who was close to Anna Wolkoff.

Lord Cottenham: journalist, motor-racing driver and scientist who worked for MI5. He was the object of Anna Wolkoff's fruitless infatuation.

Irene Danischewsky: glamorous married woman with whom Tyler G. Kent had an affair.

Comte Antoine de Laubespin: former diplomat at the Belgian Embassy in London. He was a friend and political ally of Anna Wolkoff.

Comtesse Rasseta de Laubespin: friend of Anna Wolkoff and wife of Comte Antoine de Laubespin.

Hélène de Munck: Belgian-born agent who began working for MI5 in February 1940. On the instructions of Max Knight, she infiltrated Anna Wolkoff's clique.

Duke del Monte (aka Colonel Francisco Marigliano): Assistant Military Attaché at the Italian Embassy and friend of Anna Wolkoff.

Jimmy Dickson: long-standing friend of Max Knight who recruited him as an MI5 case-officer. Also wrote novels under the pen-name of 'Grierson Dickson'.

Princess Marina 'Mira' Dimitri Romanovsky Koutouzoff: once a close friend of Anna Wolkoff, she was the daughter-in-law of Grand Duchess Xenia of Russia.

Lady Lubov 'Luba' Fletcher: Russian émigré, married to a British aristocrat. She was a friend of both Tyler G. Kent and Eugène Sabline.

Bobby Gordon-Canning: friend of Anna Wolkoff. He served as Sir Oswald Mosley's foreign policy adviser and intermediary with Adolf Hitler.

Franklin C. Gowen: diplomat at the US Embassy in London.

Lord Ronald 'Ronnie' Graham: prominent British fascist who was a friend of Anna Wolkoff and the Duke of Windsor, formerly King Edward VIII.

Francis Hemming: friend of Anna Wolkoff and her parents. He was employed as Principal Assistant Secretary to the Cabinet Office, a job that required him to attend meetings of the War Cabinet.

Thomas Hosey: a friend of Captain Ramsay and regular at the Russian Tea Rooms. He belonged to both the British Union and the Right Club.

June Huntley: American wife of the actor, Raymond Huntley. She enjoyed a close, platonic friendship with Tyler G. Kent.

Raymond Huntley: British character actor who was, together with his wife, a friend of Tyler G. Kent.

Sylvester A. Huntowski: friend of Tyler G. Kent. He was employed as a maintenance man at the US embassies in Moscow and Berlin where he boosted his income through various shady enterprises.

Tatyana 'Tanya' Alexandrovna Ilovaiskaya: the daughter of a professor at Moscow University, she was Tyler G.

Kent's girlfriend for much of the time he was based in the Russian capital.

Derek Jackson: leading scientist and ardent Nazi who was married to Anna Wolkoff's friend, Pam Jackson.

Pam Jackson: daughter of Lord Redesdale and sister of Unity and Diana Mitford, the latter of whom was married to Sir Oswald Mosley. Pamela Jackson and Anna Wolkoff were old friends.

Herschel V. Johnson: senior diplomat at the US Embassy in London. He was a friend of Max Knight's boss, Guy Liddell.

Quentin Joyce: fascist activist whose brother was William Joyce.

William Joyce (aka Lord Haw-Haw): veteran British fascist who worked for Max Knight as an MI5 agent. Just before the outbreak of the war, he fled to Germany, from where he made propaganda broadcasts on behalf of the Nazis.

Sir Vernon Kell: friend of Max Knight and Director-General of MI5.

Sir Norman Kendal: the ACC (Assistant Commissioner/ Crime) for the Metropolitan Police, based at Scotland Yard.

Ambassador Joseph P. Kennedy: ran the US Embassy in London. He was the father of the future US President, John F. Kennedy.

Ann Kent: ageing Washington, DC-based mother of Tyler G. Kent.

Tyler G. Kent: suave, womanizing junior US Embassy employee.

Gwladys Knight: first wife of Max Knight, with whom she ran a hotel on the edge of Exmoor.

Lois Knight: second wife of Max Knight. She shared a flat with him in west London.

Charles Henry Maxwell 'Max' Knight: eccentric naturalist and MI5 case-officer who ran Section B5b, which specialized in counter-intelligence operations.

General Alexander Pavlovich Koutepoff: leader of the Russian Armed Services Union, a Russian émigré organization that collaborated with the Nazis.

Guy Liddell: as Deputy Head of B Division, the counter-espionage and counter-subversion arm of MI5, he was Max Knight's boss.

Jain Marmion Aitken: London-based fascist with links to Mussolini. She became one of Tyler G. Kent's girlfriends.

Ludwig Matthias: Jewish friend of Tyler G. Kent. Employed by a Stockholm-based company, he appears to have been working as a Soviet agent.

James McGuirk Hughes (alias P. G. Taylor): served as Chief of Intelligence for the British Union, the fascist movement led by Sir Oswald Mosley.

Bertie Mills: friend of Anna Wolkoff and energetic fascist campaigner.

Desmond Morton: the man who first recruited Max Knight to work for British intelligence. The two of them later became friends. Morton went on to be appointed as a personal assistant to Winston Churchill.

Sir Oswald Mosley: a one-time Labour Party Cabinet minister, he was the brother-in-law of Anna Wolkoff's friend, Pam Jackson. He led the British Union, previously the British Union of Fascists.

Donald H. Nichols: part of Tyler G. Kent's clique, he worked as Vice-Consul at the US Embassy in Moscow. He subsequently ran a sideline with Sylvester A. Huntowski as a currency smuggler.

Christabel Nicholson: wife of Admiral Nicholson and friend of Anna Wolkoff. Besides being an admirer of Adolf Hitler, she was involved with various British fascist groups.

Admiral Wilmot Nicholson: husband of Christabel Nicholson and friend of Admiral Wolkoff. Like his wife, Admiral Nicholson was a fascist zealot and devotee of Adolf Hitler.

Guy Miermans: Belgian-based fascist contact of Anna Wolkoff.

Jean Nieuwenhuys: diplomat at the Belgian Embassy in London who was a friend of Anna Wolkoff.

Detective Inspector Joseph Pearson: officer serving with Special Branch, the wing of the Metropolitan Police that investigated political subversion within Britain.

Queen Mary: widow of King George V. She was a friend of both Captain Ramsay and Anna Wolkoff's mother, Mme Vera Wolkoff.

Captain Archibald Henry Maule 'Jock' Ramsay: friend of Anna Wolkoff, founder of the fascist Right Club and one of the driving forces behind the Nordic League.

Ismay Ramsay: aristocratic wife of Captain Ramsay and fellow believer in the fascist cause.

Enid Riddell: close friend of Anna Wolkoff. She dabbled in rally driving and was also involved with the Right Club and Nordic League.

Franklin D. Roosevelt: President of the United States.

Eugène Sabline: a Soviet agent despite being the acknowledged spokesman for the White Russian community in London.

Valentina 'Valya' Scott: beautiful, Moscow-based friend of both Tyler G. Kent and his lover, Tatyana 'Tanya' Ilovaiskaya.

Nicholas Smirnoff: friend of Anna Wolkoff, who had worked as a photographer and moved in the same fascist circles.

Molly Stanford: regular at the Russian Tea Rooms and friend of Anna Wolkoff.

Ambassador Laurence A. Steinhardt: in charge of the US Embassy in Moscow.

Fay Taylour: famous speedway, motor-racing driver and fascist activist, who became part of the coterie around Captain Ramsay and Anna Wolkoff.

Dennis Wheatley: bestselling novelist and close friend of Max Knight.

Joan Wheatley: wife of Dennis Wheatley and friend of Max Knight.

Alexander Wolkoff: elder brother of Anna Wolkoff.

Alexandra 'Alice' Wolkoff: one of Anna Wolkoff's younger sisters.

Anna Wolkoff: fashion designer and former owner of Anna de Wolkoff Haute Couture Modes.

Gabriel Wolkoff: brother of Admiral Wolkoff.

Kyra Wolkoff: youngest sister of Anna Wolkoff.

Admiral Nikolai Wolkoff: husband of Vera Wolkoff and father of Anna, Alice, Alexander and Kyra Wolkoff. Before the Russian Revolution, he served as Naval Attaché at the Imperial Russian Embassy.

Vera Wolkoff: wife of Admiral Wolkoff and mother of Anna, Alice, Alexander and Kyra Wolkoff.

Xenia, Grand Duchess of Russia: sister to the late Tsar Nicholas II, cousin to the late King George V and, by common assent, senior surviving member of the Romanoff. dynasty. She was an old friend of Anna Wolkoff and her mother.

Bill Younger: son of Joan Wheatley and stepson of Dennis Wheatley. On graduating from Oxford University, he was recruited as an MI5 case-officer by Max Knight.

Part One

Gospel of Hate

You'll never get home alive.

That is the substance of the message sent to Tyler Gatewood Kent by his mother, who has heard persistent rumours of him being assassinated. She maintains the United States government will stop at nothing to prevent him from making public what he has discovered about a conspiracy involving the US President. Recently she cabled him pleading with him not to return to America, but he criticized her for becoming somewhat unbalanced in her judgement.

Ignoring her fears, he is at this minute among a forty-eight-strong contingent of transatlantic travellers. He had anticipated crossing the pond in a luxurious style befitting someone like him, instead of which he's quartered in the disagreeably crowded passenger section of the SS *Silveroak*, a giant British freighter trailing smoke from its single funnel. His ship is due in New Jersey later this morning – Tuesday 4 December, 1945, well over three months after Japan's surrender brought the Second World War to an end. Recurrent seasickness has as yet provided the only threat to Tyler's wellbeing during the voyage.

He's a lean, self-possessed thirty-four-year-old former prep-school athlete with suave, well-groomed good looks and a muscular physique. Enough lotion has been slathered on his short, straight chestnut hair to create a crisp side-parting. His face no longer possesses its previous fleshiness. A certain cold dignity is imparted by his unflinching blue-eyed gaze. He also exudes an air of conceit, of brusque prerogative, nourished by an august Virginian pedigree, a doting mother and a fancy education.

Already his ship has passed the Statue of Liberty and entered the Hudson River. Now the *Silveroak* is nosing its way up this broad but congested maritime highway. To the left, beyond water tousled by a chill breeze, lies the New Jersey coast, smeared with a dense, low-rise urban sprawl. To the right is a view Tyler hasn't seen for almost six years – downtown Manhattan, skyscrapers mobbing the Empire State Building.

Cordial yet detached in his dealings with other passengers, his voice higher-pitched than might be expected, he has spent a good deal of time pacing the deck, lost in thought. Even so, he hasn't yet formulated any long-term plans. In the short-term, though, he will be staying with friends in New York City. He and his mother will then go down South, where he hopes to recuperate and try to forget what he has been through. On the advice of his girlfriend, whom he last saw in London fourteen days ago, he intends to shun whatever press attention comes his way. That won't be easy, however, because he isn't just another anonymous soldier or airman returning home from the battlefields and shattered cities of Europe. He is famous for the crucial role he played in a story that made front-page news around the world, a story that validates the shop-soiled adage about truth being stranger than fiction, a story that one leading American newspaper has already hailed as the greatest spy story of the war.

Just before 10 a.m. Tyler's ship approaches the warehouses, cranes and piers of Hoboken. Little by little the *Silveroak*, hull lapped by sewage-darkened water, rumbles alongside the third of these piers. Soon the gangway is lowered.

Thuggish men, who could be mistaken for gun-toting bit-part players in a Hollywood crime movie, oversee the dockers set to unload the vessel's cargo. But first a posse of uniformed Customs officials boards the ship.

Unlike his fellow passengers, Tyler isn't permitted ashore. He has to wait for over an hour before being escorted onto the pier by Customs officers.

Always a natty dresser, he is wearing a thick, double-breasted, navy-blue overcoat. It's buttoned against the cold. One of his pockets is pregnant with letters from his mother, written to him while he was overseas. Under his arm he carries a small portfolio. In his spare hand he clutches a fedora that might otherwise have been flipped off by the wind. He also has with him a temporary passport, issued by the US Embassy in London.

Guiding Tyler towards the weathered, two-storey wooden shed that runs most of the pier's length is an ageing, thickset Customs official. As Tyler marches confidently into the building, there's a flicker of movement across his peripheral vision. Seemingly unaware of the person taking aim at him, Tyler breaks into a sly, narrow-eyed smile, the expression of someone who has been in a tight corner yet believes he has emerged intact.

Six-and-a-half years earlier ...

1

On Tuesday 23 May, 1939, a diminutive, slim-waisted woman was heading for an 8 p.m. event at Caxton Hall. Among London's best-known venues for political rallies, exhibitions and registry office weddings, it lay within easy reach of where she lived and worked. Thanks to the warm sunshine, she could have been forgiven for imagining she had somehow skipped a few weeks and advanced into midsummer.

Her name was Anna Wolkoff (pronounced 'Volkoff') though she liked to introduce herself as 'Miss Anna *de* Wolkoff', the prefix to her surname projecting an aura of Gallic refinement. In keeping with this affectation, sometimes favoured by Russians of her pedigree, she rarely allowed herself to be seen wearing anything other than an understatedly chic, Parisian-style black dress. She made a habit of pinning a brooch just below its neckline.

The colour of Anna's dresses conveyed her politics, black shirts and blouses being the uniform of Italian and German fascists, not to mention their émigré Russian counterparts. Until a few years ago, such garments had also been worn by the so-called 'Blackshirts' – the British Union of Fascists, recently renamed the British Union.

Anna's discreetly elegant dress sense jarred with her bodily inelegance, a look of chastened middle age having lately supplanted her former girlish prettiness. Thirty-six years old now, she had a wide, high-cheekboned Slavic face. It incorporated a snub nose, lips as tight as a freshly stitched buttonhole and soulful green eyes, accessorized by tapering, vigorously tweezered eyebrows. Her features were framed by unruly dark auburn hair, which she was inclined to chivvy into a shortish, permanent-waved *coiffure*. Except for applying a Cupid's bow of lipstick, she tended to refrain from using make-up, not even a couple of dabs of rouge to assuage the startled pastiness of her complexion.

Further diminishing her already circumscribed allure was her stomping, resolute gait, immune to the deportment lessons she'd taken as a child. More than two decades on from those, Anna's life had been unravelling. Her troubles gave credence to that old superstition about opals bringing bad luck. A great friend of hers had, after all, paid to have an opal set into the centre of the ring she wore.

Whatever the origin of her problems, there was no disputing that 1939 hadn't started well for her. She had been given no alternative but to shut down Anna de Wolkoff Haute Couture Modes, the West End shop that sold her own creations – frocks, suits, hats, jumpers, evening-gowns, children's clothes and even plastic fashion jewellery. During its much-publicized four-year existence, her shop had transformed her into a fashion-world celebrity, fame reinforcing her belief in her gifts as a *couturier*.

The decision to wind up her business had been motivated by the discovery that her financial backer, Major Philip le Grand Gribble, wouldn't be sinking any more money into a loss-making enterprise. Her resultant feelings of anxiety, humiliation and disenchantment, threaded with anger, had surely contributed to the whirlwind deterioration in her looks. But the collapse of her business wasn't her only source of angst.

Memories of what happened to General Alexander Koutepoff still haunted her. Ranked among the most prominent of the so-called White Russians – the anti-Communist exiles – he used to be the leader of the Russian Armed Services Union, an organization that sought to depose the Communist regime in his native country. His group ran a network of espionage and terrorist cells within Russia, cells that performed missions for Germany's fascist government.

One Sunday morning in January 1930, the General had embarked on a solitary stroll through the seventh *arrondisse-ment* of Paris. When he reached the end of the street where he lived, a limousine pulled up beside him. A policeman got out and handed Koutepoff a document summoning him to police headquarters. Clearly suspicious about the provenance of this, Koutepoff wavered.

Bang on cue, another officer strode up and assured the General that he really *was* needed at headquarters. So Koutepoff ducked into the limousine, whereupon he was sedated with chloroform and driven away. Followed by a taxi carrying two accomplices, the limousine sped towards the Normandy coast. As a precaution, curtains had apparently been nailed across its windows and the inside handles had been amputated from its rear doors.

Late that afternoon the vehicles parked on an isolated beach. Two men stepped out of the limousine and lugged the sedated General over to a waiting motorboat. It then raced out to a Soviet cargo ship anchored off the coast.

Upwards of half-a-dozen people witnessed various stages of Koutepoff's abduction. There were even witnesses to him being manhandled onto the motorboat.

Getting on for a month after his disappearance, a bottle was found bobbing in the harbour at the town of Port-en-Bessin. The bottle contained a message purportedly written by him. It claimed that he was being detained aboard a Soviet ship. Reports seeped through to the British press about how he had later been taken ashore in Leningrad, sent to Moscow, imprisoned in the notorious Lubyanka jail and tortured by the secret police, who wanted him to disclose the names of White Russian agents.

In response to these articles, the Soviets had invited a delegation of western journalists to inspect the Lubyanka. Koutepoff was said to have been smuggled out of jail on a stretcher just before their arrival, then loaded onto a heavily guarded train and transferred to a monastery used for holding political prisoners. One could only speculate on the precise nature of his unenviable destiny. What remained beyond doubt was that none of his friends, family or associates heard from him again.

His abduction, so extensively chronicled in the press, had terrifying implications for Anna Wolkoff. Their potency was magnified by the disappearance of Koutepoff's successor at the Russian Armed Services Union, and by a spate of other kidnappings and attempted kidnappings of Russian expatriates. No less ferocious than Koutepoff in her hatred of Communism,

Anna regarded herself as another significant target for the Soviets. Camouflaged by the reassuring familiarity of the London streets, a gang of Soviet kidnappers might be lying in wait for her this evening. They might just be biding their time until they could drug her with a chloroform-soaked handkerchief or crack her over the head.

2

Together with around 500 other people, including a contingent of Germans, Anna exchanged the sunlit streets for a ribbon of cramped Victorian anterooms and long, windowless corridors, illuminated by the nicotine-stained glow of gaslight. Stewards with Union Jack armbands were positioned en route into the larger of Caxton Hall's two auditoria.

As a rule, the steward asked everyone to provide a password or vouch for guests, yet tonight was different. In theory at least, anyone could attend. They just had to purchase a sixpenny ticket. But the stewards had already barred several people. A couple of those had even been violently manhandled. Still, the atmosphere didn't feel as overwrought as it had at last week's meeting. On that occasion a suspected spy – working for the Communists or maybe the police – had been thrown out.

Roughly the size of a tennis court, the main auditorium featured a small stage and row-upon-row of fold-out seats, overlooked by a balcony. Anna's friend and contemporary, a striking blonde named Enid Riddell, joined her in the tightly packed audience. Enid – whom Anna had known for more than a decade – exhibited a sheen of well-bred poise, only tarnished by a slight stammer during moments of nervousness. Otherwise her infrequent utterances were self-assured and succinct. Tonight she had a much younger man with her. Barely out of his teens, Enid's escort was an ex-public schoolboy with whom she'd been knocking round a great deal lately, their relationship nurtured by a shared enthusiasm for motor racing and fascism.

Being nearly four inches shorter than Enid, Anna needed to tilt her head if she wanted to look at her friend as they were talking. Unlike Enid, she would maintain a digressive flow of animated chatter. She often expressed her opinions with blustering conviction that was, for her and other devotees of astrology, typical of those born under the star sign of Scorpio. Counterpointed by florid gestures that hinted at her temperamental nature, Anna's gruff, smoker's voice bore the accent and inflections of her native Russia, even though she hadn't visited the country in well over two decades. Her clipped delivery also carried the imprint of childhood elocution lessons.

Masses of topics were available this evening to sustain Anna's chatter. If she wanted to keep things light and inconsequential, she could gloat over the number of people there. Almost double the usual attendance. She could gossip about mutual friends. She could natter about the latest goings-on at the Russian Tea Rooms, the café-cum-restaurant run by her parents, with whom she had a close relationship. She could discuss the books she'd been reading. She could air her belief in spiritualism, clairvoyance and the supernatural. Or she could provide Enid with news of the charity ball she'd been helping to coordinate. The event – little more than five weeks away – was being held to raise money to fund summer camps in France and England for the children of poor Russian émigrés. Anna and the rest of its small organizing committee were rounding up raffle prizes as well as compiling a programme of music and ballet. Unquestionably, the highlight would be a performance by Anton Dolin and another of the stars of the Ballet Russe de Monte Carlo, who had agreed to dance a *pas de deux* from *Les Sylphides*.

Anna loved talking about the famous, influential and titled people in her orbit, people equipped to furnish her with all sorts of tittle-tattle. Just for starters there was Queen Mary, widow of King George V and mother of the current monarch. There was Queen Mary's son, King George VI, who had himself been so kind to Anna's father. There was Grand Duchess Xenia of Russia, sister to the late Tsar and, by common agreement, senior surviving member of the Russian royal family. There was the Duke del Monte, Assistant Military Attaché at the

Italian Embassy, someone about whom Anna frequently talked to Enid. And there was Mrs Wallis Simpson, now Duchess of Windsor, wife of the recently abdicated King Edward VIII. Mrs Simpson rated as perhaps the most notable of the clients at Anna's shop. Anna was fond of trotting out the line about how the erstwhile King – since appointed Duke of Windsor – hadn't fallen in love with Mrs Simpson. No, he'd fallen in love with the *clothes* Anna had designed for his wife-to-be.

If Anna was in a more serious mood, she could make one of her anxious references to being kidnapped by Soviet agents, a subject to which she returned obsessively in her dialogues with Enid. Despite sharing Anna's fearfulness about Communism, euphemistically described in that circle as 'the Red Menace', Enid treated her friend's angst with dismissive incredulity. Frightful things like General Koutepoff's kidnapping, Enid argued, simply didn't occur in London.

Equally serious but much more topical as a conversational gambit was the possibility of war between Britain and Germany. Prominent advertisements for gasmasks, bomb-shelters, water-pumps and other Air Raid Precaution equipment had been appearing in the newspapers. Beneath captions such as 'It May Never Happen but You've Got to Be Prepared', there had also been articles telling one how to remodel one's dining-room into a gas-proof refuge.

Yet more grist to Anna's conversational mill was offered by the theme of tonight's meeting – 'Red Control in the Press and the BBC'. She worried that the Communists would take over in Britain just as they had done in Russia twenty-one years earlier. By a stroke of good fortune Anna, her father and her three siblings – Alexander, Kyra and Alice – had been in London when the Bolsheviks had seized power, otherwise they might not have been alive now. They might easily have come to the same violent end as the Tsar and his family. Anna's mother, who was in Russia at the time of the revolution, only escaped at the last moment, fleeing the country with Grand Duchess Xenia and the Tsar's mother.

Any awkward lulls in the conversation between Anna and Enid could always be filled by speculating on the identity of tonight's guest speaker. The organizers of these meetings liked to keep the audience guessing on that score. In all probability, though, the speaker would be one of the regulars. Perhaps Anna and her companions would have another chance to hear the man who recently sparked such applause by urging the audience to disseminate what he called 'the Gospel of Hate' towards the Jews. Or, perhaps, they would be treated to a blast of blood-and-thunder oratory from the leader of the National Socialist League, whose scarred face – previously sliced from mouth to ear by an anti-fascist demonstrator – made him stand out from the rest of the audience. He had given a speech earlier that month about how the Jew-corrupted newspapers pandered to Soviet Russia, how Britain should follow Nazi Germany's example, how thousands of young fascists were about to be conscripted into the British Army, and how those young men should, when the time comes, put their military training to good use by overthrowing the government.

3

The big moment had arrived. In his role as master of ceremonies, a friend of Anna's took his place on stage. He was the Honourable Captain Archibald Henry Maule Ramsay, MP, known to her as plain old 'Jock'. Thin and dapper, he was in his mid-forties with receding, greased down hair that gave the impression of fingers grasping the rim of a precipice. He sported a neat black moustache, a beaky profile and a straight-backed, commanding posture. No surprise that he had been an officer in the Coldstream Guards.

He was one of the driving forces behind the Nordic League, which had staged tonight's meeting. A colleague of his on its governing council boasted about it being the sole British fascist organization in which the German dictator, Adolf Hitler, took a personal interest.

Jock had come straight from another meeting, where he and a group of his Nordic League colleagues had, it was no secret, been lobbying other MPs. He was someone whom Anna admired tremendously – so much so that she chattered about him on a regular basis. The depth of her admiration even motivated her to give voluntary support to him as a chauffeur and secretary. Often she carried documents on which the two of them were collaborating.

From the stage at Caxton Hall, Jock began his opening speech. He had an assured and patrician manner. At first he stuck to the avowed topic of the meeting, but his attacks on Communism shaded into appreciative allusions to Nazi Germany and disparaging comments about the Jews. These incited the audience to dispense shouts of endorsement and cries of 'PJ!' – 'Perish Judah!', a slogan that could be seen daubed on walls. For Anna and others who had spent time in Germany over the past decade, the slogan carried an echo of the Nazi chant of '*Jude verrecke!*' – 'Die miserably, Judah!'

No sooner had Anna's friend relinquished centre-stage than he was replaced by A. K. Chesterton,[1] the gaunt-faced, jug-eared cousin of the late author G. K. Chesterton. Funnily enough, G. K. had been part of the line-up of visiting lecturers at the Architectural Association Schools where Anna had been a student.

Bestowed with rhetorical panache, A. K. Chesterton spoke in what was termed an Oxford accent, every syllable negotiated with finely stitched precision that would have impressed Anna's elocution mistress. He delivered a long anti-Semitic diatribe. Not the casual and widespread anti-Semitism that passed almost unnoticed in those days: the quips, the contemptuous remarks about Jewish refugees from Nazi Germany, dubbed 'refu-Jews'. What Chesterton said was much more belligerent. Its targets were what he called 'greasy little Jew-boy pornographers', as well as a successful Jewish businessman whom he accused of being one of 'the trumpeters and standard-bearers of Armageddon', striving to bring about war with Germany.

The crowd around Anna responded with euphoric approval. Edging towards the climax to his speech, Chesterton called on the audience to form an anti-Jewish paramilitary unit and to rally behind a single leader.

Greeting his proposal was a chorus of 'Mosley! Mosley! Mosley!' This referred to the former Labour Party Cabinet minister Sir Oswald Mosley, brother-in-law of a friend of Anna, and leader of the British Union.

Have our people, Chesterton concluded, the necessary spiritual and mental toughness to rise in revolt against this infinite wickedness? He said that he himself was a revolutionary. And he was certain that nothing short of revolution would suffice. 'Into the streets!' he bellowed. 'Use the lamp-posts. That is the only way to deal with the Jew. In that way alone should we find ultimate peace and salvation.'

Loud clapping and cheering resonated round the auditorium as he sat down. His speech contained much for Anna to applaud, the vehemence of his anti-Semitism matching her dogmatic prejudice, so out of kilter with her eye for the subtleties of colour and texture.

Personal resentment feeding political commitment, she blamed the Jews for aspects of her life that had gone awry. She even blamed competition from rival Jewish-owned businesses for the demise of her shop. Yet the Jewish background of Leon Trotsky and other renowned Communists also led her to equate Jews with the Soviet Union. Nazi ideology gave her a convenient means of reconciling the contradiction implicit within her views. To the Nazis, who overlooked the Soviet Union's own anti-Semitism, Communism was a racial conspiracy, rendering Jewish Communists and capitalists co-conspirators.

So intense were Anna's feelings about the Jews that she blamed them for every international problem. Above all, she blamed them for destroying the Tsarist society into which she had been born and for inflicting the consequent misfortunes on her and her family, not least their exile from their home country, precise memories of which she could still recall with swooning, nostalgic delight.

4

In the presence of Anna and the rest of the substantial audience gathered at Caxton Hall, her friend Jock Ramsay introduced that evening's guest speaker. Not the leader of the National Socialist League but the monocled ex-Chairman of the Spanish branch of the British Chamber of Commerce. Though he was meant to be that evening's top-of-the-bill attraction, he couldn't match A. K. Chesterton's theatrical elan. Speaking in more measured tones, he reflected on the Spanish Civil War, which had just culminated in the creation of a fascist dictatorship under General Franco, someone he regarded as being 'possessed of more than his fair share of the nobler qualities of mankind'.

When the guest speaker had finished, Jock got up from his seat on stage and read out a letter of support from a Labour MP who apologized for not being there. Jock then rounded off the meeting by saying, 'We have heard a most inspiring speech from Mr Chesterton. I am not an apostle of violence, but the time has arrived for action, and I solemnly state that, if our present method fails, I will not hesitate to use another. The Jewish menace is a real menace. The time at our disposal is getting short ...' Now was the moment for a dramatic pause before Jock administered the *coup de grâce*. 'Take with you a resolution in your hearts to remove the Jew menace from our land.'

His closing call to action couldn't fail to strike a chord with Anna, not just because of her anti-Semitism, but also because of her belief in the power of collective action. It was a belief pithily expressed by an old dictum she sometimes quoted – 'Union is Force'. Had her parents' generation taken that to heart and not been so passive, she believed there was every chance she might not have found herself in exile.

Meetings of the Nordic League customarily ended with a rendition of 'The Horst Wessel' song, a Nazi anthem that would trigger a ripple of fascist salutes. Since tonight's gathering was – nominally at least – open to the public, its organizers preferred to round things off with an uncontentious display of patriotism, represented by 'God Save the King'.

After the music had subsided, Anna's Nordic League colleagues liked to distribute Nazi propaganda, sent to them from Germany. Stallholders also plied the departing crowd with copies of various anti-Semitic books, leaflets and newspapers, including *Action*, official mouthpiece of the British Union. Most prominently displayed of these publications was *The*

Protocols of the Elders of Zion, which expounded the vision of a worldwide Jewish conspiracy pursued over centuries.

To Anna, whose father had owned a copy since she was a child growing up in St Petersburg, *The Protocols* – a notorious forgery by the Tsarist secret police – was revelatory. Under its influence, she identified latterday conspirators in positions of power across Europe, her sense of dread surely fortified by her interest in the occult, which perceived hidden forces and arcane links beneath the skin of everyday reality. She had even reached the conclusion that the current Pope was a Jewish infiltrator. No country, she argued, could prosper until it followed the example of Nazi Germany and its courageous leader, who had already implemented vigorous anti-Semitic policies.

Within the milling throng after this evening's speeches had finished, Anna encountered someone she had not seen for more than six months – an upper-class, polo-playing thirty year old, briefly employed as a sales assistant at her shop. Establishments of that kind were famous for hiring decorative society girls, the theory being that their presence would attract their rich friends.

Instead of adopting the disdainful poses favoured by staff in comparable shops, Anna and her assistants had tried to make business feel more like pleasure. She had been on relaxed terms with her staff. As they helped with clothes-fittings, she would reminisce about the days when she too had been employed in a junior position by a London fashion house.

The presence of Anna's former sales assistant at a meeting of the Nordic League was not entirely unexpected, given that the woman mingled with the likes of Bobby Gordon-Canning. Bobby – who owned the West End building that had housed Anna's shop – was a British Union stalwart. For a while now he had been serving as Sir Oswald Mosley's foreign policy adviser and go-between with Hitler, travelling to Munich and Berlin to meet the Führer, whom he lauded as 'a fine man, a charming man'.

Exploiting her fortuitous encounter with her ex-employee, Anna invited the woman to join the Right Club, a new organization set up by Jock Ramsay. It was dedicated to exposing and combating the alleged international conspiracy about which they had just heard. Many of the club's members had voiced fears that their private lives and careers would suffer if their involvement became public, so Jock had pledged to keep its membership list secret. Anna's one-time employee wrote her name, address and telephone number on the enrolment form that Anna gave her. The form wasn't much bigger than a bus ticket. Before leaving Caxton Hall, Anna enlisted both her ex-employee and Enid in the Right Club.

Ultimately a failure in her role as a businesswoman, Anna was proving more successful as a recruiting sergeant for Jock's new movement.

5

From the rear of the US Embassy in central Moscow, Tyler G. Kent could peer down at a drab courtyard that functioned as a car park. He was currently assigned to the embassy's Translation Section. Its offices were on the fourth floor of Mokhovaya House, a six-storey building standing shoulder-to-shoulder with an outpost of Moscow State University. Handily for Tyler, his workplace shared the same floor as the Commissary, from where he could purchase tins of specially imported provisions. These enlivened what was, particularly for someone of his gourmet tastes, an otherwise monotonous diet. He and his colleagues, for the most part, dined on Soviet tinned goods, complemented by limited and irregular supplies of fresh produce from local street-markets – black bread, tomatoes, lettuce, plus potatoes no bigger than pool balls.

Dietary stodginess accounted for the way his face had filled out. Of late, he'd been wearing a dark, meticulously barbered moustache that gave him the appearance of someone older than his late twenties. The impression of early-onset middle age was leavened by the modishness of his clothes. For the spring weather he had a light, single-breasted suit with shoulder pads, wide lapels and a two-button jacket.

Aside from his first few months in Moscow, Tyler had been based at Mokhovaya House since arriving in the Soviet Union during the opening months of 1934. Leased from the Russians, it was one of countless new buildings dotting the city, which resembled a giant construction site. Mokhovaya House possessed sufficient floor-space to accommodate not just offices but living quarters for most of its American staff. No less than thirty Russians – working as switchboard operators, economic advisers, domestic servants, lift attendants, caretakers, librarians, translators, messengers, typists and interpreters – also lived there. Tyler's Russian colleagues occupied the basement, the walls of which were papered with Communist posters.

At Princeton University, where he spent a couple of years before concluding his undergraduate education in Europe, he had been exposed to a slew of similar propaganda about Communist Russia. Some of it emanated from members of the teaching staff who had undertaken Soviet-sponsored tours of the country. They gave enthusiastic lectures on what they had seen, on the country's economic progress, and on the energy and enthusiasm of the regime. Items appeared in the college newspapers, extolling the country's new education system, its improved housing conditions, its prevalent harmony and happiness. Other articles compared the American political system unfavourably with its Russian equivalent. And there were also student trips to the Soviet Union. Voluble in his opinions about most things, not just politics, Tyler had, like many youthful idealists of the period, been persuaded that the brand of Communism espoused by the Bolshevik movement was dramatically advancing the lives of a hitherto oppressed people.

Shortly after returning from the Sorbonne in Paris, at which he had studied Russian as part of Princeton's exchange programme, Tyler had heard that the US government would be opening diplomatic relations with the Soviet Union. William C. Bullitt, freshly designated as first US Ambassador to Communist Russia, was signing up staff for the new embassy in Moscow. Tyler wanted to work there, but the fact that he had not sat the entrance examination for the Foreign Service, America's diplomatic corps, reduced his chances of being hired. Due to the economic depression and attendant government cutbacks, the examination had, however, been suspended until further notice, so Tyler had used the ensuing hiatus to strengthen his qualifications. He had enrolled on courses in history and economics at Georgetown University's School of Foreign Service. Impatient to get to the Soviet Union, he abandoned his studies and applied for a clerical job at the soon-to-be-created Moscow embassy.

Without any background in clerical work, even a job like that would ordinarily have been beyond Tyler. Fortunately for him, the US Ambassador designate wasn't a career diplomat and chose not to abide by Foreign Service protocol.

Tyler secured a place on Ambassador Bullitt's team with the aid of a clutch of impressive testimonials, which exploited his family's considerable political leverage. These came from the Secretary of State, the Senator for Virginia, the Assistant Secretary of State and a previous head of the US Consular Service. In the light of all the effort required to land a place at the Moscow embassy, there was something ironic about Tyler's present dissatisfaction with his job.

Officially, he had been engaged as a Junior Clerk. At the outset he'd worked on reception in the consulate, but he had since been moved to the Translation Section, where he could even more effectively deploy his prodigious talent as a linguist. He was fluent in Russian, French, Spanish and Italian. Over and above that, he had some Icelandic and a sound knowledge of the majority of the Slavic languages. Through lessons from Truda Ganghadaran, a young Czech woman whom he had met at a party, German was being added to his repertoire.[2] Just a handful of the embassy's Foreign Service officers spoke Russian, never mind all those other languages.

In the main, Tyler's senior colleagues were fellow prep school and Ivy League graduates who were reluctant to socialize with subordinates like him. For someone like Tyler, drawn to the *beau monde*, to luxury hotels, made-to-measure suits and classy restaurants, exile from his peers could not be anything except a cause of nagging irritation.

Few of the higher-ups cared for Tyler in any event, his attitude towards them being polite if patronizing. He combined intellectual arrogance with a sense of social superiority, born out of his mother's pride in their forebears who had held high office in the Confederacy during the Civil War and fought for their country in successive wars.[3] Clerical work was, he gave the impression, unworthy of a Southern gentleman, though he had belatedly knuckled down to his duties. By way of consolation for his present status and, perhaps, to remind the higher-ups that this was just a fleeting anomaly, he liked to make references to the important people he knew in Washington, DC, Secretary of State Cordell Hull among them.

Tyler's responsibilities at Mokhovaya House extended from translating the Ambassador's press communiqués right through to preparing English-language summaries of pertinent stories appearing in foreign newspapers and periodicals. Everyone in his department clocked up punishing hours. Provided he set his mind to it, Tyler had the facility to concentrate for extended periods and, with minimal effort, assimilate the salient points from a document.

In the Translation Section, his colleagues included Gene Pressly, a near-contemporary who was also a gifted linguist. Pressly had until recently been stationed at the US Embassy in Paris, where he had fraternized with writers and artists from the Left Bank bohemian set.[4] An idealistic upholder of the principles of the Russian Revolution, he would deliver well-argued critiques of international capitalism. These no doubt needled the equally opinionated Tyler, first-hand exposure to the dismaying realities of the Soviet Union having turned him into a vocal anti-Communist.

He had grown to believe that, far from being the classless society advocated by Communism, the Soviet Union was somewhere 'medieval despotism' flourished. These newfound beliefs were palpable in his use of a dismissive American nickname for the Soviets – 'Bolos', short for 'Bolsheviks'. His contempt for Communism was so acute that he had become sympathetic to the fascist regimes in Germany and Italy. Yet he retained an obsession with the country outside his office windows.

Like Gene Pressly, Tyler's skills as a linguist were not reflected by his pay-grade, which placed him just a single rung from the foot of the eight-step clerical salary-scale. He was earning less than men with only high-school diplomas to their names. That gave him reason to feel resentful towards his employers, resentful enough to set aside his fascist sympathies and supplement his income by peddling US government secrets to the Soviets.[5]

While there was nothing secret about the material Tyler handled, his work gave him access to the binders often strewn across neighbouring desks. These brought together a haphazard cross-section of confidential telegrams, sent or received via the embassy's Code Room. Humdrum messages about visa applications could be found side by side with important cables pertaining to the tense diplomatic situation in Eastern Europe.

Sight of this privileged information was sure to consolidate the self-importance Tyler radiated. But he did not restrict himself to reading the embassy's paperwork. He also got into the habit of photographing and making illicit transcripts of it. To cap these activities, he had started helping himself to material from the bundles of documents destined for the basement furnace. As yet, his thefts appear to have gone unnoticed.

6

Above the main entrance was a large red and green neon sign: 'DOLPHIN SQUARE LETTING OFFICE. EUROPE'S MOST COMPLETELY EQUIPPED FLATS.'

Presiding over a quiet stretch of riverside road close to the centre of London, Dolphin Square consisted of sixteen interconnected blocks, arranged round a central quadrangle. This newish development was meant to be purely residential, but Charles Henry Maxwell Knight – better known as Max – had flouted the rules by setting up offices there.

Max was a tall, polished thirty-nine year old whose passion for the sport of fencing had helped to maintain his sinewy athleticism. Watchful and more than a trifle self-conscious, he possessed the pale-eyed vigilance of a bird of prey. The other prominent components of his elongated face were a bulbous-tipped nose and a full head of dark hair that had lately undergone partial silvering. Often a pipe jutted from the side of his mouth, inhibiting the skewed curvature of his captivatingly boyish smile and ensuring that his slipstream was scented with the musty aroma of tobacco.

Dressed in a mackintosh, rumpled tweeds and a brown trilby, Max could have passed for one of Dolphin Square's aristocratic residents, just back from a few days in the country. An Army captain's dress uniform was another of his favoured costumes. He told people that he was employed at the War Office. Yet he wasn't really based in Whitehall. Nor was he in the Army. His sole experience of military life had come as a teenage midshipman in the Royal Navy Reserve during the closing stages of what was still being called 'the Great War'.

He worked in a section of Dolphin Square named Hood House. As he crossed the foyer, he was liable to bump into other so-called 'Dolphinians'. Where circumstances permitted, he would enthral children with his repertoire of adroitly performed conjuring tricks.

A smooth, almost silent lift was on hand to carry him up to the sixth floor. Through the door marked '608' lay an oblong hall that had cork-flooring, which muffled his footsteps. Leading off the hall were four rooms that came with graceful, antique-style furniture. Max's flat incorporated a lounge, a tiny bathroom, a windowless modern kitchen and a thickly carpeted bedroom dominated by a double bed. The far from spacious lounge, from where he could see the roof garden on top of the residents' sports pavilion and restaurant, provided the majority of his office space.

For £145-per-annum, sufficient to rent an entire house elsewhere in London, the flat was leased under his brother-in-law's name. Lest anyone started making enquiries about the place, that name had been added to the Electoral Register. Such attention to detail was a crucial facet of Max's job.

7

There was something deceptively innocent about the way Tyler's girlfriend smiled. As she did so, her cheeks swelled, her heavy-lidded green eyes narrowed and her lips exposed perfect teeth. Small and trim with a pointed little bust, sheathed in tight sweaters, she could look beautiful when she wanted, make-up distilling her sleek attractiveness. Typically her dark hair was brushed away from her face and cut a few inches shy of her shoulders.

In contrast to most of the Russian women on the crowded pavements of Moscow, she had fashionable clothes. Her pale, short-sleeved dress, worn with a steeply angled white beret, would have drawn admiring glances on the streets of New York or Paris, never mind the Soviet capital, where most women were so drably attired. But there was no need for Tyler's girlfriend to show off her wardrobe. Not now. Not while they were in bed together.

She was the daughter of a professor at Moscow State University. Her friends knew her as Buba, Hebrew for 'little doll', a nickname that suggests she was Jewish. Tyler had his own more mundane pet-name for her, perfect for such intimate moments as this. He called her Tanya, derivative of Tatyana. Tatyana Alexandrovna Ilovaiskaya.

Whenever they got the chance, she and Tyler – who treated women with urbane Southern courtliness, undiluted by his interest in pornography and sadomasochistic sex – would stay in bed during the mornings, irrespective of whether they were at his flat or hers. Tanya had a nicely furnished place. It occupied a turreted seven-storey building with balconies looking across a picturesque district of small shops, domed churches and ornate but crumbling old blocks that had evaded the demolition crews so active elsewhere in Moscow.

Tyler's girlfriend shared her flat with Valentina Scott, a glamorous, English-speaking twenty-five-year-old Russian friend who went by the name of Valya. Along with two infant daughters, one of whom was about to join the Bolshoi's ballet school, Valya's surname perpetuated the memory of a failed marriage to a black American dancer, famous in Moscow for performing the lindy-hop. Valya and Tanya were based just a short drive from Mokhovaya House, where Tyler had a top-floor flat. Number 29. His flat was only a couple of floors above the Translation Section. Those floors commonly resonated to the sound of gramophone records. *Imported* records because Russian ones became scratched and unplayable in next to no time. A special favourite among Tyler's colleagues was Louis Armstrong's 'Shadrack', its vocals backed by a sinuous instrumental that could be hard to shake off.

Being near the bottom of the embassy's hierarchy, Tyler was not entitled to one of the bigger, more comfortable flats. He had to make do with a studio flat instead. This came with an array of unattractive government-issue metal furniture and a kitchenette where a Russian servant was available to prepare meals for him.

Everyone assumed that the servants reported to the NKVD – an acronym for what was rendered in English as the Soviet People's Commissariat of Internal Affairs, just a long-winded and euphemistic name for the secret police. But Tyler's domestic set-up could have been worse. At least he hadn't, unlike so many lower-ranking staff, been saddled with a roommate. He could have been paired off with a member of the embassy's catalogue of depressives. Two of Tyler's fellow clerks who were rooming together had reached the point where they'd strung a rope down the middle of their quarters and agreed not to cross it.

Another good thing about his accommodation was the panoramic vista commanded by his flat. It faced the colossal redbrick flank of the Kremlin, screened until lately by a row of old buildings. Through the gap between this and other architectural survivors, he could look right across Red Square. On the far side was the Church of St Basil, its distant, multiple onion-domed facade evocative of a fairytale palace.

For the frequent parades held in the Square, Tyler and Tanya had the equivalent of a grandstand seat. Under the gaze of Josef Stalin and the rest of the Communist leadership, a river of people and vehicles, accompanied by military bands playing 'The Internationale', flowed across it in geometric formations. By nightfall, though, Red Square was eerily quiet, footsteps reverberating between the buildings, floodlights illuminating giant billboards of Stalin and various Soviet heroes. A Lincoln or some other limousine could every so often be glimpsed gliding to or from the Kremlin, curtains across the side and rear windows preserving the anonymity of the occupants.

Tyler was not, sad to say, always in a position to savour his view of Red Square. On account of the shortage of space within Mokhovaya House, he kept being evicted from his home so that freshly arrived diplomats could stay there. For a while he had rented a small but costly flat from an employee of the Norwegian Embassy. And he'd even been compelled to spend an entire year living in the Hotel Metropole – three blocks northeast of Mokhovaya House. At the end of that year he had reclaimed his flat, only to be evicted again a mere eighteen days later. It was a system certain to leave Tyler feeling ill-disposed towards the US government and, more particularly, towards the higher-level diplomats, attachés and consular officials who had first call on the embassy's accommodation.

Lying in bed, he and Tanya could choose between talking in English or Russian. Both of them spoke the other's language fluently, their accents so faultless that it could be mistaken for their native tongue. While he was in Moscow, Tyler had picked up a wealth of contemporary slang, which he deployed when he spoke Russian, the idiom of the insider used by an outsider.

His gift for languages must have owed something to his father's career in the Consular Service. Over the early stages of his childhood, he had gone with his parents on postings to China, then Germany, Switzerland, Northern Ireland and finally Bermuda. Until he was eight years old, he hadn't set foot on American soil.

Way back when he and his parents were in Bermuda, he'd flaunted his precocious talent as a linguist by addressing his private tutor exclusively in French or German, languages the tutor did not understand. One summer while Tyler was at Princeton, skipping classes if the fancy took him, he had even taught himself Icelandic purely to demonstrate that it was achievable in such a short space of time.

From the giggling comfort of their bed, he and Tanya debated what information she should pass on to her employers today. She had never concealed from him that she didn't just work part-time for the Moscow bureau of a New York press agency run by a friend of Tyler. She also worked for the NKVD. There wasn't much point in Tanya attempting to convince him to believe otherwise. How else could she explain her stylish clothes, her pleasant flat, her NKVD-issue driving licence, and her freedom to mix with foreigners and travel round Europe? These were privileges denied the average Soviet citizen.

Ever since late 1936, which marked the beginning of Stalin's homicidal purges, ordinary Russians eschewed contact with foreigners. Talking to a Russian in the street, even if you were just requesting directions, was commensurate with signing a warrant for the arrest or execution of the person you had buttonholed. All over Moscow posters listed victims of these arrests. Prostitutes controlled by the NKVD were the only people who dared speak to foreigners. Whenever a new American employee rolled up at Mokhovaya House, he would be deluged with phonecalls from Russian women. And he would be approached by women loitering outside the building.

Had Tanya not been an NKVD agent, Tyler's relationship with her wouldn't have been allowed to continue. Anyone seen coming out of Mokhovaya House with a local woman who didn't work for the secret police would be followed. The woman would then be detained, and that would be the last anyone would see of her. No tearful farewells, no explanatory letters, simply an unnerving void.

Tyler had access to plenty of material from which he and Tanya could make their morning selection. Inevitably, each item forwarded to the NKVD offered both a measure of retribution for the way the State Department had treated him and a gratifying reminder of just how clever he was. In discussing what his girlfriend should feed her NKVD handlers, whose headquarters were nearby, he didn't have the option of fobbing them off with fabricated information. Give the Soviets more than the odd scrap of that kind of thing and they would soon be onto him. After all, they had many other sources within Mokhovaya House, probably allowing them to cross-reference elements of whatever he told them. Such was the embassy's porousness that it gave him a readymade excuse for passing confidential information to the Soviets: if he didn't hand the material to them, they would only get it from somewhere else.

8

Several hundred air-raid sirens had been tested one morning not long ago, their overlapping rhythm coalescing into a dismal wail that was audible across London. Until Max or his secretary opened the windows of his Dolphin Square flat, not much noise usually seeped inside. Hard to believe he was still in what was then the world's largest city.

Max had spent most of the past decade there. For the bulk of that time, he had worked for what, with a certain swagger, he called 'the show', more formally described as the Security Service or MI5, its acronymic title lingering from when it had been a department of Military Intelligence. Previously he'd been employed by MI5's twin organization, MI6, the Secret Intelligence Service – in theory, dedicated to activities outside Britain.

As Max admitted, he put his heart and soul into his job, which he considered useful *and* very pleasant. The only drawback was the low salary, though this had the virtue of being paid in crisp, tax-free £5 notes.

These days, Max ran Section B5b. Grand though its title sounded, it comprised nobody but him and his secretary, who had the pleasure of attempting to decipher his notoriously unreadable handwriting. Copious recompense for that formidable task came from the many endearing aspects of Max's personality, not least his eccentricity, highlighted by self-deprecating remarks about how mad he was. From even the dreariest of subjects, he managed to coax gentle, sometimes irreverent humour, red tape being one of his bugbears. In his dealings with subordinates, among whom he inspired devotion, he manifested consistency, enthusiasm and serene authority, traits that distracted from his reluctance to divulge much about his life outside work.

Better disposed to trusting animals than humans, he demonstrated a gratuitous relish for secrecy that distinguished him from his joyously indiscreet mother. He always tried to keep the incongruous segments of his existence separate. Going right back to his teens, he had led self-contained lives at home, at boarding school and at Tythegston Court, his uncle's ramshackle Georgian hall, where he periodically went to stay.

The house, tucked away in rural south Wales, had been in the family since the mid-eighteenth century. At one time they had owned three other houses of that size. Its pastoral surroundings, olde worlde irregularity and rooms embossed with decorative plasterwork representations of flowers, vines, candelabra and mythical beasts made it the polar opposite of the modern flat in which he found himself.

By placing Section B5b in Dolphin Square, half-a-mile from MI5's headquarters, he could enjoy a sense of autonomy and a decreased risk of security leaks. Unshakable in his belief that a secret ceases to be a secret when three people know about it, he ensured that as few staff as possible were familiar with the names of the agents he ran. Throughout the reports submitted by him to headquarters, their anonymity was preserved behind a battery of dull codenames often consisting of numbers prefixed 'M' for 'Max'.

He had to supervise the work of thirteen agents – one more than was employed by the whole of B Division, the counter-espionage and counter-subversion arm of MI5. And seven more than was traditionally regarded as the maximum that could be operated by a single case-officer without curtailing the effectiveness of each agent. Just *one* of those agents could devour an inordinate amount of time, even before they had been enlisted.

First, Max had to identify the potential recruit from the wide range of people with whom he consorted: journalists, clergymen, aristocrats, naturalists, actors, librarians, novelists, diplomats, professors, maharajahs, not to mention young refugees from Nazi Germany, who were a favoured source of agents. Max then had to insinuate himself into that person's company, begin the courtship process and, with luck, complete the recruitment. After that, Max needed to train the person in techniques for memorizing accurate descriptions of people, in how to relay information without arousing suspicion, in all the skills pertinent to what he labelled 'field investigation' – an expression imparting a pungent whiff of the countryside. Suitably tutored, his agent could be deployed against whichever group required monitoring. If agent and host group turned out to be well-matched, Max would soon be staging frequent, surreptitious meetings with his agent, during which he would receive information about the group and its members, information that had to be written down, analysed and passed on to headquarters, enabling him and his colleagues to direct the agent with greater effectiveness. As his recruit became more deeply embedded in the host organization, MI5 would have the chance not only to influence and combat its activities, but also to collect sufficient evidence to justify legal action against it.

Tot up how much time a single agent devoured, multiply that by thirteen and then add a sprinkling of conferences with MI5 colleagues and the result was a packed timetable. Such a heavy caseload inevitably compromised Max's ability to keep up-to-date with his paperwork. He was in something of a double-bind. While he knew that he could do with help in administering and supervising the work of so many agents, he also knew that he required *more* agents.

Denied additional recruits, he wouldn't be able to cover the vast expanse of important duties that fell within his ambit. In the time he had been working for MI5, the focus of his responsibilities had changed. When he'd first joined, the priority of B Division had been to place what were dubbed 'penetration agents' inside the Communist Party of Great Britain, something he achieved with spectacular success. Owing to concerns about British fascists establishing links with their powerful European counterparts, Max felt it was only natural that the emphasis of B Division's work had lately shifted from infiltrating the Communist Party of Great Britain to infiltrating the fascist groups that were popping up.

Those groups, which branded themselves 'patriotic societies', embraced organizations varying dramatically in scale. At the smaller end were the rag-tag National Socialist League and the exclusive Anglo-German Fellowship, the latter of which received backing from big companies such as Dunlop, Thomas Cook and Price Waterhouse, plus MPs and denizens of the House of Lords. Somewhere in the middle of the spectrum was the Nordic

League, laying dubious claim to 7,000 members. Numerically, the most significant of the fascist groups was the British Union, though its support had dwindled from its 1934 peak when it had boasted more than 150 branches and 34,000 members.

Despite Max's obsolete conservatism, his nostalgia for rule by a social elite and his scepticism about democracy, which gave voting rights to people lacking the education to make an informed choice, he had come to despise what he considered the 'fascist type'. Assisted by the interception of letters and the use of surveillance by MI5's Section B6, known as 'the Watchers', he and his colleagues had been amassing information about the Nordic League and comparably subversive groups. Tip-offs from two sources within the German Embassy made it clear that those groups were being infiltrated by talent-spotters from German intelligence, targeting people who might be persuaded to conduct espionage for the Nazis. Max's agents promised to be indispensable in apprehending any such spies before they could wreak serious damage.

9

At the junction between Brook Street and Hanover Square there was a fine early eighteenth-century house. Recognizing such historical idioms had been among Anna's many weaknesses as an architecture student. Since the closure of Anna de Wolkoff Haute Couture Modes, she'd been working for Busvine's, the clothes shop based in the building's ground and first floors. She had known the owner of this well-established family business for several years. He was a youngish, perpetually sunburnt man with an efficient demeanour, a disarming lisp and a transatlantic accent. Even while she'd still been running her own shop, he had commissioned her to design clothes for Busvine's on a freelance basis, garments distinguished by their idiosyncratic detailing and unusual, exquisitely beautiful materials. Nowadays, though, she was employed in a less exalted capacity.

Her job was as a *vendeuse*, just a posh word for a shop assistant, which was rather a comedown for someone of her age and social class, someone who had been the subject of a *March of Time* newsreel, someone whose clothes had graced royal garden parties and been photographed for *Vogue* by Sir Oswald Mosley's friend, Cecil Beaton. Anna was well past the age when it was deemed acceptable for ladies of her background to work in dress shops. There couldn't be many West End shop assistants of her vintage who came from families that moved in such rarefied spheres. Her mother hobnobbed with the British royal family and had been a maid-of-honour to the Tsarina. Her father had served as an admiral, an aide-de-camp to Tsar Nicholas II and a Naval Attaché at the Imperial Russian Embassy in London. He had also been installed as an honorary Companion of the Bath by King George V. On top of all that, her grandfather had owned substantial estates in Russia, built a reputation for himself as a painter, and mixed with Leo Tolstoy, Richard Wagner and other artistic greats.

Undignified as Anna's job was, she could be thankful for the elegance of her current surroundings. Chandeliers and plush green carpets communicated an impression of unstinting opulence. Still, the shop's clientele, which included her mother's friend, Queen Mary, didn't necessarily need all that much enticing. They knew what they were getting from anything that carried the Busvine's label – custom-made fabrics, immaculate tailoring and fashionable designs.

Today, as normal, Anna was working under the guidance of the shop's manageress. Convention dictated that Anna and other sales assistants addressed the manageress as 'Miss Busvine', a pseudonym calculated to burnish the firm's reputation as a family concern.

Anna complained to the manageress about feeling horribly off-colour. She said she had a jaw-ache that wouldn't go away.

Miss Busvine gave her permission to leave the shop and consult a doctor, so she set off for the German Hospital. Run by a long-standing Nazi Party member, this was, as its name implied, staffed by German doctors and nurses. One of the medics was a friend of Jock Ramsay.

Fortunately Anna had her own transport, a little two-seater Morris convertible. Roadworks outside the Gothic arches, tracery, spires and cathedral-like gables of St Pancras Station complicated what would, on most other days, have been an unexacting four-and-a-half-mile trip. Journey's end was the dreary and impoverished East End district of Dalston.

Vehicles entered the German Hospital's grounds by turning down a private drive just round the corner from Ridley Road marketplace, where the British Union staged big open-air gatherings. The Outpatients' Department was in a small building on the right-hand side. More than 200 patients each day took their places on the long wooden benches that bisected its waiting-room.

Proud of her abilities as a linguist, Anna spoke impeccable German, allowing her to use the native tongue of so many of the outpatients as well as the staff. After she had seen a doctor, she was free to pick up a prescription from the septuagenarian pharmacist, who manned a serving-hatch near the exit. His politics were in perfect harmony with Anna's.

When she got back to Busvine's later that day, she revealed that she'd been diagnosed with a streptococcal infection. As a recipe for banishing her illness, she said the doctor had prescribed an immediate holiday. Not in Britain but somewhere foreign.

She didn't, needless to say, admit that such a trip would have other benefits. It would enable her to renew her contacts with the Nazis. And it would give her the chance to gather intelligence that might prove helpful to Jock and to both the Right Club and Nordic League.

10

Yet another day had elapsed without Tyler receiving the promised message from America. During the closing weeks of last year he'd spent his biannual leave there. He had stayed with his mother in Washington, DC, its broad tree-flanked avenues, pale stone buildings, clean pavements and gleaming vistas affording a respite from the Soviet capital's grubby decrepitude. His mother still lived at 2112 Wyoming Avenue. The neighbourhood, well-stocked with comfortably retired colleagues of his father, wasn't far from Georgetown University, where Tyler had studied prior to his departure for the Soviet Union. Over a decade ago, his parents had transformed their house into lodgings for employees from Washington's many government departments. In spite of being widowed almost three years earlier, his mother – with whom he endured a strained relationship – persisted in operating the place as a boarding house. Cold-bloodedly self-centred, not to say condescending, Tyler had every reason to begrudge her demotion from Southern belle to Washington landlady.

His own spot in the socio-economic hierarchy wasn't a cause for rejoicing either. So far, his career had been a letdown compared to that of his late father. Besides serving as Speaker of the Virginia Assembly, his father had been a captain in the Second Virginia Infantry, newspaper editor, lawyer and rancher. He had also twice run on the Republican ticket for governor of his home state. And he had enjoyed a fruitful stretch with the US Consular Service, the zenith of that period being his appointment as Vice-Consul to Guatemala.

In the hope of narrowing this shameful chasm between their respective accomplishments, Tyler had made up his mind to apply for the Foreign Service, the fiercely competitive examinations for which had at last resumed. Unless he could pass those, he would be excluded from the career that birth, intellect and education had seemingly prepared him.

The exams were held in the State Department, a huge edifice that was just a brief cab ride away. His preliminary interview with the middle-aged Chief of Personnel hadn't gone well. The man had enquired whether Tyler thought himself lazy, snobbish and generally inclined to have an unduly high opinion of himself. Tyler replied that he did not consider himself snobbish, although there were some people with whom he was not keen to associate.

Courtesy of his extended tour of duty in Moscow, the Personnel Department nonetheless permitted him to bypass the written aspect of the Foreign Service examination. Yet there was no dodging the oral assessment. In readiness for that, he had ploughed through an imposing curriculum of books on history, economics and international law.

His manner noticeably more severe than it had been, Tyler also found time for many epic discussions with his mother, whose politics had previously kept pace with his own. The revelation that her fulsome view of the 'wonderful steps' being made by Soviet Russia no longer corresponded with her son's came as a shock to her. As did the news that he disagreed with her opinion that the German and Italian dictators were 'just awful bandits, safecrackers and bomb-throwers'.

Tyler could quote from personal experience with reference to Nazi Germany, which he had visited three times. When he was first posted to Europe, he'd stopped off there in transit from Washington to Moscow. And he had later spent nearly a month there – two weeks in 1935 and a further ten days in 1937.

Dexterous in the art of misrepresenting himself, Tyler convinced his mother that his fascist sympathies did not prevent him from being a staunch patriot. He and his mother ended up talking about the threat of another European war.

The Foreign Service oral exam was carried out by a panel that included Loy W. Henderson, a friend of his late father. Henderson also knew Tyler from the Moscow embassy, having served there as First Secretary and Chief Political Officer. Tyler – not renowned for his popularity among Foreign Service staff – had got on tolerably well with Henderson.

At the end of the oral exam, Tyler was told the result by the chairman of the panel. They'd failed him. Tyler had, the chairman declared, been allotted a low score because the panel was unimpressed by the superficial manner with which he had answered most of the questions. Nor did they care for the resentment he'd displayed whenever they urged greater precision. The chairman had told him they considered him a poor bet, unless he took himself in hand and renounced his superiority complex.

No hope of pursuing a career in the Foreign Service remaining, Tyler had attempted to switch from the Translation Section at the Moscow embassy to its equivalent at the State Department. The head of this small organization, entrusted with translating documents for the President and various wings of government, had wanted to put him on the payroll. As bad luck would have it, the keenness of Tyler's prospective employer hadn't been replicated by the Personnel Division. They had pointed out that Tyler lacked the mandatory Civil Service qualification. Once again, his career prospects were stymied by the US government.

Before boarding a ship back to Europe, he visited a contact in New York City, where he made a last-minute stab at finding a better job. His friend, a curmudgeonly yet benevolent type old enough to be his father, was Editor-in-Chief at the International News Service, one of three leading American press agencies that fed stories to newspapers and radio stations across the country. Its Moscow bureau already employed Tyler's girlfriend. Tyler had enquired about the possibility of being taken on by his friend's agency, the apparent imminence of war in Europe serving as an incentive to hire someone who spoke so many European languages. The problem was that Tyler's friend disagreed with all the predictions that fighting might break out any day.

Conflict or no conflict, Tyler had been told there was a good chance of there being an opening for him. Yet those assurances were beginning to sound hollow. Weeks had gone by without Tyler receiving the hoped-for job offer. At this rate he would still be in the same humble position translating US Embassy documents next Christmas and, who knows, maybe the Christmas beyond that.

11

With casual understatement befitting the hero of *The Thirty-Nine Steps* and other John Buchan novels he so admired, Max described his job as requiring him to 'keep an eye (or even two) on any undesirables'. A generous allocation of those was currently provided by the Nordic League. Since its gathering at Caxton Hall a smidgen over three weeks ago, one of the League's members had been the focus of disquieting reports. These bore out Max's belief that you should always remember to look under a log because that's where you're likely to find interesting things.

Long suspected of collusion in espionage, the man in question was Takuidi Egushi, a Japanese accountant who worked for the London branch of the Bank of Taiwan and doubled as a foreign correspondent for the leading Tokyo-based newspaper *Asahi Shimbun*.[6] He had recently returned from Munich, where he had attended a meeting with a member of Hitler's inner circle, Heinrich Hoffmann, editor of the Nazis' English-language propaganda sheet, *News from Germany*. Hoffmann had treated Egushi to a severe ticking off for even *mentioning* Captain Ramsay in a despatch to Tokyo. What so infuriated Hoffmann was the danger that the British Embassy in Japan might have somehow snaffled the despatch and warned the British government about what he viewed as Ramsay's valuable work on behalf of Germany.

Propelled by this information, Max spent part of Thursday 8 June, 1939 composing a memorandum devoted to Ramsay, though the summer heat was less than ideal for office work. Max associated this sort of day with boyhood summers in the countryside. On warm evenings he loved to spend an hour or so motionlessly ensconced near a hedgerow, listening for the dry rasp of grasshoppers and the almost imperceptible sounds of foraging voles, shrews and field mice.

Captain Ramsay – star of Max's memo – was the Unionist Member of Parliament for the Scottish constituency of Peebles and South Midlothian. Exceedingly well-connected, he was married to the eldest daughter of a viscount and numbered Queen Mary among his friends. A good many of his other friends were drawn from both the House of Lords and the House of Commons. He'd previously featured in reports on the Nordic League, detailing his rabidly anti-Semitic speeches. Some of those reports had been forwarded to MI5 by Special Branch, the wing of the Metropolitan Police dedicated to monitoring political subversion. Others had been passed on to a colleague of Max by the Board of Deputies of British Jews, a body devoted to safeguarding the civil and religious rights of the Jewish population. Fearful of the activities of Ramsay and his disciples, the Board had hired an extremely reliable former Special Branch officer to infiltrate the Nordic League. In a series of bracing reports, the officer had quoted Ramsay as saying that Britain ought to be helping Germany and Italy to wage war on the Jews, and that he may one day follow the example of the Arab Mayor of Bethlehem who had presented both his sons with a revolver and told them to shoot every Jew they saw.

'All our observers agree that this man is either a completely honest fanatic or a most dangerous mixture of fanatic and crook,' Max remarked in his memo about Ramsay. He added that the notorious public pronouncements of Willie Gallagher, the Communist MP for the Scottish constituency of West Fife, appeared mild compared to the speeches delivered by Ramsay at meetings of the Nordic League. Bubbling with annoyance and frustration, Max railed against what he perceived as the preferential treatment accorded fascists by the authorities. 'It is certain that if any member of the Communist Party made speeches like many of the speeches made by Captain Ramsay, he would definitely lay himself open to a charge of incitement to violence.'

The continued refusal of the authorities to take action appears to have goaded Max into pondering ways of smuggling an agent into the fascist coterie around Ramsay. If Max could accomplish that, his agent should be able to gather evidence potent enough to persuade the government to reconsider its stance.

12

Oppressive humidity and wilting heat made Moscow summers uncomfortable. When Tyler was not required at Mokhovaya House, he had the luxury of being able to leave town. Denied the chance to stay at the country mansion set aside for the higher-ups and their cronies – who would play tennis, go riding, use the swimming-pool and socialize with the occasional visiting celebrity such as the writer Noël Coward and the actress Mary Pickford – he'd rented a dacha outside Moscow. He paid $4,000 in Russian currency, which was way beyond the resources of anyone dependent upon the salary of a Junior Clerk Second Grade.

To transport him and Tanya there, he also purchased a car. Not just any old car, but the two-seater convertible that had belonged to Ambassador Bullitt. Tyler had since blown another $450 on replacing it with a Soviet-made Ford, bringing his initial outlay for these trips to more than half his annual disposable income. The lackadaisical character of security at the embassy ensured that nobody in authority seems to have queried how he could afford such expenditure.

His drive to the dacha led down cobblestoned streets at perennial risk of being closed to traffic while they were widened or redirected, slicing through blocks of old buildings. Another disorientating aspect of crossing town was the way that street names would change, their new names more Soviet in flavour. Tyler could not even bank on finding his way round by memorizing architectural landmarks. These had a tendency to get demolished, leaving huge craters or piles of debris. Tyler was well-advised to allow Tanya to chauffeur him through Moscow whenever possible.

As they drove across town, weaving round bone-jarring potholes, Tyler would have set eyes on things he'd never have encountered in Washington. Horse-drawn carriages known as *droshkies*. Swaying, clanking trams so overcrowded that passengers were hanging from the sides. Curious overhead stop signals, where a mechanical finger rotated steadily round the dial, from red to green. But these isolated flecks of local colour were swamped by the cheerlessness that enfolded Moscow, the drab shopfronts, the three- or four-thousand-strong queues of shoppers camping on pavements overnight in the hope of purchasing items that were easily obtainable in America. So much for the posters on most walls, emblazoned with Cyrillic-lettered slogans such as 'Thanks great Stalin, beloved friend, leader, teacher for a better, happier life'.

Awaiting Tyler and his girlfriend was a wooden dacha set in countryside rich with pasture and birchwood. They spent weekends at the dacha, which bore similarities to the quaint clapboard houses in Nantucket and Cape Cod. Often Tanya's flatmate, Valya, and her lover joined them. Valya was an unrelenting Soviet proselytizer. She worked for Intourist, the organization that supervised tours of the country by parties of gullible foreigners wanting to marvel at what masqueraded as a workers' paradise. Impulsive, quick-witted and resilient, she had the looks of a movie star. Her long black hair, curvaceous figure and dark eyes were capable of inducing a surge of queasy male yearning.

Anywhere but Moscow, Sylvester A. Huntowski – a friend of Tyler from the embassy – would not have stood a chance with a woman like that. Squat and strong, there was no mistaking him for a film star. He possessed swarthy features and a head that appeared to have been vertically compressed in a fairground mirror. Superficially at least, he didn't have a lot going for him in other regards either.

Contracted to the Navy Department as the maintenance man, who took care of the embassy's telephone and electrical systems, his salary was so small that it made Tyler's seem munificent. He nevertheless had enough cash to remain affluent while supporting Valya. But neither his generosity nor talk of marriage kept her from being on the lookout for an even more bountiful sugar daddy.[7]

Lately Huntowski had become the topic of widespread embassy gossip, branding him 'a rotten egg', neck deep in crime or espionage. What set tongues wagging wasn't just his blatant wealth. It was the fact that his money was in Russian currency: embassy regulations decreed that roubles could only be procured via the Accounting Office, a facility to which Huntowski never had recourse.

Unlike Tyler, he'd proven adept at cosying up to American government officials in positions of authority. Huntowski could even lay claim to a mysterious patron at the State Department, possibly a Soviet agent. Dismissing the Navy Department's objections, his patron had placed him in his current job.

He worked on a compulsory two-year cycle. By rights he should not have been in Moscow any longer, but he had been allowed an extra year. This had been granted as a reward for discovering a hidden microphone while working at Spaso House, official home of the US Ambassador. When the device, which appeared to have been planted by the Soviets, disappeared not long afterwards, the Ambassador had been none too pleased. Huntowski was suspected of returning the microphone to its Russian owners.

Invitations to Tyler's dacha were not just extended to Huntowski and Valya. Tyler also liked to invite other friends from the embassy. Since his days at prep school and Princeton when he'd never integrated with classmates, he had learnt how to strike up friendships. Weather permitting, he and his guests would sit round a folding wooden table in the garden at the dacha, where they could drink and chat and stroke Tanya's dog, an easy-going German shepherd cross.

Under some circumstances, Tanya would pretend not to speak English, a trick favoured by female NKVD agents who attached themselves to embassy personnel, thus encouraging the men to talk among themselves. Deprived of American sports results and other staples of male conversation, they would discuss what had been going on at work, exposing the embassy's secrets to the attentive ears of their Russian companions.

Part of the clique that could be found sitting in the garden was Donald H. Nichols. A slim twenty-six year old with a somewhat bohemian appearance, Nichols had undulating hair and a chin that he often tried to hide beneath a goatee. Until a few months back, he had, alongside Tyler, been one of the clerical minions. Now he was Vice-Consul Nichols.

Tanya and Valya would rustle up female companionship for Tyler's guests whenever necessary. A high proportion of his overwhelmingly male colleagues were, however, less interested in women than in each other. But Nichols didn't fall into that category. He and another of the obliging supply of Russian women had set up home together already.

With the exclusion of Nichols and Huntowski, Tyler's closest friend was Henry W. Antheil (pronounced 'An-tile'), who had at one point shared a flat with Tyler. Like Tyler, he could talk to Valya and Tanya in their native language.

Only a little while ago, he had returned from leave back home in Trenton, New Jersey. Still in his middle twenties, his youth exaggerated by his Lilliputian dimensions, Henry managed the Code Room through which all messages to and from the embassy were funnelled. He had worked there since he was scarcely out of high school. His elder brother, George, a famous avant-garde composer now writing Hollywood film scores, had helped him acquire the job. George had put in a good word for him with Ambassador Bullitt, who just happened to be a friend.

By virtue of his sunny disposition and matinee idol looks, Henry had become popular with the wives of the top brass. He was also assiduous in cultivating their husbands which, combined with his work in the Code Room, gave him the inside track on everything at the embassy. Drawing on these wide-ranging sources, he predicted a European war. He went on to forecast that Hitler would be the ultimate loser. 'The reason is that the damned fool will attack Russia. That's his idea, first and last. This may finish him right off, but I'm afraid not. I think we'll eventually have to get in. Russia is strong, but not quite strong enough. Hitler is going to go a long way into Europe and Russia before we start rolling him back. But he's going to get his teeth kicked in.'

These forebodings of war could not have helped Henry's quest to shake off the poor health stalking him lately. In spite of the medication and special diets he was prescribed, he hadn't been in the best of shape for many months.

Weary of life in the Soviet Union, Henry had been lobbying for a transfer. After a year or so, he'd finally succeeded. On a trip to the US Embassy in London, where he had been ordered to deliver codebooks and other confidential documents, he had made an exceptionally favourable impression. Last month – May 1939 – Joseph P. Kennedy, the Ambassador there, had secured permission to have him transferred to England. Pretty soon now, Henry would be leaving Moscow, just the latest name on an expanding list of Tyler's friends who would no longer be joining him and Tanya at their dacha.

13

The hot, dry weather, prevalent over London for more than a month, broke with the suddenness of one of those batting collapses that were, for Max and other supporters of Surrey County Cricket Club, blighting the current season. A shade after midnight on Sunday 11 June, 1939, the rain began its energetic drum solo against the roof of his home, which was a mile-and-a-half from his Dolphin Square office. During these desolate early hours, insomnia sometimes drove Max out of his bedroom and into the kitchen, pressure of work surely exacerbating his failure to stifle the flow of thoughts spawned by his subtle and probing mind.

'In the still of the night' was, he reflected, a nice romantic phrase, conjuring a mental picture of peace and silence. Like many poetic phrases, though, he believed the expression was wide of the mark. All right, you might not hear any footsteps at that hour. Nor might you hear anyone talking. Yet that didn't mean there was nothing audible. It just highlighted what he considered the miserable quality of human sensory awareness, which he regarded as little more than an enfeebled or atrophied version of the wonderful perceptions exhibited by birds and other so-called lesser species. Whatever his senses told him, Max knew there was a whirl of nocturnal activity outside the flat where he and his second wife, Lois, had lived for several years.

She was, like her precursor, a headstrong, upper-class woman. Max had first met her in a country pub. They'd been together long enough to settle into a somnolent domestic rhythm that stoked her marital discontent. On the brink of her thirtieth birthday now, Lois – approaching a decade younger than him – hungered for a more sociable existence than Max was prepared to offer. When he was not on MI5 duties or prac- tising the bass clarinet or playing what he called 'second-class cricket' or indulging in another of his hobbies, fishing being a rare pastime enjoyed by both him and Lois, they would now and again have friends round to dinner, but that was the full extent of their social life. Talking to yet more people was the last thing Max needed after a day at work. 'I wouldn't say I love my own company, though I'm not a frightfully sociable animal,' he confessed.

Their home was near the summit of a five-storey redbrick building towards the Knightsbridge end of Sloane Street. Beneath them were the offices of a women's sportswear company and an estate agency. In a characteristically idiosyncratic arrangement, he and Lois shared their sitting-room with the woman from the neighbouring flat. Her forerunner had been petrified by the tank of grass snakes that Max had installed there. Out of such irrational fears, he realized prejudice could flourish.

Ever since childhood Max had been obsessed by birds, animals and insects. So extensive was his knowledge of their lifecycles, breeding habits and assorted peccadilloes that he'd recently been awarded a Fellowship of the Zoological Society of London, which ran Regent's Park Zoo. His scientific research had also earned him fellowships of two other prestigious institutions – the Royal Geographical Society and the Royal Microscopical Society. These entitled him to style himself proudly, Maxwell Knight, FRGS, FZS, FRMS, initials that compensated in some measure for any inferiority he felt about his lack of a university degree.

He liked to believe he had an inborn gift for studying natural history as well as befriending birds and animals. They undoubtedly responded to his purposely slow, gentle movements and the reassuring pitch of his soft, breathy voice. People would, he noticed, sometimes look at him with sneering condescension when he petted his animals in public, though he got the impression that domesticated creatures derived pleasure and security from being handled like that. He was, however, at pains to distinguish himself from those people who behaved as if their pets were imbued with human emotions and intelligence. To him, such mawkishness epitomized the antithesis of understanding and affection. He viewed nature in more pragmatic terms. Nature was, he once told a young protégé, akin to some 'ghastly, wicked war'.

Its ghastliness didn't lessen the gratitude he felt towards his late father – himself a well-informed naturalist – for encouraging his love of living creatures. Growing up in what was then the village of Mitcham, which had since become a suburb of southeast London, Max kept umpteen pets. Mice, toads, lizards, rats, slow worms, tortoises, hedgehogs and all manner of birds. He still suffered twinges of guilt about the premature deaths of several of those creatures, which he had stuffed with unsuitable food.

Pets had, in his youth, afforded him a refuge from the more problematic world of humans, already tainted by his awkwardness among his contemporaries, by his parents' unhappy marriage and by the slide towards penury of his spendthrift father, a London solicitor with a penchant for whisking girl-friends off to the French Riviera. Max's mania for birds, animals and insects nowadays presented a convenient distraction from the pressures under which he laboured, the secrecy of his work adding to the burden.

His menagerie had over the past few years encompassed not only a white bull terrier – his best-loved breed of dog, 'once owned … never forgotten' – but also what, he conceded, were various 'queer or unusual pets'. He had kept an Indian mongoose ('wonderful little beast'), a spider monkey, a baboon, a couple of snakes and a brown bear cub named Bessie. He used to take Bessie for walks round Chelsea on a lead. With enduring amusement he recalled how seldom passers-by betrayed any sign that they knew what she was. Most people scarcely gave her a glance. If they commented on her at all, the standard remark was, 'What a sweet little chow puppy!'

Max's present-day menagerie included a blue-fronted Amazon parrot, which had taken a dislike to his wife, Lois, possibly because it regarded her as a rival for his attention. But his parrot need not have worried about being marginalized. Even though Lois still relished his avuncular charm, appreciated his love of nature and found his mysterious comings and goings deeply glamorous, Max's second stab at matrimony didn't qualify as a great success.

For all his susceptibility to feminine charms, he had never succeeded in consummating his relationship with Lois. Repeated visits to a specialist doctor couldn't remedy Max's impotence, the clandestine triumph of his professional life offering a corrective to his feelings of inadequacy.

Without a solution to his problem, which made Lois suspect him of channelling his carnal appetites into affairs with other women, his second marriage was liable to go the same way as his first. Not that he'd confided in his present wife about his similarly chaste relationship with Gwladys, her predecessor. He had merely told Lois how he and Gwladys had drifted apart, how he blamed himself for Gwladys's sense of isolation, for her awful fate, memories of which could do nothing to quell his insomnia.

14

Tyler had to make his own entertainment when he returned to Moscow from his dacha. Unlike his higher-ranking colleagues, he wasn't on the guest-list for the cocktail parties, luncheons, dinners, receptions and dances held in the grand surroundings of the ambassadorial residence, where he would have been able to fraternize with staff from other foreign embassies. Word had it that the guests at a recent Christmas party were entertained by three performing seals. The animals had apparently shuffled into the ballroom with trays balanced on their noses. One of these bore wineglasses. Another had a bottle of champagne on it. And the remaining tray featured a small, candlelit Christmas tree.[8]

In contrast, the likes of Tyler did not any longer even have access to the Recreation Room on the ground floor of Mokhovaya House. He and the other clerks used to be able to play billiards and ping-pong there, but the facility had since been gutted by fire. Well, not by the fire itself but by the Russian firemen who had extinguished it.

Alternative forms of entertainment were about as plentiful as Ivy League football scores in the Soviet press. Though Tyler could always take his girlfriend to the nearby Bolshoi Theatre, the lustrous glow from its tiered balconies undimmed by the chill fog of Communism, its operatic repertoire did little to inspire anyone who didn't enjoy hearing arias to the wisdom of Comrade Stalin and his decision to nationalize Russia's farms.

Seeking entertainment in the local museums was just as misguided. He was unlikely to derive pleasure from trips to the Historical and Revolutionary Museum, the Anti-Religious Museum or the alluringly titled Bolsheviks in Tsarist Penal Servitude and Exile Museum. There wasn't much fun to be had from going to see a film either because the cinemas served a tedious menu of propaganda about the post-revolutionary utopia. And the Park of Culture and Leisure was, despite its name, no more conducive to relaxation. Strolls through its riverside grounds would be accompanied by the sight of ten-year-old boys in gasmasks carrying out bayonet drill. Was it any surprise, then, that Moscow had lately acquired a reputation as an undesirable posting? To those who lacked Tyler's anthropological fascination with Soviet Russia, even the embassies and consulates in the tropics were deemed preferable.

When Tyler wasn't in bed with his girlfriend, he would catch up on his reading, do some target-shooting or have another German lesson. He had been able to practise the language on a newly acquired friend – one of the diplomats from the German Embassy.

Should none of those activities appeal to him, Tyler would go drinking, although there were only a handful of places from which to choose. Of those, he was keen on the Hotel Metropole's combined bar and restaurant.

The Metropole, where prices were steep even after the discount for paying in foreign currency, purveyed a flavour of the high life to which Tyler was so attracted. Most of the hotel's clientele, notorious for being honeycombed with spies, were representatives of Moscow's gilded youth, clad in their patched finery, the women in homemade gowns, the men typically without jackets or ties, which made them appear unconventional to western eyes. Doused by multicoloured lights, couples jammed onto the narrow marble dancefloor. At its midpoint was a pond with a fountain. So many customers had stumbled into the water that the management had lately erected a wooden guardrail. While the dancers effected bad imitations of the foxtrot and tango, performed in time to a jazz band the size of a symphony orchestra, beautiful girls hawked gas-filled balloons on cords. The diners would amuse themselves by wrapping paper round the cords, setting light to them and releasing the flame-tailed balloons, which would drift towards the stained-glass ceiling three floors above. Like a premonition of things to come, the balloons burst with the concussive volume of an artillery barrage.

Cocooned by this jovial hullabaloo, Tyler could drink vodka with his friends and mingle with the other dollar-toting foreigners for whom the bar was reserved. And he could meet one of the hotel's residents, a man known as Calligos. Part Romanian, part Greek, Tyler's contact was an agent for the NKVD and a close associate of its bloodthirsty chief.[9]

15

Someone might be following Max. Of course this wouldn't be the first time he had found himself under surveillance. With that in mind, whenever he needed a face-to-face conversation with one of his agents, he would suggest they get together for what he described with glib disingenuousness as 'a chat'. One might think they were just going to talk about the golden era of New Orleans jazz or the latest county cricket scores or the dietary requirements of baby magpies or some other mutual interest.

The chosen rendezvous would be a location where eavesdroppers would have a job overhearing anything. Max would sometimes meet his agent in a Dolphin Square flat cadged from one of his fishing cronies. Either that, or he'd nominate busy public places, such as the foyer of a cheap hotel. And there were plenty of those in the streets near where Section B5b was based. Or he would tell his agent to meet him in a specific museum, say the Natural History Museum in South Kensington. Or he would select one of the local parks, their lawns still disfigured by zigzagging trenches that served as a memento of the previous autumn's crisis when another war with Germany had been narrowly averted. Otherwise, he would arrange a get-together in a railway station buffet, the furious shushing of the tea-urn, the rattle of cutlery and china, the regular tannoy announcements serving as convenient camouflage for whatever information he and his agent cared to exchange.

Despite working in a world of ambiguity and obliqueness, Max spoke with clarity, concision and emphatic self-assurance. Always generous with his time, he gave ample backing to his agents. Fifteen years or thereabouts in his present line of work had taught him this was how one got the best out of them.

He received his reward today when the agent codenamed 'M/T' reported on a late night meeting in a function room at a London hotel. The packed meeting turned out to have been hosted by a notoriously pro-Nazi organization called the Link.[10] Supported by the Central London branch of the Nazi Party, this aptly titled group, which had more than 4,000 members in the provinces as well as the capital, provided a link between the Nazis and the many British fascist bodies.

Max's agent disclosed that Captain Ramsay was the event's principal speaker. Ramsay had trumpeted the recent forma-tion of the Right Club. Its objectives, he'd explained, were to purge Britain of Jews and cultivate an alliance with Nazi Germany, whose leader he called 'that splendid fellow with whom we should be proud to be friends'. Ramsay had announced that different levels of membership could be purchased for anything from a modest 2/6d to a bumper £25. And he had also appealed for help from volunteers possessing specialist skills.

Using the income from membership fees, he envisaged setting up branches across the country and acquiring a fleet of loudspeaker vans, staffed by gifted orators. He talked about them touring England and preaching his anti-Semitic creed. As soon as he had finished speaking, the audience rushed to enrol.

'Ramsay must have some very influential people behind him,' Max's agent believed. The agent described the Right Club as a well-planned affair, destined to become much bigger than the Link. Ramsay was aiming to hire the Albert Hall in December 1939 for an enormous rally.

16

Bearing smudgy witness to her previous trips abroad were the rubber-stamped pages of Anna's passport. She'd been to Germany, where she had tasted life under the Nazis. She'd been to France, where she had not only arranged to have fabric printed but also exhibited her dress designs at the mid-season Paris fashion shows. She'd been to Switzerland to have one of her recurrent medical problems treated. She'd once travelled to Ostend for the weekend with Enid Riddell and others, purely to have a flutter at the casino. She'd even paid an extended visit to America, where she and a friend had found work with a prominent auction house, dealing in Old Master paintings. And not so long ago she had motored down to Austria with 'Mira' Dimitri. Princess Marina Dimitri Romanovsky Koutouzoff, to be precise.

Mira and Anna had been close. The princess even used to feature in advertisements for Anna's shop. Anna had, however, fallen out with her while they were travelling through Austria. Mira's riposte had been to flounce off with a young British Army officer.[11] Naturally, Anna would not be inviting Mira to join her this time – assuming one of her rich friends could be persuaded to lend or, better still, donate the money needed to finance her proposed recuperative trip.

The obvious person for Anna to approach was her old friend, Barbara Allen. Barbara possessed sufficient wealth to bestow sizeable cheques without noticing the consequences. For many years she'd been a fixture on London's high society circuit, shuttling between debutante dances, winters in Cape Town and transatlantic voyages on palatial ocean liners. Her wealth had been consolidated by her comparatively recent marriage to a man with a thriving family firm. It provided them with an elegant, spacious house in a smart district of London.

Though her mother was a British aristocrat by marriage, Barbara had grown up in America, her accent offering a recurrent reminder of the displacement that she shared with Anna. Slight and dark-haired, she had high cheekbones, small eyes and a sharp, pinched-looking nose that might have belonged to a Madonna on a Renaissance altarpiece.

Despite the fact that she and Anna were both well into their thirties, they still addressed one another by nicknames redolent of childhood, 'Anna' becoming 'Ankin', and 'Barbara' being transmuted into 'Ba' or sometimes 'Barbee'. So close was their friendship that Barbara had rescued Anna and other members of the Wolkoff clan from intermittent financial crises. Yet Barbara's husband regarded with hostile scepticism Anna's health problems and her ability, as he put it, to stage nervous breakdowns at convenient moments.

Anna's story in this instance was that her medical condition had been kindled by the emotional duress of seeing her business go bust. She compared herself to a mother grieving over the death of a son or daughter. Lurching further into melodrama, she claimed that she'd nearly paid for the loss of her business with her life.

17

Max could be at work in about fifteen minutes. But that was only if, yielding to the extravagance he had inherited from his father, he took a cab. Otherwise he could simply turn left out of his front door and walk over to the bus-stop. En route he could pop into his local tobacconist's and replenish his supply of Empire Deluxe or whatever pipe-tobacco caught his fancy.

He needed to catch a no. 46 to Victoria Station and then pick up a no. 135. These buses came at frequent intervals. He could picture himself years ago sitting beside a lady friend in just such a vehicle. She liked to wear an astrakhan muff. On all but the coldest days, his friend would allow her pet marmoset to go out with her, curled inside it. Max recollected with amusement the incredulous expressions of fellow passengers when her pet thrust its wrinkled little face out of the muff and emitted a burst of simian chatter.

Disembarking outside the main entrance to Dolphin Square, Max could soon be ensconced in his sixth-floor eyrie. Now he had a job that he enjoyed, he applied himself to it with a level of commitment largely alien to his much younger self. Overworked though he was, insomniac fatigue no doubt making life still more strenuous for him, he had recently taken on another agent – the fourteenth such person engaged by him at Section B5b. If the anticipated war with Germany broke out, he knew he would have to enlist many more recruits. He also knew he would require help supervising the work of those extra agents.

The frustrating thing was that he couldn't go ahead and hire the case-officers he required – unless they were willing to work for nothing, which was not unprecedented. Hiring additional staff wouldn't be feasible without his department being granted extra funding. *Significant* funding. Enough to cover the new salaries. In the region of £5 a week for each agent. Around what one would have forked out to rent a furnished flat in a decent part of town.

Max was convinced that Sir Vernon Kell, veteran Director-General of MI5, had been doing everything within his compass to obtain the necessary funds. Blame for the present financial starvation and attendant inability to employ more than one or two additional agents was something Max heaped at the door of the Tory government. Little did he realize that the bigwigs at MI5 itself were behind the penny-pinching.

For now at least, he would have to make do with his existing cadre of agents. The newest recruit was a woman once known as Mrs Marjorie Mackie. After a rancorous separation from her husband, she had reverted to her maiden name of Miss Marjorie Amor. Not the most appropriate of surnames, her prematurely old, spinsterish appearance being unlikely to rouse amorous feelings. Amorousness must have played some part in her life, though, because she had a teenage son.

She was a roly-poly forty year old, her less than appealing looks mitigated by her warm personality, reservoir of intelligent conversation and fund of stories, told in a voice suffused by a Welsh accent. A few of those stories were quite ribald.

Max's mother had possessed a comparable strain of jocular vulgarity. It used to embarrass his well-to-do uncle, the squire of Tythegston Court.

As far as possible, Max had, with occasional exceptions, made a point of only recruiting people whose honesty and objectives he considered above reproach. He worked out he would get better results and also save vast amounts of time that way. Unless he could trust his agents, he would have to verify every scrap of intelligence they ferreted out.

Luckily for his newest recruit, Max wasn't going to subject her to some unpleasant initiation ritual of the type he had endured many years earlier. The ritual hadn't, of course, been staged when he joined MI5. It had taken place when he became a pupil at the Thames Nautical Training College, a floating public school based aboard an old three-masted sailing ship called HMS *Worcester*.

Through long experience of training animals, Max was aware that there were more effective techniques of imposing discipline than harshness and cruelty. The latter, he believed, never produced willing and responsive actions. In accordance with that maxim, he strove to cultivate a friendship with each of his agents. Much of his success at running agents could be put down to his facility for befriending people, the attractive but misleading guilelessness of his smile contributing to that.

He always endeavoured to adapt himself to suit his latest recruit. The process necessitated him familiarizing himself with their home life, interests, hobbies, likes and dislikes. Sufficiently self-aware to recognize how malleable his own personality was, he worried that he was in danger of turning into someone who was all things to all men, a thoroughly objectionable creature devoid of character or sincerity.

Just as methodically as he set about winning the trust of a young bird or animal, he used candour as a means of gaining his agents' confidence. He resisted the temptation to employ people under the pretext that they were, perhaps, working for a news agency. They should know right from the outset, he felt, that they were employees of His Majesty's Government. Ultimately there would, in any case, come a point when they'd have to be told the truth. Max had witnessed the detrimental effects of case-officers hoodwinking their agents about this. He sympathized with agents for feeling resentful when they discovered that they were not employed by the organization for which they thought they were working. In those circumstances they were bound to feel aggrieved and foolish. And the focus of their predictable chagrin would be the case-officer who hadn't trusted them.

Once he befriended someone, Max had the former salesman's knack of being able to manipulate that person. His genial charm disguising both a ruthlessly controlling streak and a sportsman's competitive drive, he could persuade his agents to undertake assignments they didn't necessarily want to undertake.

There were two overriding motives behind Max's recruitment of Marjorie. First of all, he would not have to fritter away valuable time training her, because she had worked on a previous MI5 operation. She was already conversant with the rudiments of undercover assignments, with techniques yet to acquire the label of 'tradecraft'. But her most salient advantage lay in the fact that she was on good terms with Captain Ramsay of the Nordic League. She knew both the Captain and his wife through their mutual participation in the Christian Protest Movement. Until only about four years ago, Marjorie had been the Assistant Secretary of this right-wing, White Russian-dominated group, which campaigned against the suppression of Christianity in the Soviet Union.

So Max asked her to telephone the Ramsays. He wanted her to renew her acquaintance with the Captain, who had become the target of Section B5b's next investigation.

Part Two

The Devil Rides In

1

They were not like ordinary employees. Years of dealing with agents had taught Max that much. One didn't just issue them with instructions and wait for these to be carried out. Max realized he was at their beck and call, not the other way round.

Come to think of it, he had also spotted a strange quirk of human behaviour exhibited by all the most talented agents. Even though they must have known that he was liaising with other MI5 recruits, they behaved as if his relationship with them were exclusive, as if they occupied the centre of his attention. He had arrived at the conclusion that he would reap the best results by playing up to their egotism. Meetings with them were certain to acquire some of the furtive intensity of an extramarital affair, his charisma and genuine concern for their welfare only amplifying that.

Since joining Max's line-up of agents, Marjorie had reported several positive things to him. Exactly as requested, she had telephoned the Ramsays. She'd spoken to Captain Ramsay's wife who had invited her to tea at their London address a few days later. They lived at an impressive house in Onslow Square. But Captain Ramsay wasn't there when Marjorie visited.

Over tea his short, sour-looking wife had a long discussion with Marjorie about politics, strident anti-Semitism and enmity towards freemasonry characterizing her hostess's pronouncements. Mrs Ramsay also told Marjorie about the Right Club. And she went on to say that the names of many of its members did not feature on any written record. Those names that did appear in writing were hidden in a locked volume. Should Marjorie wish to become a member, Mrs Ramsay stressed that there would be no danger of anyone discovering her involvement with the club.

2

Anna could start formulating plans for her holiday in Europe. She explained to colleagues at Busvine's that the trip had been made possible by a friend who had handed her a cheque, supplemented by money from another friend.

But the news wasn't *all* good. One had to admit that the timing of the trip left something to be desired. It meant that Anna would not be able to attend the big rally at Earl's Court Exhibition Hall in mid-July. *Action*, the British Union newspaper, had been advertising the event, organized as part of Sir Oswald Mosley's long-running 'Stop the War' campaign, which attempted to create the impression that the Jews were manoeuvring Britain into a war with Germany. The campaign alerted people to the likely side-effects of such a conflict: higher unemployment, profiteering, heavy taxation, rationing and inflation adding to the unpleasantness. By championing a truce with Nazi Germany, the campaign placed Anna and other fascists in alliance with pacifists and left-wingers from the Peace Pledge Union.

Her Continental jaunt may not have been perfectly timed, yet it would at least spare her the distress of seeing her business receive the last rites. More than £4,500 was still owed to the creditors of Anna de Wolkoff Ltd – a huge debt, commensurate with the cost of three brand-new Rolls-Royces. What made the whole situation so tricky was that her father and a friend of hers were among the principal creditors who had helped to bail out her business before its eventual collapse. Had her beloved father's finances been healthier, then her debt to him would not have mattered quite so much. As things stood, the Russian Revolution having stripped her family of its wealth, he could ill afford to lose over £800.

3

The party had been held a few years ago. It took place at a swish modern flat in central London. Max's host was an aristocratic young man, employed by MI5's Transport Section.[12] Most of the guests were photogenic debutantes, incapable of talking about anything other than clothes, boyfriends and forthcoming dances. Equally out of place among this youthful frivolity were Dennis and Joan Wheatley, a middle-aged couple who had latched onto Max.

Dennis's name was familiar from the newspapers and the spines of bestselling novels that straddled the historical adventure, espionage and horror genres. He and Max turned out to have plenty in common. Following their chance encounter, Max had been asked round to the Wheatleys', who liked to invite a disparate group of people for drinks at their commodious mid-Victorian house in St John's Wood. The congenial ambience of Dennis and Joan's household was enhanced by a well-stocked cellar from which Dennis – a former wine merchant – would pluck vintage goodies whenever the occasion demanded.

Parties, Max joked, always reminded him of the worst features of the Parrot House at the zoo, yet he enjoyed stepping into the limelight and telling stories, often about jazz. He talked about getting to know the members of the Original Dixieland Jazz Band when they came over to London, and about being taught to play the clarinet by the great soloist Sidney Bechet. 'One day he and I combined in a sort of jam session. He played this particular song, "Softly Awakes My Heart", on the soprano saxophone and I did my best to keep up with him.'

Nowadays Max was on such close terms with the Wheatleys that they'd taken to calling him 'uncle'. Perhaps the most surprising of the many things Max shared with Dennis was a love of John Buchan spy novels. Max had written a couple of populist novels of his own. These had found reputable publishers and earned good reviews.[13] Both novels, which propagated the belief that the British remained ignorant of the dangers lurking abroad, were crime thrillers stalked by gangsters with names straight out of Damon Runyon's short stories – Eddie the Swede, Fingers Reilly and Dumb Louie. Speaking about his novels, he said, 'They amused me. I don't know whether they amused anyone else.'

But an overlapping taste in books wasn't all Max and Dennis had in common. They had both worked for privately funded intelligence agencies. They were both so-called 'Old Worcesters', having been educated aboard HMS *Worcester*, albeit at slightly different times. They were both right-wing conservatives. Furthermore, they were both curious about the occult. All of which had contributed to the two men establishing a lasting rapport.

As an endorsement of their friendship, Max had dedicated his second novel to Dennis and Joan. He had also confided in Dennis that he worked for MI5. Risky though his candour was, someone as shrewd as Max would not have been oblivious to the potential rewards. By admitting that he inhabited the cloak-and-dagger world, he couldn't help but go up in Dennis's estimation, simultaneously feeding his own vanity and presenting his unwaveringly patriotic new friend with a token of trust.

Max had since obtained assistance from Dennis in gathering morsels of information. D'you happen to know anything about such-and-such a person? he would ask Dennis. If Dennis didn't, Max would enquire whether it was practicable for him to find out about that person without arousing comment. Flattery cementing Dennis's cooperation, Max had told him, 'When you turned your attention to literature, the intelligence department lost a great opportunity, though I fear the financial rewards in literature are greater than in the world of intrigue!'

Apt to theorize about military strategy, Dennis expected the Germans to bombard London as soon as war was declared. He subscribed to the notion that these preliminary air raids would target the docks and marshalling yards, damage to which would prevent food from being distributed. In preparation he had stockpiled about a month's supplies for his entire household. All six of them – himself, his wife, his tearaway nineteen-year-old stepdaughter and a trio of servants. He had also created a makeshift air-raid shelter in his basement, its ceiling propped up with empty champagne crates, its outer walls braced by sandbags bedded in cement. And he had constructed a couple of escape tunnels because he suspected that even a near miss from a bomb would demolish his home and leave the shelter buried beneath rubble.

Reluctant to risk getting marooned on the Continent when Germany went to war with its neighbours, Dennis had talked about scrubbing his planned family holiday to France and going to Ireland instead. But his wife, supported by his stepson Bill, who had just completed a degree at Oxford University, had persuaded him to go ahead with the original plan and drive down to the Riviera. Before they departed in early July 1939, Max agreed to keep Dennis informed of any military developments that would justify them hotfooting it back to Blighty.

4

Until she had made the pragmatic decision to become a naturalized British citizen almost four years ago, Anna had been what was termed 'a stateless person'. Her Russian passport invalidated by the Communist revolution, she had made do with a document known as a 'Nansen passport'. Issued by the League of Nations, forerunner of the United Nations, it had enabled her to leave the country, though it offered no guarantee of readmittance. Whenever she'd wanted to venture abroad, she had moreover been required to put up with the inconvenience and expense of procuring an annual Certificate of Identity. But all that was unnecessary now she possessed a British passport. She had been able to use this when she set off for the Continent several days ago.

The timing of her departure allowed her to go to the charity ball that she'd played a crucial role in organizing. It had been held at the Ritz Hotel on the night of Wednesday 5 July, 1939. Other than a potentially awkward encounter with her estranged friend, Princess Mira Dimitri, the event had gone as smoothly as one could have hoped. It attracted a large and very distinguished turnout. Grand Duchess Xenia – a friend of Anna's family – had been there, resplendent in traditional Russian costume. The Grand Duchess's son and daughter-in-law had attended as well. They had even brought with them one of the grown-up children of the exiled King of Spain.

Within a few days of the event at the Ritz, Anna had arrived in the Sudetenland, a mainly rural ex-province of Czechoslovakia. Every inch of countryside seemed to be divided into orchards and a grid of fields. Populated by a significant proportion of so-called *Volksdeutsche*, ethnic Germans, this idyllic backwater had been the epicentre of the previous year's international crisis.

Hitler's support for the campaign by the *Volksdeutsche* for their own state had come close to provoking war between Britain and Germany. Conflict had only been averted by last September's Munich Conference, at which the leaders of Britain, France and Italy had agreed to let Germany annex the Sudetenland, since renamed the German Protectorate of Bohemia and Moravia. In March 1939 – five-and-a-half months after that – Hitler seized the remainder of Czechoslovakia without retribution from Britain and her allies.

Reminders that the Sudetenland had become part of Hitler's fast-expanding Third Reich surrounded Anna, not least in the willingness of shops to accept German currency, in the signs outside restaurants and cafés bearing messages such as 'Jews Not Allowed to Enter', and in the presence of black-uniformed officers from the Gestapo, the Nazi equivalent of the NKVD. She was based in a small health and ski resort over a hundred miles east of Prague. Known as Gross-Ullersdorf by her fellow German-speakers who predominated in that area, the resort inhabited a mountain valley.

Anna had wangled accommodation at Gross-Ullersdorf Castle. More like a French chateau than an English baronial pile, it afforded a sharp contrast to her tiny mews house and the sooty clamour of central London. She sent a postcard depicting the castle to a colleague at Busvine's, proudly informing her where she was staying.

Once a great beauty, Anna's sixty-one-year-old hostess was Princess Elizabeth Amalie, mother of the monarch of Liechtenstein. Being with people of this exalted social class would prompt Anna to put on a grand, rather hearty manner. In the course of her stay, she was able to find out whether the things she'd heard about the Sudetenland were correct. She believed that the London-based press had been guilty of plying its readership with lies calculated to turn the British public against the Nazis. Her friend, Captain Ramsay of the Right Club, said the press was the tool of an international Jewish plot – another facet of the giant conspiracy Anna's father had been discussing since she was in nappies.

Princess Elizabeth Amalie obliged by delivering stories about the behaviour of the Czechs before the German takeover. They had commandeered her best farmland. And they had refused to allow the Princess or the resident workers to leave her estate without permission.

The Nazis' annexation of the Sudetenland was something that Anna also discussed with another aristocrat. Like the owner of Gross-Ullersdorf Castle, he welcomed the takeover. He explained to Anna that he had, prior to the German occupation, been so petrified of the Communists that he'd been unwilling to take off his clothes when he went to bed. She also accepted his retelling of the apocryphal story that Hitler had only sanctioned the occupation of Czechoslovakia at the request of its President, who feared a Communist coup.

As part of her investigative mission, Anna sought an appointment with Konrad Henlein, one-time fascist leader of the Sudeten Germans, now the region's Nazi Governor. Her prospects of securing a meeting with such a senior official cannot have been hindered by the esteem in which Captain Ramsay was held by the Nazis. She was granted an appointment for Monday 17 July, 1939, but Henlein ended up sending his apologies because he was summoned to Berchtesgaden, the Führer's Bavarian retreat.

In Henlein's place, Anna met the second-in-command, Deputy Gauleiter Karl Hermann Frank, a cadaverous, middle-aged former bookseller with a glass eye and a fondness for striding round the streets with a furled whip. Since the German occupation of the whole of Czechoslovakia, he had been given control of every branch of the local police, including the Gestapo.

Even compared to other Nazi zealots, his anti-Semitism and brutality were extreme.[14]

Anna's discussion with Frank lasted a little short of three hours. She subsequently bragged that he'd told her about the imminent Nazi–Soviet Non-Aggression Pact and everything that went with it. Ostensibly illogical though an alliance between such bitter adversaries was, it represented a marriage of convenience, delaying war with the Soviets until a moment of Hitler's choosing.

5

The noise was audible across London the following Friday. One could have mistaken it for the sound of distant bombs falling, yet it was nothing more sinister than the rumble of thunder. This functioned as the prelude to a cloudburst of sufficient ferocity to inundate the lawns and terraces within sight of Max's Dolphin Square office.

Apart from an initial hot spell, plus the occasional day of sunshine, the summer had so far been wet and much cooler than normal. Inevitably, the weather was playing havoc with the cricket season. The rain looked set to scupper the final day of Surrey's match against the touring West Indies side. But Max had more important matters to preoccupy him.

On the strength of the material accumulated about Captain Ramsay and associates, Max had been assigned several Special Branch officers to help investigate them. At the heart of that inquiry was the Right Club.

Well aware of MI5's dependence on Special Branch for making arrests and taking witness statements – tasks that were beyond the ambit of the Security Service – Max laid much emphasis on the importance of establishing cordial relations with senior police officers and their subordinates. Every effort must be made, he believed, to see things from their viewpoint, thus reducing the likelihood of squabbles between Section B5b and the police.

In a phonecall to Captain Ramsay's house, one of Max's Special Branch colleagues had, posing as a potential member, requested details of the Right Club. His ploy elicited a forthright letter. 'The chief aim of the Club,' the letter explained, 'is to coordinate the activities of all the patriotic bodies which are striving to free the country from Jewish domination in the financial, political, philosophical and cultural spheres.'

Some of the fascist groups whose work Ramsay planned to coordinate were named in the letter. These included the Nordic League, the Link and the National Socialist League. Another listed group was the British Union, which had last weekend staged a 20,000 sell-out rally at Earl's Court Exhibition Hall. Surely in homage to the Nazi rallies in Nuremberg, the staginess of the event had been magnified by flags, drum-rolls, trumpets, fascist salutes and vertical shafts of light.

By acting in concert, the British Union and other groups were likely to become far more prominent and effective, making Max's workload unsustainable. Intent on reducing that burden, Max was in the process of writing a letter to his friend Dennis, currently ensconced in the Riviera resort of Cavalaire-sur-Mer, almost equidistant between Cannes and Toulon. The subject of his letter was Bill Younger, the stepson whom Dennis treated less as a son than a cherished sibling.

Max knew that Bill was on the waiting list for a job at the Foreign Office. The previous year he had recruited him to spy on his student contemporaries, among whom Communism was flourishing. Bill had displayed enough flair for political investigation to qualify him for the new post that Max hoped to create at Section B5b.

'There is a possibility of a vacancy in our own office, probably of a temporary nature, salary about three-hundred pounds a year,' Max wrote to Dennis. 'This job would be for what one might term "for the duration of the crisis and/or war". It would be temporary in the sense that if suddenly there was a wonderful peace move and things really looked like settling down, it would of course be necessary for us to cut down staff and therefore the last to come would have to be the first to go. I think that the work would be exceedingly good training for the other job, and I have been given to understand that acceptance of a temporary job with us would not prevent Bill's name going back on the rota for the other job later.

'What d'you think of this idea? The advantage is that Bill would feel that he is doing something useful and gaining experience, and of course it is impossible to say exactly when vacancies may occur in the other quarter. If you would like to let me know by return post what your personal view is – that is to say that you and Joan have no objection – I will push on the matter and put Bill's name forward.'

6

During the weeks leading up to Anna's departure for the Continent, British newspapers had carried accounts of unprovoked German attacks on Polish border checkpoints. Anna decided to visit the Silesian stretch of the frontier between Germany and Poland, where she would be able to see for herself what was happening.

Overnight she stayed in the vicinity of the Sudeten town of Böhmisch-Leipa, which Czech-speakers knew as Česká Lípa. Driving through Bohemia offered the most direct route to the Silesian frontier, only Anna couldn't enter that part of Sudetenland unless she obtained a special permit. Without this, she was forced to take the long way round, which necessitated crossing the German border, something she had been doing since childhood.

Directly she entered Germany, she would have noticed any number of people in uniform. Policemen. Customs officials. Teenage boys in the Hitler Youth. Members of the League of German Girls. Fresh-faced Army conscripts wearing grey battledress. Soldiers belonging to the SS, the *Schutzstaffel*, originally formed to protect Hitler.

Other manifestations of the National Socialist regime were present on signposts and on the colourful badges that adorned people's lapels. Made from plastic, porcelain or embroidered silk, the badges demonstrated support for the party's latest

Winter Relief charity campaign. Posters advertising anti-Semitic films and lectures adorned the streets. Elsewhere, signs in parks prohibited Jews from sitting down. And signs on the edge of villages barred them from setting foot inside.

Her detour rendered less onerous than it might have been by the smooth-as-satin roads, Anna headed for Breslau, an elegant riverside city of dark Gothic buildings and wide boulevards chock-a-block with cars, buses and trams. There and elsewhere in Germany, she was liable, anywhere from 50 to 150 times a day, to be treated to 'the German Greeting', people's right arms extended in an unselfconscious fascist salute as they said, 'Heil Hitler!' Not such an unusual experience for Anna because she'd visited the country twice since Hitler had come to power. The last of these visits had taken place three summers ago when she and Princess Mira Dimitri had travelled through Germany. Between now and Anna's previous visit, the country had acquired a deceptive air of prosperity.

From Breslau, the Silesian frontier was a full afternoon's drive. But Anna found her progress halted amidst the blast-furnaces, collieries and factories of Gleiwitz, just a few miles from Poland. She lapped up pro-Nazi stories about German peasants being killed by Polish snipers. That night her sleep was disturbed by periodic gunshots.

7

Four days had elapsed since Max had written to Dennis. Over that time the weather in London had briefly perked up, seasonal warmth superseding the recent damp chill, which had been getting Max down.

In the period since her invitation to the Ramsays' house, Marjorie had remained in close touch with Mrs Ramsay, who had encouraged her to attend meetings of the Nordic League. *Most* promising from Max's point of view.

'Promising' wasn't a word that could be applied to the weather forecast, though. By the first Friday of August, which presaged the beginning of the busiest of the bank holiday week-ends, conditions were more appropriate to spring than high summer. Swarms of khaki-clad soldiers returning home on leave accentuated the impression of abnormality. It was an impression reinforced during the subsequent week.

Max and other tenants of Dolphin Square had a ringside seat for a simulated dogfight enacted overhead. Fighter planes from the Royal Air Force dived, rolled and looped as they pretended to attack a formation of bombers, which resembled a flock of migrating geese. The bombers didn't of course drop anything but a succession of white flares.

With the mushrooming sense of emergency came a moment of realization for Max. He could see that Section B5b was sure to acquire even more responsibilities. Coping with these would be out of the question for him and his secretary. The sensible move was for him to act quickly by hiring Bill Younger and others to help with the increased workload. Max couldn't, however, lay his hands on the additional funds required to expand B5b.

A couple of nights after the white flares had been dropped, the conspicuous preparations for war resumed. In the streets around where Max and his wife lived, hundreds of volunteer firemen and other Air Raid Precaution staff practised, ready for the expected air raids. Max and his fellow cadets used to carry out similar drills aboard HMS *Worcester*. On the night of this latterday rehearsal, the whole of London was subject to an experimental blackout, intended to reduce the accuracy of German bombing. Everyone had to delay going to sleep until the exercise got underway.

Blundering round in the darkness was not an uncommon event for Max. At home he insisted on switching off the lights when his pets' bedtime arrived. Sometimes he and Lois would be left sitting in a self-imposed blackout.

As Big Ben's sonorous chimes signalled half past twelve, chains of streetlamps were extinguished. The effect was still far from complete, the darkness violated by car headlamps as well as rapiers of light piercing the gaps between heavy blackout curtains.

Dazzling sunshine greeted the next morning, but the air didn't start to warm up again until the middle of the following week. After lunch that Wednesday, there was another portent of war. In the distance one could hear the steadily deepening hum of aeroplane engines. Wave after wave of large grey bombers making up arrowhead patterns were soon visible over the city. Fighters escorted them. All of the planes came low enough for one to see their markings. No swastikas, just red, white and pale blue roundels, denoting that they belonged to Britain's French allies. A series of Spitfires plunged on them, engines shrieking. Two of the Spitfires only levelled out at the final second, then hurtled across central London. Crowds congregated in the streets to watch the ensuing pretend dogfight, which was still going on when the planes evaporated in the East End haze.

By that afternoon or thereabouts, Marjorie – codenamed 'Agent M/Y' in Max's paperwork – had something more to tell him. Egged on by Mrs Ramsay, she had applied for membership of the Right Club. Marjorie had posted her subscription to Kelly Castle, the Ramsays' Scottish home, where the Captain's wife was spending a few days.[15]

The application provoked a letter, written on Monday 14 August, 1939. Mrs Ramsay's letter praised Marjorie's discretion and assured her that she would be a valuable addition to the club. Enclosed with the message was a Right Club badge, which Captain Ramsay had designed. It portrayed an eagle, wings outstretched, pecking a writhing snake, the obvious interpretation being that the snake symbolized the perceived Jewish conspiracy. Beneath the serpent lay the motto, 'For the Right'.

At last Max's investigation was under full sail.

8

Tyler Kent had been redeployed – with the State Department's say-so – from the Translation Section to the Moscow embassy's Code Room. His new workplace was on the second floor of Mokhovaya House. There, he and his colleagues were supervised by his friend, Henry W. Antheil, the Chief Code Clerk. How much longer Henry would be there, however, remained in doubt, as he was still earmarked for transfer to England.

Low-grade items of confidential information from the telegrams flowing through the Code Room were being lifted by Henry. The material, which featured statistics on German oil reserves and aircraft production, corroborated his belief in the Nazis' aggressive military ambitions. He was in the habit of relaying this information by way of coded letters to his Hollywood-based brother, who had established a sideline as a political feature-writer for *Esquire* magazine. To stop the Soviet authorities from reading his letters, Henry sent them via the diplomatic pouch. Consisting of a large satchel that was padlocked and bound with wire, the wire sealed with lead or wax, these pouches were carried by diplomatic couriers. Their cargo was immune to search or seizure. Envelopes and other packages despatched using these pouches also enjoyed exemption from search or censorship by American officials.

In general, Tyler and colleagues dealt with telegrams relevant to three sections of the embassy. Some concerned visa applications, which were the province of the consulate. Others involved the Personnel Officer, who handled anything regarding US staff in Moscow. And the remainder focused on politics, the domain of the Ambassador and his fellow diplomats.

Telegrams would often be delivered to the Code Room by the building's squad of Russian messengers, none of whom was permitted beyond the barrier erected a few feet from the door. Serenaded by teletype machines that made a tuneless din, Tyler and his colleagues had the responsibility of translating these outgoing messages into the specified codes or ciphers before sending them to their recipients. The Code Room clerks also had to decode and decipher incoming messages.

Usually, codes were named after the colour of each codebook's binding. Most frequently employed of these was Grey, formulated with non-confidential messages in mind, which was just as well because Grey provided negligible confidentiality. A good amateur cryptographer could crack it. The fact that other governments didn't have much trouble gaining access to the substance of messages sent in Grey had even been utilized as a method of spreading disinformation. Not that Tyler would have been aware of this. But he would probably have known that Green and Brown – two of the other regularly used codes – didn't offer much more security than Grey. These seemed less about secrecy than about reducing the word-count of messages and, as a consequence, lowering the cost of transmitting each telegram. A story had done the rounds about a mysterious Japanese who had delivered a missing codebook to a US Embassy. The codebook had been returned neatly wrapped, along with a courteous note. Depending on who told the story, the note explained that the Japanese had either finished with the codebook or possessed a copy of it already.

Messages requiring more than just a token gesture at secrecy were enciphered rather than encoded. While codes transformed entire words or phrases, ciphers amended individual letters and numbers, making it much harder to disinter their meaning. Documents could be enciphered or deciphered with the aid of a machine. Alternatively, strip-ciphers such as the recently adopted M-138 could be used. Each of these comprised a hundred strips featuring the alphabet in parallel to a randomly shuffled version of it. Despatches were transposed from the former to the latter, the results grouped in clusters of fifteen letters.

Yet the secrecy of American ciphers was undermined by Code Room procedure. Original drafts of each telegram were stapled to their coded or enciphered versions. Bundled together, these were then handed to a Russian messenger, who was obliged to take them down to the basement furnace, where they were supposed to be incinerated. Even if the messenger adhered to correct procedure and did not either copy or purloin selected telegrams, the hard-to-burn bundles of paper could be rescued from the furnace by the Soviet employees who loitered round it. Once the Soviets had obtained parallel copies of the original message – the so-called plain text – and its coded or enciphered counterpart, those codes and ciphers were rendered worthless.

Inside the Code Room, it had become evident by the second week of August 1939 that diplomatic activity across Moscow was hotting up. Foreign Service staff were undertaking a feverish round of talks with diplomats from other countries. At the same time a British government delegation had just arrived in town, bent on exploring the possibility of an Anglo–French–Soviet military alliance against the Nazis.

Tyler's transfer to the Code Room had exposed to his inquisitive gaze all the latest, most confidential diplomatic communications. Under that heading fell the recent telegram from one of the Ambassador's aides. The message, sent to the Secretary of State, concerned an informant within the German Embassy in Moscow. Thanks to this unnamed source, acquired some months previously, the aide had issued a warning to the American government that the Soviets would not be striking a deal with the British and French. They would, instead, be signing a non-aggression pact with the Nazis.

Fearing that the NKVD had bugged the US Embassy, the aide didn't risk dictating his message. He preferred to write it out himself. So illegible was his handwriting that the message looked as if it had been enciphered already.

Henry W. Antheil dealt with the 'For Your Eyes Only' material like this. But even if Henry didn't blab about the contents of the most confidential telegrams, Tyler still had access to them. Copies were kept in the File Room, located on the same floor as where he worked. Tyler's new position as a code clerk gave him authorization to enter this otherwise prohibited room. If he wanted to track down a specific telegram, he simply needed to go there and skim through the main index, which contained a précis of each transmission, plus a file number that would allow him to locate the corresponding folder, where he could find the entire message. He could then transcribe or even photograph it. Any message he wanted. Messages to and from the top brass – the Ambassador, the Consul-General and the Military Attaché. Messages from abroad – from the State Department, from other Ambassadors, from the President of the United States.

9

Shortly after midnight on Friday 25 August, 1939, Max dialled the number. Phoning so late at night was not the done thing, but he had reason to ignore social convention. If he delayed making the call until a more civilized hour, he might be too late.

He was ringing a poky basement flat in Earl's Court. Its impecunious tenants – William Joyce and his wife, Meg – referred to it as their doll's house. Having visited the Joyces' home in recent months, Max could vouch for the truth behind their jest. He had known William for years, the two men's field of acquaintance intersecting at multiple junctures.[16]

William once turned up at a party thrown by Dennis Wheatley, who liked to invite mismatched people to his St John's Wood soirées. Rogues, chancers and political extremists sipped drinks alongside respectable guests. What united the disparate partygoers was the power to amuse, to be 'good fellows', as Dennis branded them.

In a warped attempt to curry favour with their host, William had expressed regret that *The Devil Rides Out* and Dennis's other novels from the same series couldn't be published in Germany because one of the heroes was Jewish. He'd added that Hermann Göring, among the most prominent Nazi officials, had read all Dennis's books. William had even offered to take Dennis across to Germany and introduce him to the Nazi leadership.

Hobnobbing with Dennis was not the only area of overlap between Max and William. Many years earlier, they had both been among the 100,000-strong membership of the British Fascisti, an organization whose title acknowledged its roots in the burgeoning Italian fascist movement, led by Benito Mussolini. Support for Mussolini's brand of fascism represented a common stance in mainstream British politics during the 1920s. Later renamed the 'British Fascists', the British Fascisti had – save for its title and hatred of Communism – few affinities with 1930s fascism, specifically with Mosley's similarly titled movement, much less with Nazism. To Max, the fundamental difference between the British Fascisti and its successors lay in its respect for the constitution and elected authorities. Its title had come to suggest otherwise, but it was really an upper middle-class, conservative movement, built around dedication to King and Country, together with backing for policies such as the introduction of secret ballots to decide whether trade unions should take strike action.

The opprobrium subsequently attached to fascism led Max to assure his MI5 colleagues that he'd only joined – somewhat implausibly – at the behest of his then employer, who had wanted to gather information about the party on behalf of MI5. In 1930 he had resigned from the movement, his departure coinciding with its increasing factionalism, political irrelevance and drift towards anti-Semitism. He had announced his resig-nation with a facetious letter to the party's newspaper, assuring its members that he hadn't been dismissed for stealing the office dog's milk.

Since those days, William's allegiances had shifted many nautical miles to starboard. He had gone from the British Fascisti to the British Union and now the National Socialist League, his own negligible little group, now on the brink of extinction.

After becoming involved with the British Union, he had been added to Max's team of agents. Over the time they had been working together, Max's attitude towards William had under-gone a metamorphosis, qualified respect transmogrified into heartfelt dislike. Max had come to the conclusion that he was a pompous, conceited creature who would not shrink from using violence. He was the type of person, Max thought, who was only pleasant to people if they shared what Max termed as his 'rabid opinions' – extreme anti-Semitic, anti-Catholic opinions. His hatred also extended to jazz, Max's favourite form of music. Under the influence of Nazi ideology, William considered jazz a symptom of cultural decadence. Whenever he heard it played on the radio or gramophone, he would switch it off. Despite the tensions between them, Max regarded William as someone who might one day make history.

Before long, William answered Max's phonecall. William had a remarkably distinctive voice. It was a fastidious, adenoidal voice that carried hints of both his Irish background and the public-school education he never had.

Seemingly laying aside their disagreements, Max leaked some information picked up from official sources. The gist of what he said to William was, 'Your name's on the list. They'll be coming to arrest you.'

'When?'

But Max was unable to provide an exact date. Just sometime soon. Tomorrow, perhaps. Or maybe the day after. He advised William to go abroad. As he said this, he probably had a destination in mind – Nazi Germany, where he had been angling to place William in an undercover capacity.

'Thank you, Max.'

10

By tipping off William that night, Max had taken an almighty risk. The list, mentioned in their conversation, was after all highly confidential. Being the leader of the National Socialist League, its pro-Nazi policies implicit within its title, William was among twenty-two people featured on that list, already submitted to the Home Office for approval. Under Regulation 18b of the new Emergency Defence Regulations, which had just gone through Parliament, those people could be detained without trial. They would then be denied the full mechanism of justice, a closed hearing before an Advisory Committee substituting for a proper trial.

Max could not be certain how Sir Vernon Kell, Director-General of MI5, would react if he found out about the tip-off. Even though Sir Vernon, previously so fulsome in his praise for Max's work, was a friend and periodic dinner guest, a passion for ornithology offering a bond between the two men, their relationship might not be capable of insulating Max from the by-products of such a discovery. Max had flouted both the secrecy of the list and the chain of command. Whatever his ultimate intentions, the tip-off hadn't been authorized, so there was a danger that he might end up losing the job he loved.

Mercifully for him, the chances of Sir Vernon learning about the tip-off were slim. In the manner of a chess player, taught to think more than one move ahead, Max nevertheless took pre-emptive action in order to deflect any future suspicion he might attract.

He put his plan into practice on the morning after he had telephoned William. This entailed disseminating a cover-story. Just the kind of story that could be slipped into a conversation with a couple of his colleagues at Thames House, MI5's headquarters.

It was a modern building near Lambeth Bridge. One entered its shop-lined foyer through a stone portico, large enough to dwarf even a man of Max's stature. MI5 had been discreetly omitted from the building's directory, made up of diverse businesses as well as a squash club and a golf driving range.[17] On the top floor, which purported to house only the Texas Oil Company Ltd, the lift opened onto a huge, echoing anteroom, from where Max could amble into MI5's wood-panelled, brown linoleum-floored premises.

Guy Liddell and Francis Aiken Sneath were the colleagues to whom Max spun his cover-story. Short and dumpy, his scalp visible through hair that had long ago sounded the retreat, Guy was a smartly dressed man in his late forties, who was more often than not puffing on a cigarette. As Deputy Head of B Division, he was Max's commanding officer, a role he'd filled ever since Max had joined MI5. Guy, whose mumbled tone of voice exuded patience and humour, had lately succumbed to the wartime propensity for addressing junior colleagues by their Christian names.

Like Max, Francis Aiken Sneath was one of those lower-ranking staff. An ex-university lecturer of a similar vintage to Max, Francis had recently been placed at the helm of the section monitoring the British Union and other fascist groups.

When setting forth his case, Max was fond of the phrase, 'from experience'. It lodged a tactful reminder of his greater length of service and, by extension, superior knowledge. He pretended to treat Guy and Francis to a candid briefing on his telephone conversation with William. In view of the fact that William had been an agent of his since 1934, there was nothing irregular about such a phonecall. Max reassured both Guy and Francis that he hadn't breathed a word about William's looming arrest or given William any other improper information. But Max's reassurance was miscalculated, being more likely to arouse suspicion than deflect it.

11

The prospect of war supplying an incentive for her to return from the Continent, on Sunday 27 August, 1939 Anna began the laborious journey back from Hungary, where she'd been staying with an inordinately rich aristocratic friend. He owned an old country house, which had formal gardens and tree-lined walks. These offered Anna a heightened flavour of the genteel life that the Communists had snatched from her and her family.[18]

She didn't get home until the following Tuesday, by which time the signing of the Nazi–Soviet Non-Aggression Pact had been announced. While she was away, London had undergone a transformation. She could have been deceived into believing that her trip had lasted a good deal longer than just a few weeks.

Almost everywhere one looked, there were signs of the impending conflict. Young men in blue RAF uniforms or khaki battledress could be seen on the streets and in the restaurants and cafés. The roads were heaving with Army lorries and military despatch-riders on motorcycles that threaded their way through the traffic. And sandbags were being stacked in front of buildings, the ground floors of which had started to slide from sight, like descending passengers in cage-lifts. London's recent militarization had even inflected women's fashion, many coats and jackets having been embellished by epaulettes and braid.

Now she was back in town, Anna resumed her tenancy of the small house and garage she'd been renting for the past five years or so. It was on Gloucester Place Mews, a narrow, cobbled side-street in the heart of Paddington. Synonymous with grotty hotels and boarding houses, this wasn't the smartest of addresses. It was immensely convenient, though – close to where she worked, close to the West End, and close to Manchester Square, home of the Wallace Collection, that most astonishing repository of paintings, furniture and *objets d'art*, where she had on at least one occasion found inspiration for her work as a *couturier*.[19]

During the time she'd lived in Gloucester Place Mews, she had become friendly with most of her neighbours. They included the Deightons, the working-class couple next-door, on whose artistically talented little boy[20] she lavished some of her meagre allocation of charm. His calm, dependable mother, who used to cook for Anna's supper parties, liked to have her round for tea and a slice of cake. In affirmation of their improbable friendship, Anna had once given the woman a flamboyant hat she'd made – a velvet fez embellished by a red feather. Not the type of thing for which Anna's neighbour would ever have much use, yet the gift went down well.

Nowhere was the disparity in the social status of the two women more tangible than in the luxurious presence of a telephone in Anna's house. Without having to traipse down the road to the nearest phonebox, she could ring her parents and also catch up with Barbara Allen and other close friends such as Enid Riddell, who had summered abroad, too.

One person no longer available to field calls from Anna was Margaret Bothamley, a fellow Right Club member who had lately emigrated to Germany. Anna had been a guest at Margaret's little gatherings, held in her Earl's Court flat. Margaret – an erstwhile regular at the café run by Anna's parents – was a wealthy, grey-haired sixty year old. She'd been a founding member of the Imperial Fascist League. And she'd been Secretary of the central London branch of that emphatically pro-Nazi organization, the Link, which functioned under the overall control of a friend of Anna's father. Since Hitler came to power, Margaret had been spending several months every year in Germany, from where she had, during the autumn of 1936, made a propaganda broadcast on behalf of the Nazis.

Such was the intensity of her fixation with all things German that she liked to tell a strange, delusional story about how, when she was eighteen, she had secretly married a German named Adolf Bliebtreu. The choice of name for her fictitious husband was indicative of where her national allegiances lay, his surname roughly translating as 'Adolf Remain Loyal'. She claimed that he'd left her only a matter of days into their marriage, after which she had received letters from him for two-and-a-half years, their correspondence truncated by his death.

Margaret's get-togethers were attended by as many as ten people at a time. Her political affiliations could be discerned merely by scanning the flat. Nazi leaflets and memorabilia were all over the place. On her piano there was even a signed photo of the Führer. Tea or cocktails lubricating the predictably pro-Nazi, anti-Semitic conversation, guests would find themselves mingling with German officials as well as fellow British fascists. Anna's unashamedly pro-Nazi friend Ronnie – Lord Ronald Graham – was among the people one was likely to encounter there. Another was the self-styled Commandant Mary Allen, an undeniably masculine ex-Suffragette and British Union supporter who had founded a sizeable paramilitary force called the Women's Reserve.[21] She habitually wore its dark, peak-capped, jackbooted uniform. For years she'd been making clandestine trips to Germany to hold talks with Hitler and two of his subordinates, Hermann Göring and Heinrich Himmler.

But Margaret's parties belonged to the past, not to the revamped city in which Anna found herself. Shrugging off any travel-induced fatigue, Anna went back to work that week at Busvine's, where the new autumn designs were on sale.

Instead of her normal unobtrusive outfit, Anna marked her return by wearing an ostentatious new costume. This included a hat, kept in place by a hatpin decorated with what appeared to be diamonds and sapphires, spelling out her Christian name.

Just before setting off for the Continent, Anna had complained to one of the other shop assistants that she didn't have any suitable clothes to take with her, yet she offered no explanation for the current sumptuousness of her attire. The last few weeks had nonetheless supplied Anna with the opportunity not only to regale her colleagues with eulogies to Hitler and the Nazis, but also to indulge her habit of name-dropping and flaunting her access to privileged information. She could parrot what she'd been told about the previous year's invasion of Czechoslovakia – how it had been staged in order to forestall a planned Communist coup, financed by a cabal of Jewish-American businessmen.

No more inclined to conceal her opinions than she was to conceal the large birthmark between her shoulder-blades, reference to Jews would have been enough to precipitate one of her anti-Semitic tirades, her thoughts unimpeded by self-censorship during their neural sprint from brain to lips. Many of Anna's pronouncements were even regarded as outrageous by her fascist friends. She knew they nicknamed her 'Julius Streicher', a name borrowed from the editor of the Nazi newspaper, *Der Stürmer*, notorious for the frothing venom of its anti-Semitic invective. And she was used to hearing patronizing remarks about how she and her family had a bee in their collective bonnet about Jews. But her convictions remained impervious to these judgements. Combined with her artistic gifts and fluency in multiple languages, such beliefs – on which, as she put it, she'd been suckled as a baby – formed the core of her patrimony.

To prevent her from alienating customers at Busvine's, the manageress had banned her from talking about the Jews, Hitler or politics in general during working hours. If Hitler and Nazi Germany are so wonderful, the manageress had previously snapped, why don't you go back there?

Undeterred by this earlier warning, Anna distributed copies of the Führer's speeches to anyone in the shop who would accept them.

12

Max kept his promise. He wrote to Dennis at the Wheatleys' holiday address on the Riviera. In his playfully phrased warning letter, Max employed their pet-name for him. 'Uncle has taken a turn for the worse and, if you wish to see him before the end,' he wrote, 'you should return home at once.'

Even without access to friends who possessed government connections, one could tell that war was only days, maybe just hours, away. The newspapers had been sprinkled with ominous accounts of French citizens being evacuated from Germany, Polish anti-aircraft batteries opening fire on a German plane, German troops massing near the Polish border and Polish military convoys heading through Warsaw. Also there had been stories concerning the British government's reaffirmation of its guarantee to support the Poles if they were attacked.

13

On the ground floor at the Architectural Association Schools in Bloomsbury, there used to be a special office set aside for students who had sustained disabilities during the First World War. Anna only needed to cast her mind back to the occupants of that office to be reminded of the human price of military action.

By the morning of Wednesday 30 August, 1939, preparations for the next war had become even more conspicuous on the streets around where she lived and worked. Giant molehills of sand had sprouted from the pavements overnight. Passers-by watched teams of volunteers shovelling it into sandbags. Other men were boarding up – and, in some cases, bricking up – windows. Still others were busy painting white lines down the centre of roads and on traffic islands, pavement edges, trees and lamp-posts. These markings had the purpose of assisting motorists during the blackout.

Every now and then, men working in the street perpetuated the recent craze for pidgin German by shouting phrases such as 'Ach! Mein patience exhausted ist.' Heavy traffic meanwhile rolled past. There were lorries laden with sand and timber. And there were cars displaying a hotchpotch of signs. 'Air Defence Priority.' 'We have joined the National Defence Transport Group.' 'ARP' – Air Raid Precaution.

Whether any of the defences on such prominent display would shield people against German weaponry was a moot point. During her trip to Czechoslovakia, Anna had heard stories about that country's supposedly impregnable fortifications. The aristocratic owner of a porcelain factory told her the Germans had, after the occupation of Czechoslovakia, requested permission to test their artillery against one of the gun emplacements on his estate. He'd said that a single German artillery shell had pulverized the target.

14

Max still hadn't received a reply to the letter posted to the Wheatleys' address on the Riviera. Any grounds for concern were, however, soon banished. Unaware that Max had tried to warn them, Dennis and family resurfaced in London on the final day of August. They turned out to have been on a leisurely gourmet detour through France. Dennis had also taken the opportunity to revisit the First World War battlefields where he'd served as an artillery officer. But he had been disappointed to find few landmarks he recognized. All the same, he was delighted to have squeezed in one final happy week in France before, as he described it, the curtain of war came down.

Unlike Dennis, Max didn't have firsthand experience of the muddy carnage of the Western Front, of war's boundless capacity to lend substance to even the most grotesque of nightmares. Max had nevertheless just been given a preview of coming attractions. This had occurred within the improbable confines of Regent's Park Zoo, which he had visited frequently over the years. As a child he often went there with his father, who had been chummy with several of the staff. They would show Max behind the scenes and even let him get quite near the alligators, orang-utans and other animals.

In his latterday role as one of the fellows of the Zoological Society of London, which ran the place, he bore some of the responsibility for the excruciating decision that had been taken to destroy a substantial part of the Zoo's magnificent collection. As a means of safeguarding against the risk of bomb blasts releasing dangerous insects and reptiles into Regent's Park, all the poisonous snakes, boa constrictors and black widow spiders had received a death sentence. So too had a young African bull elephant who could not be rehoused elsewhere. A similar fate awaited most of the inhabitants of the aquarium, which was being drained lest an explosion unleashed almost a quarter-of-a-million gallons of water on surrounding roads.

The zookeepers couldn't be blamed for looking so visibly shaken by the slaughter now underway. Max knew how heartbreaking animal bereavement was. He had once owned a spider monkey that had died of pneumonia after only a couple of months. It was, he thought, quite the most lovable and delightful of creatures. He never saw her bite or even *attempt* to bite anyone. Lodged in his memory was how she had, during her final illness, gently gripped his fingers as he'd stroked her. Then she had held them near her chest. She had, he was certain, wanted to show him the source of her pain. When she'd died in his arms, tears welled up in his eyes. Desperate to preserve his stance as a scientific pragmatist and to resist joining the ranks of what he scornfully labelled 'dyed-in-the-wool sentimentalists', he liked to think those tears were a product not just of grief but of frustration at his powerlessness to alleviate the monkey's suffering.

15

The streets near Anna's house were noisier than ever on the morning of Friday 1 September, 1939. Since seven o'clock, police in loudspeaker vans had been driving round broadcasting instructions. These were directed at the excited herd of children flowing past the Gloucester Place end of Anna's street.

Yet there was nothing unexpected about the present turmoil. Details of this exodus had featured in the previous day's newspapers, several of which Jock Ramsay dismissed as 'Jewspapers'. Across the city, thousands of children were being shepherded to prearranged assembly points, from where they could be evacuated to safer parts of the country.

Sharpening the piquant aroma of impending danger, posters declaring 'HITLER INVADES POLAND' had by late afternoon appeared on newsstands around the West End. Recently, newsstands had been doing a frantic trade, queues of people forming as the vendors shouted the stop-press headlines. 'Latest! Latest! 'itler just sent for a couple of aspirins!' one of them had been calling out the other day.

News that Warsaw and other Polish cities were being bombed and that Nazi troops were advancing into Poland through the borders with Germany and Slovakia came as no surprise to Anna. The repercussions of the invasion were correspondingly predictable. Both Britain and France had already mobilized their armies.

The sense of crisis was redoubled by the Civil Defence Department leaflet dropped into the letterboxes of all households that day. Patently intended to reassure, the leaflet offered advice on what to do in an air raid. It featured soft-soap about how well-built British houses were and how the chances of suffering a direct hit were just one-in-a-hundred. But any recollection of the newsreels and press reports on the wars that had already disfigured the 1930s hinted at how hellish things would be for the survivors. Mangled corpses everywhere one looked. Piles of rubble. Water bubbling out of ruptured mains. Smoke and flames. In retrospect, the wars in Spain and China were beginning to appear no more than provincial try-outs for the West End production about to open any day now.

From dusk that evening, the government imposed a nightly blackout. This was a new experience for Anna, who had been on holiday when the blackout rehearsal had been staged. Without the streetlights, the brightly lit window-displays, the illuminated interiors of passing buses or the inviting glow seeping through the curtains of nearby houses, busy roads were reduced to nothing but a roiling stream of voices. Every now and again, the darkness was broken by a match fizzing into life, perhaps yielding a fugitive glimpse of some up-lit face, cigarette-in-mouth, cheeks hollowed like an El Greco Christ. The darkness was also relieved by flashes of lightning and an almost full moon that slid out from behind rapidly emptying rainclouds.

Supplementing the moonlight were few permissible sources of artificial light. Traffic signals, now just dim red and green crosses. Blinkered side and rear lights on vehicles and bicycles. Fuzzy red lights marking pedestrian refuges. And torches carried not only by pedestrians but also by the uniformed commissionaires who stood outside the grander hotels, double layers of tissue paper creating abbreviated, threadbare beams.

When Anna had been at boarding school near Worcester, 'Out in the dark' was among the perennial options for the English composition exercises set by her headmistress. As befitted the school motto, *Vi et Virtute* – 'By Strength and Courage' – the headmistress also urged them to defy the tradition of mutely decorous femininity and express their opinions. Weekly lectures on world affairs were scheduled in an attempt to persuade Anna and the others to take an interest in politics, the lecturer's voice customarily counterpointed by the negligent click of the girls' knitting-needles. Anna's former headmistress might not have approved of the character of Anna's political beliefs, but she would surely have been proud of the diligence with which Anna continued to implement the principles learnt all those years ago.

Even though the Germans had just invaded Poland – the third country they had subsumed in as many years – Anna didn't hold Hitler responsible for what was going on. She accepted the Nazi line that the Poles were the true villains, their final provocation being the previous night's armed occupation of the radio station in Gleiwitz, the town where Anna had heard all those stories about Polish snipers. In truth, the entire incident at the radio station was staged by the SS, using concentration camp inmates dressed as Polish soldiers, the dead bodies of whom provided counterfeit 'proof' of Polish aggression.

16

Meetings with colleagues at MI5 headquarters had just become a lot less convenient for Max. What used to be a short journey there from Dolphin Square was now a six-mile trek. Only the previous Sunday, Guy Liddell, Sir Vernon Kell and the rest of the staff had decamped from Thames House to the most improbable premises in west London – His Majesty's Prison Wormwood Scrubs. MI5's move away from central London was motivated by the need for more office space.

Getting to MI5 headquarters would have been much easier had Max been able to drive. Unlike his late brother, who had contested the Royal Automobile Club's Tourist Trophy road races, Max had never been remotely interested in cars. At least he could reach Wormwood Scrubs by tube. Its castellated and turreted entrance, which looked like the entrance to one of those toy forts popular during his childhood, wasn't far from East Acton Underground Station.

Beyond the gates, there was a small courtyard and a flotilla of large, dimly lit mid-Victorian buildings whose previous occupants had departed. Even the prisoners in the hospital wing were no longer there. Inmates with three months or less remaining of their sentences had been told they were eligible for release, at which point everyone in the hospital had made a miraculous recovery.

Each of the prison's accommodation blocks had a central atrium lined with cells, linked by staircases and layer upon layer of filigreed iron walkways. Female members of MI5's staff, whose underwear would otherwise have been visible from below, were permitted to don trousers, formerly an outlandish conceit. Wafts of their perfume couldn't do much to counteract the lingering stench that permeated the place. Max's colleagues had arrived last week to discover part-filled chamber pots in cells destined to be their offices.

Further differentiating these rooms from run-of-the-mill offices were tiny, barred windows, too high up the wall to provide a view. Cumbersome iron doors with no handles on the insides were another distinguishing feature. Visitors such as Max had to be careful not to shut the door behind them when they arrived for meetings. Do that and they would find themselves locked inside until an observant colleague came to their rescue.

Where confidential information was being bandied about, face-to-face meetings were preferable to phonecalls, which might be overheard by a switchboard operator at a local telephone exchange. Today Max was in conference with Sir Vernon, who had coined an amusing term for these trips to Wormwood Scrubs. He called them 'scrubbing', which made it sound as if he spent his days on his hands and knees like some meaty-armed charlady.

Sir Vernon was just over twenty-five years Max's senior, though the difference in age seemed greater. Max's tall, upright frame projected an impression of hearty good health, whereas Sir Vernon resembled some genial and timorous Edwardian scholar, his little oval pince-nez and neatly clipped moustache playing a part in that. Between asthmatic coughing fits, which rattled his frail physique like a sash-window in a gale, he treated his staff with courtesy and paternalistic care that tended to arouse deep affection.

His conversation with Max dealt with the wave of raids being carried out by Special Branch. These were targeting people on the MI5 list, whose detention without trial had been sanctioned by the Home Office. Hearing that one of those people – William Joyce of 38a Eardley Crescent – had evaded arrest, Max wasn't in a position to express anything other than feigned surprise.

When the police had gone round to this address, it had been vacant aside from William's mother, sister and another woman, who were busy tidying the place. William's mother told the police that he and his wife, Meg, had already left the country. If his mother was to be believed, they'd taken the train to Dover, then caught the cross-Channel ferry. On the assumption that the Irish Republic would remain neutral during the coming war, they'd previously been planning to flee to Dublin. Meg had, however, talked her husband into going with her to Berlin instead.

Max had first attempted to get William to move to Germany several years earlier. The idea had been for William to join the Nazi Party, obtain German citizenship and carry on working as an MI5 agent. But William, who looked favourably on the Nazi regime as an ally in the fight against Communism, had rejected Max's proposal. By dint of the recent tip-off, Max had finally got his way: he had an agent in Berlin, armed with plausibly anti-British credentials. Yet there was scant prospect of William being persuaded to spy on the Nazis.

To allay Sir Vernon's concerns about Special Branch's failure to arrest William, Max did his best to downplay its significance. 'Joyce is not a danger,' he insisted, the warm, soothing timbre of his voice tailor-made for situations such as this.

17

At 11.15 a.m. on Sunday 3 September, 1939, Prime Minister Neville Chamberlain began his well-advertised radio broadcast. Weary defiance pervading his manner, he said, 'I am speaking to you from the Cabinet Room in Downing Street. This morning the British Ambassador in Berlin handed the German government a final note stating that, unless we heard from them by eleven o'clock that they were prepared at once to withdraw their troops from Poland, a state of war would exist between us. I have to tell you now that no such undertaking has been received and that consequently this country is at war with Germany.'

Following the Prime Minister's broadcast, Anna was informed by Busvine's that they no longer required her services. There wouldn't be much demand for evening-dresses and ball-gowns anymore, so the company had to reduce its costs. Enraged by the offhand manner of her unforeseen dismissal, Anna grumbled about how her two-year employment contract had been discarded as if it were merely some out-of-date railway timetable.

Still, she had the comforting knowledge that she and her fellow White Russians were a versatile bunch. Look at her parents. They didn't just run a café. At one stage her father had worked for a firm of coal merchants. Then there were all those former officers in the Tsarist Army, earning a crust as taxi drivers. But the prize for the most inventive career-change surely deserved to go to that erstwhile colleague of Anna's father. He went from being an Admiral in the Russian Navy to making ladies' hats. Running him a close second in the versatility stakes was Anna's paternal grandfather who had, after the Communists snatched power in Russia, reinvented himself as a professional watercolourist.[22]

In Anna's mind, the demonstrable adaptability of herself and her family was a wellspring of pride. She reacted to her sacking from Busvine's by applying to become a Russian translator. Offering a potentially rich source of the type of inside-information she treasured, the job was based at the London headquarters of the RAF's Advanced Air Strike Force. This recently created organization had just established an outpost in France alongside the infantry units of the British Expeditionary Force, there to bolster the French defences.

While Anna waited for a response to her application, she cast round for stop-gap employment that would at least cover her day-to-day expenses. She enrolled in the Auxiliary Fire Service, which was desperate for recruits. Before she could be officially inducted into the Service, though, she had to travel across town for a medical examination.

Already purged of children, sporadic chalk-marks on walls and pavements affording a heart-rending reminder of them, London had undergone yet more changes since the Prime Minister had made his announcement the other day. Buses and taxis had become much less frequent. A ring of over a hundred silver-skinned barrage balloons, their wire tethers designed to bring down low-flying enemy aircraft, beaded the distant skyline. Posters explaining what to do in the event of a poison gas attack had been pasted up. Yellow squares of detector-paint, sensitive to mustard gas and other chemical weapons, had appeared on postboxes. And gasmasks in neat shoulder-slung boxes or canvas cases were being carried by most people.

Despite repeated gripes about her health, Anna passed the Auxiliary Fire Service medical. Unlike most other female recruits to the AFS, she was not assigned a position as a clerk or telephonist. Being an experienced driver who owned a car, she was allotted the rank of Category D Auxiliary. In that role she would be responsible for driving vans and using her Morris convertible to ferry officers around town and tow little grey two-wheeled water-pumps, which the AFS staff referred to as 'appliances'.

The job paid a small weekly salary of £1 17s. 6d. Added to that was an allowance for the use of her car. She would also be entitled to half-price haircuts in many West End salons and to three restaurant vouchers a day, worth sixpence apiece. But these vouchers wouldn't make much difference. Even the most basic meals cost ten times that.

Along with the vouchers, Anna was handed a fire service respirator and a signed chit. The latter had to be presented to an authorized retailer, from where she would be issued with a dark-blue AFS uniform. It featured a brass-buttoned tunic that had epaulettes and a belt-cinched waist. An AFS badge filled the spot where the left-hand breast pocket might have been. The badge was embroidered in precisely the same shade of scarlet as the packaging for the new Elizabeth Arden beauty set.

To accompany the tunic, Anna had a choice between peg-bottom trousers or a long skirt. These came with a peaked cap – which she wore at a fashionably acute angle – plus a pair of what could only be termed 'sensible shoes'. Graceless black things made from stiff leather. Until they were broken in, Anna was bound to get blisters whenever she wore them.

Her uniform also included a voluminous double-breasted greatcoat, made from material that possessed all the flexibility of a mahogany sideboard. Ironic considering that she had spent so much time working with exquisite fabrics such as red-spotted organza, black damask and, of course, that pale silk with the fleur-de-lys design printed in what was advertised as 'Blue Anna'.

To complete her AFS uniform, she was ordered to provide a white shirt, black tie and fawn stockings. Not exactly the most flattering of ensembles. It was all a far cry from the autumn collection she'd been about to unveil at her shop this time last year. The collection had sent the fashion correspondent from *The Times* into raptures. 'Lovely.' 'Ravishing.' 'Romantic.' Those were just some of the words used — words capable of supplying emotional sustenance through hard times.

18

Max rang up Dennis and broke the news. He announced that William Joyce's digs had been raided by Special Branch and that William had fled the country. Then Max asked Dennis whether he'd ever met William. It was a question to which Max knew the answer.

No doubt eager to avoid being linked to something scandalous, Dennis replied that he didn't recall encountering William.

'Oh, yes you do,' Max corrected him. 'He was at one of your parties.'

Having challenged Dennis's conveniently vague memory of William, Max teased him by concocting a story about how the police had found a rather interesting file when they'd scoured the fugitive's home. The subject of that file was a certain Mr D. Wheatley. Max deadpanned an account of how it contained a document William had drawn up for the Nazis. He went on to explain that the document identified Dennis as a useful collaborator once the Germans had occupied Britain. And Max even claimed there was a recommendation that Dennis should be appointed *Gauleiter* – local Nazi Party leader – for northwest London.

Confident that Max knew him well enough to realize this wasn't true, Dennis laughed off what Max told him. Without conceding that the whole story was nothing more than blokeish joshing, infused by an element of cruelty and competitiveness, Max turned the laughter into a duet. Ever the game-player, Max's amusement may have been enriched by the awareness that he'd just demonstrated why *he* worked for MI5 while Dennis merely *wrote* about espionage.

19

Her AFS enrolment completed, Anna was posted to 'Sub-Station V', one of numerous makeshift fire stations housed in requisitioned buildings. It lay only a brief drive from her home. By going via Marble Arch and onto the wide sweep of Park Lane, she could make the most of her car's acceleration. When she'd almost reached Hyde Park Corner, Anna needed to veer left into the compact network of streets on the fringe of Mayfair, an area with which she was well-acquainted.

Earlier in that decade she had lived in a beautiful Arts and Crafts-style house there. She was old enough to remember what Mayfair had been like before it was colonized by exclusive little shops, blocks of flats and hulking great hotels. The area had been dominated by privately owned mansions of the type where her uncle Gabriel used to attend lavish supper parties and dances. Known to her as 'Gavroche', he was an effeminate, self-deprecating homosexual. He'd been a diplomat at the Imperial Russian Embassy in London and a fixture in high society, his circle encompassing Lady Cynthia, the first wife of Sir Oswald Mosley. Like so many other people, he had joined what were designated 'the self-evacuees' abandoning London, only he hadn't merely decamped to some English country town. He had abandoned his house in Kensington and fled to neutral Switzerland. Well away from danger – for the time being at least.

Sandwiched between two small shops, one selling cakes, the other antiques, Sub-Station V was on Down Street. Anna's new workplace had until recently been a seedy garage called University Motors.

Except for a few professional firemen, Anna's new work-mates consisted of barely trained men and women under the command of the Station Officer, distinguished by his yellow cap-badge. The men were being put through parade-ground drill and being trained in how to extinguish fires using the station's two mobile water-pumps.

Nobody seemed to have the foggiest idea what they were doing. To make matters worse, everyone was dog-tired. If the expected air raids had taken place right then, a large expanse of the West End would have gone up in flames.

Soon Anna got into conversation with a switchboard operator, based in the Watch Room. AFS Watch Rooms routinely echoed to the staccato buzzing of the switchboard and the sound of women's voices delivering instructions, laced with acronyms and Fire Service jargon. One heard just as wide a cross-section of accents as one heard at British Union meetings, some of those accents broad Cockney, others *terribly* refined, class boundaries eroded by tentative camaraderie.

Anna's new acquaintance was a tough young Australian Egyptologist who had been on holiday in France when the imminence of war had compelled her to seek refuge in England. She detested her job on the switchboard. Ever since her family had first shared a telephone-line in Melbourne, she had loathed phones. Her feelings about them had, she declared, been reinforced by her experiences at Sub-Station V.

Much like Anna, she was marking time until she could wangle a better job. In her case, she was waiting to see whether her application to work for the foreign languages section of the Ministry of Information's Postal and Telegraph Censorship Department had been successful. Happily for Anna, that was one of the places where Jock Ramsay was itching to procure a sympathetic contact.

With evangelical tenacity, she spent the next few days trying to persuade the switchboard operator to join the British Union and accompany her to meetings. A fair number of the male activists from local branches of the party had been called up for military service, so the onus was on Anna and other female supporters to fill the void and promote Mosley's 'Stop the War' campaign. In temporary abeyance since the final days of August when the movement had staged a couple of big open-air rallies, the campaign was about to start again. So far, however, Anna's determined efforts to recruit her acquaintance from the Watch Room had been rebuffed.

20

A colleague of Max's over at Wormwood Scrubs had cultivated a well-placed informant within the German diplomatic corps. His informant said that Hitler would attempt to land a knockout punch against Britain as soon as war was declared.

Within minutes of the Prime Minister's dramatic broadcast last Sunday, the prediction appeared to have come true. An impending attack was heralded by the eerie mating-call of air-raid sirens. Yet those sirens had been a false alarm.

That was four days ago, during which the doom-laden prophecies of Max's friend, Dennis Wheatley, hadn't come to pass either. Not a single German bomb had fallen on Britain, several more false alarms heightening the sense of relief.

One could have succumbed to wishful-thinking, to conjecture about how all the previous talk about bombing and gas-attacks might have just been alarmist claptrap. Nonetheless one could not help but feel a spasm of pulse-quickening anxiety whenever one heard a vehicle accelerate and then suddenly decelerate in a busy street, the concurrent gear-change engendering a plaintive yowl that rose and fell like an air-raid siren's opening notes.

For Max and other animal lovers, the atmosphere of trepidation, of death stalking the city, was intensified by the sight of queues of people outside veterinary surgeries, waiting to have their pets put down. Once the bombs started falling, London would – so the theory went – be no place for domestic animals. Shrouded by tarpaulins that drew attention to what they sought to conceal, stacks of dead creatures were accumulating on the pavements in front of those surgeries. Had Max achieved his boyhood ambition to become a vet, he might have found himself wielding the fatal syringe.

In spite of the nagging fear that hung over London, the sense that the capital was enjoying nothing more than a stay of execution denied so many of its domestic animals, Max was pressing on with his work, only his efforts were being hindered by the situation at MI5 headquarters.

Section B7 – Francis Aiken Sneath's department – should have been handling the paperwork for the investigation of Captain Ramsay and associates. B7 was in a shambles, however. No good expecting *them* to help with the administrative side of things, Max realized. He'd have to deal with the paperwork as well, though that wasn't something for which he had been prepared by his schooling aboard HMS *Worcester*.

His path from there to an expensively furnished office in Dolphin Square had been circuitous by any standards. After leaving the Royal Navy Reserve, he had been a paint salesman, a clerk at the Ministry of Shipping and a sports master at a boys' prep school in the genteel London suburb of Putney. He'd then found freelance employment with the IIB, the Industrial Intelligence Bureau, his opportunistic ability to beguile strangers and cultivate potentially helpful alliances fostering his successful transition from sports master to spymaster – to games that lacked well-defined rules and etiquette.

Set up by a prosperous businessman with MI5 links, the IIB was funded by the Federation of British Industries as well as the Ship Owners' and Coal Owners' Associations. The IIB endeavoured to obtain advance warning of industrial unrest, arising from subversion by anarchists, Communists and Irish Republicans. Max had deployed his social skills to create a network of around a hundred spies from all walks of life.

His experience at the IIB had prepared him for the role of Director of Intelligence for the British Fascisti, where he had honed what were, he acknowledged, very specialist skills. He had run undercover operations. He had established cells within factories. He had put together intelligence files. And he had kept tabs on the organization's internal security.

Through a recommendation from a leading member of the British Fascisti, he'd been approached by Desmond Morton, an MI6 officer who had since become a friend. On an initial three-month trial basis, Max had been added to Desmond's small team of so-called 'Casuals', mostly entrusted with travelling round Britain verifying information that had been obtained abroad. Max's former employer at the IIB had granted him permission to take his network of agents with him to MI6.

Under Desmond's supervision, Max had used those agents to explore ties between various British-based Communist groups and the Comintern – the wing of the Soviet regime committed to fomenting world revolution. He had impressed Desmond by his honesty and by the speed with which his agents had burrowed into the designated groups. It was excellent preparation for what he was doing now. He just had to hope that Marjorie infiltrated the Right Club as speedily and effectively as her predecessors had infiltrated their Communist targets.

21

Anna had got the job as a Russian translator for the RAF's Advanced Air Strike Force, but the acceptance letter didn't specify when she would begin. She could extract a measure of solace from the knowledge that she was not the only person being kept waiting. Quite the contrary. Waiting was a tiresome ritual to which most Londoners were growing accustomed. Waiting for buses. Waiting for taxis. Waiting for the latest news. Waiting for bombs to fall.

Left to count off the days until she switched jobs, Anna carried on reporting to Sub-Station V. Since being posted there, she had needed to acclimatize to the shift system. 9 a.m. until 6 p.m. or 6 p.m. until 9 a.m., each shift preceded by a roll-call. Over the so-called night watch, she and her colleagues – who had been ordered to bring bedclothes with them – were permitted to nap in the upstairs dormitory above where the mechanics used to work. For the first few nights, they'd been disturbed by a succession of visitors expecting to find the prostitutes formerly based there when the garage was closed for business. Another impediment to sleep was provided by the drone of patrol aircraft. Occasional moments of relaxation also had a tendency to be ruined by groups of Home Office officials who would ring the fire-alarm and time the speed of response.

Those heavy AFS uniforms were coming in handy now. Last week the temperature had plummeted. Since then, it had been downright glacial overnight. That and the profusion of tweed coats and knitted dresses in the shops left one in no doubt that autumn was taking up residence.

Now the French couture houses had switched to producing military uniforms, London finally seemed to be acquiring its own distinctive style, the emphasis being on warmth, practicality and home-produced materials. Pleated skirts, long sleeves, high necks and simple, unembellished hats offered an abrupt transition from those bell-shaped skirts and hand-embroidered evening-dresses that had been so voguish last season. Suffice to say those weren't the kind of garments one could envisage Anna's tomboyish acquaintance from the Watch Room modelling off-duty.

In recent days, Anna had persisted with her efforts to recruit the woman to the fascist cause. Her endeavours had, however, just been brought to an unproductive end by the news that her acquaintance had been transferred. Not to the Ministry of Information's Postal and Telegraph Censorship Department, but to another fire station.

Anna had many things to take her mind off this small failure. Lately the AFS had been keeping her so busy that she hadn't even had time to maintain her prolific correspondence with friends and family. Her life was largely devoted to training. First-aid. Keep fit. And lectures on poison gases. These reputedly smelt like almonds, geraniums and pear drops, yet their effects were horrible – burning, choking, blistered skin, collapsed lungs, symptoms guaranteed to ensure that one paid attention to the lectures on how to use the AFS-issue gasmasks. Tight-fitting rubber contraptions that made one's skin feel clammy.

Memorizing the layout of the West End was also part of the training for Anna and other AFS drivers. To prepare for tests on the fastest routes across town, they were instructed to walk or drive round the area both during the day and at night, their clean uniforms apt to provoke derisory remarks from members of the public. Sometimes people even shouted after them, '£2 a week for doing nothing!' – a comment notable not just for its unfairness but for its fiscal inaccuracy.

Driving through the blackout, especially without the aid of moonlight, was a tricky task. One could find oneself creeping along Park Lane when one thought one was going down Piccadilly. The darkness was hard on the eyes as well, hard enough to induce headaches. Deep shadows, which seemed to indicate open spaces, would gradually announce themselves as buildings. What appeared to be a traffic-light could evolve into an Air-Raid Warden. Then there were those motorists who made life so dangerous by clinging to the white lines down the centre of the road. And there were those homicidal maniacs – troubling numbers of them – who drove at breakneck speeds. Others even insisted on overtaking. It was a miracle that even more people weren't killed on the roads.

Walking through the blackout was a hazardous business, too. One was left to grope one's way along familiar streets rendered labyrinthine and eerily unfamiliar. One's fingers were like those of a blind person reading Braille, their tips tracing the contours of a wall, alert for changes in texture. Shins kept grazing the kerb. Ears became attuned to the sound of voices and approaching vehicles, to the cautious rhythm of footsteps, to the tap-tap-tap of walking-sticks, to the liquid babble emanating from busy restaurants and pubs. Shoulders were perpetually braced for the next of those bruising, confidence-sapping collisions with another disorientated pedestrian or, worse still, something solid – a building, a postbox, a parked car or a wall of sandbags, objects strewn across the city with apparently malicious intent, their presence leading to comments about suffering from 'the blackout blues'.

Daylight divested those same streets of their newfound malice, yet it could not return them to pre-war normality. True, one continued to catch passing glimpses of that old horse-drawn delivery van with 'Scotts, the Hatters' written along the side. In place of cockaded top-hats, though, its driver and footman now wore steel helmets. Many of the mansions around Down Street had meanwhile been vacated, their shuttered windows as blank as the eyes of a corpse. On the main shopping thoroughfares, 'TO LET' signs had germinated. Duckboards had been placed across the sandbags that lined doorways.

Handwritten 'Business as usual' placards had popped up. And exposed glass had been criss-crossed by strips of gummed paper, sometimes made to resemble a Union Jack, sometimes conveying chipper little messages. 'Keep smiling.' 'Chin up.'

Elsewhere one caught sight of the British Union insignia – a circle with a lightning flash inside it – scrawled across walls, together with the words 'Mosley' and 'Peace'. Rival government posters declaring '*Your* Courage, *Your* Cheerfulness, *Your* Resolution Will Bring Us Victory' were also springing up. Such jaunty confidence on the part of the authorities was, to Anna's mind, entirely misplaced.

22

In excess of 1,500 miles away, Tyler and his Code Room colleagues at the Moscow embassy were working round the clock. The extra work was generated by an increase in the quantity of cable traffic. Much of this originated from the senior diplomats elsewhere in Mokhovaya House. Ever since the Germans had invaded Poland a little over two weeks ago, the building had been suffused by a ceaseless hubbub.

But Tyler wasn't in the Code Room at that moment. He was heading through the embassy, something he'd done thousands of times before, yet he had reason to feel a tremor of apprehension today. Not that he tended to show any outward signs of anxiety. Why Ambassador Laurence A. Steinhardt had summoned him was a mystery with potentially daunting ramifications. Beyond an initial welcoming handshake, the likes of Steinhardt did not commonly have much to do with such junior staff.

Whatever the reason for the summons, it had to be important. Perhaps the Ambassador was going to reprimand him for something. It wouldn't be the first time Tyler had been censured by the higher-ups. His most recent brush with authority had involved him being given a warning by former Ambassador Bullitt for neglecting his work in favour of the rival attractions of the bar at the Hotel Metropole. And previously Loy W.

Henderson – Chief Political Officer in those days – had admonished him for something that had occurred before Tyler had even arrived at the embassy. During his voyage from America to Europe, he'd propositioned a fellow passenger, who turned out to be the secretary to a friend of President Franklin D. Roosevelt. While she had been swimming in the ship's pool, Tyler had slipped a note inside one of her shoes. The note had suggested an evening together, but his boldness had won him nothing more than a tête-à-tête with Henderson.

Maybe today's summons was unconnected to either liquor or libido. Maybe the Ambassador had heard that Tyler had been passing information to Tanya. Were that the case, Tyler might get dismissed from the State Department. He might even find himself facing a criminal charge.

Ambassador Steinhardt's office was on the third floor, directly above the Code Room. Smooth in manner as well as appearance, he was a tall, slim forty-six year old. He had dark eyes and black, thinning hair, his saturnine features at odds with the effervescence of his personality. Far from unmasking Tyler as a spy, Steinhardt informed him that he was being posted to another embassy. He would be taking the job in London that had, at the request of Ambassador Kennedy, earlier been allotted to Henry W. Antheil, the Moscow embassy's Chief Code Clerk. Steinhardt was putting Tyler in a difficult position because the arrangement torpedoed his friend's plans. At least Henry would not be stranded in Moscow. Rather than being transferred to London, he was being sent to Helsinki.

Garrulous and personable, Steinhardt may well have set out the factors behind Tyler's London posting. Suggestions later surfaced that the Russian authorities had requested his removal, owing to his openly negative comments about the Soviet regime. What Steinhardt would not have known was that, in all likelihood, the Soviets *wanted* Tyler to be assigned to another embassy, London being the plum spot. If they could place a spy within the Code Room of the London embassy, that spy would be immeasurably more valuable than a spy within its Moscow counterpart, where information was easy to obtain.

The importance of the London Code Room derived from its function as the clearing-house for communications between Washington, DC and America's European consulates and embassies. Afforded access to these cables, the Soviets would have a crucial diplomatic advantage over the United States and, to a lesser extent, European countries whose manoeuvrings were exposed by the American cable traffic.

However, Steinhardt's announcement about the move from Moscow to London was couched, Tyler did not find the prospect unduly enticing. Though he had friends in the English capital and liked it enough to have spent a portion of his last but one biannual leave there, he didn't want to live in London, a powerful disincentive supplied by the probable German attack on the city.

Exiting Steinhardt's office, Tyler took the highly improper step of trying to engineer an alternative posting back to America. He did so by cabling the State Department at 4 p.m. that afternoon. The recipient of his message was Loy W. Henderson. Tyler hoped his late father's old friend might set aside past differences and pull a few strings on his behalf. The telegram read, 'What chances transfer to Department. Kent.'

23

Innumerable childhood hours prowling the countryside around Tythegston Court, his uncle's home, had taught Max how to be what he termed 'a nature detective'. The primary skills for this were applicable to his job with MI5. He'd identified those as an ability to fit evidence into a logical pattern and the refusal to evolve seductive theories running counter to that evidence. Careful observation and a patient approach to the accumulation of facts were the other skills he'd acquired.

Marjorie Amor had not so far added to his stockpile of facts about Captain Ramsay's activities. Tomorrow – Thursday 14 September, 1939 – marked precisely a month since she'd been issued with her Right Club badge. Attempts to reintroduce herself to the Captain had made no headway, though. Outside of a series of fruitless phonecalls to his house, she had nothing much to report.

Becalmed investigations like this lent weight to Max's staunch refusal to employ agents on a payment-by-results basis. He believed that would only encourage them to exaggerate, misrepresent or even invent material. Where agents required financial support, he preferred to give them a monthly stipend. Cash on the nail. That way they would not be penalized for circumstances beyond their control. He liked to tell recruits that he fully understood that there would be days, weeks, sometimes entire months during which they'd glean little of value.

Until Marjorie made progress – assuming she ever did – Max had plenty to keep him busy, hard work offering sanctuary from the sexual void at the heart of his marriage. He was currently putting together the latest in a series of reports destined for the Central Registry, the department that administered MI5's gigantic, cross-indexed filing system. In those write-ups he could apply the serious naturalists' principle of trying to discern behavioural patterns within accumulated observations.

Report-writing was fundamental to his job. As Jimmy Dickson, his friend at the Ministry of Labour, had pointed out, 'The work of the Secret Service is not the sort of thing which one reads about in novels, where beautifully dressed men, wearing little silver badges on their braces, put drugs into the wine of ravishing Balkan princesses on the Côte d'Azur.'

Max's latest report marshalled his knowledge of the Nordic League. Already the subject of a fat dossier, the League was an offshoot of the White Knights of Britain, also known as the Hooded Men – equivalent to the Ku Klux Klan in America. It had been founded in 1935 and had since spawned at least three London branches. Two more were in the process of being set up. Its headquarters was the Druids' Memorial Hall on Lamb's Conduit Street, where a big papier-mâché model of Stonehenge occupied the stage.

Every Monday evening until not long ago, this had been the venue for meetings of what Nordic League members had started referring to as 'the Stonehenge Debating Society'. These drew crowds of between 60 and 200. Placards bearing anti-Semitic slogans hung from the walls while records of fascist marching songs blared out.

Among the recurrent speakers at the Druids' Memorial Hall was a Hitler-worshipping Australian who liked to castigate Britain's 'Judaised Parliament and press'. Other stalwarts included a representative of the Arab League who had, at a recent meeting, delivered a well-received talk arguing for 'extermination' as the answer to the perceived 'Jewish Problem'. Regular speeches had also been made by Captain Ramsay and other members of the Nordic League's governing council. One of those council members posed the rhetorical question, 'Must every saviour be crucified by the Jew?' His praise for the Nazi leader had, on other occasions, been reiterated by a colleague who had – with laughable, pseudo-religious fervour – described Hitler as 'that man of God across the sea, that great Crusader who had re-established honour and dignity among the German people, a man for whom one would be proud to die'.

During another of the Nordic League meetings, the same speaker had held forth on the possibility that he and his fellow fascists might 'one day snatch the reins from that effete and corrupt body now in power at Whitehall'. He'd then given full vent to his anti-Semitism – prejudice that was not yet against the law, not unless racial hatred shaded into incitement to commit murder.

Besides organizing these gatherings, which sometimes concluded with chants of 'Heil Hitler!', the Nordic League had arranged multiple screenings of an imported Nazi propaganda film. What rendered the organization even more sinister and worthy of Max's attention were its links to the Nazi Party. For a start, two of the League's founders appeared to be Nazi agents. Right after a League meeting, one of them was observed driving straight to the German Embassy for a late-night briefing. Over that summer, the League's other founder had visited Germany, where he had held a meeting with someone whose name had previously cropped up. That someone was Heinrich Hoffmann, the Munich-based Nazi propagandist and intimate of Hitler. An invitation to go on the payroll of the Nazis' Propaganda Ministry had reportedly stemmed from the meeting. Unrelated MI5 surveillance had also exposed another connection between the Nazis and the recipient of that invitation. Last autumn he had received a visit from a former German naval officer sent across the Channel to gather information about Britain's readiness for war.

There were suspicions that a couple more of the Nordic League's most active members were Nazi agents as well. Fuelling those suspicions, one of the men had stated that all genuine friends of Germany should be prepared to carry out espionage. But the documented links between the League and the Nazis did not stop there.

Of the contingent of Germans who used to attend the Druids' Memorial Hall meetings, the most prominent just happened to be a Nazi Party member. And the Australian who regularly spoke at those meetings had been contributing pseudonymous articles to Nazi newspapers. In addition, a representative from the League's governing council had gone to Berlin to attend Hitler's birthday celebrations. For good measure there had been a report that the League sought approval from the Nazi Party before issuing propaganda leaflets.

With the help of Customs officials at the port of Harwich, yet another link had emerged. Back in the autumn of 1938, a German posing as 'an author of philosophical works dealing with religion' had disembarked there. The German visitor – who worked for the *Völkischer Beobachter*, the Nazi Party's official newspaper – turned out to have been provided with a letter instructing him to make contact with the League.

Max's so far unfinished report on the League mentioned that its regular gatherings at the Druids' Memorial Hall had ceased. He noted that a few key members had nevertheless convened there two days ago. In the course of the meeting, a reference had been made to the 'most important work' being continued by Captain Ramsay and the group's leaders. It was a statement loaded with significance because the League had, only the previous week, been reported to have contemplated 'sabotage arrangements'.

24

Loy W. Henderson issued a swift response to Tyler's telegram. 'Apparently no vacancies for person of your qualifications in Department at present,' Henderson wrote. Something pointed and breezily condescending could be discerned in that reference to 'your qualifications'.

Tyler did not even have the option of taking up the matter with Henderson's boss, Secretary of State Cordell Hull, whom he'd known since he was three years old. As a young lawyer, Cordell had lodged with Tyler's parents. But there was no point in cabling the Secretary of State because he'd already counter-signed Henderson's telegram.

Writing to Henderson had always been a long shot. Aside from the friendship that had existed between him and Tyler's father, there was no reason why he should do Tyler any favours. Not after all the trouble Tyler had caused him over the past few years. They had got off to a bad start. And matters had not been improved by Tyler's attempt to order a consignment of high-powered air rifles from a New York-based company. He and his Moscow friends had only wanted to use the rifles for target practice, yet Henderson had been dragged into a protracted legal debate between the embassy, the State Department and the manufacturer over the legality of exporting firearms to Russia.

The disappointing news that Tyler could not avoid being posted to London was compounded by the revelation that the transfer came with an appreciable wage cut, explained by the lower cost of living there. His drop in salary would be rendered even sharper by the loss of the favourable allowance that was built into the dollars-to-roubles exchange rate available to American staff at the Moscow embassy.

Sometime over the next few days he would be leaving town. He was indignant at the way he was being hustled out of the Soviet Union 'without being able to express any wishes on the subject'. In the short time at his disposal, he would have to gather the possessions he had accumulated. While he'd been in Moscow, he had built up an extensive library of scholarly titles in almost two-dozen languages, in tongues as diverse as Swedish, Japanese and Arabic. If he wanted to take these books to London, he would have to negotiate various obstacles. First, he would have to seek permission from the Soviet authorities. And even if they granted that, he would have to pay a small fortune in shipping costs, on top of which he would be vulnerable to Russian export duty – an arbitrary figure occasionally amounting to more than the retail value of an item.

Since Tyler had no urge to remain in England for long, he delayed confronting these problems. Instead, he left his books in the Store Room at the embassy, from where he could have them forwarded to his next-but-one destination.

He also decided to leave behind a small, locked briefcase. One of his colleagues was persuaded to deposit this for him in the embassy's safe. Tyler said he would have it sent to London via the diplomatic pouch at some later date. By using the pouch, he could prevent Customs officers from opening his briefcase and seeing its contents.

25

The breakthrough occurred on Thursday 21 September, 1939. After who-knows-how-many phonecalls from Marjorie to Captain Ramsay, spaced over nearly a month and a half, Max's patience was rewarded. Finally, Marjorie had got through to Ramsay and arranged to meet him.

Her report provided Max with the equivalent of the specimens he examined under a microscope, poring over every detail, alert for anything significant. She described her encounter with Ramsay. It had occurred at his mother's house on the edge of Hyde Park.

Around four years had gone by since their paths had crossed when they'd both been campaigning for the Christian Protest Movement, but Captain Ramsay had told Marjorie that he remembered her. Perhaps he was just being polite. He'd added that his wife had been saying complimentary things about her.

Marjorie announced that he'd gone on to tell her about his decision to refrain from staging public meetings on behalf of the Right Club. Officially at least, the club had ceased to exist. Unofficially … well, that was another matter.

Ramsay had informed her that he was planning to pursue the club's objectives in secret – so secret that only he knew the names of its members. From now on, the club would operate within other organizations. Government ones.

Underlining the need for discretion, Ramsay spoke about his desire to propagate the club's message by distributing leaflets. He presented Marjorie with a sample and promised to give her more.

She and Ramsay went on to discuss the international situation and the prospect of her volunteering for some form of war work. At that point, he confided in her about having club members in most government departments. Censorship and the Foreign Office were the exceptions. Marjorie then cleverly alluded to her influential friends – people who might wangle her a job in Censorship, though she made no promises on that score.

'If you could help us there, it would be very useful,' Ramsay remarked without disclosing what he wanted her to do. He simply said that Censorship was under the control of a Jew and that it would be good to have somebody there who was 'Jew-wise' – an approving tag applied to anti-Semites by British fascists. Also he remarked on the importance of placing people like that in as many different institutions as possible, enabling them 'to spread the truth by word of mouth'.

Just prior to saying goodbye, Marjorie enquired whether, in the event of revolution breaking out across Britain, Right Club members would be ordered to follow the British Union leader, Sir Oswald Mosley.

'Certainly not,' she recalled him replying. 'Before such a situation arises I shall be in touch with all the members and you will then be told who is your leader.'

Marjorie's account of her conversation with Ramsay impelled Max to set about trying to get her a job in MI5's Military Censorship Department. By having a word with one of his contacts at Wormwood Scrubs, he might be able to find something for her, but he knew from experience that taking additional people into one's confidence was not especially desirable. Sooner or later they would have to let a colleague of theirs into the secret. And then that colleague might confide in someone else. And so forth – until the agent's cover would be as effective as a broken gramophone record.

Instead of using the back-door method to land Marjorie a job at MI5 headquarters, Max decided it would be safer for her to apply for it in the normal way. No sense in telling her potential employer that she was already working for Section B5b. So he arranged for the name and address of the official in charge of appointments to be despatched to her, along with a specimen letter and job application form. She was expected to copy the contents and post them to the nominated address.

Max now had to bide his time and hope she got the job. If she did, it would demonstrate to Ramsay how valuable she could be. Once she started the job, Ramsay might try to exploit her access to confidential government material. Batches of made-up information, mixed with the genuine article, could be used to win his trust.

26

Even indoors, the blackout felt as if it was in force. Due to the new low-voltage electricity supplied throughout Britain, once dazzling light bulbs emitted only a half-hearted glow, the residual light scarcely sufficient to illuminate the features of a supper companion, let alone the entire room. Right now Anna was dining with Francis Hemming, a middle-aged friend whose austere features were well-suited to such low visibility. He had a block-like head, finely pleated skin beneath his eyes, and a hairline as wispy and uneven as a worn clothes-brush. Looks aside, he was a fascinating man. In some respects he was a paragon of the conventional Englishman, yet one did not have to be in his rumpled, peevishly amusing presence for more than a few minutes to twig how unorthodox he was. One soon noticed his disinclination to observe the social niceties. He would get straight to the point.

Before the war, Francis and his wife had moved in the same fascist circles as both the erstwhile German Ambassador to Britain, Joachim von Ribbentrop, and the onetime First Secretary to the Belgian Embassy, Comte Antoine de Laubespin, who was an associate of Anna. For over ten years the Hemmings had moreover been frequent visitors to the Russian Tea Rooms, the west London café-cum-restaurant that her parents ran. The Hemmings had become quite close to Admiral and Mme Wolkoff. It was astonishing that Anna hadn't crossed paths with either Francis or his wife until about four months ago when they had been introduced to her while lunching at the Tea Rooms.

Francis's unorthodoxy extended to his choice of wife – his second wife at that. Definitely not the kind of woman one would expect a senior civil servant to marry, she was a former stage actress who used to be the mistress of Wyndham Lewis, the Hitler-supporting artist and writer. She had also worked as a fashion correspondent, though she had a somewhat mannish taste in clothes.[23]

But this evening Anna was unable to talk to her about the fashion world because she'd already joined the evacuees fleeing town. In the wake of her departure, Francis had briefly rented a room from Anna's parents. He had since moved to lodgings with some friends of the Wolkoffs.

Though Anna did not share Francis's obsession with entomology in general and butterflies in particular, they still had a great deal to discuss over supper. The war was the obvious topic despite the uneventful course that it had so far taken. As someone who had served in the trenches and been severely wounded, Francis could speak from experience about the pain, waste of life and barbarity of war. He was capable of supporting his arguments with evidence culled from his career within the inner sanctums of Whitehall as well.

Since leaving the Treasury's Economic Advisory Council, he'd been appointed Principal Assistant Secretary to the

Cabinet Office. His duties included taking minutes at the daily meetings of the War Cabinet, attended by Prime Minister Neville Chamberlain and senior ministerial colleagues, among them Winston Churchill, First Lord of the Admiralty. These gatherings conferred on Anna's friend inside-knowledge of government policy and the progress of the war.

27

Max's hitherto reluctant paymasters had decided to grant Section B5b the extra cash it so urgently required – enough to cover the wages for a couple of case-officers. Their presence would go some way towards easing the burden on Max and his secretary. Max had lately been feeling under particular pressure, though he knew he wasn't alone in that respect.

True to MI5's tradition of recruitment through personal contacts, promoting a reliance on men from public-school backgrounds, Max used the additional funds to employ his friend, Jimmy Dickson, whom he had known for more than a decade. Jimmy was the same age as Max. They had some of the same interests, too. Pulp fiction, criminology and novel-writing were among those.

Jimmy wrote crime and espionage thrillers – books such as *Soho Racket* and *Gun Business*[24] – that appeared under the nom de plume, Grierson Dickson. In his last but one novel, he had cheekily assigned some of Max's foibles to the villainous spymaster at the centre of the story.[25]

By employing Jimmy, Max was returning a favour dispensed the previous year when he had successfully put Max up for membership of the Authors' Club. Max's days as a published novelist may have been fast receding, but the club offered a convenient venue for work-related meetings over a meal or a glass of something. It wasn't far from the various government ministries, including the Ministry of Labour, where Jimmy had, until his transfer to MI5, held a senior post.

Friendship and favours aside, what made Jimmy so suitable for recruitment was, in Max's opinion, his fascination with subversive movements and sound knowledge of the problems faced by MI5. His professional background would also come in handy. He used to work as a fraud investigator. It was a job that had brought him into contact with Metropolitan Police officers who were battling London's large-scale inter-war drug trade. Confident that Jimmy would not require much training, Max had arranged for him to be seconded to B5b, where he'd be expected to set up his own network of agents and supervise his own investigations.

With Dennis Wheatley's approval, Max bestowed the lower-ranking of the two new posts on Dennis's stepson, Bill Younger. Dennis asked Max for a job as well, encouraged no doubt by Max's previous flattering comment about how MI5 had lost a great opportunity when he'd chosen a literary career. But Max tactfully sidestepped Dennis's request by assuring him that the best way he could assist the war effort would be through writing novels that would take people's minds off the loneliness and other hardships they were enduring aboard ships and in Army camps and ARP posts.

Tiny in stature, childhood polio bequeathing him a slightly withered arm, Bill Younger would not have been in demand by the armed services. What he lacked physically, he made up for intellectually. His family's recent trip to France had coincided with his being awarded a first-class degree. Not that degrees and diplomas were things upon which Max placed much value, Max's own lack of academic qualifications probably influencing that judgement.

He believed that 'the academic mind', as he put it, was suited to the broad research sometimes required by case-officers. Yet it wasn't ideal, he thought, for the task of running a group of agents, each of whom diverged markedly in their personal characteristics, virtues and failings. He'd noticed that few people of Bill's educational attainments possessed the necessary grasp of human nature. And they didn't, from what he had observed, have the prerequisite ability to get on with all categories and classes of people.

Bill certainly got on with Max, the gap in age and education bridged by their mutual fascination with detective novels, their literary ambitions,[26] and their curiosity about reincarnation and other phenomena beyond the material world. In supervising trainee case-officers such as Bill, Max treated them with the same maternal fussiness he expended on the abandoned fledglings and baby animals that he so often reared.

Even though Bill had previously worked as an agent, he was, Max realized, still too inexperienced to make a substantial contribution to Section B5b. Max estimated that Bill would not be able to take a full caseload for another six months, perhaps. Maybe longer. Bill was nonetheless deemed ready to perform follow-up work sparked by an unrelated investigation.[27]

All over town on Friday 22 September, 1939 – no more than a fortnight after Bill had joined Max at B5b – one heard people talking about how London was in for a weekend of bombing. Everything pointed towards it, they said. The appearance of dozens more barrage balloons gave substance to the rumours about thousands of enemy aircraft massing on the Dutch border.

Being targeted by German bombers was something with which Max was familiar. While he had been a cadet aboard HMS *Worcester*, moored not far from the mouth of the Thames, German aircraft would fly overhead en route home from attacks on London. The ship had twice had bombs dropped on her. One of these had hit its target but failed to go off. And the other had detonated near the starboard bow, inflicting no damage yet shaking the boat as vigorously as a percussionist playing the maracas. Max would be lucky to enjoy a third such narrow escape.

28

Before leaving Moscow that Saturday, Tyler notified his superiors of an incident that had occurred six weeks earlier. Driving through town, he'd collided with a drunken Russian pedestrian, who had sustained a broken leg. Tyler said he did not object to the embassy paying reasonable compensation if they felt so inclined, though he pointed out that the pedestrian was entirely at fault.

Under Soviet law, Tyler had committed a grave offence. It brought him within the jurisdiction of the State Automobile Accident Inspectorate, which could enmesh him in the Kafkaesque nightmare of Soviet bureaucracy, of waiting in line to see officials who would redirect him to appointments with other officials in other buildings in other parts of town. The incident had also offered the NKVD a chance they would not spurn, blackmail being integral to their modus operandi. That much was plain from the experiences of Anthony J. Barrett, Tyler's former Moscow drinking buddy, who had worked at the embassy as a Quartermaster's Clerk.

The NKVD had burst in on Anthony and taken pictures of him in a compromising position with at least one other man. Anthony had been given seventy-two hours in which to make a choice. Hand over the US military ciphers or else serve a lengthy prison sentence.

In theory, the man's diplomatic passport should have furnished immunity from prosecution, but the NKVD disregarded such legalities. Tyler's friend – who liked to address him by the ironic nickname of 'Pucia', Corsican dialect for 'shorty' – had been in a tearful panic, babbling about how he'd been a fool, how everything had been his fault. He'd told the top brass what had happened. In double-quick time, they had arranged for him to leave Moscow that night.[28]

Yet there wasn't much of an incentive for Tyler to follow his example and report any attempted blackmail. Not after the way Anthony had been treated by the State Department. They'd sacked him as soon as he got back to America. From a selfish point of view – and Tyler was nothing if not self-centred – a single course of action lay open to him. Strike a deal with the NKVD – his freedom in exchange for the US government telegrams he had stolen.

29

Smoking presented Max with a moral dilemma. Anyone in possession of a modicum of common sense knew that tobacco took up valuable cargo-space aboard transatlantic ships – cargo-space better allocated to food or munitions. Yet the government earned vast tax revenue from tobacco. Wags relished pointing out that Britain would have no trouble financing the war if everyone in the country did their patriotic duty by drinking or smoking to excess.

In that sense Max's friend, Dennis, had been doing his duty for years. He'd just taken Max's advice and started a new novel. Aiming to create 'an up-to-the-minute spy story', he sought accurate background material about the world of contemporary espionage. Since his stepson, Bill Younger, was far too discreet to reveal anything about the goings-on at MI5, who better to contribute the necessary raw material than Uncle Max?

Within the plot of Dennis's novel, the real-life operation against Captain Ramsay and the Right Club found a partial echo. The book was poised to follow its handsome and resourceful hero on a secret mission to Germany, where he would conduct the type of infiltration being carried out by Marjorie. His mission would be to penetrate the Nazi Party. Once inside the party, he would overthrow Hitler and bring about a negotiated peace with Britain.

Away from the world of make-believe, London had been untouched by air raids between Friday evening and Saturday morning. The city had nevertheless changed overnight with the introduction of petrol-rationing for taxi-drivers and private motorists. Its roads were denuded of most of the usual traffic. Suddenly the West End was a paradise for jaywalkers. And the fug of exhaust fumes had disappeared altogether on some streets.

30

An equestrian statue of Tsar Alexander III, surely among the most improbable survivals from the pre-Soviet era, guarded the entrance to the October Station. Inside, its concourse and platforms generally teemed with peasants cradling their possessions.

Tyler boarded the *Red Arrow* express. Whoever had named it must have been colour-blind because the locomotive was painted *blue*. Promoted as Russia's answer to the *Broadway Limited*, the train linking New York and Chicago, it was scheduled to depart just after midnight. Twelve hours hence – at lunchtime on Sunday 24 September, 1939 – it would be arriving in Leningrad, at which point Tyler could make his connection to Helsinki. Ordinarily, he'd have gone through Warsaw and on to Berlin, only that route was closed now Poland had become a war zone, where the Germans and their Soviet allies were currently dividing the territorial spoils.

With typical Communist disdain for the truth, Tyler's train shuffled along the track less like a *Red Arrow* than some felt-slippered Muscovite old-timer. Its relatively new rolling stock, where men and women found themselves bunked in the same sleeping cars, nonetheless represented a marked improvement upon your standard-issue Russian trains.

Regardless of the age of the rolling stock, what never seemed to change was the pungent clutter that festooned the tables between the seats. There would without fail be some black bread, some cigarettes and a tin of anchovies, the lid peeled back. There would also be servings of roast chicken wrapped in newsprint, dark grease stains flecking stories about rising crop yields and industrial output, stories that elbowed aside the murder mysteries, political analysis and sex scandals seen in the American press.

Before Tyler boarded the train, Anthony J. Barrett, his disgraced former colleague, had written from the United States to urge him to put Tanya to work buying diamonds and premium quality furs, which could then be smuggled out of the Soviet Union. His friend boasted about turning a tremendous profit

– corresponding to some three months' wages – on the items concealed in his own baggage when he'd left the country. Those items included a sapphire ring purchased on his behalf by Tanya.

Covetous of the trappings of wealth and the easy money that would give him access to them, Tyler had grounds for devoting serious consideration to his friend's plan. One didn't have to be a criminal mastermind, however, to realize that it came with a fatal flaw. Anthony had only been able to smuggle all those things through Soviet Customs because the top brass at the embassy, in their desire to give him a cover-story for his sudden late-night departure, had nominated him as a diplomatic courier. And Customs officials were of course forbidden to search couriers' luggage. Tyler would be granted no such distinction, so he wouldn't have a hope of getting undeclared valuables through Customs. The Soviets would escort him off the train at the frontier and examine his luggage so meticulously they'd even take down the names in his address book.

At any rate, Tyler did not have to rely on smuggling as a source of the additional funds required to keep him in the manner to which he aspired. Just so long as he had access to confidential US government documents to pass across to the Soviets, he would have plenty of money, self-interest trumping his fascist sympathies.

31

Only a year or two back, Max had spent a fondly remembered day on the Isle of Sheppey with an artist friend.[29] Lurking near a wide, flat expanse of countryside, the two men had peered skywards at a succession of short-eared owls. These were hunting the voles that lived in the tussocky grassland.

But things had changed since that day. Any skyward staring was now inevitably tinged with anxiety, the circling specks overhead less likely to be birds than German aircraft. Through what remained of the weekend, however, none of the predicted enemy bombers materialized over London.

Come Monday morning, the city's empty roads lent the rush-hour an aberrant flavour. Max was due at a meeting to chew over the threat posed by the Nordic League and British Union, Wormwood Scrubs presenting the obvious venue. For meetings of more than a couple of people, the prison cells were too small, so the Gym or Library tended to be used instead.

Max would be joined at today's conference by Guy Liddell, Francis Aiken Sneath and two junior colleagues.[30] All but one of Max's companions had witnessed the brutality of the Nazi regime from close-up. Francis had been a university lecturer in Germany, his marriage to a German woman amplifying his unease about what was happening to her country. Despite possessing no irrefutable evidence to support his theory, he was rightly convinced that Hitler had been promoting the spread of fascism by funding the British Union.

In readiness for the meeting, Max had yesterday submitted a discussion document to Guy Liddell. The document was designed to bring him up-to-date with the latest intelligence on both the British Union and Nordic League. Supposedly disbanded, the second of those organizations had staged several recent gatherings. Few of its members were prepared to fight against Germany. Captain Ramsay and various associates were moreover planning to disrupt the war effort. Secure in their perverse belief that the Jews were behind the current 'misunderstanding' between Britain and the Nazis, Ramsay and his supporters intended to distribute anti-Semitic circulars and stickers among MPs, in clubs and through the armed forces. These freshly produced leaflets not only accused 'World Jewry' of instigating the war, but also refuted the Prime Minister's assertion that Hitler could not be trusted.

What made the activities of Ramsay and his cronies so unsettling was the news that he had been in touch with Sir Oswald Mosley, leader of the British Union, many of whose members appeared to have been infiltrating the War Reserve Police. Ramsay had approached him with a proposal to initiate cooperation between his movement and the Nordic League.

Further cause for alarm had been offered by Max's colleagues from Special Branch. Just three days ago, they'd come up with a report concerning the Right Club. The report described how the club had been enlisting the support of sympathizers within the armed forces. Serious discussions had, it alleged, even taken place about the possibility of staging a *coup d'état*. This new report commented on the impression among British fascists that the Right Club would make brisk advances if the Duke of Windsor, thought to share the organization's ideals, could be persuaded to become its figurehead. But there was, apparently, pessimism among the club's members that the Duke would risk committing himself to such intrigue.

32

It was now Tuesday 26 September, 1939 – exactly a week since Max had paid what was in danger of turning into a disastrous visit to HM Prison Wandsworth. He had been there to conduct his second interview with William Joyce's twenty-two-year-old brother. Quentin Joyce, who was being held under Regulation 18b of the Emergency Defence Regulations, worked for the Air Ministry, which oversaw the RAF. He also belonged to William's organization, the National Socialist League.

During a ninety-minute interview, Max had grilled Quentin about his long-standing friendship with a known Nazi agent, about the substantial sums of money Quentin had received from the man and about the letters Quentin had sent him in Berlin. These were sprinkled with cryptic phrases and references to 'stamps'. As Max had pointed out, 'stamps' were, in espionage parlance, a synonym for 'maps'. Quentin had nonetheless kept up the pretence that he and his Nazi pen-friend were engaged in the entirely innocent pursuit of collecting valuable postage stamps.

Until today the repercussions of Max's trip to Wandsworth had not manifested themselves. His problems began with a report that Special Branch submitted to Francis Aiken Sneath and a junior colleague. It concerned the interrogation of William and Quentin's sister. Under questioning she'd revealed that Quentin had been 'greatly encouraged' by last Tuesday's visit from an unnamed MI5 officer. She had said the officer was the same person who had advised William to leave England if he wanted to avoid being arrested.

Francis and the junior colleague who had read the report expressed concern that Special Branch was prepared to treat the statement at face value. Nor were they too pleased by the implicit assumption that an MI5 officer had acted in such an irregular fashion. When they quizzed Max about the Special Branch document, he reminded them that he'd wasted little time in reporting the telephone conversation between himself and William Joyce, which had occurred late on the night of Friday 25 August, 1939. 'Of course,' he added, 'it is hardly necessary to state that there was no question of Joyce having been warned or given improper information.'

Covering himself against further enquiries, Max fired off a memo after the meeting. His memo was to his immediate superior, Guy Liddell. 'You will recollect,' he wrote, 'that I had a telephone conversation with William Joyce a few days before war broke out and I had every reason to think that he would have informed his brother or some member of his family of this conversation.' Max went on to admit that he'd told Quentin about the phonecall to William. But he emphasized that he'd mentioned this purely as a strategy for breaking the ice with Quentin. He wrapped up the memo by denying once again that he had tipped-off William.

33

Tyler took the steamer from Helsinki to Saltsjöbaden, a fashionable and attractive, though slightly out-of-season resort about eighteen miles from the Swedish capital. Most likely in the chic, waterside confines of the aptly named Grand Hotel, where he rented a room, he encountered one of the daughters of a local shipping magnate.[31]

Playing up to his proud Southern lineage – which, he boasted, went back to Pocahontas, the Algonquin princess – Tyler would, with the chivalrous flourish of someone very sure of himself, kiss the hands of women to whom he had just been introduced. He possessed a knack of enveloping strangers in measured charm, of projecting a cultivated air of indolence redolent of moneyed leisure. Members of the opposite sex tended to respond to his poise, implicit in which was a sense of his own attractiveness.

He won himself a dinner invitation from the shipping magnate's daughter. On a sheet of hotel notepaper he jotted down details of the arrangement: 'Floragaten 1 through kitchen 8pm.'

Located in the centre of Stockholm, which could be reached via a half-hour ride on a little electric train, the address was a huge, dormer-windowed mansion at the intersection between two streets – Floragaten and Karlavagen. In days gone by, his hostess's ageing, moustachioed father had served as Swedish Consul-General to Siam, so Tyler could trade stories with the old man about diplomatic life.

A sightseeing tour of Stockholm was also laid on by Tyler's hostess. Nearly six months in Russia, where the necessities of life were scarce, rendered the variety and abundance of the city's shops unfamiliar. Stockholm had a well-trodden tourist itinerary that took in the National Museum, the Royal Palace and the Skansen Open-Air Museum, at which antique buildings from all over the country had been re-erected. To the strain of peasant fiddlers playing folk tunes, visitors could climb an old redbrick tower that offered a glittering view of the city's constituent islands, linked by bridges and a relay of ferries.

After several days in the Swedish capital, Tyler headed for the Central Station and boarded the train to Oslo. With him was a short, plump, well-dressed man, the cast of whose dark-complexioned features looked Turkish. In reality Tyler's companion was a Jewish-German named Ludwig Matthias, now a naturalized Swede, his change of citizenship indicative of his opposition to the Nazi regime. Passionately anti-Semitic though Tyler was – prejudice embraced by a high percentage of Americans – he had the ability to conceal these feelings any time the situation required it.

Ludwig seems to have been an NKVD agent ordered to chaperone Tyler, a business trip to London on behalf of a Stockholm-based firm affording legitimate cover. From Oslo, the pair took the train bound for the port of Bergen. Its carriages, divided into mahogany-panelled compartments, were luxurious, which was just as well because a thirteen-hour journey lay ahead of Tyler and Ludwig.

Their train crossed an idyllic valley prior to embarking on the gradual ear-popping ascent towards the distant snowy peaks. Dense woods converged on both sides of the track. By and by, the trees thinned out, exposing a big fjord. Later this was replaced by snowfields, tiny ski resorts and a rocky wasteland that beckoned the eyes towards a mighty glacier.

When the train clattered into the cold, rainy port of Bergen, chiefly made up of modern grey stone buildings, Tyler – and probably Ludwig, too – found comfortable overnight accommodation in an old hotel. It looked onto a peaceful square, where a bronze statue of a violinist played silently against a backdrop of fir-clad hills, mountains and a funicular railway.

For the next stage in their trip to London, the two men embarked on a B & N Line steamer, due to dock in Newcastle upon Tyne twenty-two hours from then. On concluding the North Sea crossing, they appear to have caught the same train. Its long, scenic route took it within sight of a number of villages and towns that echoed the rustic, anglicized Gothic buildings of St Alban's, the American prep school where Tyler had studied. His schooling made him part of the establishment yet also apart from it by virtue of his status as a scholarship student.[32] Only a decade had passed since he had left St Alban's, but he had packed a lot into that time, many of his experiences unlikely to endear him to the Episcopalian priest who'd been his headmaster.

At length Tyler's train slithered past the back gardens of scores of terraced houses before coming to rest beneath the giant arched canopy of King's Cross Station. There, he alighted amid the smoke and steam and deafening locomotive noises. Between the platforms and the exit was a news-kiosk. Articles about the Spanish Civil War had filled the newspapers when he had last been in London. Today they were filled with stories about another war. 'THE PERFIDY OF HITLER', trumpeted the front page of the *Evening Standard* on the night of Tyler's arrival, Wednesday 4 October, 1939.

Before long, Tyler – who had parted from Ludwig – was on the verge of entering the Cumberland Hotel, a vast, nine-storey art-deco structure. Facing it were both the Marble Arch monument and Hyde Park. The latter used to be populated by nursemaids pushing prams and by people lying in deckchairs. Not any longer. Since Tyler's last visit, the park had been bisected by trenches and dotted with anti-aircraft guns that protruded from sandbagged emplacements.

Dominating the Cumberland Hotel's stylish foyer was a big luminous clock, inset into the wall. Beneath its slender hands lay the streamlined reception desk where Tyler had to register. Though the Cumberland didn't aim for an upper-crust clientele, it was still outside Tyler's price range. His reduced salary, converted from dollars into British currency, brought him just £11-a-week less tax, leaving a shortfall that needed to be bridged by payments from the NKVD.

A quiet, impressively equipped room awaited Tyler. It had an en suite bathroom, a telephone, a lever that adjusted the central heating and a button that summoned room service, luxuries far beyond the hotel where Tyler had stayed when he first arrived in Moscow. Guests at that seedy establishment used to joke that you had to pay extra if you didn't want to share your room with rats. Pay extra and you still got the rats.

34

Ever since war had been declared, British radio stations and newspapers had dropped the weather reports, the explanation being that these might assist the Germans. So next morning Tyler was left without guidance in deciding on the most suitable outfit for the day ahead.

On exiting the hotel, he encountered tepid, breezy weather and skies as leaden as they were during his previous visit to

England. This time he carried with him an official letter from Moscow, confirming that his salary had been paid until close of business on the Friday before last. He had been instructed to hand over the letter as soon as he got to the embassy, which was a short walk from his hotel.

Grosvenor Square was Tyler's destination. Mostly taken up by a railinged oval park rimmed by smoke-darkened mansions, it did not bear much resemblance to the squares in Washington, DC or New York City. The embassy shared a couple of interconnected pastiche Georgian houses with other outposts of the American government, comprising the Department of Agriculture, the Commercial Attaché's office, the consulate, the War Department and US Customs. Both houses had grand porticoes, the first of them functioning as the entrance. Each morning a bus pulled up there and deposited a group of Tyler's colleagues, garrisoned at Headley Park, a stately home some way outside London. There were vague plans to move the embassy there when the Germans started bombing the city.

In the embassy's foyer was a desk invariably manned by a uniformed doorman with a Cockney accent. He directed dozens of visitors – mainly anxious European refugees seeking American visas – and apportioned cheerful greetings to fellow staff. Almost 200 people worked there, many more than at Mokhovaya House. Women were barely represented in the Moscow embassy, yet here they made up a small but conspicuous proportion of the workforce. The staff had modern offices on the first three floors, above which were several flats rented to people who had nothing to do with the American government.

Tyler found himself under the direction of Rudolph E. Schoenfeld, a balding senior diplomat who liked everyone to address him as 'Rudy'. He issued Tyler with two Yale keys. These granted entry to the Code Room, where Tyler would be putting in eight-hour shifts: 8 a.m. to 4 p.m., 4 p.m. to midnight or midnight to 8 a.m. But Tyler was no stranger to long hours.

One reached the Code Room by walking up to the second floor and through the Index Bureau where the walls were sheathed in cabinets and neatly shelved box-files. Supervised by an older woman who was painfully shy in the company of men, three young women toiled at separate desks, each with her own manual typewriter.

Employees had it impressed upon them that the Code Room door should be locked at all times. The Code Room was off-limits to everybody but Tyler and the other code clerks and telegraph operators, plus that day's Duty Officer. Two code clerks staffed it on weekdays. Its principal features were a large safe and an even larger desk, home to stacks of paper and more typewriters.

Since the embassy in London acted as the channel through which messages were conveyed between Washington, DC and America's other European consulates and embassies, the room that Tyler had just entered was far busier than its Moscow equivalent. Tyler's chief responsibility was to use the codebooks – stored in the safe – to translate the flow of messages. In one crucial regard, his duties differed from those he had performed in Moscow. This lay in an unusual assignment passed down to him by the embassy's most senior official, Joseph P. Kennedy, US Ambassador to Britain.

Lean, middle-aged and balding, with reddish-grey hair and round-framed spectacles behind which his blue eyes flitted like tropical fish in an aquarium, Kennedy was a blur of ambition, energy, confidence and abrasive charm. Before taking up his current job, he had been a businessman, his multimillion-dollar investments encompassing a Hollywood movie studio. He and one or two of his devoted entourage could on occasion be glimpsed strolling through the embassy. Junior members of staff such as Tyler were expected to acknowledge him with a respectful 'Good morning' or 'Good afternoon, Ambassador'.

At Kennedy's behest, Tyler was entrusted with making typed copies of selected documents from the files, documents intended to aid the composition of the Ambassador's memoirs. Now Tyler had access to all of the American telegrams between Europe and Washington, DC, dating back to 1938.

On the morning Tyler reported for duty, Grey Code was being used for an important transatlantic message, forwarded by Ambassador Kennedy. The message had come from a member of the British government – Winston Churchill, First

Lord of the Admiralty. It bore the heading, 'Strictly Personal and Most Secret for the President and the Secretary'.

Directed at President Roosevelt and the US Secretary of State, Churchill's message concerned the policing of the Neutrality Zone that the President had imposed across United States territorial waters a month earlier. Within that Zone, foreign vessels were prohibited from undertaking military operations.

Approximately an hour later, another message from Churchill was delivered to the Code Room. Written by the Deputy Chief of the British Naval Staff, this second telegram presented specific suggestions regarding the Neutrality Zone. Despite the message's purported secrecy, Tyler was supposed to send it using the Grey Code. Not a rational choice for anything you didn't want the Germans to decode. In this instance, though, Grey held one significant advantage over the much more secure strip-ciphers. That lay in the knowledge that messages to and from Washington, DC had to be routed through a British government-run cable facility. As Tyler's bosses must have guessed, all of these messages were passed from there to British cryptographers. Supplied with copies of American cables in both the original text and the coded version, the British would have been able to understand any subsequent messages sent in that code. Had Tyler's bosses insisted on employing one of the strip-ciphers, they would have provided the British with the tools to crack that cipher. By using Grey, long since compromised, Tyler's employers would preserve the assumed effectiveness of the strip-ciphers.

A short time after beginning work in the Code Room, Tyler resumed his practice of copying as well as stealing items of correspondence despatched by telegram. His duplication activities were lent a patina of legitimacy by the orders relayed to him from Ambassador Kennedy. These entailed plucking specific messages from the File Room cabinets and typing up copies of those messages. Whenever he did that, he would load an extra sheet of carbon paper into his typewriter, enabling him to produce a duplicate for his own purposes, too.

Left alone in the Code Room on a frequent basis, he could slip the stolen documents inside his suit pockets. Even if he was working by himself, though, there was always the fear that one of the telegraph operators or perhaps the Duty Officer, who strode in and out of the room, might catch him helping himself to US government paperwork.

Getting stolen documents out of the building was easy. Other than the daily checks on the codebooks and ciphers, not to speak of the rigorously enforced rules on locking the Code Room and allowing only authorized staff inside, little in the way of security existed at the embassy. There weren't even bag or body searches. Tyler could just breeze past the doorman, taking with him another cache of confidential paperwork that served as his open sesame to the luxuries for which his upbringing had prepared him.

Part Three

Stop, Look, Listen

1

Late on the afternoon of Sunday 8 October, 1939 – three days after his arrival – Tyler was sitting in the residents-only lounge of the Cumberland Hotel. Wooden panelling and rich-hued marble lined this amply proportioned room, its air of modish luxury accentuated by angular-patterned carpets as well as boxy little settees and easy-chairs. Through its windows was a view of the street.

In Moscow, things were at their busiest on Sunday afternoon. But in London the shops and pubs were closed then, breeding an atmosphere of joyless ennui, not helped by the current damp, cloudy weather.

Ludwig Matthias, Tyler's travelling companion, wandered into the hotel's lounge at about five past six, looking particularly dapper. After a brief chat, he and Tyler went down to the large, softly lit basement restaurant, their movements rippling across a geometric collage of mirrors.

The city's restaurants had changed in subtle ways since Tyler's last visit. Uniformed customers now proliferated. And there was a new live-for-the-moment atmosphere.

Over the ensuing half-hour, sufficient time for a leisurely coffee, dispensed by one of the pink-and-brown uniformed waitresses, Tyler and Ludwig sat in the restaurant. They had a lot to talk about. Since their parting at King's Cross Station, Ludwig had been through the foreign visitor's obligatory ritual of going to the Aliens' Registration Office to notify the police of his presence in London. He had also been conducting a series of errands. In case anyone from MI5 or elsewhere was shadowing him, he had taken regular precautions, entering and exiting addresses via different routes.

At 6.45 p.m. Tyler and Ludwig vacated the restaurant and made their way up to Tyler's room, where they could talk without fear of being overheard. They stayed there for no more than a few minutes before returning to the lounge. Ludwig filled out a telegram form, then he and Tyler headed back through the hotel. Pausing at the Despatch Desk, Ludwig arranged for the telegram to be sent to Stockholm.

Outside the hotel, he and Tyler hovered in the cold dusk while they debated where to have dinner. They settled on Jermyn Street, which offered a choice between four famously good but wallet-thinning eateries, patronized by ambassadors, film stars and millionaires. As they set off through the nascent blackout, Ludwig clutched the bulging envelope that Tyler had given him upstairs – an envelope big enough to hold a sheaf of US Embassy documents.

2

Lately the BBC hadn't been broadcasting up-tempo jazz, Max's preferred brand of music. Whenever one switched on the radio and tuned in to the Home Service, one would find oneself listening to announcers who sounded as if they were auditioning for the Voice of Doom, their announcements interspersed by a rather staid musical ragbag. Sea-shanties. Old English folk songs. Renditions of what were characterized as 'familiar and well-loved melodies', played on a cinema organ of all things.

If Max fancied a mood-lifting burst of Jelly Roll Morton, Sidney Bechet or Mildred Bailey and Her Alley Cats, he had to listen to the Continental stations. These broadcast from places such as Paris and Luxembourg, places imbued with an aura of exoticism for English people, most of whom had travelled no further than Blackpool or Southend. Yet Max did not share the belief that anything foreign was automatically superior to its English equivalent. Where music was concerned, he bridled at the suggestion that foreign musicians were better than home-grown ones.

He had long been a keen musician himself. Soon after the First World War, he'd established his own dance band, its line-up recruited from other former officers who had served in the armed forces. Recently he had taken to boasting about how ahead-of-its-time his band had been. It was, he claimed,

'London's first small, hot combination'. Happy to cultivate his reputation for eccentricity, he also liked to tell the story of how, back at the flat in Chelsea where he had once lived, he used to accompany a record of 'Beale Street Blues' on his clarinet, the music vying with a cacophonous chorus produced by three of his pets – a bulldog, a baboon and a bear cub.

During the past few days, music broadcast by the radio stations at Hamburg, Bremen, Cologne and Zeesen had been punctuated by what was becoming a famous preamble: 'Germany calling, Germany calling, Germany calling.' The same sinister voice, which was apt to pronounce the first word as 'Chair-mini', then listed the frequencies of these stations and said, 'You are about to hear our news in English.' There followed a dose of Nazi propaganda in the form of a news report and a scripted opinion piece, read by the sinister-voiced man.

Among English listeners, his scrupulous upper-crust delivery earned him the nickname of 'Lord Haw-Haw', a moniker initially shared with another of the Nazis' English-speaking broadcasters. Though Lord Haw-Haw's real name was never mentioned, his voice would have been unmistakable to Max. It belonged to none other than William Joyce, with whom Max most likely remained in contact.[33]

3

Unwilling to settle for the cheaper off-the-peg suits that were gaining in popularity, Tyler began to run up an enormous tailoring bill.[34] His tailor had a workshop above offices in Soho, a district of low buildings and narrow streets. These hosted innumerable restaurants, pubs, market stalls, factories, brothels, off-licences, bakeries, delicatessens and cafés, plus after-hours clubs that were as well-hidden as speakeasies, the associated signage emblematic of a teeming cosmopolitanism found nowhere else in London at that date.

Tyler's new outfitters loaned him one of their pattern books while he decided what he wanted. Fine tailoring was something with which he had a seasoned familiarity. The upper-class students alongside him at Princeton were no less attentive to the cut of their clothes than the subjects they were studying. Nowadays Tyler favoured single-breasted suits. In terms of colour he liked grey, black or navy-blue cloth, his taste extending to fashionable little flecks and chalk-stripes.

With his perfectly fitting suits, he presented a strikingly suave figure at the US Embassy, where custom-made clothes were ordinarily the preserve of the most senior staff. He did not just acquire a tailor in Soho, though. He also obtained accommodation there.

Rents for halfway decent flats in that part of town were even higher than the charges levied by the Cumberland Hotel. For the same rent exacted only a half-mile away, a tenant would have less space. He would have windows that presided over a vista of urban decay. And he would be liable to find himself with antediluvian plumbing, the kind that made wheezing, tubercular noises each time he switched on the tap.

But Soho did have its advantages. It was close to the embassy for one thing. Moreover, it was bustling, hospitable, disreputable and captivatingly varied. When Tyler walked through it, he would see prostitutes trawling for customers. He would see scrawny children and bleak, dustbin-lined alleyways, He would see bookshops with discreet window-displays, hinting at their capacity to fulfil his taste in pornographic photos and sadomasochistic books. He would see clusters of people chatting on the pavement. And he would hear snatches of French, Italian, Yiddish and Chinese along with the whir of sewing machines in nearby workshops and street-corner hurdy-gurdies clattering through instrumental renditions of the latest hits.

Stricken by loneliness now that he was separated from Tanya and his Moscow friends, Tyler would all the while be jostled by competing smells, by the sour tang of refuse, by a multitude of aromas not often encountered in London. Turkish cigarettes. Freshly ground coffee. Salami. The yeasty fragrance of newly baked croissants. If he closed his eyes, Tyler could just about kid himself into believing he was back in Paris, though the truth could not be eluded for long.

Experience of life in wartime Britain did nothing to mitigate his dissatisfaction with his latest posting. He soon started contemplating possible escape routes. Financial rather than ideological motives being behind his theft of US government documents, he felt under no obligation to retain his current access to the communications pipeline between London and Washington. Ideally, he wanted to return to Moscow or land a job in Berlin.

4

Anna had received some frustrating news. In a development sure to nurture her sense of malign forces exercising a covert influence over events, the RAF had deferred her pending appointment as a translator for the Advanced Air Strike Force. Compelled to rely on her measly AFS salary, she did not have much choice but to relinquish her little mews house. On Friday 13 October, 1939 – three weeks short of her thirty-seventh birthday – she decamped to her parents' flat in the genteel grandeur of South Kensington, the district that hosted London's principal White Russian colony.

Much as she adored her parents, moving in with them felt such a retrograde step. Eighteen years after she'd last lived with them, the thought of becoming their lodger was humiliating. As if she hadn't been through quite enough already. She'd been stripped of her business, her wealth, her status, her looks and now her home, each successive loss inevitably deepening her bitterness and resentment.

Still, the prospect of moving to South Kensington wasn't without its consolations. That part of town was at least familiar – somewhere associated with happier times. When she had first moved to England at the age of ten or eleven, following her father's appointment as Naval Attaché at the Imperial Russian Embassy, Anna and family had lived at another property in the area. And she had later had her own studio-flat there as well.[35]

From Gloucester Place Mews to her new home was a three-mile journey through warm, intermittently sunlit streets, populated by women in the new-style hooded overcoats and by growing numbers of cyclists. Nonchalantly pedalling alongside roaring lorries as well as dray-horses towing carts was a class of people one never used to see on bicycles. Fashionable ladies in snoods. Young girls in slacks. Besuited bureaucrats.

Suits were something Anna did not enjoy designing. What on earth was the point, she thought, of trying to compete with the English at a game where they are quite frankly unbeatable?

Her journey concluded at 18 Roland Gardens, a large Victorian house owned by a retired German hotelier who occupied all but its basement. Situated on a residential street near the café-restaurant her parents ran, their flat was entered via a steep, twisting flight of steps directly off the pavement. These ushered one down to a long, dark passage and a doorway leading to a cluster of dingy rooms where Russian was the preferred language. Corseted in those rooms were not only Anna's parents but also her indolent twenty-eight-year-old sister, Kyra, youngest of her three siblings.[36] Kyra's far from beautiful looks incited uncharitable remarks by other members of the Russian émigré community.

The flat yielded a tangible reminder of how cruel fate had been to the family since the days when they had lived in that house in Gledhow Gardens, since they'd owned that mansion in Pskov and that estate in Balovnevo, with its orchards, its forest and its long drive fringed by birch trees. Before the revolution, her parents had been able to employ servants, throw lavish parties and purchase almost any frippery they desired.

Displayed on the walls and shelves of their current home were paintings and drawings by Anna and her paternal grandfather, whose erudition and wide-ranging talents led her to regard him with awestruck reverence. Thinking about him was sufficient to make her overbearing self-confidence evaporate, leaving her with a sense of her own artistic and intellectual shortcomings. Her grandfather had been a successful artist, a doctor of philosophy, a musician and a scientist, to say nothing of his literary career, his art historical output garnering the admiration of the painter, John Singer Sargent.

While Anna produced deftly characterized portraits, executed in tentative post-Impressionistic dabs of colour, her grandfather specialized in meticulously detailed, sugary landscapes and city-scapes, painted in an even earlier idiom. These included sunsets on the Nile, and views of the waterways and piazzas of Venice, where he had owned a palazzo abutting the Grand Canal. His pictures were signed, 'A. N. Roussoff', a pseudonym embraced to avert confusion with another artist who bore his surname. Anna was immensely proud of the fact that three of his pictures were in the collection of the nearby Victoria and Albert Museum, where her middle sister, Alice, had once worked.[37]

Sharing the basement flat's wall-space were examples of the less conventional artistic output of Anna's mother, Mme Vera Wolkoff. She used tinted rags and appliqué needlework to portray scenes from Russian life, scenes that encompassed a group of Communists crucifying a child. She also created slightly sinister portrait dolls depicting people as diverse as the late Empress of Russia and the dancer, Anna Pavlova. Mme Wolkoff's work had been the subject of several exhibitions, supported by numerous prominent members of the aristocracy, not to mention the late King George V and his wife, Queen Mary, who had bought some of her creations.

Even before Anna moved in, the Wolkoffs' art-lined flat resounded to the forceful opinions of its occupants. Like Anna, her parents and sister Kyra blamed the Jews for the family's present circumstances and consequently voiced their approval of the Nazis.

When Anna's father, Admiral Nikolai Wolkoff, wasn't vent-ing his prejudices, he demonstrated the humour and sparkly bonhomie that made him popular, especially with women.[38] He had gained a reputation in the past as a wine-quaffing philan-derer. Short, plump and bespectacled, he was due to turn seventy next summer. He had white hair and a beard trimmed in the style of the last of the Tsars.

Mme Vera Wolkoff was inclined to behave more like his adju-tant than his wife. In heavily German-accented Russian, she referred to him as 'The Admiral', these recurrent allusions to his former eminence patching his frayed dignity.

Nigh on a decade younger than her husband, Vera was a well-padded yet energetic woman of palpable intelligence. She had an enduringly aristocratic manner, and a command of English that fell far short of the Admiral's. Protracted exile had not destroyed her belief that the old order could be restored in Russia once the Communist government was ousted. Most of her husband's friends and acquaintances were either involved in espionage or had connections to the intelligence services, so she was well-placed to pick up news of any progress towards that objective, Hitler and the Nazis offering her best hope of attaining it.

Deprived of servants until the family's declining fortunes could be reversed, Mme Wolkoff had taught herself to cook traditional Russian dishes. Anna believed that Russian women, along with their French counterparts, had an innate gift for cooking, necessity awakening a dormant talent in those who had never previously had to make even the simplest of dishes. Her mother now prepared delicious food, the aroma from which suffused the flat.

There was, Anna had noticed, a deep-rooted Russian obsession with food, an obsession that was, she thought, so brilliantly satirized in the short stories of Nikolai Gogol. She remembered childhood journeys on the train between Germany and Tsarist Russia, filled with homeward-bound passengers who, as they approached the frontier, would talk about little else but the culinary delights awaiting them at the next stop. Promptly the train pulled in, they would join the undignified rush to the station buffet. Anna could still picture the tables there, one of them covered with a white cloth and laden with plates and cutlery, the other dotted with bottles of vodka in ice-buckets and with plates of food: borscht, sturgeon in aspic, smoked sprats marinated in oil, caviar on rye bread, grated chicken. Not common-or-garden chicken but meat from those distinctively flavoured birds, reared on seeds from the forests of Siberia. And of course there would be the dish everyone had been talking about beforehand – a steaming plate of *Smolenskaia kasha*, which Anna regarded as a quintessentially Russian example of gastronomic poetry.

However comforting the prospect of home-cooking was for Anna, it did not lift her sense of failure. In sympathy with her darkening mood, the weather abruptly changed. Within hours of her taking up residence at 18a Roland Gardens, the extended summer ended. It was replaced by a monsoon-like downpour, overcast skies rendering her parents' flat gloomier than ever. She did at least have the option that Sunday of escaping to the opera house on Kingsway, where the British Union was staging another of its mammoth rallies.

5

All weekend the downpour didn't let up. On the streets near where Tyler worked, it damaged many of the recently constructed walls of sandbags. A high proportion of those became so saturated that they burst. Others just leaked their contents.

Despite the weather, which curtailed his spare-time options, Tyler hadn't yet got round to telling his devoted mother that he'd arrived safely. There was nothing new about his failings in that respect. 'I am a rotten correspondent in the best of times,' he would declare, this uncharacteristic self-deprecation masking his callous narcissism, his disregard for the feelings of others.

Even after the weekend downpour abated, streams of silted rainwater meandered across rubbish-strewn pavements. That Monday the drying streets near the US Embassy were clotted with people dismantling sandbag walls. Once these had been taken down, they were reconstructed on raised planks.

Towards the end of the 4 p.m. to midnight shift in the Code Room, another letter from Winston Churchill had to be cabled to President Roosevelt via the US Secretary of State. Churchill had not signed the telegram, preferring to employ the transparent pseudonym of 'Naval Person'. Again, Grey was the code selected for relaying his message to Washington.

'Our accounts of Hitler's oil position make us feel he is up against time limits,' Churchill had written. The telegram argued that Hitler would soon have to launch the anticipated offensive.

6

There was a message for Tyler. It came from Secretary of State Cordell Hull, the political protégé of Tyler's late father. Cordell had, in the absence of any word from London, been asked by Tyler's mother to check that he was all right. For a man of Tyler's age, there was something deeply embarrassing about being the focus of such maternal solicitude. Anyone would think he was still at prep school.

Nudged by the telegram from Cordell, Tyler wrote to his mother to inform her of his safe arrival in London. His letter, sent via the American diplomatic pouch, also mentioned that he had met an old friend of hers from her home state of Virginia.

Were he not feeling quite so lonely, he might not have wanted to spend time with a friend of his mother. Coincidentally, her friend, Mrs Bette Straker, was a member of the American Women's Club, positioned close to his new workplace. He'd already become acquainted with the woman on a prior visit to England. The elderly but energetic widow of an insurance actuary, she had lived for more than thirty-five years in a north London suburb.[39] Even now she still talked about her upbringing in 1890s New York, about those distant days when the streets of Manhattan were dominated by hansom cabs.

Though Bette inhabited liberal, feminist circles, well-disposed towards the Soviet Union, she socialized with many of London's vociferously anti-Communist Russian émigrés. Under her wing, Tyler received an entrée into that community, among whom the growing possibility of a Soviet military assault on Finland presented cause for outrage. In anticipation of such an attack, the Finnish government had already begun to evacuate Helsinki and another of its major cities. Tyler's old boss, Ambassador Laurence A. Steinhardt, was being deployed as an intermediary between President Roosevelt and the Soviets. Last week the President had sent them a message expressing his 'earnest hope' that nothing should occur which might 'affect injuriously the peaceful relations between Soviet Russia and Finland'.

In the company of Bette, Tyler received an introduction to Admiral and Mme Wolkoff. His mother's friend served alongside Mme Wolkoff on the organizing committee for the Russian Red Cross Society's Christmas Bazaar.

The Admiral was impressed by Tyler's fluent Russian and references to having lived in Moscow recently. First-hand knowledge of contemporary Soviet life afforded Tyler an opportunity to win the approval of Admiral and Mme Wolkoff by telling stories validating their hatred of Communism. Truda Ganghadaran, his former German teacher, who used to talk about her experiences at every opportunity, was an ideal source of such stories. When Tyler had met Truda, her husband – an Indian engineer – had still been around. Not for long, though, because he was soon hauled off by the Soviet secret police. Four-and-a-half months pregnant, Truda's passport was confiscated and she'd been prohibited from leaving Moscow. What fate had befallen her husband, the Soviets would not initially disclose. They waited six months before notifying her that he'd been found guilty of spying. For that, they had executed him. At the time of Tyler's departure from Moscow, Truda was still there, living in fear of being arrested as well.[40]

7

Max was accustomed to scrutinizing the weather and registering its fluctuations. A couple of weeks had passed since the downpour marking the delayed transition from summer to autumn. London had subsequently been swathed in perpetual twilight, smoke from thousands of chimneys only adding to this. Chill gusts of wind emphasized the change. These shepherded fallen leaves along pavements and gutters untouched by any street-sweeper's broom.

Still, as the newspapers gleefully observed, the capital had escaped lightly in comparison to the French border. Torrential rain had created swampy conditions for the British Expeditionary Force, stationed there in anticipation of the Nazi offensive that never seemed to come. Feeling wet and cold was something Max had often experienced as a cadet aboard HMS *Worcester*. He and his shipmates had slept on draughty bunks that could end up being drenched if anyone forgot to close the hatch. And they were regularly ordered to furl and unfurl the ship's sails, a chore that could take up to six hours in stiff winds, icy spray from the sea increasing the burden of the canvas, which thrashed about with the muscular vigour of a freshly landed trout.

Like the expected assault on France, there had been no sign of the predicted air raids, unless one took into account a single half-hearted attack on the Forth Bridge in Scotland. A leading insurance company had even started laying odds on the war being over by Christmas. Yet the civil defence measures lingered and the gossip about a German invasion persisted.

Irrespective of the time of day, Max could neither enter nor exit Section B5b's Dolphin Square offices without passing idle groups of uniformed first-aid workers. They were there because the building's underground garages had been transformed into one of London's major casualty depots. Colour-coded lines had been painted on the numerous paths visible from where Max worked, each colour indicating where certain types of casualties should be taken.

With Bill Younger available to pursue follow-up enquiries and provide what was growing into a close and supportive friendship, Max was meanwhile supervising the operation against Captain Ramsay and the Right Club. On Wednesday 25 October, 1939, Marjorie had been over to Onslow Square to call on the Captain's wife. In conversation with Mrs Ramsay, Marjorie mentioned that she'd succeeded in finding a job with MI5's Military Censorship Department.

Some of the Right Club's friends in the War Office and Admiralty had been removed from their posts, Mrs Ramsay said, so it was splendid news that Marjorie had got into the Military Censorship Department. But Mrs Ramsay did not pursue the matter, preferring to talk about other things. She divulged that Captain Ramsay knew someone at Scotland Yard who had talked about meeting an MI5 officer with an interest in discussing the British Union. No names were mentioned by

Mrs Ramsay, though. She also said that her husband had been warned that he should take great care not to lay himself open to action by the authorities.

Such leakage of sensitive information from Scotland Yard bore out Max's belief in keeping the activities of his agents secret from the police. Except in rare cases, he thought, a secret agent should remain secret, operating independently and unknown to the Metropolitan Police or any other force.

According to Marjorie, Mrs Ramsay hadn't just crowed about the Right Club's informant within the police. She'd also spoken about the club's well-connected aristocratic members. These included the aviation expert, Lord William Sempill, who was part of its governing council.

For the past fifteen years he had been under investigation by MI5, his activities documented in an array of paperwork that fattened his file like one of those bloated pets, the sight of which so nettled Max. Until war had broken out, Sempill had been mixed up with the Link and the Anglo–German Fellowship, organizations now disbanded. As Max's colleagues at Wormwood Scrubs would have been able to confirm, there was evidence that Sempill had been supplying the Japanese with top-secret technological information about the construction of aircraft carriers.

Besides gloating about the titled members of the Right Club, Mrs Ramsay referred to meetings of the club's 'Inner Circle'. These were held at her house every Wednesday evening. She quizzed Marjorie about the possibility of getting time off work on those evenings, the inference being that an invitation to join the Inner Circle might be forthcoming.

8

Through a Jewish colleague with whom he was friendly, Tyler got to know June Huntley, another American expat, her name masking her Russian parentage. Just a little older than him, she was a petite, charming woman with long hair, a beguiling smile and a shapely figure, her sharp dress-sense heightening her attractiveness. Tyler's new acquaintance had a hard-to-quench taste for alcohol and a habit of talking about the theatre to the exclusion of pretty much everything else. Her husband, Raymond, was an up-and-coming character actor who had appeared in films such as *Knight Without Armour*, starring Marlene Dietrich.[41]

Within the twinkling of a heavily mascaraed eye, June and Tyler were close, platonic friends. He confided in her about how few people he knew in England, how he'd never wanted to be sent to London, how he didn't care for Britain and the British, how he would *love* to secure a posting to Berlin.

He was aware that life in Germany was hard for American embassy staff, yet he envied the young, Berlin-bound code clerk whom he had met earlier that month. The knowledge that the other man would happily have swapped places with him made the situation even more galling.

When he wasn't doing the 4 p.m. to midnight shift in the Grosvenor Square Code Room, Tyler became a regular evening guest at the Huntleys' ritzy address, which happened to be within easy walking distance of the US Embassy. He had lengthy conversations with June's husband, who possessed an air of curt authority, fostered by an immaculately trimmed moustache and a voice that erred towards the astringent. Their discussions were spiced up by Tyler's anti-British pronouncements and by his prediction that the Germans would take over America and create a fascist regime there.

9

Anna's social life provided a respite from the dreariness of the weather, her depressing domestic circumstances and her work as an AFS driver. Off-duty she had slipped into the habit of dining with Francis Hemming, her recently acquired friend, whom she could probe about what he'd witnessed while taking minutes at War Cabinet meetings.

Their meals together contributed to the weight she was putting on, the slight cushioning around her jawline offering a clear manifestation of this. It was what the beauty columnists described with euphemistic tact as 'a contour defect', which could supposedly be rectified by the new Face Moulding Treatment, promoted by the Elizabeth Arden salon, where one of Anna's friends worked.

As well as dining with Francis, Anna was spending time with Johnny Coast, a boisterous and temperamental twenty-two-year-old colleague from the Nordic League, who travelled up to town from rural Kent. Ever since resigning from his job as a merchant banker, Johnny had been casting round for an alternative career. Well, less of a career than a vocation, something he loved doing. And he certainly loved going to Soho restaurants, though it was doubtful anyone would pay him to do *that*. He loved going to the ballet at the Royal Opera House in Covent Garden, too.

Mention of ballet would have teed up Anna for references not just to Alicia Markova and the other famous dancers associated with her fundraising event at the Ritz last summer, but also to her uncle Gabriel, who used to work at the Royal Opera House. Her uncle had at one time been in a similar situation to Johnny, yet things hadn't turned out badly for him. When the revolution had put paid to his job at the Imperial Russian Embassy, he'd been compelled to find a fresh career. He had ended up in a lucrative, much-lauded role as a costume and set designer.

The difficulty of finding one's true calling was something with which Anna also had copious experience. Right from the early part of her childhood, she had been encouraged to express herself through acting, writing and painting. After leaving the Dorset boarding-school where she'd completed her secondary education, she had been among the first female students to enrol at the Architectural Association. She had, however, frittered away a fortune in tuition fees by chalking up unsatisfactory results in her exams and then dropping out at the end of the initial year.

Unlike Anna and her uncle, Johnny Coast was yet to find his métier, though politics presented a viable option. Ferociously anti-Semitic in the views that spouted from his toothy features, he was part of Captain Ramsay's fascist clique. While Anna supported both Ramsay and Sir Oswald Mosley, her friend had become sceptical about the British Union's leader. 'Under no circumstances can he be considered a serious political proposition, but merely a dago comic who is a safety valve,' Johnny claimed. 'Blast him, for he has likeable qualities, including a fine straight left and a wrist and nerve of steel in a scrap!'

Johnny had a weakness for this sort of outburst. Intolerant though Anna was and steadfast though she remained in her backing for Mosley, she carried on seeing her young friend.

10

Hostilities had been declared less than two months ago, yet the war – its geographic scope yet to justify billing it the Second *World* War – was already beginning to leach into most aspects of life. Its impact was palpable even on the news-kiosks in Tyler's neighbourhood, paper-saving measures having dramatically slimmed the periodicals and newspapers. Those publications shared display-space this morning – Tuesday 31 October, 1939 – with a booklet published by the British Foreign Office. In the booklet were firsthand accounts, mostly by Jewish prisoners, about the torture and brutality being perpetrated inside Nazi concentration camps. People were reading it on all the rush-hour buses and Underground trains.

London's rush-hour buses had, ever since Tyler's arrival, been almost as packed as their Moscow equivalents, pressure on the transport system ratcheted up by the continued closure of so many West End tube stations for unspecified protective work. Rumour had it that they were going to be used as air-raid shelters. But there still hadn't been any air raids – just another false alarm. This had originated yesterday with a single, doleful siren, located somewhere east of Grosvenor Square.

Ambassador Kennedy hadn't seen fit to create a shelter beneath the embassy, so each time a siren sounded Tyler and his colleagues had to hurry out of the building and round the corner onto Grosvenor Street. Refuge was afforded by the huge basement of Molyneux, an haute couture dress shop less than 200 yards away.

Yesterday's siren was counterpointed by other rooftop sirens, by smaller ones installed on passing squad cars and by short blasts from policemen's whistles. After about ten minutes, the noise had climaxed with the sirens breaking into the continuous, baleful caterwauling that denoted the 'All clear'.

When Tyler turned up at work today, he took the opportunity to appropriate another confidential document for his burgeoning collection of stolen US government paperwork. As with many of the other exhibits in his collection, this would have been of particular interest to the Soviets. It comprised a letter from Guy Liddell to the Washington, DC office of the Federal Bureau of Investigation. Liddell had requested information from the FBI about two Soviet spies, one of them British, the other American, both active in the United States. Tyler may well have known both individuals because they were living in Moscow at the same time as him.

Instead of retyping the letter, he stole the file copy, thus helping the two agents and their Soviet masters by removing from the embassy's records any trace of their activities.[42]

11

It was nigh impossible to avoid noticing that the corridors and other communal areas at Dolphin Square were much emptier than they had been. Copious numbers of Max's fellow Dolphinians must have either been called up for military service or moved to somewhere less likely to have bombs raining down on it. This exodus from the capital, which wasn't just confined to Dolphin Square, could be inconvenient. Max would have grown accustomed to telephoning people and being informed by the operator that he had dialled a 'Ceased line'. Where government contacts in Whitehall were concerned, one would often hear an unfamiliar voice say that Mr Bloggins and his entire department had been transferred to Northumbria. Obstacles of that nature were bound to make Max's work even more time-consuming.

A major element of his MI5 duties still consisted of overseeing Marjorie's infiltration of the Right Club. Her next report put him in the picture regarding her recent visit to Onslow Square to see Mrs Ramsay. During the visit, which occurred on the evening of Friday 3 November, 1939, conversation had again turned towards Marjorie's job in the Military Censorship Department. At Max's bidding, Marjorie told Mrs Ramsay about the layout of the department, the nature of her work and the opportunities she had for moving round the building.

Greedily snaffling the bait, Mrs Ramsay asked Marjorie whether she ever got the chance to meet people in other MI5 departments.

Marjorie replied that the staff canteen at Wormwood Scrubs provided the only such opportunities.

Captain Ramsay's wife then said, 'Yes, I think when it comes to the showdown you will have work to do.'

12

Such was the air of military stasis, one heard people making facetious references to 'the Second Bore War', a punning allusion to the two Victorian conflicts between Britain and the Boer rebels in South Africa. Tyler's daily journey from Soho to Grosvenor Square nonetheless coincided with a spate of West End postboxes being set ablaze. But the Germans weren't the culprits. Those were Irish Republicans protesting against what they viewed as the British annexation of Northern Ireland.

In advance of Thanksgiving, Tyler stole an additional US government document from his Grosvenor Square workplace. Marked 'Secret', this had been sent by Guy Liddell to a member of the embassy's senior staff. Liddell's intention was for the letter to be forwarded to the appropriate authorities. It warned the Americans about a Soviet agent living in New York City, from where he was directing espionage against Britain. The letter also requested a search of home and business addresses associated with that agent. Such raids would, the letter assured its recipient, furnish material beneficial to both British and American intelligence.

Again – in a likely bid to sabotage the tip-off, which threatened the continued effectiveness of key Soviet agents – Tyler removed the embassy's file copy.

13

Occupying the centre of Brompton Square was an expansive, oblong communal garden, ringed by attractive four- and five-storey Georgian terraced houses. An old friend of Anna's family had once lived there.[43] Just across the square was the house where Johnny Coast and Anna were heading. No mistaking it because the place had distinctive Romanesque-style windows.

Anna loved to flaunt the younger men she sometimes cultivated, so she was taking Johnny round to meet Major Philip le Grand Gribble and his wife, Anthea May. She had first befriended the Gribbles when she'd been looking for someone to finance the dress shop she wanted to open. Until then, she had been selling her clothes privately, designing garments on an individual basis for each client, never repeating herself. Philip – who was twelve years her senior – had ended up providing the capital she needed. She had rewarded him with a 49 per cent shareholding. Even though Philip had since lost his entire investment, they remained on good terms, the only sign of tension being between Anna and his wife.

Fed by an eclectic career, spent running farms in South Africa, serving in the Army, working as a women's magazine journalist, as well as writing novels and short stories, Philip displayed a facility for colourful reminiscences. 'When flying in the East, I have several times seen the same ghostly happening,' one of his fund of anecdotes began. 'The first occasion was in 1916 when

Sir Pierre van Ryneveld, who now commands the Air Force of the Union of South Africa, and I set off from El Hamman, on the Mediterranean coast, to reconnoitre a distant oasis. For some way we followed the coast and I well remember in the haze of the early morning I was starting to see a third machine in formation keeping pace on my left. I felt a moment's superstitious dread before I realized that the pilot who flew at my wing tips, circled in a *grissaille* frame, barely tinged by rainbow colours, was my own reflection who waved his hand and dipped and banked as I did. On comparing notes later, I found that Sir Pierre had also flown beside his own ghost.'

Never shy of expressing himself, Philip gave the Nazis his unconditional support. Yet Anna's decision to take Johnny round to Brompton Square was not, in hindsight, an inspired move.

At the outset, he behaved with conventional decorum. Unable to sustain that, he became embroiled in a furious political disagreement with Philip's wife, who found herself the target of his savage temper. The time was fast approaching, he told her, when she and her ilk would have their throats slit. In a final menacing aside, he said he was *looking forward* to that day.

14

For obvious reasons a simple two-minute silence replaced the long-established wolf's howl of sirens that would otherwise have sounded across London at eleven minutes past eleven on the morning of Sunday 11 November, 1939. Paper poppies, invoking the flowers that dotted the Flemish graveyards in which so many of Britain's Great War casualties had been buried, nevertheless blossomed not only from people's lapels but also from the radiators of passing vehicles. Among the so-called 'glorious dead', commemorated by those poppies, was one of Max's schoolmates, who had gone down with his ship. Max's brother was another of the war dead being remembered.

The prospect of sombre-voiced headmasters reading out fresh lists of ex-pupils who had given their lives for King and Country rendered this year's Armistice Day all the more poignant. Lest anyone forget that further British bloodshed was on the agenda, Wednesday morning's newspapers circulated stories about the first bombs to land on home soil. Not in London but in the Shetland Isles. The attack hadn't exactly left a trail of devastation, though. It had damaged an empty house and blown out the windows of several crofts. But that was the full extent of it.

15

Little by little Tyler was burrowing into London's Russian émigré community. He soon struck up a friendship with a Russian who had taken Polish citizenship. On learning that his new friend was a long-standing acquaintance of Eugène Sabline, former Chargé d'Affaires at the Imperial Russian Embassy, Tyler nagged him for an introduction.

Despite the embassy's belated closure, following the British government's decision to open diplomatic relations with the Soviet Union fifteen years ago, Sabline remained the spokesman for the London-based White Russians. Tyler's desire to obtain an introduction probably stemmed from Ludwig Matthias naming Sabline as a convenient conduit for passing stolen US government documents to the Soviets. In White Russian parlance the former Chargé d'Affaires was 'a reverse radish' – white on the outside, red on the inside. By establishing a legitimate social connection to him, Tyler's encounters with Sabline would acquire an illusory air of innocence.

16

Special Branch had compiled a report for Max and his MI5 colleagues. It identified Captain Ramsay as one of the leaders of several fascist and anti-Semitic groups who had attended a conference on Armistice Day. The conference had taken place at

Sir Oswald Mosley's London home, just a little way from Dolphin Square. Mosley and the others had debated the possibility of pursuing their objectives through cooperation. Only vague agreement had, however, been reached on that score.

Also noted in the report was the ferocity with which Mosley had attacked the government. He'd slated it for its alleged mistreatment of a British Union activist detained under the Emergency Defence Regulations. Belittling the well-documented concentration camp atrocities described in the recent Foreign Office booklet, Mosley accused the government of hypocrisy. Ramsay offered to raise the matter in Parliament.

The report on the meeting at Mosley's home was the fruit of a jovial and effective partnership Max had established with the Special Branch officers assigned to the Right Club case. His dealings with Scotland Yard could scarcely have been further removed from his adversarial relationship with the police when he had been working for Desmond Morton at MI6. This time round, Max was delighted to have avoided trouble of that sort. Good teamwork was, he knew, essential to the success of an investigation.

17

Anna had a supply of personalized stationery, evocative of her relatively affluent past. Balanced ostentatiously above her initial was the silhouette of a crown.

On a sheet of this smart notepaper, she began a sprawling letter to the writer, Louis-Ferdinand Céline, whose novel, *Journey to the End of the Night*, she had read and admired when it was first published in French several years earlier. As she explained, her admiration for him had grown since the subsequent release of his two anti-Semitic tracts, *School for Corpses* and *Trifles for a Massacre*. These carried sham evidence of a Jewish conspiracy implicating the Vatican, the British secret service and the Comintern – the Soviet organization set up to stimulate world revolution.

In her letter Anna mentioned that she had just lent *School for Corpses* to a Member of Parliament. Though she didn't give away the MP's name, it was obviously Captain Ramsay. She told Céline that she and the MP wanted to obtain and then publish evidence verifying his conspiracy claims. Whatever material he had about British intelligence and the head of MI6 would, she added, be especially helpful as she and the MP were compiling a dossier on him.

18

It wasn't long before a further shipment of information from Marjorie was being unloaded on Max's quayside. She revealed that Mrs Ramsay had gone round to tea at Marjorie's furnished flat. Actually, it was less of a flat than a bed-sitting room. It had the virtue of coming with its own telephone-line, which made keeping in touch a lot easier for Max. The flat was in a seedy part of town, just down the road from Notting Hill Gate tube station. Not the natural habitat for someone of Mrs Ramsay's social standing. A few years back, another of Max's agents – a young woman who had infiltrated a Communist spy-ring – had taken rooms near there.

Over tea Mrs Ramsay probed Marjorie about the Military Censorship Department. Was it keeping her busy? And, if so, what was she doing?

When Marjorie explained that they were engaging extra staff, Mrs Ramsay said, 'With languages?'

'Yes – and without.'

Mrs Ramsay asked if Marjorie knew where those additional staff would be deployed.

In reply, Marjorie said of course she did – that was her job.

'Do you have access to many people?' Mrs Ramsay enquired.

Marjorie told her that she had the freedom of every room in her section.

'Captain Ramsay thinks you will be most useful when the time comes,' Mrs Ramsay reiterated. 'We think that there will be a Communist rising and then we shall have to take over. Mosley has tried often and hard to get Jock to join in with him and – this is for your private ear – he promised him Scotland. But I asked Jock about this and he is firmly resolved on two things. No pogroms of Jews. That is unnecessary. And no joining with Mosley.'

Judging by the general tone of the ensuing dialogue, the Right Club appeared to have another contact in the Military Censorship Department.[44] Were Marjorie's suspicions correct, it was just as well that Max had been given comparative autonomy from the rest of MI5.

19

The meeting place was no more than a ten-minute walk from where Anna lived. Straight up Roland Gardens, its pavements bordered by large houses. A distant barrage balloon usually hung over the T-junction ahead. She had to veer right onto Old Brompton Road and past the familiar haphazard palette of high street businesses. Then she had to turn left at the ladies' hairdresser.

Short hair – either shingled or permed into a so-called 'Baby Boy Bob' – was in fashion. And one could well understand why, because it was eminently practical. It retained its shape even after it had been crushed beneath an AFS cap like Anna's.

As one approached the Harrington Road turning, one caught a first glimpse of the Russian Tea Rooms. Often Johnny Coast's bicycle was parked outside, several parcels strapped to the back. Made up of two cramped, rather shabby dining-rooms adorned by a portrait above the fireplace of Tsar Nicholas II, the Russian Tea Rooms bore no resemblance to the splendour of its near-namesake in New York. It was furnished with bentwood chairs and approximately a dozen small tables draped with oilcloths. Vases of flowers stood on the tables, from where one had a view across the street. Queensberry Hall, home of a famous ballet school for children, was opposite.

When Anna's mother had, with financial backing from British friends, launched the Tea Rooms in 1923 – a few years prior to its American counterpart – she'd served not only teas but also what were dubbed 'light luncheons'. Since there was a demand for suppers as well, she kept the place open during the evenings now, last orders being around 9 p.m.

The food was prepared in a steamy and unpleasant basement kitchen where Mme Wolkoff toiled alongside a Russian cook. From the subterranean kingdom inhabited by these two women, Anna's father emerged at frequent intervals, cheerfully distributing a range of items, in those days all somewhat exotic to the English palate. Homemade yoghurt, containers of which were available for delivery to local customers. *Pirozhki* – pastries stuffed with meat, potatoes or cheese. Glasses of lemon tea. Caviar and blinis. Borscht. Depending whether Anna's parents could get hold of the requisite sugar, currently in short supply, there was also the menu's star attraction, *tyanuchki*, a sublime caramel-like dessert. 'Only one Russian woman in London knows how to make it,' the Wolkoffs would tell customers. With a surge of nationalistic pride, Anna recalled how non-Russians would pass approving comments when they sampled dishes like this.

If anyone asked for wine or, perhaps, beer to accompany their food, Admiral Wolkoff had to explain that the Tea Rooms wasn't licensed to sell alcohol. But customers were, of course, at liberty to go and buy a bottle from the Anglo–French Wine Stores, little more than half-a-dozen doors up Harrington Road. Unfinished bottles would, whenever customers requested, be kept until their next visit.

Witty, extrovert and flirtatious, Anna's father was surprisingly well-suited to the role of host and waiter. His mother had been English, accounting for the unaccented fluency with which he spoke the language of his present home country, occasional lapses into idiosyncratic phraseology betraying his foreign background. Just as he'd once discoursed knowledgeably about naval munitions, he now enlightened customers – many of whom had become friends – about the origins and respective merits of different varieties of caviar.

Already a magnet for extreme anti-Semites and Nazi sympathizers, for White Russians and fascist daytrippers from outside London, the Tea Rooms was the chosen rendezvous for Anna and her Right Club cronies. In late afternoon or evening, they would gather for food and conversation.

Female members of the group were encouraged to purchase a Right Club uniform. Designed by Anna, this consisted of a coat, dress and hat. Each item was available in a selection of colours. So far, however, these ensembles – for which Anna charged £3 10s – had not lived up to their potential as a lucrative sideline. She'd sold less than half-a-dozen of them.

Central to the Right Club contingent that joined Anna's table at the Tea Rooms were five of her friends. One of them was Johnny Coast, their relationship having survived the scene he had made when she took him round to meet Major Philip le Grand Gribble and his wife.

Another of Anna's group was Enid Riddell, who had been with her at the Nordic League's Caxton Hall rally. Enid rented a little, ultra-modern flat slightly over a mile from the Tea Rooms, where she'd been a loyal customer since before the war. Glamorous even without appreciable cosmetic assistance, she had a button nose, grey-blue eyes and blonde hair, styled in a long bob. Much of her adult life had been spent gallivanting round the French Riviera. Her biggish monthly allowance from her grandmother – supplemented by generous handouts whenever necessary – had always enabled her to shun the rigours of marriage and employment at the same time as paying for the expensive clothes and jewellery she wore. Court shoes. Fine silk stockings. Blue or sometimes pink blouses that contrasted with her predominantly black wardrobe. Some of her outfits had been made by Anna. The rest of her clothes came from Harrods and her jewellery from Cartier, shops way beyond Anna's present circumscribed budget.

Also included in Anna's Tea Rooms quintet was Anne van Lennep, a British woman of Dutch extraction, who was a resolute supporter of both the Right Club and British Union. Heavily built, her large eyes set into a moon face, her girlish complexion belying the fact that she was in her late thirties, she had sandy hair and a penchant for funereal clothes, worn with flamboyant hats.

The remaining member of the gang was Molly Stanford, who referred to Anna somewhat deferentially as 'Miss Anna'. Molly was in her mid-forties, though she looked older. She had a long, pointed nose, a thin, angular body and a fondness for brown clothes. From her nearby home, she pottered over to the Tea Rooms for all her meals. She and Anna shared a couple of friends, one of whom was Margaret Bothamley, now living in Berlin. Via a British fascist based in Brussels, Molly was conducting an illegal correspondence with Margaret.

Under Anna's guidance, the Tea Rooms set embarked on what were innocently termed 'sticking parties'. These had begun when Johnny Coast brought with him the first in a series of parcels containing gummed labels known as 'stickybacks', many of them as large as a paperback novel. Printed on each label were paragraphs of artfully conceived anti-Semitic propaganda, headlined by slogans such as 'This is a Jews' War!'

At night the group from the Tea Rooms would venture into the blacked-out streets. Over previous weeks there had been stories in the London newspapers about women being assaulted and robbed under cover of darkness, so Anna and friends were well-advised to stick together. Enid offered to drive them in her car, but they preferred to walk. They traced preassigned routes diagrammed on little maps produced by Anna. Every so often they would scuttle into hotel lavatories, where they'd use the washbasins to dampen the backs of the labels. Vying for space with Communist stickyback squads, they would leave a trail of propaganda on phoneboxes, noticeboards, lamp-posts, bus-stops and signs denoting pedestrian crossings.

20

British Summer Time had been extended by six weeks as a means of allowing people to travel home each evening without being inconvenienced by the blackout. Consequently, the clocks weren't due to go back until tomorrow – Sunday 19 November, 1939. The date was doubly significant for Max because it marked the anniversary of an event that had left an enduring imprint on him, an occurrence that yielded suitable material for his avid philosophical debates with friends about whether life held any purpose.

As an innocuous prologue to this past event, he'd received a note from his then wife, Gwladys. He and Gwladys had long since separated, yet they remained on affectionate terms. She was a warm, vivacious, sporty woman, who played cricket and rode to hounds with her local hunt. Max had first met her during the 1920s when they had both been senior members of the British Fascisti – while Max had been in charge of intelligence, Gladwys had been Director of the Women's Units. They had also been fringe members of the Bright Young Things, the liberated, party-loving set whose antics were memorialized by Evelyn Waugh in his popular novel, *Vile Bodies*. Since her separation from Max, Gwladys had lived in the Somerset town of Minehead, where she ran a hairdressing and manicure salon.

Three years ago to the day, she had taken the train to London from Bath, where she was having treatment for sciatica. She registered at a room in the Overseas Club and sent Max a note: 'Sweetheart, just arrived for a few days' shopping. Will you give me a ring in the morning to see what we can fix up – not too early, as I will be having breakfast in bed and will not be leaving here until after 10am, Love, G.'

Instantly Gwladys's message reached him, Max telephoned the club and asked to speak to her. But the housekeeper said she was taking a nap. Anxious to chat with his wife, he rang several more times that evening. The last of these calls was a touch before eleven. When the housekeeper told him that his wife still hadn't surfaced, he asked the woman to rouse her. Returning to the phone after a brief interval, the housekeeper said that she couldn't wake Mrs Knight.

Max went straight to the Overseas Club, where he also tried and failed to wake Gwladys. From the bottles of medication beside her bed, it was apparent that she had overdosed on aspirins, combined with the barbiturates she was using to relieve her sciatic pain. So Max summoned a doctor, who arranged for Gwladys – unconscious but still alive – to be moved to a nearby hospital. Over the coming hours Max obtained help from a leading authority on poisons. Unfortunately, the specialist was no more successful than anyone else at reviving Gwladys. Powerless, Max watched as she developed what was diagnosed as pneumonia, harbinger of that horrendous moment when, aged just thirty-seven, she died.

The ensuing coroner's inquest did nothing to blunt Max's grief. Never comfortable talking about his private life, he had been obliged to put up with questions about his marriage. And he'd even had to suffer cross-examination by the barrister working for Gwladys's estranged and embittered mother. The barrister exploited the occasion to disseminate his client's unsubstantiated theory that Max had somehow engineered Gwladys's death in order to inherit her sizeable savings. Predictably, the inquest spawned extensive articles in the press, coupled with headlines such as 'MYSTERY DEATH OF AUTHOR'S WIFE'.

What had happened to Gwladys remained a source of anguish for Max. If their marriage had not been such a lamentable failure, they would not have been living apart and she would not have been so lonely. That was what really gnawed at him – the thought of how unhappy she'd been, a symptom of her unhappiness being her tendency to launch zestfully into a sentence and then allow it to fade into disconsolate silence.

On the Monday after the anniversary of her death, the war continued its gradual, seemingly inexorable encroachment into every aspect of life. That day there was a government announcement regarding the imminent rationing of butter, sugar, bacon and ham. More ominously, the heavy and insistent drumbeat of anti-aircraft fire was audible early in the morning. It came from somewhere towards the east. Yet it didn't prove the overture to an air raid. Instead, the barrage stopped and everything carried on as before. The evening newspapers provided an explanation. A single German bomber had strayed over the Thames Estuary, provoking a fusillade of such intensity that the aircraft turned tail.

21

Tyler and his colleagues were filing out of the US Embassy and down the front steps. Among them was Ambassador Kennedy, who appeared increasingly gaunt and unwell. He stood at the top of the steps while Tyler and the majority of the others fanned along the pavement.

Like one of those borrowed summer days you get in Washington, DC during the autumn, today was unexpectedly warm and bright – warm enough for Tyler to relinquish his overcoat. He wore a dark single-breasted suit in combination with a white shirt and tie.

Across the street from where he and the others were standing, a photographer had rigged up a tripod with a large, boxy plate-camera set on it. To look through the camera's viewfinder, the man needed to duck beneath an old-fashioned black hood. He had been commissioned to take a picture that could be presented to the Ambassador as a keepsake. The official line was that the Ambassador would be leaving London on Wednesday 29 November, 1939, for a Christmas break in the United States. If the souvenir photo was anything to go by, though, Kennedy had been handed a one-way ticket.

Nobody would be surprised to see President Roosevelt using Kennedy's poor health as a pretext for replacing him with someone whose views on America's role in the European war were not at such conspicuous variance to his own. Going by the telegrams that had passed through the Code Room, Roosevelt was – at the very least – sympathetic towards Britain. Kennedy, however, was a vigorous proponent of the doctrine of 'isolationism', of keeping America out of the war. His isolationist stance, shared by Tyler, had been embedded in US law since the summer of 1935. Not only did Kennedy believe that it would be a miscalculation for America to become entangled in the conflict, but he also hoped the Chamberlain government would enter into peace negotiations with Germany.

Staking a prominent spot in the photo that was about to be taken, Tyler parked himself at the front, about ten yards to the right of the Ambassador. Tyler almost blocked out the young woman behind him. She was left peeking over his shoulder. Immersed in the crowd yet somehow removed from it, he posed for the camera with arrogant self-assurance. He had the bearing of someone convinced of his own invulnerability, someone maybe relishing the knowledge that he'd made fools of the Ambassador and the rest of the top brass.

22

Anna remembered how, when she was growing up, all the children of her acquaintance, boys and girls alike, had been given miniature cookers for Christmas. These were beautifully made things on which one could prepare an entire meal. With barely suppressed rancour, she observed that such gifts had in retrospect been fortuitous. They'd trained an entire generation of Russian émigrés for lives spent in the kitchens of restaurants across Europe.

By the final week of November 1939, Christmas decorations were visible in the windows of West End shops. The more exclusive retailers favoured dwarf trees made from white feathers. On a less cheerful note, posters had popped up all over the place warning, 'Don't help the enemy! Careless talk may give away secrets.' And the newspapers were carrying stories about the ever more likely assault on Finland by the Soviets.

Whenever one took the time to wander into the shops, one saw lots of women buying Christmas presents for husbands and boyfriends in the armed forces. This year, though, Anna had other things to occupy her mind besides the festive season, not least the illness she'd contracted. It had a whole colour-swatch of symptoms. Feverishness. Loss of voice. Halitosis. Throat pain. Difficulty swallowing.

Her illness was diagnosed as septic tonsillitis. She blamed it on her present working environment. Recently, she had been transferred to another of the AFS stations. Several of these hastily improvised outposts made Down Street Sub-Station feel like the Ritz. The sleeping quarters sometimes consisted of nothing more than a concrete basement floor. In lieu of proper bedclothes, one was issued with a single blanket, a suitcase doubling as a pillow.

Employers who disregarded the wellbeing of their workforce infuriated Anna. She had been on the receiving end of that sort of shoddy treatment before. As an apprentice dressmaker, she had toiled in a basement overrun with rodents. To add insult to injury, her workroom used to flood during rainy periods. Needless to say, the employees at Anna de Wolkoff Haute Couture Modes did not – as she liked to remind people – have to put up with such ghastly conditions. Quite the reverse.

AFS regulations entitled Anna to four weeks' sick-leave before being compulsorily discharged from her job, yet she didn't wait that long. She preferred to follow the impetuous example of droves of dissatisfied AFS women resigning in protest against conditions at the fire stations.

Once the symptoms of her illness receded, dressmaking offered the most obvious alternative means of earning a living. But work of that nature wasn't easy to find anymore. A stroll through the West End would reveal why. Most women these days gave one the impression that being neglectful of their appearance was something they regarded almost as an emblem of patriotism. Small wonder that nine out of ten people in Anna's line of work were unemployed.

23

For Max and fellow ornithologists, there was reason to feel excited. A grey shrike, one of Continental Europe's rarest birds, had been spotted on the outskirts of London. That wasn't, however, the only bit of interesting news for Max.

On Wednesday 1 December, 1939 – six days after the Soviet military offensive against Britain's Finnish allies had begun – Marjorie went to tea with Mrs Ramsay. Yet again, Marjorie's hostess mentioned well-placed Right Club contacts, this time within MI5 as well as the police. Referring to the latter, she said, 'The main body are with us, but there is a bad patch up above – although, even there, we are not without help.'

Marjorie was introduced to Anna Wolkoff over tea at the Ramsays' house. Wolkoff told Marjorie that she was a dressmaker, but she hadn't been getting much work lately. She said she was weighing up whether to seek a favour from a close friend – the long since retired head of naval intelligence. With his backing, she thought she might be able to secure a position in the Ministry of Information's Postal and Telegraph Censorship Department. In her report Marjorie expressed the opinion that Wolkoff was vetting her.

Wolkoff ended up inviting Marjorie to supper at the Russian Tea Rooms. A quick glance at the map would tell Max that the Tea Rooms backed on to where MI5 had been based when he had first transferred from MI6. Both the Russian Tea Rooms and Anna Wolkoff were familiar to Max. Eight months earlier they had been the subject of a tip-off from an agent run by a colleague. Codenamed 'Source U.35', the agent[45] had named the Tea Rooms as a meeting place for Nazis. Besides which, he referred to Wolkoff as 'a staunch Nazi propagandist'.

Max – who loved this sort of intrigue – responded by submitting a request for the Watchers to place the Tea Rooms under surveillance. Frustratingly, though, his request was batted away with a memo so offhand as to shade into rudeness. The memo read, 'It hardly seems worthwhile having any special observation on this restaurant. Even if it is a meeting place for Nazis this is not a particularly significant fact.'

Now Wolkoff had been linked to his current investigation, Max's first port of call was to ring Wormwood Scrubs and see whether the Central Registry had anything salted away on her. In theory, one of the women there – the so-called Registry Queens – just had to go through the card indices. These featured a 'Precautionary Index' of 'persons potentially dangerous to National Defence'. From there, she could obtain the reference number of a 'PF' – a 'Personal File' – on Miss Wolkoff, then fish out that file and get a 'DR' – despatch-rider – to deliver the file to Dolphin Square.

The trouble was, the Registry wasn't a patch on how it used to be in the days when Max had joined the Security Service. There were gaps in the system where files had not been returned by case-officers. Filing-cards had been lost. New ones had not been indexed. And some of the filing-cabinets were overflowing. In any event, the whole system was somewhat antiquated when one compared it to the punchcard filing systems being introduced by big business, yet one couldn't hold the Registry Queens responsible for the situation. Their duty was only to *maintain* the system. Not that there were enough of them to keep on top of things.

Section B6 – the Watchers – offered a speedier alternative to the Registry. A request was duly submitted to B6 to make discreet enquiries about Anna Wolkoff. Mercifully, they didn't reject the application. But the results of their enquiries were comparatively unenlightening – just a thumbnail biographical sketch, which covered the failure of Wolkoff's business, her job at Busvine's, her subsequent work for the AFS, her successful application to become a naturalized British citizen, plus her friendship with Johnny Coast. This reference prompted a call for B6 to make similarly cautious enquiries about him as well. Alas, even the most rudimentary information proved elusive.

24

At last Tyler's persistence paid off. His recently acquired White Russian friend succumbed to his nagging and agreed to introduce him to Eugène Sabline, ex-Chargé d'Affaires at the Imperial Russian Embassy in London. Along with his friend, Tyler was invited to Eugène's home at 5 Brechin Place, South Kensington – an address habitually mispronounced by émigré Russians as 'Brrr-etch-in Place'. Part of a row of soot-coated five-storey houses with musclebound porticoes, the building had been given a Russian name that defied precise translation, even by a linguist of Tyler's calibre, the nearest English analogue being 'The Russia House'.

The address did not just function as a home for Eugène and

his wife. It also served as unofficial headquarters of the émigré community. Ornamenting its front door was a double-headed eagle, symbol of Tsarist Russia, a Janus-faced motif that inadvertently signified the duplicity that lay beyond.

Fluid charm masking his native shiftiness, Tyler's host had small, inquisitive eyes and a bald, almost spherical head. He was a short, tubby man in his middle sixties. His younger, dark-haired wife looked frail and undernourished next to him, a lopsided smile enhancing her consequent air of vulnerability. Yet she was an experienced hostess with a sociable personality that made her perfect for the role.

Eugène expressed amazement at Tyler's command of Russian, though Tyler's host was bamboozled by the contemporary slang that laced his sentences. The Sablines did most of their entertaining in a large downstairs room where they and their guests dined on the type of Russian food to which Tyler was so partial. Dotted with elegant furniture rescued from the Winter Palace in St Petersburg, the room also contained a grand piano that the composer Sergei Rachmaninov had played. Above the mantelpiece hung a gilt-framed portrait of Catherine the Great, which helped to give visitors the impression that they had strayed into pre-Revolutionary Russia.

Guests were shepherded round the piano, where they could join their hosts for impromptu renditions of traditional songs from the *Rodina* – the Motherland. Invited to talk about the house in which they found themselves, Eugène would tell the story of how he and his wife had moved there on the day the British government had granted the Soviet Union diplomatic recognition. Before handing over the old embassy to the Communists, he'd clambered onto its roof and lowered the Tsarist flag for the last time.

In deference to the belligerent anti-Communism of many members of London's White Russian colony, Eugène pretended not to be on speaking terms with the Soviets. He was nonetheless conducting illicit meetings with Soviet officials, during which either stolen US government paperwork or a summary of that paperwork could be exchanged for the British currency Tyler required to maintain his otherwise unaffordable way of life.

25

There was already a file on Anna Wolkoff over at MI5's Registry. It featured the report from the agent who had identified her as 'a staunch Nazi propagandist' and also referred to a tip-off given to that agent by a contact who moved in high-society fascist circles. The contact alleged that Wolkoff was participating in espionage. What made her even more deserving of additional scrutiny by Max and his sidekick, Bill Younger, was that her parents – Admiral Nikolai Wolkoff and Mme Vera Wolkoff – had files on them as well. These reached back more than twenty years.

Vera Wolkoff's dossier catalogued her work between 1917 and 1919 as a courier for the anti-Communist White Russian forces during her country's civil war. The documentation mentioned her receiving a suspicious telegram sent from Vladivostok, incorporating what appeared to be code.

Altogether more extensive and pertinent allegations were to be found in Admiral Wolkoff's file, which divulged that he had been under spasmodic investigation since 1915, soon after his posting to England as Naval Attaché. Intelligence-gathering occupied a prominent role on the list of an attaché's traditional functions, so he was bound to attract MI5 scrutiny. While the Great War was raging, he'd been suspected of communicating with Germany via Stockholm. And he'd been regarded as pro-German and anti-British – attitudes mirrored by his daughter Anna, then only thirteen years old. On hearing about the death of Lord Kitchener, the British Secretary of State for War, she had been reported as having made the gleeful remark, 'Now the English will get it ...'

During his tenure as Naval Attaché, there had been allegations that Admiral Wolkoff was guilty of embezzlement. The shadiness of his activities increased after he'd lost his job and the Communists took control of his country. In 1922 he'd been named as one of the five coordinators of the Russian Imperial Counter-Revolutionary Group, which ran a network of anti-Communist agents and hoped to overthrow the Soviet regime.

He'd also been involved in several fishy commercial enterprises, none more so than the Endoto Syndicate Ltd, of which he had been a director. There were strong grounds for believing that the firm, linked to an equally dubious company that had been selling fraudulent mining concessions in Abyssinia, existed as a front for gun-running.

As recently as June 1939, he'd been the subject of an instructive report by an MI5 officer, who had written: 'I went to the Russian Tea Rooms last night and found Admiral Wolkoff more bitter than ever against the Jews, about whom he lent me a book entitled *Spotlight on the Jew* and tried to get me to buy another. In the course of the conversation it turned out that he had visited the German Embassy the previous afternoon where he had seen some films shown by Frau Dirksen, wife of the Ambassador. Fitz Randolph, the present attaché, comes to the restaurant fairly often and he and the Admiral appear to know each other quite well, so that it was probably Fitz Randolph who got him the invitation to the embassy.

'Admiral Wolkoff was very pleased when I said that I still thought this country and Germany should be friendly towards one another. He said that he was telling Russians that the only chance of salvation for Russia lay in Hitler assuming a dictatorship there.

'I hardly see what danger Admiral Wolkoff can be, but think that if a little money was put in his way, he would find it quite easy to reconcile his conscience with anything he could do for the Germans by persuading himself it was for the good of humanity!'

His friend from the German Embassy, cited earlier in the report, was the American-born Dr Henry S. Fitz Randolph, who attempted to sound more German these days by calling himself Dr Sigismund Fitz Randolph. A member of the Anglo–German Fellowship, one of the pre-war fascist groups that Max had kept an eye on, the doctor was an enthusiastic supporter of Hitler. It appeared that his enthusiasm was reciprocated because he was among Hitler's first appointees to the now defunct German Embassy in London. Until the outbreak of war, Dr Fitz Randolph had served as Press Attaché there, reporting directly to the Nazi propaganda chief, Josef Goebbels.

Such wide-ranging documentation about Admiral Wolkoff and his daughter pointed towards them being 'fifth columnists', a term derived from the Spanish Civil War. In an effort to spread panic within Republican-controlled Madrid, a Nationalist general had claimed that he had four columns of troops converging on the city and a *fifth* column of Nationalist sympathizers inside it, ready to assist.

Fears of a British equivalent had recently been fed by reports that had percolated through to Max's boss, Guy Liddell, about mysterious lights, which seemed to be signalling to German aircraft. Some of those lights had been spotted near the port of Harwich on the dates when enemy planes had dropped mines in the harbour.

To assist Max's investigation of Anna Wolkoff, permission was sought to intercept letters posted to 18a Roland Gardens. Hardly in keeping with the teachings of Max's old headmaster on HMS *Worcester*, who had tried to instil in his pupils respect for the rights and property of others.

Before the Post Office was prepared to intercept letters, a warrant had to be obtained from the Permanent Under-Secretary of State at the Home Office. In the past Max and company had experienced difficulty securing warrants against British-based fascists. MI5 had even been refused an application to monitor Sir Oswald Mosley's post, despite the fact that Mosley had not long before undergone a private marriage ceremony witnessed by Hitler in Goebbels's drawing-room. An equally disappointing response had greeted MI5's request for a warrant against the London offices of the Nazi Party.

Max was in luck today. For a limited period the Permanent Under-Secretary of State at the Home Office issued a warrant giving him permission to have the Wolkoffs' post steamed open, photographed, carefully resealed and then delivered to its intended recipients.

26

Tyler's resentment at the way he had been forced to leave Moscow was undiminished. He hankered after a return there, his discontent with life in London offering an incentive. But his aim was not to go back to the Moscow embassy, where his friends, Sylvester A. Huntowski and Donald H. Nichols, were still based. Instead, he wanted to become one of the foreign correspondents stationed in the Soviet capital – men with whom he'd rubbed shoulders at the bar of the Hotel Metropole.

Beyond a spell as editor of his prep-school newspaper, Tyler had no journalistic background, yet that shortcoming could, to some degree, be offset by his fluency in Russian. Subscriptions to *Pravda* and *Izvestia*, the leading Soviet newspapers, gave him a means of sustaining his grasp on both the country's language and politics.

Pro-Nazi, anti-British and anti-Semitic though his own politics were, Tyler struck up what might prove an advantageous friendship with a Jewish New Yorker, who ran the London Bureau of the *New York Times* and espoused wholeheartedly anti-Nazi and pro-British opinions. Tyler and his gregarious, boundlessly obliging Jewish contact took to eating together at the Barcelona, a small, unpretentious and inexpensive Soho restaurant. Owned by an eager-to-please Spaniard, it was a haunt of exiled left-wing veterans of their country's recent civil war. George Orwell – famous enough to arouse a shimmer of excited comment – numbered among those customers. They dined on authentic Spanish cuisine.[46] Sweetmeats and a rich almond-laden form of nougat called *Turrón de Alicante* were just two of the house specialities. In spite of all the time Tyler and his new dining companion spent eating at the Barcelona, he failed to parlay their friendship into a job as a foreign correspondent for the *New York Times* – or any other publication.

27

While helping to train staff from MI5 and Special Branch, Max had often been asked to describe how agents should be recruited. The only snag was, he couldn't think of any golden rules. Mind you, he had noticed his colleagues seemed to treat *not recruiting women* as just such a rule. He frequently heard it said that women are less discreet than men, that they are guided by their emotions instead of their brains, that sex will sooner or later get in the way of their work. Yet none of those generalizations held water in his experience. Women had, after all, pulled off many of the world's greatest espionage coups.

If anything, Max believed women were better suited than men to working as agents. He could quote the example of the operation he had directed against the Soviet spy-ring that was stealing British naval blueprints from Woolwich Arsenal. The spies might never have been caught but for the sterling work of the young woman at the heart of the investigation. She had spent well over six years living under the kind of pressure certain to test the mettle of the strongest men.

There were signs that Marjorie would prove a worthy successor. Only eleven days before Christmas, she had something quite significant to tell Max. The subject of her report was a visit from Anna Wolkoff to her Notting Hill flat. Wolkoff had spoken about being a friend of a chap named Francis Hemming. She said he was a Right Club sympathizer, though he wasn't willing to admit that publicly.

Marjorie also told Max that Wolkoff had bragged about making a trip to Germany and Sudetenland the preceding summer. Wolkoff claimed to have met various leading Nazis on her travels. Rudolph Hess, the Führer's Number Two, was among them. Plus she referred to Konrad Henlein, Nazi governor of Sudetenland, in suspiciously familiar terms.

Before leaving Marjorie's flat, Wolkoff had mentioned how she'd gone round to Captain Ramsay's house for breakfast that morning. She needed to present him with a document of some sort, though she didn't elaborate on its contents. He required it urgently, she said.

What was apparent from the reports available to Max was that Wolkoff's involvement with Captain Ramsay posed a tangible threat. As Guy Liddell had already been informed, Ramsay was due to attend a secret session of the House of Commons, scheduled for Wednesday 13 December, 1939.

Notes on Ramsay were promptly given to Sir Vernon Kell, head of MI5. The intention was for them to be forwarded to the Permanent Secretary of the Treasury, who doubled as Head of the Civil Service. Rated among the Prime Minister's closest confidants, the Permanent Secretary was asked to relay the paperwork to Neville Chamberlain, who could then discuss it with colleagues. The notes argued that Ramsay should not be shown sensitive government information, because he would be liable to leak it to the Nazis.

28

Tyler got into the habit of using the American Club. Membership – popular with fellow Embassy staff – was open to US citizens, punctual payment of the subscription being the other prerequisite.

Sited on the northeast corner where White Horse Street met Piccadilly, the club inhabited a nineteenth-century mansion that radiated an aura of the opulent living to which Tyler was drawn. From the foyer, he could wander into the pine-panelled card room, its walls decorated with portraits of the club's past presidents. He could also take a seat in the reading room where he could peruse newspapers and magazines from back home. And he could ascend the gracefully coiled stairway that led into the bar and dining room. White-jacketed waiters, flitting this way and that beneath a twinkling chandelier, distributed a range of American culinary specialities to the clientele. Until just before dusk when the windows had to be blacked out, there was a fine view of Green Park.

Presumably in this setting, Tyler encountered Anna Wolkoff's high society American friend, Barbara Allen, who administered the club. Three months pregnant with her second child, she harboured opinions that distinguished her from the majority of the club's patrons. Its exclusively male membership tended to be fiercely pro-British and vocal in their criticism of the defeatist attitude of Ambassador Joseph P. Kennedy. Prior to decamping to America a couple of weeks back, Kennedy had often voiced what he saw as the inevitable scenario, where the Germans defeated the British and French.

Barbara Allen shared Kennedy's attitude, her conversation witheringly dismissive of England and the English. For her and Tyler, this yielded an important area of consensus. But the two of them could not as yet become better acquainted because she and her husband were going away for a short time. Unlike Tyler, who would be working over Christmas, they had the option of spending the holiday period away from London.

29

Denied either the petrol allocation that accompanied her AFS job or the cash for expensive blackmarket fuel to swell her meagre petrol ration, Anna could no longer drive round town in her black Morris whenever the fancy took her. But she didn't require a car to get to Brechin Place, where she was due to attend the Russian Red Cross Society's annual Christmas Bazaar. From her parents' flat, she could walk there in three or four minutes.

As ever, the bazaar was being held at the home of Eugène Sabline and his wife. Over the past decade-and-a-half, they had often used the Russia House for these fundraising events. Anna enormously admired Eugène for what she saw as his adroit and indefatigable work on behalf of their Motherland and its traditions.

Having been to these charity events before, she knew what to expect. Backed by the choppy rhythms of a balalaika band, numerous aristocratic women would be running stalls decked with toys, hand-painted glassware and a disparate range of goods imported from Russia, everything from cigarettes to perfume, from paintings to early nineteenth-century lace.

By attending the bazaar, Anna was lending support to her mother, who was on its organizing committee. This featured various friends of the family, among them a German baroness, whose husband – a long-term Nazi Party member – had already been interned.

At the Russia House, where the stubborn defence being mounted by the Finns against the Soviet invasion warranted appreciative comment, Anna chanced upon a widowed British aristocrat with fascist connections. Treating Anna to an effusive build-up that described her as 'a great dressmaker' and the daughter of Admiral Wolkoff, former Naval Attaché at the Imperial Russian Embassy, the woman then introduced her to Mrs Dolly Newnham and Mrs Christabel Nicholson.[47] Anna had come across neither of them before.

Of the two strangers, Dolly Newnham was the least assertive. Genteel and elderly, she had grey hair and a pair of thick-framed spectacles that dominated her face. Her tall, dark-haired companion proved closer to Anna in both age and temperament. Christabel Nicholson had a liking for broad-brimmed hats and stylish clothes. Meeting a famous fashion designer such as Anna was a cause of excitement for her, transmitted through a loud voice with an upper-crust accent. She had a high-handed yet loquacious manner, a sense of intellectual superiority pervading what she said. In one of those 'Small world, isn't it?' coincidences that help to transmute chitchat into something more substantial, she turned out to be the wife of a retired British admiral who was a friend of Anna's father. Christabel's husband had frequently talked about Admiral Wolkoff.

Politics provided another link between Anna and her two new acquaintances. As it happened, Mrs Newnham – a pious Roman Catholic – hated Communism and belonged to a minor fascist group with which Anna's friend, Johnny Coast, was involved. Like a number of erstwhile Suffragettes, disillusioned by democracy, Christabel had become a fascist, too. She and her husband had joined the Anglo–German Fellowship and the Link, membership of which encompassed friends of Anna and family. Lately the Nicholsons had been regulars at meetings convened by Information and Policy, another fascist group with which some of Anna's friends were associated.

Until a few years ago, Christabel had been employed by London County Council to carry out medical and psychiatric examinations of schoolchildren. More recently, though, she'd been qualifying as a barrister. Seldom averse to delivering caustic generalizations, to which her past employment lent spurious authority, she believed in the low intelligence of the British people, and in the concept of Britain's mental, physical and moral decline, hastened by what she referred to as 'cheap and nasty amusements'.

Besides sharing Anna's admiration for Hitler, she agreed with her opposition to the war against Germany and her scepticism about Britain's prospects of victory. She also shared Anna's fanatical anti-Semitism. Even outside the sphere within which Anna and friends moved, such sentiments had become more common over recent months, exacerbated by crude propaganda in the fascist press about Jewish refugees taking British people's jobs and scrounging off the state.

Flattering Christabel's vanity, Anna gave every sign that she was in awe of her new acquaintance's intellect. By the time Anna exited the Sablines' house, the foundations for a friendship with Christabel had been installed.

30

During the lead-up to Christmas Day, grimly determined shoppers, some of them pausing to buy battery-powered torches from kerbside vendors, thronged the pavements around Tyler's flat. Scores of children, whose evacuation from London had been reversed, were also in evidence. Few schools had reopened so a fair number of those youngsters had been left to run wild.

After dark the nearby hotels, nightspots, restaurants and cinemas were permitted to advertise themselves with little neon signs, the frail glow from these dissolving in the icy darkness. Night-time temperatures well below freezing had given rise to comments about the cold. For Tyler, however, the weather did not merit any complaints. He had experienced much worse through those long, dark winter months in Moscow when sunrise wasn't until 10 a.m. and dusk arrived at 4 p.m. Another trait that distinguished wintry Moscow from wintry London was the mist that never seemed to abate, mist that cued the slow-motion boom of ships' foghorns, mist thick enough to shroud the accoutrements of war. Heading down the street, Tyler could bask for a few seconds in the illusion of peacetime normality. That illusion tended to be banished by the sight of something emerging from the murk as stealthily as an image on a photographic negative plunged into developing fluid. Next thing you knew, a stack of sandbags slunk into sight. Or you became aware of the metallic glint of a barrage balloon looming overhead.

Back in the Soviet Union, the official attitude towards Christmas had been oddly inconsistent. Santa Claus figurines could still be purchased, yet there was a sign fixed to the shrine near Mokhovaya House declaring, 'Religion Is the Opiate of the People'. Unsurprisingly in view of that, Christmas Day was treated as just another working day.

That same ethos held sway in the Code Room at Grosvenor Square. As Tyler passed through the neighbouring Index Bureau, impeccably attired as ever, he had got into the habit of flirting with one of the young women stationed there. Dependably polite and friendly in her response, she gave Tyler no encouragement.

On Christmas morning another letter from Winston Churchill to President Roosevelt found its way to the Code Room, where Tyler set about translating it into Grey Code, a process that took less time than the higher-security codes. The letter, due to be cabled to Washington, DC, was a response to complaints about HMS *Exeter* and other Royal Navy warships flouting the new, expanded version of the Neutrality Zone – the Pan-American Safety Zone – that had been imposed across

North and South American territorial waters. These violations had culminated in the scuttling of two German ships: a merchant vessel just off the American coast and the German warship *Graf Spee* at the mouth of the River Plate in Uruguay.

Churchill apologized for the 'trouble about recent incidents', adding, 'We cannot always refrain from stopping enemy ships outside international three-mile limit when these may well be supply ships for U-boats or surface raiders, but instructions have been given only to arrest or fire upon when out of sight of American shores ...' His message went on to explore the repercussions of the sinking of the *Graf Spee*. 'Generally speaking think war will soon begin now,' Churchill wrote. 'Permit me to send you, Sir, all the compliments of the season.'

Tyler copied the message and smuggled his copy out of the building.

31

Jimmy Dickson, Max's friend and colleague at Section B5b, had a theory about what the two of them were doing. Their work was so engrossing, he reckoned, because it drew on 'that old man-hunting instinct'.

Despite the holiday atmosphere prevailing over Christmas and New Year, the investigation of Wolkoff and the Right Club continued. Marjorie reported seeing a Right Club member swanning round the Telephone branch of the Postal and Telegraph Censorship Department. Helpfully for her, he'd been wearing the kind of badge Mrs Ramsay had given her last summer. The man sporting it turned out to work there.[48]

More material for Max came from someone who used to lodge with Anna Wolkoff's parents. 'Alexander, the son, is probably too interested in his business to mix himself up with political activities,' Max's informant declared, 'but there seems no doubt that the remainder of the family, Admiral Wolkoff, Madame Wolkoff, Anna, Alice and Kyra, are very sympathetic, unless their opinions have changed during the last few weeks, to the

Nazi regime, much more so than they are to this country ... I lived in Admiral Wolkoff's house for some months in 1920, and have seen him and his family from time to time every year since then. He gives the impression that he has not really very much love for England, although he has a certain amount of English blood in him and I should not be surprised to hear that he had worked or was working against this country, if it were made worth his while financially. The same probably applies to his daughters.'

Another fresh contribution to Max's files arrived courtesy of the Home Office warrant enabling MI5 to intercept letters addressed to the Wolkoffs' flat. Shortly before the New Year's Eve festivities, a letter had been sent to Admiral Wolkoff by Anna's brother, Alexander. It reiterated an earlier warning, which Alexander had passed on to the Admiral, from an inside source who had disclosed that British officials took a dim view of the Admiral's behaviour. Alexander's latest fretful letter described how an even more senior source had just repeated the same message to him in forthright terms. What was obvious, Alexander stressed, was that Admiral Wolkoff's outlook could be seen as treacherous and that he risked imprisonment if he did not curb his behaviour.

In an appeal to reason, Alexander reminded the Admiral of his English ancestry and urged him to nail his colours to the mast of his adoptive country at a time when it was engaged in a life or death struggle. Anna's brother went on to plead with their father not to flaunt his anti-Semitism, not to voice pro-Hitler sentiments, not to allow Nazi sympathizers to patronize the Russian Tea Rooms and not to get into political discussions with people he didn't know. Alexander also begged Admiral Wolkoff to ensure that the rest of their immediate family – Anna in particular – adhered to that advice. Thoughts of Anna led him to comment scathingly on the news that she had apparently been angling for a job in the Postal and Telegraph Censorship Department. He expressed disbelief that she could be so foolish as to imagine that the government would want to employ someone such as her.

32

During daylight hours since New Year the temperature had seldom heaved itself far above freezing. Meteorological experts were already declaring this the coldest beginning to any year for the best part of half-a-century. To add to the wintry gloom, there seemed to be a growing feeling that the war with Germany would be a long-drawn-out affair. One no longer heard so much wishful-thinking, so many stories about unrest among the German populace, about someone with a niece who knew the Foreign Secretary who said everything would be over by the spring.

1940 had not got off to the start Max might have desired in other respects either. On Tuesday 3 January, the Home Office completed the latest phase of its review of the detention orders that he and his colleagues had obtained just before the outbreak of war. Evidence against twenty-four of the detainees had been given the once-over by the Home Office Advisory Committee, the recommendations of which were bound to irritate Max. A quarter of those prisoners were being freed, and another four were nominated for release subject to restrictions.

Within a couple of days of the committee delivering its findings, Max received an even more serious setback. It took the form of a blunt memo from headquarters about the Wolkoff inquiry, which had been going on for more than six months.

'Anna Wolkoff is known to share her father's strong anti-Semite views,' the memo read. 'I do not think there is any reason to suspect her activities, and I do not think it is worthwhile making any further enquiries at present.' Its author ended by ordering Max to shelve the Wolkoff investigation.

33

Tyler's colleagues at the US Embassy in Grosvenor Square found themselves at the centre of what promised to escalate into a major dispute between the American and British governments. It had to be handled in the absence of Ambassador Kennedy, who was on sick-leave back home. This brief spat arose from the British insistence that the Royal Navy had the right to search neutral ships. By doing so, the British aimed to impede the delivery of goods intended to assist the German war effort. A US merchant vessel called the *Moormacsun*, which was bound for Norway, had as part of that policy been forced to detour into a Scottish port and then been searched, triggering a flurry of telegrams between Washington and the Code Room at Grosvenor Square.

Comparable scrutiny was not, providentially for Tyler, applied to the cargoes of documents that he smuggled out of the embassy. From early January 1940, he had to ferry these on a new route between work and home.

He'd just moved to a boarding house in Paddington, where there weren't many people on the streets or frequenting the small shops that punctuated them. Large numbers of the local boarding houses and hotels added to the prevalent air of desertion by advertising vacancies at 'Special War Terms'. Capitalizing on just such a cut-price deal, Tyler had rented what was billed as a 'luxury suite' in a 'quiet exclusive house'. For this he paid the easily affordable sum of £5 a month. In Moscow, where rents were extortionate, the same flat would have commanded a far higher figure.

As his new landlady – an ageing widow who lived on the premises – was keen to remind prospective tenants, flats in her house had never been vacant before the war. Indeed, they'd attracted a very select clientele. Two of the five flats had been rented to peers of the realm.

But circumstances had obliged her to reduce the rent and provide Tyler with a series of extras: London newspapers, complimentary cigarettes, not to speak of the bed-making services of the resident maid.

Just in excess of a mile separated the US Embassy from Tyler's new flat, which was at 47 Gloucester Place, one of a long sequence of four-storey terraced houses with elegant facades. Returning from work or elsewhere during the blackout, Tyler had to avoid tripping over the steps. When he reached the front door, there was, however, no need for him to fumble about in the darkness while he tried to find his key. That was because his landlady always left the door on the latch.

Nine, maybe ten paces down the narrow, windowless hall and he reached the foot of a staircase insufficiently wide for him to pass another of the tenants. The first flight of stairs brought him to a tiny landing, where he had to turn left through a door to which no key was available. Privacy could only be guaranteed by bolting the door from the inside.

Beyond was a big, high-ceilinged room. It served as a combined bedroom and lounge. Furnished with a writing desk, a large table, plus a wardrobe, Tyler's flat had tall, thin windows that faced a line of near identical houses.

Through a set of double-doors lay his private bathroom, undoubtedly something of a treat in those days, its luxuriousness diminished only by an icy draught. Shared bathrooms had been a feature to which he'd become accustomed while living in his studio flat at Mokhovaya House. On one occasion an old colleague of his in the Moscow Code Room had returned to find a two-foot-long fish swimming in the bath. The fish turned out to have been put there by his Russian servant in preparation for cooking next day.

Despite the absence of a lock on the door to the Gloucester Place flat, Tyler stashed mounting numbers of stolen embassy documents there. His Moscow experiences had left him complacent about the chances of being investigated. Under headings such as 'Germany', 'Czechoslovakia', 'British Cabinet' and 'Churchill', he filed the documents in a series of folders. He kept these in a brown suitcase, which he stored in his wardrobe, ready for when he needed them.

34

Max considered the memo about Wolkoff, previously sent to him from headquarters, 'rubbish and misleading'. By reason of her Nazi contacts, her friendship with an MP, her complicity with subversive political groups, her habit of hoovering up information, her father's past involvement in espionage and his ability to smuggle messages to Germany, she was, Max believed, a 'most dangerous' woman.

Obedience to those in authority was something his naval training had been dedicated to teaching him. But he scribbled a shirty response to the memo from headquarters. His reply spurred a colleague to write 'Hear! Hear!' alongside this on the memo.

Instead of telling Marjorie to drop the Wolkoff component of her work, Max allowed her to continue. Emphasizing the urgency of the situation in which they were operating, yet more anti-aircraft fire could be heard several mornings later from the direction of the Thames Estuary.

35

Plenty more information relating to Wolkoff soon reached Max. Its starting point was Wednesday 11 January, 1940, when she had turned up at Marjorie's door. Obviously in a confiding mood, Wolkoff let slip that the Duke of Westminster – one of Britain's richest men – had given a sizeable sum of money to the Right Club. His donation was said to be £1,000, equal to the annual employment costs of up to five people. The gift had to remain confidential, Wolkoff explained, because the Duke had not yet decided to align himself publicly to the fascist cause. Anyone as knowledgeable as Max about the world of British fascism would, however, have had no doubts about the ideology of the Duke, who had been a leading member of the Link.

Wolkoff also spoke about her continued desire to land a job in the Postal and Telegraph Censorship Department and about the possibility of bringing influence to bear on Princess Alice, Duchess of Gloucester, whom she'd known since they were at boarding school together. Nowadays Wolkoff's schoolmate was married to the Duke of Gloucester, third in line to the British throne. In that context Wolkoff mentioned someone who worked as the Duke's equerry – his senior aide. Wolkoff professed to have enjoyed some success in converting the equerry to the fascist viewpoint.

On the Tuesday after Wolkoff's visit to the Notting Hill flat, Marjorie reciprocated by popping round to 18a Roland Gardens. She and Wolkoff were joined there by Johnny Coast, newly enlisted as a private in the Coldstream Guards. Marjorie said that Wolkoff had talked about how prominent members of the Right Club were urging Captain Ramsay to try to involve General Ironside, Britain's highest-ranking Army officer, rumoured to share their beliefs.

36

Tyler followed up his pre-Christmas lunch at the Russia House by phoning Eugène Sabline and paying further visits there. When they were together, Tyler complained about how dull he found life in London. He said he would not mind returning to Russia or maybe going to Germany. Life in a totalitarian country was, he added, more interesting than in a democracy.

Heavily committed to the Chiswick-based Anglo–Russian Sports Club, which hosted regular social events, Eugène tried to relieve the boredom by introducing Tyler to some of his friends. In line with the old Gregorian calendar, they were poised to mark the dawn of 1940. Tyler was invited to the club's New Year's Eve Ball, staged on Friday 20 January at the Hyde Park Hotel, just across the street from Knightsbridge tube station.

Well over 200 dancers could be accommodated in the hotel's ballroom. As they swirled round, the revellers needed to be careful not to collide with either the four bulky pillars near the centre or with chatting onlookers. Burst pipes had become a recurrent subject of conversation. You heard so many stories about people who had left town in September but forgotten to turn off the water and drain their pipes. And now they'd returned to find collapsed ceilings and flooded houses. Plumbers seemed as scarce as butter.

That night Tyler encountered a twenty-nine-year-old redhead of the type who was even more strictly rationed. Boosting her manifest appeal were a curvaceous figure and an effusive personality, its charm deriving from a zestful cocktail of self-dramatization and wistful humour, infused by a mournful quality familiar to readers of Russian novels. Irene Danischewsky was her name. Even though she had been brought up in England, Irene – her name anglicized from 'Irina' – proved capable of talking with Tyler in fluent Russian, her intelligence evident in her conversation. She and her parents and their two other children, both grown-up, had been fortunate enough to leave their native country in advance of the revolution. Irene's aristocratic father, whose family used to own an estate just outside Moscow, had been part of a delegation that had journeyed to England to buy military equipment, only to be left stranded by developments back home. For more than two decades he'd supported his family by working as a London cab driver.

Unlike her staunchly conservative father or ardently socialist brother, the latter of whom had taken part in demonstrations against Mosley and the British Union, Irene possessed no interest in politics. She and Tyler discovered a more basic rapport, sexual attraction coexisting with the ability to find shared humour in life's trivia, to sustain effortless, pleasant chatter that made time pass with disconcerting speed. Potentially blocking the route from flirtation to romance was Irene's husband, a Jewish-Russian businessman who was also present at the Hyde Park Hotel's ballroom. He and Irene shared a flat close to Kensington Gardens, the phone number of which was soon harvested by Tyler.

37

A long overdue letter from Louis-Ferdinand Céline arrived. He apologized to Anna for the delay in responding to her. The delay had, he explained, been due to him being beset by court cases provoked by his recent book, *School for Corpses*.

But he didn't answer the questions Anna had, at Jock Ramsay's behest, asked him about MI6 and the alleged Jewish conspiracy.

'I hope to be in London for two days in early April and will not forget to pay you a visit,' Céline wrote. Then he added, 'I should be pleased to meet your friend, the MP.'

The implication was that Céline, wary perhaps of having his correspondence snooped on by British intelligence services, would only answer Jock's questions in person.

38

Every morning before Christmas, the song thrushes and starlings had been particularly vocal around London. Now one scarcely heard them. What with the heavy frosts and the shortage of food, both species must have suffered badly. Years of study had taught Max that birds were exceedingly sensitive to heat and cold, but the apparent decline in the starling population did not have the most urgent claim on his attention. Not when he had a fresh report from Marjorie to assimilate.

It informed him of a conversation she'd overheard between Anna Wolkoff and a Right Club friend called Molly Stanford. From what they had been saying, Marjorie twigged that Wolkoff and the other woman were somehow managing to correspond with Margaret Bothamley who was living in Berlin. Marjorie also told Max that Stanford was in possession of some of Bothamley's papers.

The connection between Wolkoff and Bothamley was far from unexpected. Bothamley's name had repeatedly cropped up in pre-war Special Branch surveillance of British fascists. She was a regular at the Russian Tea Rooms, a supporter of the Nordic League and a pro-Nazi activist, for which she had been paid handsome 'lecture expenses' by the Nazis. Her continued correspondence with Wolkoff and Stanford did nothing to quash the belief that the two London-based women were members of the much-talked-about Fifth Column.

Clearly, Wolkoff gave the Right Club leader a means of communicating with Berlin. Marjorie's prearranged trip to his home in Onslow Square last week served to spotlight the danger implicit in that discovery.

When Marjorie arrived at the house, Mrs Ramsay was at home, but her husband telephoned to explain that he'd been waylaid at the House of Commons. In her husband's absence, Mrs Ramsay asked Marjorie to obtain a photograph of an order that the War Office was said to have issued. Any such leaked government documents could, of course, now be passed on to the Nazis by Wolkoff.

39

Tyler met up with Irene Danischewsky again, the encounter rapidly culminating in sex. He and Irene – who was at first heedless of the potential consequences – embarked on an affair, their trysts restricted to daytime when her husband was at work. Further constraints were imposed by Tyler's schedule at the US Embassy. Unless he was assigned either the 4 p.m. to midnight or midnight to 8 a.m. shifts, he did not have the opportunity to see Irene during the daytime.

If possible, she would arrive at his flat around 9 a.m. and spend the morning with him, bodily warmth offering sanctuary from the wintry draughts. Married though she was, Irene's love-making resembled that of a diffident young girl, not ready to try out the manoeuvres described in Tyler's copy of *The History of the Rod*, a nineteenth-century sadomasochistic sex primer. Neither he nor Irene was prepared to discuss such matters, his general reserve leaving her reticence about sex unchallenged.

As a form of instruction, he showed her some of his collection of pornographic photos. Yet even these failed to coax his new girlfriend into being more sexually adventurous and demonstrative.

He and Irene were just as uncommunicative about other things. So devoid of personal disclosure was their conversation that they might as well have been strangers. Passion spent, Tyler would often part from Irene towards the end of the morning, having first explained that he had arranged to meet someone for lunch. Whom he was meeting, he never revealed.

40

Anna scheduled a sticking party for the next full moon, which would lessen the difficulties imposed by the blackout. Enid Riddell and Anne van Lennep, her friends from the Russian Tea Rooms, continued to be regular companions on these nocturnal jaunts. The group was enlarged by four other Right Club members. One of those was Captain Ramsay's son. Another was the wife of a Midland industrialist who had a house in the environs of Kelly Castle, the Ramsays' Scottish estate. And the third recruit was Mrs Dolly Newnham, whom Anna had encountered for the first time at the Russian Red Cross Society's Christmas Bazaar. Now Anna and Mrs Newnham would exchange warm greetings whenever their paths crossed.

Mrs Newnham, her speech interspersed by expressions of decorous outrage, turned out not only to be a friend of Sir Oswald Mosley's wife, but also to live on the same street as Anna. Enthusiastic though Mrs Newnham was about the sticking parties, she didn't hit it off with Johnny Coast, who carried on supplying Anna with labels, many of which were stored in the Wolkoffs' flat.

The other recently acquired member of the stickyback team was Bertie Mills, a forty-two-year-old friend of Anna from the Nordic League and the Link, where he used to work alongside Margaret Bothamley. He had broad shoulders, brushed back hair and an ebullient way of speaking that tolerated no interruption. Once upon a time the British Consular Service had employed him in Africa and South America. But he was currently jobless and inhabiting a bedsit near the Wolkoffs' home.

As Bertie may have told her, he'd lately attended a meeting

with Captain Ramsay, Sir Oswald Mosley and other leading fascists. The gathering had been precipitated by a desire to amalgamate the Right Club, the British Union and sundry fascist parties, creating a single more potent force.

Over the short term, Bertie hoped to use his fluency in multiple languages to infiltrate one of the government's Censorship Departments. Brazenly pro-Nazi and anti-Semitic, he was convinced that the government would soon be toppled by a revolution, and that Germany was 'bound to wipe the floor with England and France'.

For Anna, Bertie and the others, South Kensington Underground Station – half-a-mile from the Russian Tea Rooms – marked the beginning of that evening's stickyback itinerary. They needed to take the eastbound District Line from there. Waiting in the blue half-light used to illuminate the platforms, most of which were in semi-darkness, one caught sight of the flashes from the live rail beneath each oncoming train.

Evening rush-hours on that line were notoriously unpleasant. Men seldom any longer surrendered their seats when women wriggled onto the train. Its unlit carriages juddered and swayed as they entered the tunnel. Glowing cigarette-tips bobbed in the sudden blackness, which was impregnated by the smell of unwashed hair, pipe tobacco, brilliantine and stale sweat, the occasional furtive whisper of conversation affording the sole distraction. Wherever one went at the moment, people were coughing – an incessant, rasping cough, symptomatic of a new strain of flu that was doing the rounds.

At least Anna and friends only had to travel three stops before getting off at St James's Park, the name giving her an associative link to her childhood, a time-machine back to St James's School for Girls, to the minutiae that comprises the warp and weft of memory, to windows overlooking the Malvern Hills, to vases overflowing with Michaelmas daisies, to currant buns eaten within the swimming-pool's disinfectant haze ... It was all so far removed from air-raid sirens, gasmasks, sandbags and the blackout.

Anna's sticking party had to get from the station's recently modernized, marble-clad ticket hall to nearby St James's Park.

Darting into the ladies' lavatories in the park, they could use the washbasins to moisten the backs of their gummed labels. The stickybacks were then ready to be applied to convenient surfaces along a route that began not far from there. Anna's first obvious target was the office of the Protestant British Israel League.

Her carefully planned route channelled them down a succession of small streets, where the buildings were silvered by the moon. One could not walk through the blackout lately without seeing the glow of dozens of phosphorescent flowers. These had been treated with luminous paint before being slotted into the buttonholes of men and women alike.

Several of the streets on Anna's route hosted shops bearing Jewish names. Mendel Kanner. Barnett Finkle. Isador Kauffman. Names that were a silent provocation to Anna.

Beyond the factory on the corner of Grosvenor Road was the immense frontage of Grenville House, riverside wing of Dolphin Square. Anna's friend, Lord Cottenham, whom she nicknamed 'Cotty', had a small flat on its ninth floor. Not so long ago, Cotty – a thirty-six-year-old writer, broadcaster, pilot, racing driver and former lecturer at University College London – had been *more than just a friend*. Anna had harboured such an intense passion for him that she could even recall the date on which they had first met. Thursday 20 October, 1938.

With his errant wife, tragic childhood, physical courage and aristocratic trappings, prominent among these being a butler, Lord Cottenham was an alluring yet vulnerable figure. Sadly, their relationship served to demonstrate the wisdom of the old Russian saying that 'love will creep where it cannot go'.

Though things had not developed the way any woman in her position would have wished, Anna looked back fondly on the blissful times they'd enjoyed together. And she remained grateful to him for the interest he had shown in her novice literary efforts and for his continuing friendship. Only a little while ago he'd invited her and a mutual friend – who was a close associate of Mosley – round for a drink before the three of them went out to supper.

Past the terraced riverside garden opposite where that sherry party had taken place, Anna and her stickyback team had to turn onto Tite Street. Under orders from Anna not to put up any more labels, they had to make for Anne van Lennep's flat on Paradise Walk, which signalled the end of their evening's work. Inside the flat were large quantities of Margaret Bothamley's possessions, abandoned when she had moved to Berlin.

Bent on disseminating the fascist message across a wider area, Anna drew up plans for another stickyback expedition. Next time her group would be split into pairs and allocated their own routes. Half-a-dozen of these were drawn up. They covered much of central London. Numerous tube stations along the District Line were targeted. Ready for the impending expedition, Anna issued a list of instructions to her Right Club companions.

➤ Assign each person a specific role – finding the way or putting up the labels or keeping watch.
➤ Try to memorize the directions, so you always know the next couple of turnings.
➤ Check there's a gap between you and the previous two-person team.
➤ Make sure you're not walking on the light side of the street, otherwise you might be spotted putting up labels.
➤ Do your best to keep moving.
➤ Refrain from pasting the labels on walls, because the glue won't stick to them.
➤ Look for pale-coloured noticeboards and other places on which to daub slogans.
➤ Never speak to any of the other teams.
➤ Keep your eyes peeled for shadowy entrances, where policemen might lurk.
➤ Start talking about the weather if you see a police constable approaching. Indicate the direction of approach with a line such as 'I gather there's a chill coming in from the west.'
➤ Get back to Anne van Lennep's flat for twelve that night.
➤ Leave her flat in couples to avoid drawing attention.

41

Letters from members of the public, some of them anonymous, had begun to pour into MI5. These were presumably encouraged by newspaper scare stories about the Fifth Column, which was blamed for a series of mysterious explosions at a gunpowder factory on the outskirts of London. Max knew that each allegation should be followed up, even if the results showed it to be as unfounded as those recent claims that lights were being used to signal to German aircraft.

He told his friend Dennis Wheatley about one such baseless allegation. This concerned a soldier who was caught with a slip of paper bearing a list of foreign names such as Heinrich Hauser and Serge Orloff. Max's anecdote had a droll conclusion at odds with the prevailing anxiety. He said he'd pointed out to his MI5 colleagues that the names on the list belonged to characters in Dennis's detective game, *Herewith the Clues*, which had been released last year.

Many of the tidal wave of letters about suspected Fifth Columnists asked MI5 not to involve the police, so Max and his agents – practised in penetrating subversive organizations – were deemed especially suitable to make the requisite enquiries. But Max, even now he had Bill Younger and Jimmy Dickson alongside him, didn't have time to pursue these in parallel to his existing work. Nor could he obtain assistance from other MI5 departments as they had no appropriate staff available. Conscious of the urgency of the matter, he submitted a request to Sir Vernon Kell, asking for permission to recruit and train a few officers to wade through the Fifth Column allegations.

42

Since their encounter at the Christmas Bazaar, the nascent friendship between Christabel Nicholson and Anna had flourished. Anna was now a periodic supper guest at the

Nicholsons' home. They lived in Ashburn Gardens, just a few streets from Anna's current abode.

Entered via a short flight of black-and-white-tiled steps that led under a stout portico, their building faced a small, oblong park, rimmed by plane trees. Christabel and her husband, Admiral Wilmot Nicholson, had a roomy ground-floor flat with views of the garden at the back. In these surroundings she and Anna could explore their interest in the supernatural. Christabel claimed to have sighted a ghost at the Hampshire manor house owned by her husband's family. She said that the apparition was a sad-faced woman in white, who strolled out of the house and down the drive. On separate occasions other people had reported hearing the disembodied sound of swordfighting from that part of the garden. Stories about a duel being fought there between two brothers encouraged Christabel to theorize about how the duellists and the woman in white were connected. Perhaps the duel had been fought over her?

Anna and Christabel were not just united by their fascination with the supernatural. Both women also nursed a passion for military and political tittle-tattle. Predictions about the likely course of the war reached Christabel from her friend, Major-General J. F. C. Fuller. A leading figure within the Nordic League and British Union, Fuller was a pioneering military theorist. Before the war, he had supplied intelligence reports to the Nazis. Christabel held his opinions in high esteem.

She also liked to drop references to the fact that she knew General Ironside, the commander of Britain's military forces. Often she would quote negative stories he had told her about their country. She repeated these with the same relish with which she delivered peppery assessments of people she disliked. The working classes were 'thick-skinned and inconsiderate and only fit to be servants', she declared. Other targets for her scorn were three pro-Soviet MPs. She said they deserved to be treated to that ancient Roman punishment of being 'sewn in a sack with a viper and a cockerel and drowned in the Tiber'.

Happier grounds for conversation were provided by her memories of an all-expenses-paid trip that she and her husband had taken to the 1936 Olympic Games in Berlin. They had been guests of the Nazis, who made a great fuss of them. She and Admiral Nicholson even had the pleasure of a one-hour audience with the Führer. 'As a woman he impressed me one way, as a doctor he impressed me another. As a woman he was very beguiling ... I watched him for his voice and his gestures and his blood pressure whilst I was sitting by him. He is an extraordinary young-looking man. He shouts and talks and gets quite excited with never any quickening of the breath. He will be quite violent, and then perfect relaxation between. I have seen that day after day when the man has been speaking. I am sure he owes a great deal to that, that he can relax entirely, smile pleasantly and dissociate himself entirely from what he had just said.'

Through this encounter, Christabel had come to believe that Hitler was 'a very good man ... the kind of man we need in England'. Last year she had reaffirmed her belief by hosting a supper party to celebrate the Führer's birthday, her guests including a senior Nazi diplomat.

But the gabbled exchanges between Anna and Christabel returned with unfailing insistence to a single theme – the Jews. It was a topic to which Admiral Nicholson could contribute, his anti-Semitic opinions leading him to burden his references to 'the Chosen Race' with a heavy cargo of sardonic distaste.

Addressed by his wife as 'Nic', he was a slender, hawk-nosed martinet in his late sixties – fractionally under twenty years older than his wife. He had a pompous demeanour and an old-fashioned turn of speech, accommodating phrases such as 'silly ass'. Being a long-standing friend of Anna's father, whom he had first met at an Anglo–Russian naval reception before the Great War, Admiral Nicholson treated Anna as a surrogate daughter rather than merely a fresh acquaintance. Anna reciprocated by treating him in a manner indicative of fondness and respect.

Straying briefly from her racial and political obsessions, Anna complained to Christabel about the pain she was suffering in her knees and elbows. Christabel examined her and diagnosed 'septic joints'. Aware of how impoverished Anna had become, Christabel spared her the expense of paying for prescriptions and instead doled out appropriate medicines. These came from the drug samples Christabel was still given by pharmaceutical companies even though she was no longer a practising doctor.

Christabel's kindness to Anna did not end there. It extended to commissioning dressmaking work and trying to find other customers for her. Yet Anna remained short of money, her predicament not helped by the way inflation was further eroding her spending power, which served as a reminder of how far she had fallen in little more than a year. One just had to go back to the Christmas before last to reach those halcyon days when she still presided over Anna de Wolkoff Haute Couture Modes.

Her business had occupied a gorgeous old building at 37 Conduit Street, its spacious, high-ceilinged rooms adorned by Robert Adam-style mantelpieces and plaster ceilings. Flanking its entrance were a pair of huge bronze lamp standards with art-deco light-fittings in the shape of flames. Outside was a blue plaque announcing that it had been the home of the early nineteenth-century Prime Minister, George Canning, forebear of Bobby Gordon-Canning, Anna's friend from the British Union. What had once been the Prime Minister's drawing-room functioned as the showroom where models strutted and posed in her flamboyant creations, each assigned its own name – 'The Naughty Nineties', '*En voyage*', 'Intrigue' and 'Escapade', the last two of these names hinting at Anna's extracurricular activities.

If Anna had learnt anything from the vicissitudes of her life, it was the speed with which one's fortunes could fluctuate. Prosperity could transform into poverty, success into failure, power into powerlessness – and vice versa. Soon enough, she might find herself enjoying similar privileges to Christabel as a guest-of-honour during the Nazis' victory parade through the West End.

43

Freezing temperatures had set in over the weekend, leading to more carping about the weather. By the standards Tyler had experienced in Moscow, however, the morning of Sunday 29 January, 1940 almost qualified as a fine spring day. Light overnight snow had nonetheless conspired to reduce the traffic to a sluggish pace. This gave Tyler and anyone else who happened to be crunching across the West End a chance to read the new, boldly lettered government slogans on the sides of the buses. 'BLACKOUT,' these read, 'BEFORE STEPPING OFF THE KERB – STOP – LOOK – LISTEN. SAFETY FIRST.'

Within the relative comfort of the Code Room at the US Embassy, Tyler used the Grey Code to encrypt a succinct communication from Winston Churchill – 'Naval Person' – to President Roosevelt. Headed 'PERSONAL AND SECRET', the letter attempted to alleviate the diplomatic row sparked by the Royal Navy's interception of the American freighter, *Moormacsun*.

'I gave orders last night that no American ship should, in any circumstances, be diverted into the combat zone round the British Islands declared by you,' Churchill had written. 'I trust this will be satisfactory.'

At 4.05 p.m., Tyler despatched the message to Washington, DC.

Early next day he was presented with another confidential message from Churchill that had to be translated into the distinctly unconfidential Grey Code and then wired across the Atlantic. This latest message, which Tyler sent soon after midday, clarified its predecessor and urged that Britain's privileged treatment of American shipping – likely to antagonize other neutral nations – should be kept secret.

Tyler subsequently took home a typed transcript of the first telegram and a carbon-copy of the second.

44

In his Dolphin Square base, Max had the luxury of central heating and little chromium-plated electric bar-fires to parry the midwinter cold. By the morning of Monday 30 January, 1940, the snow furring the neighbouring rooftops had disappeared as abruptly as it had descended.

London appeared to have escaped lightly in comparison to some parts of the country. There were reports of fifteen-foot snowdrifts on Exmoor. Until six years ago or thereabouts, Max's late wife, Gwladys, had run a small hotel on the edge of the moor. He used to go down there at weekends. During the winter he'd sometimes help the local farmers hunt for sheep buried in snowdrifts. He'd take with him Lorna, his Great Dane, who was adept at sniffing out sheep. He remembered an occasion when he and Lorna had been joined by Gwladys's bulldog, which revelled under the name of Fatty. Max had only brought Fatty with them to give it some exercise. In spite of its snub-nose, which he'd never credited with sensitivity to smells, Fatty – itself a source of pungent odours – had guided them to several sheep. Fatty was, Max thought, a remarkable dog in many ways. It could catch mice as well as any cat. If a mouse darted behind a piece of furniture, Fatty would crouch nearby and wait with the same patience that Max and his colleagues stalked their human prey.

When Max arrived at Dolphin Square, he risked a potentially uncomfortable encounter with Sir Oswald Mosley. Each morning the British Union leader could be seen walking through the foyer of Hood House. Mosley had just rented two adjoining flats on the seventh floor. Almost directly above the premises occupied by Section B5b. He must have been using them as office space. Part of the potential awkwardness of chancing upon him lay in the fact that he and his acolytes had become the antithesis of everything Max regarded as wholesome.

For Max and colleagues, the threat from the British Union escalated dramatically that Monday when Special Branch infiltrated a gathering of the party's London District officials. Mosley's deputy used the occasion to highlight the party's role as a revolutionary movement and to speak about the imminence of that revolution. In characteristically grandiloquent style, Mosley himself then declared the time was coming for 'the sweep forward, which the movement would make, as their brother parties in other countries had made when their hour of destiny struck'. The Special Branch officer who attended the meeting remarked that 'Underlying the whole of his speech there was a strong hint of a march to power by armed force.'

45

Even when Tyler was not required for the 4 p.m. to midnight shift in the Code Room, he couldn't spend the evening with Irene. Her husband was sure to become suspicious if she wasn't home when he returned from work, the upshot being that Tyler spent many of his evenings with Eugène Sabline instead.

Tyler's friend introduced him to the cocktail-party circuit, to polite conversation with White Russian aristocrats over glasses of black velvet or highballs or whatever else they were serving their guests. For soirées of this nature, one of which was held near Tyler's flat,[49] Eugène squeezed into evening dress and a wing-collared shirt, his jacket embellished by a crisp white handkerchief and a row of Tsarist-era medals. He would normally have a voluminous attaché case with him, which he would snap open at the apposite moment. Lining the case were attractive wooden cigarette-boxes, each inlaid with regimental insignia and Imperial Russian crests. The boxes had been made in a workshop run by Eugène. It gave employment to otherwise destitute fellow exiles. He would charm sympathetic guests into purchasing the boxes.

Eugène and Tyler formed a regular trio with Lady Luba Fletcher, a middle-aged Muscovite who was likely to be receptive to Tyler's accounts of his experiences in her hometown. She had fled Russia twenty-one years ago, her departure hastened by her first husband's participation in a botched attempt to overthrow the Soviet regime.[50] Nowadays she owned a West End dress shop and a big house in Kensington, shared with her new husband, an aristocratic former Army officer. Their honeymoon had taken them not only to Nazi Germany but also Budapest, talk of their trip enabling Tyler to swap notes with her on their experiences of both places.

Oddly enough, Tyler had holidayed in Budapest just a few months after Luba and her husband. He had made the trip during his biannual leave from his job in Moscow. The Hungarian capital had represented his final port of call on a tour embracing England, Italy and Yugoslavia. But his memories of Budapest were not the stuff of nostalgia. A mere three days after checking into a luxurious hotel, he had contracted influenza, plus an ear abscess. Such was the severity of his condition, he ended up being transferred to a hospital where the doctors had operated on him. Afflicted by a high fever, he had then been laid up for nigh on three months in a Budapest clinic, his time there enlivened by a two-week visit from Tanya, who was trusted sufficiently by her NKVD handlers to be allowed to leave the Soviet Union.

Via Lady Luba Fletcher, Tyler gained access to the smart set that colonized upmarket establishments such as the Berkeley, Savoy and Ritz hotels, where most of the female clientele had abandoned evening-gowns in favour of more practical get-ups. Tyler, who admitted to being fickle in his dealings with women, now became acquainted with a prominent member of that raffish crowd, namely Princess Mira Dimitri, friend of Eugène Sabline and erstwhile friend of Anna Wolkoff.

Bright and unscrupulous, this beautiful, doe-eyed twenty-seven-year-old gossip-magnet had a thirst for vodka only exceeded by her thirst for sexual adventure, which she pursued with equal lack of discrimination. Her mood, always a product of how much alcohol she'd consumed the previous night, veered from optimism to deepest pessimism. Whenever anyone mentioned the Soviet Union, she could be relied upon to conjure a tone of sneering pity. She favoured an alliance between Britain and Germany against the Communists.

Many an evening she could be found with her tiny, buffoonish husband in the restaurant at the Berkeley Hotel. Liable to play practical jokes on their companions, her husband was one of Grand Duchess Xenia's sons. Hitherto resident in grace-and-favour accommodation within Windsor Great Park, provided by the late King George V, Mira and husband had a small house near Tyler's flat. They had just returned from a few months on the Riviera where, despite their venomous anti-Semitism, they'd been sponging off a Jewish family whom they had befriended. Neither of them possessed much money, so they prowled the Berkeley in the hope of cadging meals from the well-to-do contacts they groomed. Key participants in the Dimitris' louche clique[51] included Princess Marina of Greece and her husband Prince George, better known as the Duchess and Duke of Kent.[52] The Duchess had become one of the most celebrated members of the British royal family, her stylish clothes spawning many a trend in haute couture.

Situated midway along Piccadilly, the Berkeley – where the Dimitris and their friends cavorted – was exorbitantly expensive. A single meal would set a diner back as much as a pure wool Burberry overcoat. While one dined, one could watch couples dance to the house band, which started playing about eight thirty each evening, the melody affording temporary reprieve from the cold, dark world outside.

46

Few jobs were, Max recognized, quite as stressful as the job being undertaken by Marjorie. He only needed to cast his mind back to his pre-war operation against that Soviet spy-ring to realize how an agent's health could be eroded by the strain of leading a double life. The woman deployed on the case spent four years cut off from most of her friends. Eventually she had suffered a nervous breakdown. Marjorie could easily undergo an identical fate.

Given the risks taken by agents and the sacrifices they made on behalf of their country, Max was annoyed at the way so many government officials seemed to pigeonhole them as unscrupulous and dishonest people with dubious motives. He'd noticed how the phrase 'secret agent' tended to be spoken with a tone of contempt, yet he believed that spies often exhibited some of the finest human virtues.

His approving attitude towards Marjorie and her ilk seemed to be shared by members of the public. Since the launch several days ago of Dennis Wheatley's extensively advertised new novel, *The Scarlet Imposter*, written at Max's behest, the book was on the way to becoming a colossal bestseller. If the work of Marjorie and Section B5b's other agents succeeded in encouraging government officials to match the public's evident admiration for secret agents, then Max would feel as if his career had achieved something worthwhile.

By assigning a second agent to the Right Club operation, its dependence on Marjorie and its resultant vulnerability could be decreased. Max was nevertheless aware that the use of multiple agents on the same inquiry might lead to problems. Where his agents weren't fully conversant with what was happening, they were likely to fritter away time by reporting on each other. All the same, Max could see plenty of reasons why he shouldn't tell one agent about the presence of another. Not because he didn't trust them, but because they might betray their connection by exchanging meaningful glances or even a surreptitious wink. He also decided that agents were better off working on their own because the others wouldn't, if one of them was rumbled, inevitably be unmasked as well.

Despite these fundamental complications, Max had just recruited a second agent to work on the Right Club case. Enlisting undercover staff had become much harder since the onset of war. He and his colleagues were, after all, fishing in the same pond as the armed forces and various government departments.

The new agent's name was Hélène de Munck. Only twenty-five years old, she came with the highest references. She was a protégée of a wealthy woman[53] for whom she used to work as a housekeeper-cum-personal secretary. Hélène's sponsor inhabited the same milieu as Max's colleague in Naval Intelligence, Ian Fleming, years away from achieving fame as the author of the James Bond novels.

Hélène was somewhat on the short side and favoured the kind of garb that ensured she did not stand out – grey flannels with a striped grey scarf. She was tough, versatile and enthusiastic, but she didn't look the picture of good health. There were shadows around her eyes that showed up against her pallid complexion, which itself contrasted with her black hair.

Max arranged for Hélène to commence work on Wednesday 1 February, 1940. An agent's preliminary training was regarded by him as being of the utmost importance. Yet he had been so busy since last autumn that he found it hard to devote sufficient time and attention to new agents.

Pivotal to Hélène's recruitment was his belief that each agent should be compatible with the target of each investigation. For the past few years she had been an acquaintance of Admiral Wolkoff and a sporadic visitor to the Russian Tea Rooms. Diligent study of Anna Wolkoff's file – of the personal characteristics, the strengths and weaknesses so far exposed – had moreover revealed that Hélène and Anna enjoyed acres of common ground. Like Anna, Hélène had been born abroad, not in Russia but in Belgium. And she'd gone to school in Britain like Anna. Hélène had travelled widely on the Continent as well. She was also multilingual. She and Anna crossed over in other ways, too. They both lived on the fringe of the aristocratic British world, yet they weren't really part of that world. Further ballast was added by Hélène's self-confessed anti-Semitism. No acting would be required if she got into conversation with Anna and other Right Club members.

Best of all, Hélène had an academic interest in spiritualism, the occult and clairvoyance, which, according to Max's dossier, fascinated Anna. Max decided that his new agent was well-placed to exploit that, because she had what he considered an uncanny skill at discerning someone's personality from their handwriting.

Of the many things he had learnt from his experience with wildlife, the potency of temptation was among the most readily transferable. As a child, he'd once reared a young magpie that had found bright objects irresistible – a trait that was, he maintained, inborn throughout that species. With a view to placing equivalent temptation in Anna's path, he gave Hélène instructions to stage an apparently chance meeting with her, the Russian Tea Rooms offering the most believable setting for such an encounter. So Hélène started eating meals there. Not so often that she aroused suspicion, mind you.

She was instructed to smuggle an allusion to the occult into any ensuing chitchat between her and Anna. That would then enable Max's new agent to mention her character-reading skills, which she was supposed to accentuate to the point where they strayed into the realm of psychic phenomena.

From past experience, Max knew that penetration operations of this nature were most effective if one could engineer a situation whereby the target solicited the assistance of the agent, not the other way round. His operation against the Communist spy-ring had kicked off that way. After nearly six years of mixing with London's pro-Soviet faction, his agent had been approached by the leader of the ring and invited to work for them.

Were Hélène to succeed in penetrating the Right Club in similar fashion, Max realized that her motives might at some point be questioned by Anna and friends. But that was when Anna and Captain Ramsay would surely remember that Hélène hadn't thrust herself forward. Far from it. Outward reluctance to join an organization always lent credibility to an agent, Max reflected.

47

That Thursday Christabel Nicholson became a member of the Right Club. She fell in with Anna's suggestion that she should buy one of the club's uniforms. She even ordered the matching hat, prompting Anna to make an appointment to visit Christabel's home for a fitting.

Gone were the days when Anna could afford to employ a specialist assistant to handle this essential chore. Gone, too, were the days when she could be so profligate with fabric. Acres of material had been needed to make that eighteenth-century-style evening-gown with the voluminous hooped skirt, which she'd designed a few years ago for her friend, Pam Jackson, sister-in-law of Sir Oswald Mosley.

Christabel's husband was on hand to help select the colour of Anna's latest, altogether less extravagant creation. In the event that Anna did not have any leftover rolls of fabric, her customers had to make their selections from the official wartime colour chart. Only a matter of months back, she'd been able to offer them a range of more than 600 colours, but now the choice was limited to ten shades.

At fittings Anna had a tape-measure draped conveniently round her neck. She would emit bursts of inattentive chatter as she gently rotated her client, frowning over the position of the broad-stitched seams and taking rapid measurements. If the seams were too tight around the neck, armholes or elsewhere, she would mark where they had to be adjusted. She would then box up the garment, take it home, unpick all of the tacking and restitch it with painstaking care, by which point the seams were ready for pressing, a laborious job that often had to be repeated two or three times. But she was sufficiently experienced in the art of couture to realize that a well-pressed garment would look ten times better.

Sure enough, Christabel was delighted with the outfit. It was, she pronounced, just the sort of smart-looking thing one could wear to a cocktail party. She thought the hat was jolly pretty, too.

48

Tyler was still spending frequent mornings with Irene at his flat. When he didn't have a lunch engagement, they would often go for afternoon walks through the bleak, leafless streets, his conversation as guarded as the city itself. Sometimes he and Irene would end up at tourist sites, including London Zoo, then drawing only sparse crowds. Among its remaining star attractions was a long-maned African lion, apt to deliver the occasional playful bite to his small cub, which responded with a soft noise not unlike laughter.

Even as Tyler and his new girlfriend wandered around the Zoo, they could not get away from the war. In case any dangerous animals escaped during an air raid, rifle-toting marksmen were patrolling the grounds. Many of the enclosures were empty and the restaurant had been locked up. And walls of sandbags screened the mouths of the pedestrian tunnels, linking the two halves of the Zoo. Inside, the tunnels were fitted with benches and electric lighting, so they could be used as air raid shelters – perfect for a passionate clinch. While Irene's passion was accruing operatic depth, Tyler could marshal only enough romantic ardour to camouflage his glacial indifference, his preparedness to jettison her at a moment's notice.

Being seen together at the Zoo or elsewhere in the West End, much less kissing in public, was freighted with danger for Irene. Her original spirit of recklessness diffusing, she had become fearful that her husband would learn about her affair with Tyler. But the chances of running into her husband – who worked for his family's import-export business, headquartered near West India Docks, well away from most of the tourist sites – were mercifully slim.

Irene and Tyler remained at far greater risk of bumping into one of her family or a friend of her husband. Feasible candidates abounded. High on that list was her brother-in-law, whose job as Director of Publicity at Ealing Film Studios was bound to take him into the centre of town.[54] Irene's brother, who worked as a musician, was someone else they might come across. The same applied to her taxi-driver father who might glimpse her and Tyler from his cab. And she couldn't rule out crossing paths with her sister, Olga Mallett, a recently married, sometime chorus girl who moved in elite West End theatrical circles. If Tyler and Irene encountered Olga, there was the consoling possibility that Olga might be more understanding because she too had a weakness for adultery.[55]

49

Three days after Christabel Nicholson's enrolment in the Right Club, the Ramsays hosted another meeting at their London house. Marjorie, who was there with Wolkoff and several others, let Max know what had taken place. She told him that Captain Ramsay and his wife made remarks implying that there was a member of the Right Club in the Ministry of Economic Warfare.

Created last autumn, the ministry sought to undermine Germany's financial and industrial sectors by enforcing a naval blockade that would prevent the importation of vital goods. Max's friend and former boss at MI6, Desmond Morton, held a senior post within this key organization. Through Desmond, who casually fed him morsels of information that might prove advantageous to Section B5b, Max would have had an inkling of how much sensitive material could be gleaned from the ministry and from MI6, which shared the same building. Desmond himself would also have made a worthwhile target for Right Club snooping because MI6 was supplying him with top-secret briefing documents.

As well as drawing attention to the possible infiltration of Desmond's organization, Marjorie told Max that Captain Ramsay had grilled her for nearly three hours. She quoted some of the questions he'd asked her, and the answers she had given.

'Do you know any people in MI5?'

'Probably by sight through seeing them in the canteen, but that is pure guesswork.'

Ramsay enquired whether she'd ever been into their offices.

'No.'

'Have you many Jews round you?'

'About three at the outside.'

Marjorie remembered Captain Ramsay asking whether she could provide the names of the Jewish employees in the Censorship Department. She went on to recount another snatch of dialogue between herself and Ramsay.

'Are the Censorship moving and, if so, where to?'

'I do not know.'

'Can you give any opinion from gossip overheard, as to whether the war will be called off?'

'I do not know.'

This exchange had, she informed Max, been followed by a discussion about ways in which the Right Club's membership could be boosted. There had been a proposal that Marjorie should evaluate potential recruits through what was described as 'a sort of study circle on the Jewish question'. New members shouldn't be accepted until they'd completed a vetting period of three months.

At that, conversation had reverted to the subject of the department where Marjorie worked. She recalled being asked, 'Do you ever get the chance to pick up titbits?'

'Only very seldom.'

Then the Captain had said, 'Do you think you could influence the younger girls?'

'Not much in Wormwood Scrubs. There are only two at most in a room, and I have no access to the typing pool, but I will try.'

'We are not out for mass membership,' Ramsay had replied. 'We want quality, not bulk.'

50

Tyler received a hurriedly scrawled note from Barbara Allen, the woman who administered the American Club. 'We are back in London now,' the message read. 'I wonder if you are not already engaged could you come round for a cocktail tomorrow evening about 6 o'clock? I have asked some other compatriots of ours …'

She and her husband had a house on an imposing Georgian crescent only a mile from the US Embassy. Barbara's husband, who was employed by the London division of his family's printing and advertising firm, turned out to possess family connections to the British Union. His firm had, until just prior to the war, been in partnership with Mosley on a project to set up a radio station, broadcasting from the Channel Islands. And his brother – a former Conservative MP – had been secretly bankrolling Mosley's movement. Barbara's brother-in-law had, however, since fallen out with the British Union leader.

When it became apparent that she was fascinated by London's Russian émigré population, Tyler – whose vocabulary had acquired an Anglicized tincture – suggested a jaunt round the capital's Russian restaurants. Barbara, now several months pregnant, consented to his plan.

Inevitably, the tour would not take long because there were few such establishments. As Barbara was in a position to tell him, most of London's Russian restaurants had the life expectancy of a fruit fly. The same sad story had been enacted many times. It starts with a Russian émigré borrowing some money, with which he leases premises and equipment. Word gets around that the food is simply *marvellous*. Every bit as good as that little place in, say, Odessa or St Petersburg. The restaurant is soon heaving with customers, many of them Russians who eat on credit, promising to pay next week. Only next week comes and the account still hasn't been settled. But the restaurateur doesn't have the heart to turn away his Russian creditors who linger for hours, nursing their drinks while they talk to their friends. Then the owner gets into conversation with them, brings over a complimentary bottle of something and joins them. Within weeks an estate agent's sign has appeared outside the restaurant and the proprietor is casting round for some alternative means of making a living.

51

There had been a very revealing conversation between Marjorie and Molly Stanford, Wolkoff's friend from the Russian Tea Rooms. Max got wind of it from Marjorie. She said that Stanford wanted to send a letter to a contact in Belgium. During the conversation Stanford told Marjorie that she didn't want the letter to go through the normal censorship procedure, which had been implemented alongside other wartime emergency measures.

Knowing that Marjorie worked in the Censorship Department, Stanford asked if she'd mind doing her an enormous favour. Would Marjorie be able to sneak her letter through the system?

Naturally, Marjorie said yes, so Stanford gave her an envelope addressed to 'Monsieur Price'.

Max arranged for it to be opened and its contents photographed, but the message remained uncensored before being resealed in its envelope and posted to Belgium.

When Price – or whoever the ultimate recipient was – laid eyes on the letter, he or she would inevitably assume it had somehow circumvented the usual system. By fulfilling the favour asked of her, Marjorie's status within the Right Club – and her concurrent value to Max – was certain to be enhanced.

52

Anna had bagged one of the five-shilling tickets being sold from the big old building on Great Smith Street that housed the British Union's bookshop and national headquarters. Her ticket bought her a place at the party's London Administrative Area Luncheon, due to be held at the Criterion Restaurant early next month.

She'd dined there before. Four summers ago, it had been the scene of an extraordinary revelation by a friend who had been lunching with her. That friend was the late Arthur Kitson, an elderly Lothario and fellow anti-Semite, who sometimes masqueraded as Sir Arthur Kitson or even the Honourable Arthur Kitson. Not long before their visit to the Criterion, Anna's friend – an inventor, engineer, monetary reformer and undischarged bankrupt – had been employed by the Nazis as an economic adviser. Over lunch Arthur had told her about a plan to murder King Edward VIII – future Duke of Windsor. Arthur had spoken about documents that were on their way from America, detailing the assassination plot. He'd wanted to know whether Anna could deliver these to the King via her mother's friend, Grand Duchess Xenia, who had been close to the King's father.

Poised to embark on a Continental motoring holiday with Princess Mira Dimitri, Anna had assured Arthur that she'd do what she could. On the Monday before she and Mira departed, she had met Arthur again. He had presented her with a letter addressed to 'His Majesty The King'. As requested, she had passed this on to the Grand Duchess.

En route across the Continent, Anna and the Princess had stayed at an inn near the Austro–German border. Immediately they'd arrived there, the innkeeper had asked them if they had heard that an attempt had been made to assassinate the King of England.

Responding to the news, Anna had said, 'So soon!' Her response must have been fed back to the German authorities because later that evening, while she and Mira were in their room, Anna had received a message telling her to go downstairs. She had found the local *Gauleiter* and several other Nazi officials waiting for her. They had ended up questioning her about her apparent foreknowledge of the assassination plot.

But the plot had by then reached a farcical climax. After the Trooping the Colour ceremony in Hyde Park, a man had shoved his way to the front of the crowd. Instead of firing his revolver, he had hurled it at the King, who had suffered no injuries. The man had meanwhile been collared.

Anna explained to her Nazi interviewers how she'd known about the plot. When they discovered that she was a zealous anti-Semite, they invited her to join them for supper, during which she heard that Franz von Papen, the German Ambassador to Austria, had been earmarked as the next Ambassador to Britain.

Rarely missing a chance to talk about her proximity to the centres of power, she had since told the story of how she'd lectured her Nazi supper companions on von Papen's shortcomings. She said the *Gauleiter* had assured her that he'd pass on her opinions to Hitler, whom he would be seeing in a few days' time. When she trotted out the story, she gave the impression that *she* was behind von Ribbentrop's appointment as Ambassador in place of von Papen.

53

Max was given the go-ahead. Granted permission to hire additional case-officers, he finalized his list of candidates with suitable attributes and experience. Detective skills were highly desirable, but he did not anticipate signing up any policemen. What deterred him from hiring ex-coppers was that he had noticed how few of them possessed the common touch. Since his recruits would need to interview a large and varied selection of people, he decided they had to be just as comfortable talking to a duke or a dustman.

He employed four new staff, all with pukka, military credentials. There was a soldier-turned-stockbroker, whom he had found working with Marjorie in the Censorship Department.[56] Then there was a man who had been seconded from the Army after being injured in a training accident.[57] And there was a First World War veteran who had made a name for himself as an explorer.[58] Completing the quartet was a young aristocrat who had come to Max's attention some years before the war.[59] Max sensed that he would be more help to MI5 than the armed forces.

With the objective of teaching these recruits about intelligence work, Max had secured authorization to set up a spy school for them at Wormwood Scrubs. Despite Section B5b's backlog of work, he was insistent that none of the quartet should undertake assignments on behalf of his department until they had been properly trained.

He had witnessed how disruptive the training process could be. At the beginning of the war, headquarters had recruited large numbers of staff without a smidgen of intelligence experience. Busy colleagues of Max's had ended up neglecting their own jobs in order to tutor those recruits. Other colleagues had sometimes had no choice but to carry on working and let the new recruits pick up knowledge as best they could. In many cases the results were, as Max put it, more easily imagined than described.

To avoid duplicating this chaotic state of affairs, he had mustered a rota of volunteer tutors from headquarters. All of them were generous enough to contribute to a programme of lectures, delivered while they were off duty. Max was therefore able to minimize disruption to the Right Club investigation and the rest of his work, which remained plentiful enough to make him feel under appreciable stress.

54

Except for Irene Danischewsky, whose infatuation with him was enriched by rapturous respect, Tyler welcomed only occasional visitors to his flat. That helped to keep Irene ignorant of the other women in his life. When she wasn't with him, Tyler – whose waking hours had grown as tangled as some epic German sentence – would spend his free time with Luba Fletcher, Barbara Allen, Mira Dimitri or June Huntley.

June had not long ago taken him to a party, where she had introduced him to Jain Marmion Aitken, a well-heeled and well-connected twenty-three-year-old friend. Jain made a show of agreeing with everything Tyler said to the pair of them. She was nevertheless proud of what she termed 'woman power', of the resourcefulness of women who shared her New Zealand background, of their ability to perform traditionally male tasks, everything from driving an ambulance to repairing a faulty engine or salting a newly butchered pig. Unconditionally pro-fascist, she flaunted her close ties with a mistress of the Italian dictator, Benito Mussolini.

For the evening of Wednesday 14 February, 1940, which St Valentine's Day flavoured with romance, Tyler lined up a date with Jain. In the eyes of someone so drawn to old money, her youthful allure was inevitably burnished by the fact that she consorted with the likes of Lady Violet Astor, who had married into one of America's most eminent families and was a confi-dante of Ambassador Kennedy.

The setting for Tyler's date with Jain – candid in her belief that Kiwi women 'love to play' – was just a few streets from where he worked. Jain didn't have far to travel either. She lived in a newish flat towards the southern edge of Mayfair – so different from New Zealand, from those remote farms she had visited, farms where itinerant girls of her age were housed in caravans.

Darkness had long since fallen by 7 p.m. when Tyler was due to see her at Claridge's, which society people like her rated as one of the three finest hotels in the world. It had made the news lately because the Duke of Windsor had stayed there during his recent trip to England. Beyond its sandbagged entrance, revolving doors palmed guests out of the frigid blackout and into a subtly lit world of art-deco sumptuousness, where the wealthy patrons were reflected in a slew of mirrors with vaguely Chinese designs engraved on them.

Tyler had arranged to dine with Jain in the long, arcaded restaurant, within which stylized botanical paintings and models of pagodas sustained the oriental theme. Claridge's wasn't only famed for the quality of its cuisine but also for the size of its bills. A two-course meal of, say, duck à l'orange followed by peach melba would have cost Tyler more than a month's wages after subtracting rent and tax. With outgoings like that, he had to keep on augmenting his regular income.

55

Over the third weekend of February 1940, which brought news of Soviet military progress in Finland, Marjorie submitted her latest findings. She disclosed that one of Captain Ramsay's contacts had warned him that he was under close investigation and should be extremely careful in the immediate future. She also notified Max of the fact that Wolkoff and the Russian Tea Rooms group were putting up stickybacks nearly every night, their activities now encompassing so-called 'window-slashing'. This involved scratching graffiti across the windows of shops, the word 'Jew' being a window-slasher's favourite.

Bertie Mills was named by Marjorie as an energetic participant in these activities. Marjorie added that Mills had asked

Wolkoff – who claimed to have connections to Sir Vernon Kell – whether she could provide any information about the head of MI5. The entire discussion had, Marjorie told Max, been conducted in French, presumably because Wolkoff and Mills assumed nobody else would understand it.

Thanks to his involvement with the Nordic League and the Link, Mills was already the subject of an MI5 file that extended back to January 1939. It showed that he had worked in Nazi Germany – first for a steel company and later as a tour guide. Since his return to Britain, he'd been involved with a litany of British fascist groups. He was closely associated with both Captain Ramsay and Sir Oswald Mosley, too. His file also revealed that he had, almost a year ago, been in touch with a Hamburg-based organization that distributed Nazi propaganda.

56

Now that Tyler had established a friendship with Barbara Allen, she no longer addressed him as 'Mr Kent'. Instead, she called him 'TK'.

She and Tyler were not yet finished with their gastronomic tour. Next on their itinerary was the Russian Tea Rooms. Owned by the parents of one of her dearest friends, it rated as by far the longest-surviving of the town's Russian eateries. It had been there for more than a decade-and-a-half – ever since the days when Barbara's mother was hosting debutante dances for her. Yet it didn't look like it would hold out much longer.

Customers were not exactly queuing to claim seats at the dozen or so tables that dotted its two rooms. Tyler gauged it as rather a modest, dingy little place.

At the Tea Rooms, Barbara introduced Tyler to her friend, Anna Wolkoff, whose parents he had met under the auspices of Betty Straker. It was surprising that he and Anna hadn't until then encountered one another, since they knew a number of the same people.

Tyler found 'Miss Wolkoff', as he addressed her, bright and fun to talk to, their mutual love of fine food purveying an easy starting point. His diminutive new acquaintance was one of those women whose emotions were as easy for him to parse as a sentence in a Spanish primer. When she regarded someone as attractive, she would, with every semaphored gesture and gushing utterance, betray both her interest and her neediness. For a ruthlessly calculating ladies' man of Tyler's experience, that left her vulnerable to his practised charm, which he could switch on and off.

57

The long cold spell finally abated on Tuesday 20 February, 1940. Max received an update from Marjorie the following day. 'Captain Ramsay,' she informed him, 'has decided that a room or some rooms shall be taken to run a sort of social club which need not be registered as a club, where raw recruits can be entertained and led gently towards the ideas and aims of the Right Club.'

Wolkoff had been placed in joint charge of the quest to find suitable premises. Marjorie added that Right Club members were being encouraged to recruit local shopkeepers. Jewish-owned businesses such as the Marks and Spencer chain of department stores were meanwhile placed out of bounds to members. Bringing her report to a close, Marjorie stated, 'It is understood that Captain Ramsay is compiling a special black-list of Jews who are to be dealt with "when the time comes".'

58

Anna had just obtained a back-issue of *Truth*, the strongly anti-Semitic, anti-war, anti-Churchill weekly newspaper edited by the husband of her Right Club friend, Dolly Newnham. On the inside pages Anna spotted an article headlined

'REFUGEES AT LARGE'. It emphasized what its anonymous author perceived as the serious problems caused by the Jewish refugees entering Britain from Germany.

The article, its anti-Semitism veiled by a tone of apparent objectivity, provided Anna with an excuse to get in touch with Sir Vernon Kell. She had met him last winter at a supper party thrown by Lord Cottenham, the subject of one of her intense crushes. By contacting Sir Vernon, she might be able to secure additional material for her friend and Right Club colleague, Bertie Mills, who had requested information from her concerning the Director-General of MI5.

If the warnings previously given to her brother and Captain Ramsay about an investigation of her father and the Right Club were accurate, her letter might also serve to wrongfoot any such inquiry. Writing a chatty and helpful missive to the head of MI5 was, after all, hardly the behaviour of a woman hell-bent on undermining the government.

During the supper party at which Anna had encountered Sir Vernon, there had been a heated discussion about the influx of refugees. Sir Vernon had admitted to having taken a keen interest in that topic for many years. Reintroducing herself to her fellow guest, Anna spent part of Thursday 22 February, 1940 penning her letter to him. It informed Sir Vernon about the closure of her shop and other misfortunes she had suffered since they'd met. With the letter, she enclosed her freshly acquired copy of *Truth*. She pointed out that it contained an article dealing with the subject they had discussed at Lord Cottenham's supper party. And she expressed hope that Sir Vernon would find *Truth* just as interesting as she had.

59

On the same day Anna wrote to Sir Vernon Kell, a pair of Irish Republican Army bombs – one of them concealed in a wastebin, the other in a cloakroom – detonated near Tyler's flat. In the evening papers, it was reported that the bombs had wrecked a couple of shopfronts and injured a good many people, two of them severely.

These blasts offered Tyler, always a grudging London resident, a foretaste of what life would be like when German bombs started falling. At least the top brass at the embassy had finally seen fit to convert its basement into a proper air-raid shelter.

Inside forty-eight hours of those IRA bombs going off, Tyler tried to engineer a transfer to Germany, something he had attempted while he'd been living in Moscow. Such a transfer would now reunite him with his old pal, Sylvester A. Huntowski, who was being posted to the US Embassy in Berlin. From there, Huntowski was poised to launch a currency smuggling racket, which exploited their friend Donald H. Nichols's present role as a diplomatic courier shuttling between Berlin, Bucharest and Moscow. By moving to the German capital, Tyler would lose access to the valuable documents flowing through the London embassy, but he and the others stood to pocket fat wads of cash from this new scheme.[60]

With customary disregard for protocol, Tyler didn't seek to obtain a transfer to Berlin by going through the normal chain of command. Instead, on Friday 24 February, 1940, he wrote directly to Alexander Kirk, US Ambassador to Germany. He drafted a long, wheedling letter proposing a job swap with the young, Berlin-bound code clerk who had stopped off at Grosvenor Square last October. 'I recall that when he passed through London on his way to Berlin,' Tyler wrote, 'he at that time said he would prefer to be in London.' Tyler also mentioned hearing that the other Berlin-based code clerk 'has had enough of it in Germany'.

Since there was no postal service between there and Britain, Tyler sent his letter via the American diplomatic courier. He was optimistic about getting the transfer he craved. That prospect led him to contemplate smuggling his collection of stolen documents to Germany. Maybe he could use his friendship with one of the German diplomats stationed in Moscow to help negotiate the sale of his collection to the Nazis.

Part Four

No Turning Back

1

Captain Ramsay was taking precautions. Marjorie reported that he'd requested help in pre-empting whatever legal action the authorities were planning against him. She advised Max that Ramsay wanted Right Club members to move the incriminating supply of stickybacks and other fascist propaganda out of his house in Onslow Square.

Using this information, Max could get in touch with Special Branch and ask them to obtain a warrant to raid Ramsay's London address. The decision was, however, taken not to do that. Any such activity might nudge the Right Club leader towards the belated realization that Marjorie was spying on him.

Perhaps the most intriguing and potentially crucial aspect of her recent findings concerned an occasion when she had been with Anna Wolkoff in the Russian Tea Rooms. Wolkoff's father had come over to them and pointed out a young man sitting elsewhere in the restaurant. She had then gone across to speak to him. On her return, she told Marjorie that he was a most interesting person, who worked at the US Embassy. Before that, he had been stationed at its counterpart in Russia. Anna talked about how he'd been there for around five years and spoke magnificent Russian. In passing, she described him as sharing 'our way of thinking'. His name, Marjorie believed, was something like 'William Tolly'.

For Max, there was a sense of déjà vu about this discovery. Less than a year ago, he had initiated the deportation of another suspected German agent who had cultivated a source within the US Embassy. When he heard about Wolkoff's contact, he got in touch with the Foreign Office and requested a copy of the official list of US Embassy employees. But Max didn't warn the Americans that one of their staff might pose a grave security risk.[61]

2

Compliments of Marjorie, there had been news of an important development.

She'd met Anna Wolkoff in the Russian Tea Rooms at lunchtime on Saturday 25 February, 1940. Marjorie and Wolkoff had gone back to the Roland Gardens flat to have tea together. Rich material for Max's case-notes was garnered from the time Marjorie spent with her. Wolkoff confided that she knew Jean Nieuwenhuys, Second Secretary at the Belgian Embassy in London. Through him, she said she was able to use the Belgian diplomatic bag to send letters to the Continent, evading British censorship. Logic dictated that she must have something to hide.

Her letters were addressed to a friend of Nieuwenhuys. That friend forwarded them to their destinations. It was a clever way of bypassing the censorship process. Of course, this had weighty ramifications in view of what Max already knew about Wolkoff and her links to Ramsay and other influential people.

Wolkoff told Marjorie that she'd posted a letter through the Belgian diplomatic bag only last week. She said the letter had been sent to William Joyce. Mention of Joyce – recently identified by the British press as the Nazi broadcaster nicknamed 'Lord Haw-Haw' – gave the discovery of her channel for illicit communications an extra frisson of danger.

Apparently her letter to Joyce had described the activities of the Right Club. Enclosed with it was a separate missive from her friend, Molly Stanford. The addressee of this second letter was Monsieur Price, a name familiar to Max. It had featured on the letter Stanford had previously asked Marjorie to smuggle through the censorship process – the letter Max had opened and then photographed.

3

Frequent references to the goings-on at the Russian Tea Rooms and to Admiral Nikolai Wolkoff had led Max to place the restaurant under periodic observation. The fruits of his surveillance were not reaped until Monday 26 February, 1940, the day after Marjorie's encounter with Anna Wolkoff. His undercover skills eclipsing his literary talents, Max's agent outlined the latest of several visits: 'On this occasion got somewhat pally with wife of above, an elderly aristocratic, motherly lady, who has faith in the restoration of the old regime, if Stalin regime is overthrown, lamented the sad plight of the White Russian refugees all over the world, but are grateful for the refuge they enjoy in this and other countries, and are proud to possess a large number of influential friends in this and other countries. The old admiral is not very talkative, and somewhat cautious as to who he is talking to, new customers are eyed up suspiciously.'

It looked as if the Admiral had heeded the earlier warning contained in that letter from his son, Alexander – the letter that had been intercepted a few weeks ago.

Max's spy went on to describe the other customers in the Tea Rooms. 'A couple of French-talking individuals next to my table, and a couple of foreigners, one I believe to be the man whom I saw emerging from the Russian Trade Delegation Building, Hatton Garden, but would not swear to it, though gathered from other sources that Red Russian agents keep an eye on such places.'

At the Tea Rooms, Mme Wolkoff gave Max's spy a leaflet advertising the Russian Red Cross Society's Easter Bazaar, due to be staged at the Sablines' home. Mme Wolkoff was, according to the leaflet, part of the organizing committee.

Midway through his report, the spy noted that a percentage of the proceeds from events of this nature went towards anti-Communist propaganda. He also observed that the base-ment of the Sablines' house was being used for occasional meetings of what he dubbed 'the White Russian Movement', an amalgam of anti-Communist groups. The most prominent of these, he stated, was the fascist Brothers of the Russian Truth, which offered training in espionage. From his experience of intelligence operations in pre-war Germany, he knew that the Brothers had long-established links to German fascists.

He added that the heads of the White Russian movement hoped they might be able to cajole the Nazis into turning against the Soviet Union. That was why they maintained contact with Germany through neutral countries such as Belgium. 'Some of the ex-Tsarist heads are somewhat inclined in sympathy with the Nazis still,' he explained, 'and one may find one or two spying here and in France for the Nazis in return for some Promised Land.'

4

Studious though he was, Tyler loved being outdoors. Now the days had grown a touch warmer and drier, periods of bright sunshine proclaiming the arrival of spring, he had an incentive to take Irene Danischewsky on daytrips out of town. Extra motivation came from the desire to avoid running into her husband or members of her extended family.

Getting away from London also vastly reduced the danger of Tyler suffering any awkward encounters with his women friends, whose existence he had never disclosed to Irene. Of those, the woman with most potential to create problems for him was Jain Marmion Aitken, their date at Claridge's having been followed by other such dates together. Not that he regarded her or Irene as anything more than expendable components of a city that held 'no particular interests' for him.

Fortuitously he and Irene didn't have to risk using crowded bus or train stations when they went on excursions. Tyler could, instead, afford to hire a chauffeur-driven car from a firm based a mile or so from his flat. Escaping the surreptitious complexities of his London life, he took Irene for rural drives, during which she relaxed in his company. Yet his conversations with her remained circumspect. Like some top-of-the-bill actor who endowed his chosen role with persuasive assurance, he still succeeded in convincing her that he was a good man, a man of integrity, a man who detested the Nazis.

5

Max didn't have to wait long. On Tuesday 27 February, 1940, Marjorie supplied her next significant consignment of intelligence about Wolkoff and the Right Club. By that stage her investigation of Wolkoff – lately in defiance of orders – had regained official backing.

Her report mentioned a woman by the name of Fay Taylour who had, on Mrs Ramsay's recommendation, been admitted to the Right Club. Max and colleagues were well-versed in Taylour's recent activities. She had just returned from the Irish Republic – a neutral country – where she had made anti-British speeches and been in touch with a Roman Catholic priest who was a leading exponent of the Judaeo–Bolshevik conspiracy theory.

Courtesy of a Home Office warrant, more damning material about Taylour had already been secured. 'I love Nazi Germany and the German people and their leader,' she had written to the Right Club activist, Bertie Mills.

In spite of the mounting seriousness of the reports on Wolkoff's circle, Max was struggling to obtain another warrant to intercept post being sent to her at the Roland Gardens flat. His MI5 colleague, Francis Aiken Sneath, came to his rescue by composing a supportive memo to the Home Office.

Later that day Max's warrant application was finally approved. Yet Max only needed to talk to his boss, Guy Liddell, about Home Office warrants to realize that they were not without their disadvantages. Guy had submitted a complaint about them to Jasper Harker, head of B Division, the MI5 counterespionage section. As Guy had discovered, the implementation of these warrants was deplorably haphazard.

The Post Office turned out to be opening only about 10 per cent of the letters and packages sent to addresses for which a warrant had been granted. Investigations were being severely hampered as a consequence. Still, even one-in-ten letters sent to Wolkoff's address might bring to light something valuable.[62]

6

Next day, another of Max's agents – codenamed M/W – reported having tea with Bertie Mills and two other men. They'd gone to the café adjoining the British Union's headquarters. While they were there, Mills said that the Hotel Rembrandt, which was a stone's throw from South Kensington tube station, would no longer be hosting Right Club meetings. Henceforth these would instead be held at St Ermin's, an exclusive restaurant just a few yards from Caxton Hall.[63]

In Marjorie's bulletins on the Right Club, there had been no mention of the Hotel Rembrandt. Max could draw certain conclusions from that. Either Anna Wolkoff didn't know about these meetings or else she wasn't telling Marjorie everything about the club's activities.

To accentuate the frightening impression that Wolkoff constituted only a small component of a well-organized Fifth Column, a new Nazi radio station, apparently based in Britain, had begun transmitting the previous Sunday. The station, audible with minimal interference, was called the New British Broadcasting Service. It carried a medley of propaganda talks and music. Presenting itself as a station run by renegade patriots, opposed to the war, their nationality emphasized by the use of such home-grown signature tunes as 'Annie Laurie' and 'Auld Lang Syne', it wrapped up its broadcasts with a rendition of 'God Save the King'.

7

'Strictly Personal and Confidential for the President from Naval Person', the message began. That evening – Wednesday 28 February, 1940 – it was given to a colleague of Tyler in the Code Room at the US Embassy. The contents of the message had the power to cause political embarrassment to both Roosevelt and Churchill. It confirmed that Britain was favouring America over other neutral countries, whose ships were being forced into the Scottish port of Kirkwall, where they were being searched and compelled to show 'navicerts' – naval certificates guaranteeing their cargo was not destined for Germany.

Tyler didn't bother transcribing the message. He simply helped himself to the carbon-copy made for the embassy's records. Then he smuggled it back to his flat on Gloucester Place, where it joined a growing hoard of US government documents. So exhaustive was his collection that he had accumulated every message going into or out of the Code Room for entire months.

8

Anna did not have to venture far from the Russian Tea Rooms to buy the latest issue of the British Union newspaper. The little shop across the road from the Victoria and Albert Museum always stocked it. One of the recent issues carried an announcement about the party's London Administrative Area Luncheon being sold out, so Anna had reason to feel glad she'd already snaffled a ticket.

She was among nearly 450 guests heading for the Criterion Restaurant on Friday 1 March, 1940. The Criterion faced cold, windswept Piccadilly Circus, which had been transformed by the war. No longer was one confronted by the familiar glare of flashing neon advertisements for well-known brands. Other bloodless casualties of war were the statue of Eros and its accompanying fountain, which had occupied the traffic island in the centre. They had been replaced by a stubby wooden obelisk. Even the talkative gaggle of straw-hatted cockney flower-girls, who used to gather round the fountain, had gone. For months now, their spot had been usurped by a disorderly ring of soldiers, sailors and their lady friends, as well as gawping provincial daytrippers.

Encouraged by the British Union hierarchy to address one another by their surnames, Anna and fellow activists funnelled through the entrance to the Criterion and up the staircase. Within the assembled throng were titled aristocrats, pensioned Army officers and the renowned writer, Henry Williamson, whose good-looking, dolorous features often stared out from newspapers.

Various friends of Anna were going up to the second-floor function rooms, too. Those friends, soon ensconced in the Grand Hall, included Muriel Whinfield, who was also a friend of the Mosleys. A fifty-two-year-old former parliamentary candidate for the British Union, she had come up from her home in Hampshire with her ailing husband, a retired lieutenant colonel. She spoke in such a self-consciously refined manner that one might have assumed she was a dowager duchess. Quite a contrast to the Wolkoffs' friend, Grand Duchess Xenia, a genuine aristocrat who eschewed those same airs and graces.

Prone to eulogize 'the pluck and determination of our Blackshirt men', Muriel was unstinting in her criticism of democracy. She yearned for what she saw as the National Socialist nirvana, though hopes of reaching that via the electoral process were dwindling, as the British Union's minuscule vote at the previous month's by-election had demonstrated.

Also present alongside Anna were a couple of friends from the Right Club. There was Captain Ramsay's son, who had accompanied her and Enid Riddell to the Nordic League meeting at Caxton Hall last year. And there was Lord Ronald Graham, a tall, fair-haired, pillow-cheeked ex-naval officer, known to his pals as Ronnie. Despite his relative youth – he was only in his late twenties – the sour tang of scandal hovered around him, thanks to his being named in a well-publicized case that had reached the divorce court. Ronnie was a great chum of the Duke of Windsor.

Before the war, Ronnie had also been close to a London-based Nazi diplomat, famed for doling out copies of Hitler's autobiography. Politics always dominated the conversation between Ronnie and his friends, who all believed in the justice of the Nazi cause and its inexorable victory. He liked to drink champagne toasts to the Führer, to talk in rapturous detail about his meetings with Hitler and other senior Nazis, and to reminisce about what he considered the wonderful spectacle presented by the Nuremberg rallies.

Another juicy topic for tabletalk was offered by Muriel Whinfield's absent son – a fellow British Union activist. Rumoured to have been on his way to Germany to contribute to the English-language propaganda broadcasts, he had recently been arrested in Switzerland, where he'd been involved with a couple of Nazi agents.

Justifying the five-shilling ticket price for today's event, the guest of honour was none other than Sir Oswald Mosley. In imitation of Mussolini and Hitler, Mosley was referred to as 'the Leader'. Within the pseudo-religious rituals of fascism, the entrance of The Leader bestowed an unfailing excuse for ham theatricality.

Mosley was roughly the same height as Ronnie Graham, but the resemblance stopped there. A slim, handsome man in his early forties, who exuded charismatic egotism, Mosley looked more Italian than English. His neatly trimmed moustache and black, swept back hair lent him a certain caddish brio.

Seated close to him on the top table was Commandant Mary Allen who, like Anna and Ronnie, used to attend Margaret Bothamley's tea parties. Mary had just been installed as the organization's Chief Women's Officer, an appointment sure to nourish her native conceit.

Besides bringing close proximity to Mosley and the rest of the leadership, Anna's ticket purchased a multiple-course meal. Like all British restaurants, the Criterion was excluded from the system of food rationing. No coupons had to be relinquished, yet one couldn't, even by dining in such exclusive places, avoid the shortages of certain ingredients. One really noticed these during the final course when far fewer cheeses were available, cream was dispensed in measly quantities, and those little iced cakes were nowhere to be seen. Nowadays one also had to make do with a single sugar-lump to sweeten one's coffee.

The instant Anna and the rest of the diners were served their last course, Mosley got to his feet. He was greeted by a surge of cheering. Fists clenched in a typically pugilistic stance, he leant across the table and said he was glad to see so many friends. Invariably he began in a soft voice, the confiding timbre of a practised orator. His voice rising in volume, he was soon berating the British government for ignoring what, he claimed, were the reasonable peace terms proposed by Hitler just a few days ago. He explained to Anna and the rest of his enthusiastic audience that Germany wanted a free hand in its former colonies and Eastern Europe. Germany did not seek world power. Of that, he said, he had been assured, a calm and rational tone conferring authority on this portrait of Nazi intentions.

He then expanded on his criticism of the war and the British government. The war was, he believed, the product of an international Jewish conspiracy.

Again, the audience cheered.

In an oratorical trick that brought to mind the German dictator, Mosley was almost yelling as he approached the climax to his speech. 'The British Union,' he said, 'offered the only possible solution. The whole system of government would have to be changed before any real progress was made, and it was up to the British people to make their choice.' There was no halfway house in the struggle for National Socialism, he added, his implicit message being that the British people had a choice between democracy or fascist dictatorship. 'The British Union,' he went on to declare, 'would either triumph or perish. There would be no compromise, no turning back. The battle was on and would be fought to the bitter end ...'

A tremendous swell of applause washed through the room when he stopped speaking.

9

Since learning about Anna Wolkoff's link to the US Embassy, Max had been informed that she appeared to have a second contact there – someone by the name of Kent.

If Max filled in the Americans about Wolkoff's connection to Kent and Tolly – the man previously mentioned – both men were sure to be questioned. They would also probably be transferred to jobs where they'd have no access to sensitive material. Were that to occur, it would be tantamount to Max standing upwind of a badger. His scent would alert the creature to his presence. Wolkoff would likewise know something was afoot if her contacts at the embassy were either interrogated or sidelined. Max's entire operation would then be brought to a premature and unsatisfactory conclusion.

Even if the Americans could be persuaded to play a waiting game, to delay grilling the suspects and to allow them to remain in their current posts, there were a couple of potential hitches. First, there was the danger that American officials might discuss the matter with the Foreign Office, itself the subject of an investigation into leaks and alleged penetration by enemy agents. Then there was the giant question mark over the allegiances of Ambassador Kennedy, who had, despite earlier indications to the contrary, just reclaimed his London post after an extended holiday in the United States. As the fount of notoriously pessimistic statements about Britain's military prospects, he seemed less like a friend than a foe.[64] It was, furthermore, public knowledge that he had, during the summer before hostilities broke out, engaged in unauthorized talks with Nazi officials.

Preferring to sidestep these security concerns, Max refrained from warning the Americans about Messrs Kent and Tolly whom, he soon discovered, were the same person. Instead, he persisted with the tactic of patiently accumulating information about Wolkoff and her associates. As part of that approach, Section B6 – the Watchers – kept the Russian Tea Rooms under surveillance. Not that B6 had sufficient manpower to keep anywhere under observation for long.

While that was happening, Max uncovered more about Jean Nieuwenhuys, Wolkoff's friend at the Belgian Embassy, who had reportedly been smuggling her letters to the Continent via his country's diplomatic bag. Max was apprised of a meeting between Nieuwenhuys and Admiral Wolkoff. Their encounter had apparently created friction between Anna and her father, who said he thought that Nieuwenhuys was Jewish and that she was a fool to have trusted him.

10

A distinguished visitor was due at the US Embassy in Grosvenor Square on Sunday 10 March, 1940. Privy to all of the most secret diplomatic communications between Washington and the various American embassies and consulates across Europe, Tyler would have known about the impending arrival of Sumner Welles, Assistant Secretary of State in the Roosevelt administration. Now on the final leg of a journey that had already taken in Rome, Paris and Berlin, Welles had been assigned the role of President Roosevelt's Special Envoy. He was set to register at Claridge's Hotel, site of Tyler's recent date with Jain Marmion Aitken.

Tall and self-assured, Welles fetched up at the embassy a short while after midday. He was whisked off for a working lunch with Ambassador Kennedy.

If you believed the stories in the evening newspapers, which were being delivered to Tyler's flat, Welles was on a peace mission designed to canvass the views of the British, German, French and Italian governments. But he hadn't brought with him from Washington any specific proposals, save for a nebulous statement about the power of free trade to eliminate international tension once hostilities had ceased.

With regard to the success or otherwise of his talks, Welles issued no communiqués to the press. His reluctance to keep them informed gave rise to him being tagged 'Sumner the Silent'.

To those in the know, his peace mission represented little more than a stalling tactic by the President, who feared an imminent German military offensive. Roosevelt was of the opinion that the British and French would be better placed to withstand the onslaught if it could be deferred for even a week.

11

That Tuesday Max received a memo from Section B3. The message came from a colleague who was aware of his investigation. His colleague wrote, 'It will be remembered that some time ago there were reports in the press of a station broadcasting defeatist and pro-German propaganda in English which did not appear to have been operated from Germany. Information has been received from a very delicate source that Anna Wolkoff has some knowledge of this and according to her the station operates between 50 and 51 metres.' The New British Broadcasting Service was, of course, the station that transmitted within that wavelength. 'On Sunday last, 10 March,' the memo continued, 'a soldier in uniform was in Wolkoff's Russian Tea Rooms, Harrington Road. He was talking with Anna Wolkoff about this station and appeared to know something about its workings.'[65]

Previous assumptions that the station might be operated from within Britain had, however, been scotched by the BBC Monitoring Service, created to transcribe foreign radio broadcasts. 'Wireless bearings taken on the station,' the backroom boys at the BBC pronounced, 'are not inconsistent with a position in Germany – it is certainly to the east of this country.'

If Max's MI5 colleague acted on the erroneous memo from Section B3 about the New British Broadcasting Service, there was a danger that the eight-month investigation of Wolkoff and the Right Club might be jeopardized. To avert that disastrous prospect, Max wrote a note at the bottom of the memo, which he sent back to B3. 'Would you speak to me before actually doing anything?' the note read. He signed it, 'M'.[66]

12

Tyler had met Anna Wolkoff a second time, his Soviet connections offering motivation for his urge to worm his way into her affections. Soviet intelligence routinely monitored London's Russian émigrés and sought to penetrate any fascist organizations to which they belonged.[67] For the past five months at least, the Soviets had been trying to find out more about the goings-on at the Russian Tea Rooms and about Anna's father whom, they believed to be in contact with both the Nazi Party and British fascists.

As Irene could attest, Tyler had an effective method – quite unconscious, perhaps – of piquing the romantic interest of women. He would first entice his victim with charm and sophistication, not to speak of his facility for moulding himself to the company he was keeping, be it Jewish or anti-Semitic, fascist or anti-fascist. Then he would let their emotional fervour collide with an impenetrable wall of dignified reserve worthy of the romantic hero in a Hollywood movie, his detachment implying whatever the woman desired it to imply. All being well, the woman would come away feeling impressed, challenged or intrigued by him, those responses complicated by a dash of sympathy.

On the surface at least, he and Anna hailed from very dissimilar backgrounds, yet their divergent experiences yielded potent underlying affinities. Chief among those was their awkward position as exiles, not just geographical exiles but social exiles as well, thwarted people disbarred from the gilded lives that had once appeared their birthright, resentment being a conspicuous by-product. Added to that, both of them had a tendency to seek solace from their current circumstances through allusions to their influential connections to the upper echelons of society.

In spite of Tyler's growing rapport with Anna, he still referred to her as 'Miss Wolkoff'. Like her father, she was always keen to talk about Russia and hear about present-day life there. Tyler's previous posting equipped him to sate that curiosity.

And he now had another source of reliable, even more up-to-date Russian news.

On Monday of that week an American journalist, who had been in Moscow at the same time as Tyler, had briefly appeared in London. Tyler's acquaintance had just witnessed the most severe food shortage in the Soviet Union since the famine of 1933, yet Soviet censors had prohibited him from reporting on any facet of it. 'The Soviet leaders of today,' he declared, 'are doped by their own propaganda, and the Kremlin has brought the level of intelligence of all Russia down to its own.'

Such a caustic assessment of Stalin's regime would have appealed to Anna. She would also have basked in the news that emerged on Wednesday 13 March, 1940. The Soviets, unable to conquer the Finns, had signed a peace treaty with them.

Vehement in his anti-Communism and ostensibly unequivocal in his anti-Semitism, Tyler seemed a perfect match for Anna. His custom of erasing from his conversation any reference to other girlfriends would have sprinkled petrol on the emotional flames.

13

Last weekend the police had raided the homes of two of Anna's friends from the Tea Rooms – Molly Stanford and Anne van Lennep. These raids formed part of an investigation into the illegal correspondence with Margaret Bothamley in Berlin. Piles of Margaret's possessions, stored in Anne van Lennep's flat on Paradise Walk, had been confiscated.

Anna was fortunate that her own home hadn't been raided, because she too had been in touch with Margaret. The raids lent credence to a warning Anna was given next day by her brother, Alexander.

Recently he had been seconded from his job as Publicity Manager at Shell Oil to a post with the Ministry of Information, the government's propaganda arm. There, he was working for Major Sir Joseph Ball, an unscrupulous former MI5 officer,

Conservative Party fixer and confidant of Prime Minister Neville Chamberlain. Sir Joseph secretly ran *Truth*, the anti-Semitic, anti-Churchill, pro-fascist newspaper that had so impressed Anna. More to the point, he maintained strong links to the Security Service.

From a colleague at the Ministry of Information, Sir Joseph being the obvious culprit, Anna's brother had received a tip-off, which he passed on to her. It warned that she'd find herself behind bars if she persisted with her campaign of subversion. A couple of times previously, Alexander had relayed comparable warnings, but the tone of this latest message was more emphatic and menacing. In a barbed aside, he added that his recent application to become a British citizen wouldn't have been turned down had she taken the advice he had given her only a couple of months ago – advice that she should keep quiet about her anti-Semitic, pro-Nazi opinions and throw her support behind the British war effort.

Anna was incensed by what her brother told her. The British government's decision to turn down his application struck her as unjust because Alexander had, like her, spent most of his life in Britain. She felt that the decision smacked of inconsistency, too. Why should *he* be denied citizenship when it had already been granted to her?

Some measure of compensation for the annoyance caused by Alexander's letter was proffered by her embryonic relationship with Tyler. She and the American had met again, leading her to gush schoolgirlishly about it to her friend, Johnny Coast, who was poised to be sent abroad with his regiment. She told Johnny that she'd made 'a wonderful new contact' at the United States Embassy, an amalgam of intrigue and sexual attraction stoking her excitement.

14

For some years Max's line-up of agents had featured Lionel Hirst, a thirty-five-year-old London estate agent whose codename was 'Special Source'. He and his wife, whose parents were German, lived within spitting distance of Gunnersbury Park tube station. Justification for his codename was furnished by his successful penetration of four fascist groups – the Link, the English Array, the British Union and the Right Club. That said, Lionel hadn't played any comparably *special* role in the operation against Anna Wolkoff and friends.

His first noteworthy involvement came on Thursday 14 March, 1940 when he tipped off Max about the participation of Wolkoff in Molly Stanford's illegal correspondence with Margaret Bothamley. Lionel briefed Max on the letters, which he had seen. In common with previously intercepted fascist communications, Wolkoff and Stanford employed a rudimentary code to disguise the meaning of what they were writing about. 'Germany' was transmuted into 'father', 'England' into 'mother', 'Jews' into 'germs' and 'Jewish influence' into 'skin infection'.

Three days after Max had received the briefing from Lionel, those coded messages acquired even more threatening implications. On the 1 p.m. BBC radio news bulletin, there was an announcement that German bombers had attacked the British fleet as it lay at anchor in Scapa Flow on the north coast of Scotland. The official statement from the Admiralty conceded that more than a dozen aircraft had reached their target, yet only a single warship had been damaged. Fourteen people – seven civilians and seven naval personnel – had been wounded, though. And another civilian had been killed.

15

In the week since the warning letter from her brother, Anna's sense of outrage had been marinating. She now believed she was being victimized by the Judaeo–Bolshevik conspiracy about which Jock Ramsay so often preached.

Additional grounds for discontent were provided by the malign influence of the war. During the past seven days alone it had manifestly diminished the lives of her and her family. With the advent of meat rationing, Russian dishes such as *basturma*, *kotletki* and *shashlik* became a rare delicacy. Demand for offal – liver, kidneys, hearts, tripe, all excluded from rationing – had accordingly increased, raising the price of even these humble replacements. Anna's parents had also been confronted by the news that the local council would soon be levying an extra 14 per cent tax on both their flat and the Tea Rooms – money they could ill afford.

Finding an outlet for her exasperation, Anna devoted part of Monday 18 March, 1940 to writing a longish, deeply disingenuous letter to Sir Vernon Kell, who had sent a polite response to her previous communication. She told him about the warning she'd received from her brother. In what was probably another bid to wrongfoot MI5, she assured Sir Vernon that she had nothing to do with any form of subversion. Distorting the truth to portray herself as a wounded innocent and a true patriot, she even denied her involvement in politics. But she did admit to being an anti-Semite, her admission presaging a sustained rant that portrayed the Jews as a demonic breed committed to instigating a Communist revolution in Britain. Just because she was anti-Semitic didn't, she argued, mean she was a Nazi sympathizer. She concluded by requesting Sir Vernon's advice on how she should respond to the warning she had been given.

Her letter elicited a swift reaction, which suggested the authorities were treating her complaint seriously. Anna was invited to discuss her concerns at the War Office the following afternoon.

16

Nearly four weeks had passed since Tyler had applied for a transfer to Berlin. To date, there had been no response from Ambassador Alexander Kirk. Unless Tyler was prepared to resign from his job in the Code Room and lose access to confidential material, it looked as if he would have to remain in London.

Over the coming Easter weekend he'd already drawn up plans to escape to Bexhill-on-Sea. The town was some five miles along the coast from Hastings, which had childhood associations for him. During the interlude between his father's consular postings to Northern Ireland and Bermuda, Tyler and his parents spent a couple of years there.

His friend, June Huntley, had made a reservation for him at the hotel in Bexhill where she had been staying these last two weeks. Tyler was due to join her that Friday. Instead of braving the packed trains, he would be motoring down to the coast in the car he'd recently purchased. As a side-effect of petrol rationing, there were some bargains on the market. Tyler had been free to take advantage of the situation because he could procure a regular petrol allocation through the embassy.

He had acquired a Ford Model 68 Cabriolet – a snouty-looking two-seater sportscar. Even on the second-hand market, these commanded steep prices. It would have set him back in the region of a month's wages.

The car added playboy glamour to his trips out of town with Irene. On sunny days he could roll back its soft-top and let the wind blow through their hair.

London was at present under a dense layer of cloud. But Tyler had sufficient familiarity with the English climate's muddled syntax to realize that the weather might be entirely different come the Easter break.

Sauntering through the Index Bureau at the embassy during the lead-up to the holiday, Tyler had his customary chat with the young New Yorker who worked there. He told her about his forthcoming trip. With casual aplomb, he asked whether she'd care to join him. The two of them, he suggested, could go out sailing with some of his friends.

She thanked him very much before saying that she had unfortunately made other arrangements for Easter.

17

Dull, drizzly conditions prevailed on the afternoon of Anna's meeting at the War Office. Trafalgar Square, already disfigured by long, windowless redbrick air-raid shelters, cheek-by-jowl with the boarded-up fountains, never looked at its most appealing on days like that. In abrupt contrast to the weather were the cheerful spring fashions lately adorning the streets. Women had taken to wearing real snowdrops, daffodils or other flowers around the brims of those little straw hats that were all the rage. Brightly coloured frocks, gloves and shoes had become fashionable, too.

On either side of the broad expanse of Whitehall were the immense edifices that housed the main government departments, their ground-floor windows screened by sandbags, their aura of secrecy and gravitas enhanced by a thicket of radio masts. Anna soon entered the War Office, a smoke-tarnished, skull-capped Edwardian citadel. It had a cavernous, mosaic-floored interior and a domed stairwell punctuated by classical columns. Distinguishing the styles of these had been among Anna's few strengths as an architecture student.

She was, before long, face to face with Sir Vernon Kell, whose health had evidently deteriorated since she'd met him at Lord Cottenham's Dolphin Square flat. Today they were joined by a man of around her age. He was introduced as Captain King from the War Office.

18

The man who had just greeted Anna Wolkoff was not an Army officer. Nor did he work for the War Office, as he liked to pretend. Nor was his surname 'King', though he often used that alias. His real name was Max Knight.

Prior to Wolkoff's arrival, he and Sir Vernon had discussed how they should handle their meeting with her. They found themselves at once relinquishing some of the initiative, however, when she showered them with gratitude for agreeing to see her. Max was struck by what he regarded as her plentiful yet superficial charm. Loath to give her the impression they'd been over-eager to convene the meeting, he told her that, while Sir Vernon was perfectly willing to hear what she had to say, their primary goal was to identify the person who had warned her brother. That person had, he stressed, no doubt claimed quite wrongly to have access to official information. He observed with delight how this last remark appeared to take the wind out of Wolkoff's sails.

She replied that, naturally, she could appreciate the matter from their point of view, but he would have to pardon her for being more concerned with her own side of things.

Max asked Wolkoff whether she would be good enough to explain to him precisely what her brother had said to her.

Rather than give a direct response, she replied that Alexander had repeated to her almost the same warning she'd previously received from Prince Kyril Scherbatow, former private secretary to the late Sir Henri Deterding. Now there was a name that was bound to ring bells for Max. Alarm-bells. When Max had recently interrogated a fascist detainee at HM Prison Wandsworth, Deterding – Alexander Wolkoff's erstwhile boss at Shell Oil – had been named as one of the financial backers of the British Union. Deterding's veneration of Hitler, his anti-Semitic views and his fiscal support for the Nazi Party lent credibility to the assertion. Through his contacts with the chief Nazi ideologue and leader of the party's foreign affairs department, Alexander Wolkoff's one-time boss had even had a member of the German Foreign Office assigned to his staff. Since retiring from the post of Shell's Chief Executive in 1936, Deterding had moved to Germany where he had befriended Hermann Göring, one of Hitler's right-hand men. At Deterding's swastika-decked funeral – under a year before war broke out – a Nazi functionary had laid wreaths from Hitler and Göring, as well as delivering a brief tribute from the German leader.

Continuing her response to Max's question, Anna Wolkoff said that Prince Scherbatow had more than once warned her that her anti-Jewish activities would land her in trouble. The last of those warnings had, she said, come only the previous night when she'd chanced upon the Prince at a cocktail party. He had mentioned to her that a certain member of London's Russian colony had told him that she was attracting 'undesirable attention' on the part of the authorities. But the Prince had refused to divulge the name of his informant.

Wolkoff then regaled Max and Sir Vernon with a protracted digression, which entailed her trotting out the life stories of both Prince Scherbatow and Sir Henri Deterding. Ultimately, Max steered her back onto the subject of her brother, only she had little to add to what she'd written in her letter. She insisted that Alexander's motive for warning her was probably concern for his own position at the Ministry of Information, plus anxiety that her activities might prevent him from becoming a naturalized British citizen.

When Max responded to what she had said, he adopted a tactic formulated beforehand by Sir Vernon. He declared that it was absolute rubbish for anyone to suggest that expressing one's views on what he termed 'the Jewish question' could be the cause of holding up the naturalization of a relative. For Alexander to pass on information that had supposedly been given to him by a person with access to official sources was, Max added, much more likely to get him into trouble than her anti-Jewish activities.

Wolkoff reacted by brandishing the name of the former head of naval intelligence, whom she labelled as a close friend. She said he'd cautioned her three years ago about opposing the Jews.

Max suspected that Wolkoff had an ulterior motive for mentioning her friend: to remind him and Sir Vernon about the powerful people she knew. Her remarks contributing to his belief that she was a plausible, clever and cunning woman, Max enquired whether she had any idea who told Prince Scherbatow that she was under investigation.

After a moment's hesitation and apparent embarrassment at naming a friend – embarrassment that Max interpreted as wholly bogus – she said she thought Prince Scherbatow's informant might have been a man she knew from the Russian Tea Rooms. Yet she could provide no credible reasons why that man should have been the source of the tip-off.

Regaining the initiative, Wolkoff quizzed Max about the attitude of the authorities towards herself and other like-minded people. He was impressed by her skill at distorting the facts until she appeared quite harmless, if a trifle eccentric. She was, he concluded, a first-class liar. Had he not been so well informed about her activities, he felt sure that she would have made a complete fool of him.

Talk of the official attitude towards British-based fascists such as herself inspired Wolkoff to give Max and Sir Vernon a garbled account of the Special Branch raid on Anne van Lennep's flat. Of course Max knew all about the raid, which had been conducted as part of the investigation into van Lennep's illegal correspondence with Margaret Bothamley. Known to be an enthusiastic Right Club and British Union activist, van Lennep had also attracted MI5's attention through her close friendship with a German baroness who, right up until leaving England just before the declaration of war, had been strongly suspected of working as a Nazi spy.

During Wolkoff's account of the raid, she referred to a man who had accompanied the raiding party but wasn't wearing police uniform. Max couldn't help finding this amusing because he was the man in plain clothes.

For a brief interval the focus of Max's conversation with Wolkoff shifted back to the tip-off she had been given by her brother. She then asked Max about the legal position regarding the propaganda material being distributed by her and friends.

He told her that he thought their position was made abundantly clear in the Emergency Defence Regulations. She knew as well as he did, Max said, there was – within the limits of the law – complete freedom of speech and expression of opinion in Britain. The law, he pointed out, merely proscribed activities that were either criminal or which could be proved to be detrimental to the defence of the realm or prosecution of the war.

This offered the cue for Wolkoff to confess that she was 'an ardent stickyback performer'.

Pretending to find her admission endearingly comical, Max said that sort of thing didn't fall within his province. He went on to say that he thought the offence lay not in the stickybacks themselves but in the places where they were put up.

She replied by asking whether it was an offence to hold anti-Jewish views.

That was rubbish and she knew it was, he reiterated. He said she could think what she liked about Jewish firms such as Lyons and Montagu Burton. Were she to throw a brick through the window of one of their shops, she'd be punished for wilful damage, not for her views about Messrs Lyons and Burton.

His explanation prompted her to become conciliatory. She professed to understand the situation clearly now.

Max was quite convinced by the time she left the War Office that her purpose, both in writing to Sir Vernon and during the interview, had been to put up a smokescreen regarding the activities of her and her fascist associates. She had, he decided, also been trying to sniff out indications as to how the authorities were likely to deal with them. He hoped he hadn't given anything away.

When he settled down to produce a detailed report on his meeting with Wolkoff, he began by writing, 'It was a real pleasure to cross swords with someone of that calibre.'

Her activities echoed those of the treacherous, foreign-accented librarian in his friend Dennis Wheatley's new sequence of stories that were being serialized in the *Daily Sketch*. The librarian, who lived in London but whose true loyalties rested with Germany, handed out Union Jack bookmarks impregnated with bubonic plague. Shades of the poisonous anti-Semitic propaganda distributed by Wolkoff and friends.

19

After she had departed from the War Office, Anna mulled over her encounter with Sir Vernon Kell and the man she knew as Captain King. She came away with the impression that they'd persist with their investigation, so she set about trying to deter them.

On a sheet of her headed notepaper, she penned a curt letter to Captain King. Under the pretext that she had suddenly remembered something important she should have told him, she mentioned saying to her brother that she planned to submit a written complaint if she received any more such anonymous warnings. She omitted the name of the person to whom she intended to complain. But she assured Captain King that he would be able to guess whom she had in mind. The obvious candidate was the former head of naval intelligence, whose name she had dropped during her visit to the War Office.

20

Led to believe that Tyler mirrored not only her opposition to the war but also her pugnacious anti-Semitism, Anna had already confided in him about the Right Club. She arranged to take him to supper at Jock Ramsay's Onslow Square home. Tyler might prove a useful contact, she assured Jock.

Jock's house, which had been modernized some years before he and his wife purchased it, formed part of a tall Victorian terrace not far from the Russian Tea Rooms. It was even larger than it appeared from the street. Downstairs were a succession of reception rooms, not to mention a light and airy dining room.

Inevitably, conversation between Tyler, Anna and their host turned to politics. The dominant theme was hostility to Jews and Communists. Expert in moulding himself to suit the circumstances, Tyler soon found himself debating the fundamental causes of the war. He took issue with Captain Ramsay about the origins of the conflict.

Next morning Tyler and Anna returned to the scene of the dinner party. Following on from the previous night's discussion, Tyler told Ramsay that he had acquired a collection of documents dating back to 1938, documents setting out the political manoeuvring in advance of the war. Tyler asked the Captain whether he'd like to see them.

'Yes, I would.'

21

Max was beginning to enjoy the benefits of having two agents plugging away on the investigation of Wolkoff and her Right Club friends. Exactly as he had planned, Hélène de Munck's anti-Semitism and interest in the occult provided a bond with Wolkoff that he could exploit. Wolkoff had already given her a supply of stickybacks. Late on Wednesday afternoon, there was another significant moment in the nascent friendship between the two women. That moment occurred when Wolkoff visited Hélène's flat for tea.

Intrigued by Hélène's putative gifts as a clairvoyant, Wolkoff arranged to sample them. For the ensuing demonstration, Hélène didn't use a crystal ball. As she explained to Max, she copied a technique sometimes employed by fortune-tellers. Her method involved staring at a piece of silver immersed in water. Wolkoff was very taken by the results.

Once the session had been completed, Wolkoff started bragging about having agents all over the place, agents who were working against the Jews in England and America. She told Hélène that she wasn't an opponent of the British. 'To hate the Jews is not to be pro-German,' she said. 'I admire Hitler, but I want the English to do their own washing.' She proceeded to ask whether Hélène was likely to be travelling to Belgium to see her family.

Hélène said that was quite possible, though no specific date for the trip had been fixed.

In response Wolkoff asked her to get in touch as soon as everything was confirmed. Wolkoff wanted Hélène to meet someone in Belgium – someone named Guy Miermans – and collect what was described as an important anti-Semitic document. Since the authorities were, Wolkoff told her, unlikely to allow this to be brought into Britain by conventional means, Hélène would have to smuggle it through Customs.

Top left (1): Sold as part of Anna Wolkoff's spring 1938 collection, this black-and-white crêpe dress features Mongolian-style sleeves, matching gloves and a Shantung Baku hat.

Top right (2): A 1937 portrait of Captain Archibald Maule Ramsay, taken at Bassano Ltd, a prestigious West End photographic studio.

Bottom right (3): Anna Wolkoff, photographed for her British Certificate of Identity, issued in January 1931.

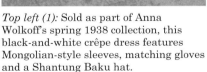

Top (4): The front of Anna Wolkoff's shop, located at 37 Conduit Street in the West End of London.

Bottom (5): Film still from unused footage for a *March of Time* newsreel, in which Anna Wolkoff carries out a dress-fitting at her shop, *c.* 1937.

Top (6): Tatyana 'Tanya' Alexandrovna Ilovaiskaya *(left)*, pictured with Donald H. Nichols *(middle)* and Valentina 'Valya' Scott *(right)*, *c.* 1939.

Centre left (7): Tyler Kent's German teacher, Mrs 'Truda' Ganghadaran, *c.* 1939.

Bottom right (8): Portrait drawing of Tyler G. Kent, September 1940.

Left (9): Drawing of an outfit from Anna Wolkoff's summer 1937 collection. The outfit comprised a white organdie blouse worn beneath a black silk suit with a pattern of white, red, green and blue stripes, composed of little flower designs.

Right (10): Drawing of a white turban, available from Anna Wolkoff's shop. The turban – worn with earrings created by the Parisian designer, Dilkusha – was fastened by a crescent-shaped, pearl-embellished clip.

Above (11): Tatyana 'Tanya' Alexandrovna Ilovaiskaya *(middle right)* posing with Donald H. Nichols *(middle left)*, Valentina 'Valya' Scott *(left)* and Sylvester A. Huntowski *(right)*. Note the shadow of the photographer's head – probably Tyler Kent's – on Valya's skirt.

Left (12): Promoted as an 'Aphrodite dress', this classical Greek-inspired evening gown was part of Anna Wolkoff's summer 1936 collection. Both the dress and its accompanying scarf were made from white shirred chiffon.

Above (13): A British Union member sells a copy of the party's newspaper in front of Victoria Station, 1938.

THE RIGHT CLUB

Wardens	£25 and	£10-10-0 p.a.
Stewards	£5 and	£5 p.a.
Yeomen	£1-1-0 and	£1-1-0 p.a.
Keepers	10/6 and	10/6 p.a.
Freemen	2/6 and	2/6 p.a.

Above left (14): An ivory damask evening gown designed by Anna Wolkoff. Its bodice is edged with pleated scarlet chiffon, which also sheaths the straps and forms a cascading train.

Above right (15): Card listing the different levels of Right Club membership and the annual cost of each of them.

Above (16): Northerly view across the central quadrangle of Dolphin Square. The middle block on the righthand side is Hood House, where Max Knight had a flat on the far corner of the sixth-floor.

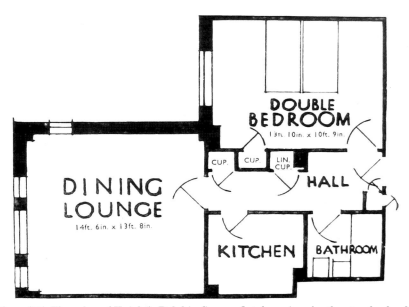

Above (17): Floorplan of Knight's Dolphin Square flat, luxurious by the standards of that period. It came with a pastel-toned bathroom suite, furniture from Maple & Co, central heating, a 'four-programme radio', as well as a kitchen that included fitted storage cabinets, coloured linoleum and an upmarket fridge and cooker.

SOHO RACKET

Recommended by the CRIME BOOK SOCIETY

by GRIERSON DICKSON

DENNIS WHEATLEY writes:
"Tremendous pace from start to finish. I predict a big name for Grierson Dickson as a crime book author" "One of the most brilliant and effective openings that we have seen in any thriller"—*Glasgow Herald*

Top (18): One of a series of portraits of Max Knight, taken in 1934 by the renowned British photographer, Howard Coster.

Bottom left (19): MI5's Thames House headquarters led off the huge seventh-floor foyer, depicted in this drawing, 1930.

Bottom right (20): Advertisement for the 1935 debut novel by Max Knight's friend and colleague, Jimmy Dickson, who wrote under the name of Grierson Dickson.

Above (21): Princess Mira Dimitri, photographed by Norman Parkinson for the front cover of *The Sketch*, a popular British high society magazine.

Top (22): Fay Taylour driving an MG Midget at a London racetrack, August 1936.

Bottom (23): These Russian tea rooms at 31 Carnaby Street in Soho – pictured around 1929–30 – once offered an alternative to the Wolkoffs' sinister establishment.

Above (24): Corner of the Central Court at the Cumberland Hotel.

Above (25): Still from a newsreel showing Ambassador Joseph P. Kennedy arriving at the US Embassy in Grosvenor Square, August 1938.

Right (26): Bill Younger striking a jokey pose in the guise of his crime-writing alter ego, William Mole, c. 1957.

Above left (27): Max Knight entertains one of his menagerie, *c.* 1962.

Above right (28): Margaret Bothamley's German identity card, 1943.

Left (29): Ministry of Information safety poster, 1939–40.

Top (30): June Huntley posing with Tyler Kent's crashed car, March 1940.

Above left (31): Joan Miller, the MI5 secretary who assisted Max Knight with his investigation.

Above right (32): Colonel Francisco Marigliano, Duke del Monte.

Above (33): Police mugshots of Tyler Kent, Sunday 27 May, 1940.

Left (34): Freshly disembarked in America on Tuesday 4 December, 1945, Tyler Kent and his mother are escorted through the crowd by two former New York Police Department detectives.

MAXWELL KNIGHT

O.B.E., F.L.S.

✦

Taming and Handling Animals

✦

Top and middle left (35 & 36): Max Knight pictured with Goo, the rescued bird that became the subject of his 1955 book, *A Cuckoo in the House*. Having been hand-reared and trained to hunt for its own food, Goo was released back into the wild.

Top right (37): Clara Kent, *c.* 1975.

Left (38): The dustjacket of one of Max Knight's many post-war books on natural history.

Above right (39): Max Knight's friend and MI5 colleague, Jimmy Dickson, posing for a publicity photo to promote *Murder By Numbers*, his pioneering 1957 study of serial killing.

22

By arrangement with Tyler, Captain Ramsay called at his flat. Tyler characterized Ramsay as a fine specimen of an English gentleman – a backhanded compliment in view of Tyler's low opinion of England and the English. 'Not too heavy on the intellect,' was his condescending judgement.

While Ramsay was at the Gloucester Place flat, Tyler did something to ingratiate himself with Anna and ease his passage into the Right Club. He showed Ramsay where he kept the paperwork stolen from the US Embassy. In his role as a Soviet agent infiltrating the Right Club, there was, however, nothing to be gained by exposing more than a carefully vetted selection of documents.

'You can come in and look at them if you like when it suits you,' Tyler said. He gave his visitor a preview of some of the material, too.

Exhibiting a preposterous level of trust in someone he had just met, he then explained to Ramsay how to get into the flat. No keys were required because the front door was kept on the latch and the door to his flat could be locked from the inside only.

He added that Ramsay was welcome to store anything he wanted there. It was an offer that demonstrated his awareness that Ramsay might have things he didn't wish the police to find if they raided the house in Onslow Square.

23

Tyler posted a brief letter to Captain Ramsay shortly afterwards. With the letter, he sent a press cutting about the growing popularity of *The Protocols of the Elders of Zion*, the anti-Semitic conspiracy tract whose contents Anna treated as unimpeachable fact. In a gesture of political solidarity, Ramsay had given Tyler a copy.

On Thursday 21 March, 1940 – the day before he had arranged to travel down to Bexhill – Tyler also wrote to Anna. Knowing that she was a smoker and, presumably, that she was broke as well, he'd pledged to get her some cigarettes. Like other US Embassy staff, Tyler had access to Chesterfields, a specially imported brand. He wrote:

> Dear Miss Wolkoff (or Anna?),
>
> I am enclosing a few Chesterfields which I promised you. It's not very much but when our next shipment comes in, I hope very soon, I shall be more generous.
>
> I am driving down to the south coast early tomorrow morning for the Easter holidays and expect to be back in London on Tuesday next at which time I hope to see you and make the acquaintance of more of your interesting friends.

To that, he tacked on a couple of sentences in Russian, which gave the letter a confiding tone. He signed it 'Anatoly Vasilievich', a pseudonym borrowed from the prominent anti-Communist, Anatoly Vasilievich Baikaloff, one of Eugène Sabline's closest London-based friends.[68] Tyler's choice of nom de plume indicated that he was Anna's political ally. It also contained an oblique reference to his own ideological shift from left to right as Baikaloff had, like him, once been a believer in Communism. Rather than being an in-joke with Anna, the pseudonym was perhaps conceived as Tyler's own private joke, a self-admiring token of what he looked upon as his intellectual superiority.

24

Marjorie had been round to see Anna Wolkoff at the Roland Gardens flat. During her visit, Max's agent heard about the interview with Captain King. There was no sign that Marjorie knew the name in question was an alias of Max. She remarked that Wolkoff seemed to think the trip to the War Office had been rather successful.

But Marjorie's report didn't stop there. She added that she'd bumped into Wolkoff again later that day. Wolkoff had been with Mrs Ramsay at the Onslow Square house. There, Mrs Ramsay talked about Right Club contacts in the higher reaches of the British Army. Her contacts predicted that Britain would form an alliance with Germany and fight against Russia.

The ensuing discussion between the guests had, according to Marjorie, gravitated towards conjecture about the number of Jews working in the Ministries of Supply and Information. Soon afterwards Mrs Ramsay's husband arrived home. He and Wolkoff exited the room for a private debriefing about her interview at the War Office.

In the meantime Mrs Ramsay got into conversation with Marjorie. Mrs Ramsay mentioned that she and her husband were poised to head up to their castle in Scotland. The two women debated ways in which letters between there and London could be exchanged without being intercepted. Eventually they agreed that Marjorie should write to Mrs Ramsay at Kelly Castle, telling her 'how interesting things were in England'. This would signal that a letter, addressed to 'Mrs R. Mackie', would be waiting for Mrs Ramsay at Dundee Post Office.

When Captain Ramsay concluded his tête-à-tête with Wolkoff, he raised the possibility of Marjorie offering her services to MI5. He also made it clear that he rated her and Wolkoff as two of his best aides-de-camp. Having praised Marjorie's usefulness to the Right Club, he stressed that she mustn't do anything rash, which might endanger her position within the Military Censorship Department.

25

The weather wasn't yet warm enough to justify peeling back the roof of Tyler's soft-top sportscar when he set out for Bexhill on Friday 22 March, 1940. Due to that weekend's special Easter holiday petrol allowance which swelled people's last reserves of fuel, the principal southbound road had become surprisingly crowded. Packs of cyclists were barrelling towards the coast alongside the motor vehicles.

As he drove south, where the weather became overcast, Tyler added to his record of mishaps behind the wheel by crashing his sportscar. He damaged the radiator grille, snapped the front bumper and left one of the freestanding headlamps dangling like an eyeball dislodged from its socket. Yet he was still able to join the traffic pouring into Bexhill, where many of the hotels and guesthouses displayed 'No Vacancies' signs and the pavements were swarming with holidaymakers – masses of servicemen and their girlfriends, to say nothing of the predictable families with children. In a reflection of the national mood, the majority of the women were wearing muted-looking dresses.

Pretty soon Tyler found his way to the place where he would be spending the weekend with June Huntley. The Digby House Hotel turned out to be a quiet residential establishment occupying a four-storey Victorian terraced house just down the street from the Home of Rest for Ladies of Reduced Circumstances.

Assuredly not a lady of reduced circumstances, the Londoner who ran the hotel was there to greet Tyler. She had him complete a registration form that asked for his name, nationality and identity card number.

His room abutted June's. The whole place was a comedown after some of the swanky establishments he'd patronized, such as the vast St Gellert in Budapest, which had an outdoor swimming-pool that had a wave-making machine and a poolside dance-band.

With his smart clothes, soft Southern drawl and gentlemanly manner, Tyler scored a hit with the proprietress of the Digby House Hotel and her diminished contingent of staff. More than could be said for June, who had affronted the woman's rigid sense of propriety by getting drunk in her room with male friends.

June had brought along her cat, a sturdy ginger creature. He shared her room, which featured a large bay window with a prized ocean view, or at least a sliver of an ocean view. To the left was the Hotel Metropole, never likely to be confused with its racy Moscow namesake. Beside it was an even larger building, whose streamlined white concrete walls and balconies would not have appeared out of place on some American beachfront. Through the adjoining gap, Tyler and June could see the English Channel. But the visibility, impaired by fitful drizzle, wasn't good enough for them to make out France, where the Allied armies were still awaiting the expected German assault.

That evening June took Tyler across the road to the Hotel Metropole. Requisitioned for use as RAF accommodation, it had been stripped of carpets and other relics of its Edwardian heyday. Their absence exaggerated the flavour of dilapidation, conjured by bare floorboards and a broken lift.

June introduced Tyler to Peter Humphreys, a trainee RAF sergeant garrisoned there. Her friend was in his late teens. He had deepset eyes, crinkly hair and a physique that led people to refer to him as 'Hunk'. Tyler impressed Hunk with his charm, his studied indolence, his plentiful supply of cash and his boast that he spoke seven languages.

Together with another RAF sergeant, Hunk had become June's drinking partner. In an improbable series of coincidences, Hunk knew her husband and she had known Hunk's father, Cecil Humphreys, when she was living in America. His father had been a supporting actor in numerous films, the latest of which was *Wuthering Heights*, starring Laurence Olivier.

Next day the weather exhibited signs of improvement, sunshine interspersing light showers. Buses laden with holidaymakers kept on rolling through the streets. Unbroken lines of parked cars fringed the road down to the marina.

As planned, Tyler set out for the beach at the western edge of town. Overlooked by cliff-top houses was a solitary shed that functioned as clubhouse for Bexhill's tiny band of yachting enthusiasts. Numbered among those were the friends Tyler had mentioned to his young colleague at the US Embassy.

From the beach, he and his companions had to slide their wooden dinghy into the water, across which small motorized fishing boats frequently puttered. Once the dinghy had been launched it could exploit the southwesterly breeze. There was just enough wind to fill the dinghy's sail and send it skating across the grey water.

Ever since boyhood Tyler had enjoyed sailing. He took Hunk out with him in the boat, where he could practise tips from the yachting manual he had left in Moscow with so many of his books. That weekend he spent a substantial portion of each day bobbing around off the Sussex coast.

When Tyler and friends were ready to call it a day, they just had to navigate their boat as near to the beach as possible and then wade ashore. By hitching her up to the cable-winch next to the clubhouse, they could haul her up the beach.

Back on dry land, Tyler and June went drinking with Hunk on Saturday evening. In this instance they shunned the bar at the Metropole. Nor did they venture into the local pubs, which were packed with holidaymakers. Instead, they tried one of the town's members-only clubs.

Hunk brought with him the other RAF sergeant from June's heavy-drinking circle. Known to them as 'Smithy', their friend was Wilfrid Duncan Smith, a twenty-six-year-old trainee pilot with dark, retreating hair. He'd been the manager of a tea plantation in India. More recently, he had worked as a car salesman. That night he was accompanied by a woman whom he presented as his wife, though that seems to have been no more than a convention-appeasing fiction. Her attendance didn't moderate his alcohol consumption.[69]

Saturday evening's get-together proved such a success that Tyler and June repeated the arrangement at a different club next day when Tyler turned twenty-nine. Birthday or no birthday, throughout the weekend he went halves with June on the cost of round after round of beer and whisky.

Despite being in the company of two British servicemen, the tenor of much of his conversation was critical of Britain. He said the country shouldn't wield so much influence. And he argued that it ought to become a republic like America.

Hearing about Tyler's earlier mishap with his sportscar, Smithy expressed interest in purchasing the damaged vehicle. They arranged to meet in London to discuss the sale.

26

Anna had been talking to Francis Hemming's wife. Initially part of the wave of evacuees fleeing London, Mrs Hemming had since returned to the capital. She loved gossip, which she referred to as 'chit', abbreviated from chitchat. She also had a penchant for deploying what were, outside her coterie, generally regarded as shocking turns of phrase. At any moment she could spice up a bland conversation with a reference to 'an amusing fuck' she'd experienced. But she had more significant things to discuss with Anna.

She'd asked whether Anna would be prepared to teach German – the language of Britain's potential occupiers – to Francis. Anna had then arranged to have Francis round for regular lessons at the Roland Gardens flat.

Unable to resist flaunting her connections, she told Marjorie that Francis had, through his job in the Cabinet Office, given her the lowdown on a recent scandal. This focused on the Ministry of Supply, the government department entrusted with equipping the British armed forces.

Items had appeared in the newspapers about certain employees at the ministry who were alleged to have demanded bribes to influence the provision of lucrative contracts. Scotland Yard was currently undertaking an inquiry into those allegations, which had been the subject of a parliamentary debate as well. Amidst much publicity, three people had been dismissed from their jobs at the ministry. Two of them, as last Wednesday evening's gleeful talk on the New British Broadcasting Service had highlighted, bore Jewish surnames guaranteed to incite another of Anna's fierce monologues.

27

Tyler was supposed to remain in Bexhill until next Tuesday. In a fit of pique, triggered perhaps by one of his periodic arguments with June, he checked out of his hotel at 6.30 a.m.

on Monday 25 March, 1940.[70] Tellingly, June wasn't there to see him off.

In the days after his return to the capital, where people had started referring contemptuously to 'the Phoney War' being waged by their government, Tyler met up with Smithy, the trainee pilot intent on purchasing his sportscar. He and Smithy, an expert car-mechanic, then tied up the sale.

Around that time, Tyler received a parcel containing two books. It came with a note from Captain Ramsay, thanking Tyler for the press cutting about *The Protocols of the Elders of Zion*.

'I am so glad the *Protocols* are finding readers,' Ramsay wrote, enclosing a couple more copies.

28

To reinforce Wolkoff's confidence in Marjorie and Hélène, Max instigated a clever ploy. His scheme was only practicable because he'd been the beneficiary of a giant stroke of luck – something he wasn't too proud to acknowledge.

Impressed by Hélène's apparent occult gifts, Wolkoff presented her with a sample of someone else's handwriting and asked her for a character-assessment of whoever had written it. Max's good fortune lay in the discovery that the handwriting didn't belong to a stranger. It belonged to Marjorie, about whom he and his colleagues already had biographical details. Scraps of these could be fed to Hélène who, in accordance with Max's preferred working methods, remained unaware that Marjorie was also one of his agents.

Purportedly relying on nothing more than close scrutiny of the handwriting sample, Hélène was able to impart an uncannily perceptive analysis of the author's character. So perceptive were her insights that they functioned as a convincing endorsement of her otherworldly powers. Max now had the opportunity to manipulate Wolkoff through her belief in what Hélène said.

29

At 7.15 p.m. on Thursday 28 March, 1940, Radio Bremen broadcast another of William Joyce's talks. It offered Anna a shiver of recognition. Within Joyce's broadcast, which attacked the British government, was some gossip that appeared to have been culled from the message she had sent him last month via Jean Nieuwenhuys, her contact at the Belgian Embassy. The gossip, quoted in an obvious attempt to stoke class antagonism, centred on the home village of her friend, Muriel Whinfield, who had been at the recent British Union luncheon.

'Girls from well-to-do families – who are being trained in Alton, Hampshire – came along like a host of invading Amazons,' Joyce said. 'They insisted on taking possession of one bedroom and sitting-room each, even if such accommodation could only be obtained at the cost of crowding a whole family and their goods into the kitchen. These charming young locusts have made a deplorable impression on the population.'

30

Tyler used a pencil to take down the phone number. 'KEN 7714.' He wrote it on the back of an unused Telegraph Form from the Code Room. The number belonged to Anna and family. She had invited him to her parents' flat, a sure sign that she regarded him as a serious suitor. Embracing the nom de plume featured in his letter to her, she started calling him Anatoly – proof of their tightening bond.

By the side of her phone number, Tyler penned abbreviated instructions on how to get to Roland Gardens. He was told to catch the no. 30 bus. Its route took it close to where he lived. The nearest stop was more or less in front of a shop advertising itself as a 'Bust Support Specialist'. Tyler also happened to be quite adept in that field.

His bus headed onto Oxford Street, passed the Cumberland Hotel and then worked its way through Knightsbridge and South Kensington. He just had to wait until the first stop beyond the Christian Science Reading Room before stepping off the vehicle and completing his journey with a brief walk down Roland Gardens.

Surrounded by the paintings and other mementoes of Russia that decorated the Wolkoffs' flat, Tyler re-encountered Anna's father. Now was his opportunity to win her family's blessing as well as strengthening his relationship with Anna. So he tried to impress them by conveying the notion that he had worked in Moscow not as a mere Code Clerk but as a Junior Secretary – a fully fledged diplomat, this self-awarded promotion also leavening the embarrassment he felt about his lowly status.

Anna's brother, Alexander, who didn't live far away yet seldom visited, was among the family members present. Somewhat older than her, Alexander had a difficult relationship with their father, the tension between them exacerbated by Alexander's reluctance to assist their harassed and overworked mother by laying the table or washing up. Politics yielded another recurrent point of discord. In contrast to his parents and siblings, Alexander wasn't prepared to support the fascist cause.

But Tyler hit it off with him, the mechanism of conversation lubricated by overlapping interests. Like Anna and their father, Alexander shared Tyler's fascination with Russia, where Anna now believed that Soviet communism would, even without German intervention, end up mutating into National Socialism.

Tyler had lately acquired another fount of news about present-day events in the Wolkoffs' homeland. At a concert last month he had been introduced to a middle-aged Russian émigré who worked at the Wellcome Medical and Historical Museum.[71] He'd since been round to dinner with her and her unscrupulous brother, who had just landed a job with the BBC Monitoring Service. The job entailed supervising the staff responsible for transcribing and recording radio programmes broadcast within the Soviet Union and other countries.

Russia wasn't the only interest Tyler shared with Alexander. They shared an enthusiasm for the cinema, too. Anna's brother could speak from personal experience of the film industry, albeit not the glamorous end of the business. He was now employed by the Ministry of Information's Films Division, which supervised the production and distribution of short propaganda films.

Getting to know Anna and family didn't just bring Tyler the opportunity to talk about movies and reminisce about Russia. It also brought a significant practical benefit. Though he had disposed of his sportscar, Tyler still needed access to a car if he wanted to continue driving Irene on amorous daytrips. Purchasing one of the vehicles advertised in the evening newspapers supplied by his landlady was the self-evident solution. But Anna held the key to a much simpler and less risky answer to Tyler's problem. She sold him her two-seater Morris convertible. The deal made perfect sense. As things stood, her car wasn't doing her much good because she couldn't afford to tax or service it. Petrol was, in any case, becoming impossible to purchase for ordinary citizens like her. This way she would still be able to use the car because Tyler was open to the idea of letting her borrow it.

31

By arrangement with both Anna and Jock, Marjorie had already moved out of her flat in Notting Hill Gate and rented somewhere with sufficient space for private meetings of as many as a couple of dozen Right Club activists. Her flat could also be used for staging interviews with prospective members.

More or less equidistant between the Wolkoffs' home and the Russian Tea Rooms, Marjorie's new digs were at 24 Manson Mews. Anna paid her a call on the afternoon of Friday 5 April, 1940. Even if she walked at a somnambulant pace, Anna could get there from Roland Gardens in less than ten minutes, short enough to elude a sequence of downpours of sufficient ferocity to leave blossom spattered across the pavement.

Anna entered Manson Mews through a grand arched gate, but the street itself was narrow and cobbled, with a series of unexceptional little houses on either side. She made for the entrance to no. 24. Contrary to what had been decided during an earlier meeting at the Tea Rooms, none of Marjorie's guests bothered with the agreed password. This was 'Freeman', the alias by which the Right Club women referred to their leader, who sometimes tried to disguise himself on the telephone by introducing himself as 'Mr Freeman'.

The door to no. 24 led up to a three-room flat immediately above a row of garages. Joining Anna at the party, held in a large bed-sitting room, which Marjorie called 'the parlour', were more than twenty other Right Club members and their friends.

Molly Stanford – one of the Tea Rooms clique – was among those enjoying a genteel afternoon tea. So too was Richard 'Jock' Houston, a tough-looking thirty-six year old with close-set eyes and dark, corrugated hair. He had been at a previous Right Club meeting, staged at Apsley House on Hyde Park Corner, home of the 5th Duke of Wellington, who had acted as chairman. Jock Houston was also familiar from those Nordic League gatherings at the Druids' Hall, where he had some-times been in the audience and sometimes been on stage.

Fast-talking and combative, he possessed a strange hybrid cockney-Glaswegian accent. Though he and Anna disagreed about the British Union, which he had grown to despise, there were plenty of things about which they could agree, not least their admiration for the Führer, their belief in the Judaeo–Bolshevik conspiracy and their opposition to the war. Slaughter, starvation and the arrival of a National Socialist regime would, Jock maintained, be the war's ultimate consequences.

With him that afternoon was his awestruck middle-class girlfriend, Mollie Hiscox, whom he liked to address as 'my precious'. Seven years his junior, she was a diminutive, plain-looking, sandy-haired woman, given to continual refer-ences to 'my beloved Führer' and to declarations such as 'We were born in the wrong country'. Right up to the previous summer she had augmented her ample inherited income by organizing tour parties to Nazi Germany – what she glibly described as 'jolly private parties of young people'. Among her German contacts was a former British Union member who worked for Heinrich Hoffmann's Munich-based Foreign Press Office, which had supplied the Nordic League with Nazi propaganda.

Part of the crowd clustered in the parlour alongside her and Anna was Fay Taylour, a political protégée of Anna's friend, Bertie Mills. Fay had been in Germany until just a week before war was declared. Besides being a member of the British Union, indicated by the brooch she wore and by the half-dozen copies of *Action* that she carried round with her, she'd belonged to the Right Club for about six weeks. She had enrolled in tandem with a shamelessly pro-Nazi friend of hers, whose job as a civil servant rendered him a potentially fruitful contact.

Like Anna, Fay was unmarried and in her late thirties. Unlike Anna, though, she had the benefit of a private income. Another conspicuous dissimilarity between the two women lay in the fact that everyone seemed to regard Fay as being attractive – what men dubbed 'a very presentable girl'. Dark-eyed and plump-cheeked, she had a sinewy physique and short auburn hair, invariably concealed beneath a hat.

Guided by looks alone, one would never have believed that she was a famous motor-racing driver and speedway rider who had broken the lap speed record in front of 30,000 people at Wembley Stadium. 'Flying Fay', the press called her. She could tell Anna and the others innumerable anecdotes from her past, her effectiveness as a storyteller curtailed by her tendency to digress, her use of plummy expressions such as 'dash it!' underlining her well-heeled background. Moreover, she could regale Anna and company with stories about her time in Germany, where she had got to know several Nazi officials and made a broadcast from the same Berlin propaganda station as William Joyce. Yet one could not always decipher what she was saying.

Other guests with whom Anna could mingle included Thomas Hosey, a coarse, rather conceited man who worked in the motor trade. He was a friend of Jock Ramsay as well as being a regular at the Tea Rooms and meetings of the Nordic League.

During that afternoon's party, he signed a Right Club enrolment form and paid for the lowest level of membership.

He made no secret of his plans to assist the probable Nazi invasion by letting German parachutists help themselves to his fleet of vehicles. 'It would be too bad, wouldn't it, if I happened to lose the keys to the garage one night and someone found them ...'

Also in the parlour that afternoon was a tall, dark, anglicized German in his early twenties, who aspired to become an actor.[72] Urbane though he was, he got into a disagreement about Sir Oswald Mosley with another of Anna's companions. Refuting the suggestion that Mosley had suitable credentials to become Britain's dictator, the young German reeled off a list of disqualifying factors.

The party was well advanced when a door opened and Jock Ramsay stepped into the room. As if Marjorie were a component in some expensive tinplate toy, powered by an ingenious clockwork mechanism, his arrival caused her to leap from her chair and call out, 'The Leader!'

32

Probably fulfilling the role of Anna's escort, Tyler had been invited to the Holborn, a famous restaurant so named because it loomed over the junction between High Holborn and Kingsway. The building was a huge, richly ornamented Victorian affair. From the enclosed yard at the back, where Tyler could leave his car, the side entrance offered the most convenient access to its warren of anterooms, staircases and ceramic-tiled corridors. These linked its smoking room, buffet, oyster bar, restaurants and function rooms.

Tyler's host was Sir Oswald Mosley who had good manners, immense charm and a surfeit of self-confidence. Among the other guests, already sitting at the table, was Anna's friend, Bertie Mills, whom Tyler hadn't previously met. But the circumstances of their first encounter weren't propitious. Mills was asked to relinquish his seat for Tyler. Like as not, the request came from the gloating Anna, keen for her beloved Tyler to sit beside her. With grudging courtesy, Bertie let Tyler take his seat.

33

Early on the morning of Tuesday 9 April, 1940, the BBC Home Service announced that the Germans had invaded Norway and Denmark. Not that the BBC was Anna's only source of up-to-date news. She was still listening to the Nazi propaganda broadcasts by William Joyce and others, from which she took notes on the latest developments, alert for discrepancies between the German and British bulletins.

One certainly noticed glaring differences in how the occupation of Norway and Denmark was being portrayed. 'The German Army has taken over the armed protection of these countries,' the 9.45 a.m. broadcast by Radio Deutschlander began. 'For this purpose, this morning strong German forces of all units of the German Army have moved into these countries ...'

However the Nazis' motives were interpreted, the emerging news from Scandinavia marked the end of the Phoney War and the beginning of what Tyler's countrymen would call the shooting war. News of the German assault coincided with a message Anna received from her friend, Ronnie Graham, who was anxious to introduce her to one of his friends.

Responding to Ronnie's message, she met him around eleven that morning in the Russian Tea Rooms, where business was so lacklustre that the place was barely ticking over. These days her father had been forced to take on the job of making yoghurt and delivering jars of it to customers, a chore that he and his wife could once afford to delegate to an errand boy.

When Anna arrived at her parents' restaurant, Ronnie introduced her to a man named Hughes. James McGuirk Hughes. Ronnie's friend, who was a few years older than Anna, had a bald, cannonball head and suet-pudding features, on which a small moustache floated. He did have a disarming smile, though.

Along with the two men, Anna sampled the refreshments on offer and exchanged anti-Semitic small talk. But Ronnie couldn't hang around because he had a train to catch. While he went up to the counter to pay their bill, Anna was left alone with Hughes, who said, 'Would you be prepared to do anything to help in the cause of anti-Semitism?'

She replied that she'd be willing to do *anything* to harm the Jews.

'Have you ever sent anything to the Continent through a diplomatic bag?'

Anna's response was cagey: 'Well, if it's very important I might be able to get it sent.'

Without delay Hughes pulled a sealed envelope from his pocket and handed it to her.

34

The envelope was addressed to William Joyce. For Anna, the name didn't just carry associations with broadcasts from Germany. It carried more personal meaning. She and Joyce shared a great many friends. Until he had decamped to Berlin, he used to be a near neighbour of one of her father's Russian chums – a fellow Right Club member.[73] Like her, Joyce had been at Caxton Hall for the meeting of the Nordic League last spring. And he had spoken at the League's previous meetings. Before Christmas she had – via Jean Nieuwenhuys, her contact at the Belgian Embassy – sent a letter to him about the Right Club.

Written on the envelope Hughes had just handed Anna were the words, 'Rundfunkhaus, Berlin', Germany's equivalent to BBC headquarters. Smuggling the letter out of Britain wouldn't be easy. Not unless she ignored her father's warning that she shouldn't have anything more to do with Jean Nieuwenhuys, who provided her usual route for letters to the Continent.

Anna asked Hughes what was inside the envelope.

'Oh, some good anti-Jewish stuff, I believe. Can you send it?'

Ronnie was still at the counter, his back to her. Anna didn't want him to see the envelope, so she had to make a swift decision before he turned round and came back to their table. She slipped the letter into her bag. Then she and Hughes accompanied Ronnie to the station.

In the afternoon she went round to Onslow Square to see Jock Ramsay. Though she told him about meeting Hughes, she didn't mention the envelope. Hughes had earlier disclosed that it contained a letter from a friend of Joyce.

Jock cautioned Anna against Hughes. She heard from Jock that Hughes used three aliases and should not be trusted.

35

Precisely as they had been during the early days of the war, the streets that evening were eerily quiet, contributing to the general unease. Most people seemed to want to stay at home and listen to the radio in the hope of picking up more news on what was unfolding in Norway and Denmark. Flouting the stay-at-home trend, Anna went back to the Tea Rooms.

Her father was there, talking to Hélène. Suddenly he came over to Anna and told her that Hélène had made a casual reference to having a friend at the Romanian Embassy.

Curiosity whetted, Anna permitted her father to usher her over to Hélène. The two women had a fleeting conversation before Anna asked Hélène about the Romanian. Anna wanted to know whether he was in a position to get a letter to Germany.

Hélène said she thought that might be possible. She added that he had, after all, sometimes been kind enough to forward the letters she'd written to her uncle who lived in Romania.

'Why didn't you tell me this before?' Anna said. Disregarding Jock Ramsay's earlier advice, she reached into her bag and pulled out the letter addressed to 'Herr W. B. Joyce'.

Hélène explained that her friend at the Romanian Embassy

was due to leave the country within the next forty-eight hours, so they would be working against the clock.

But Anna was reluctant to hand over the letter. Not until she had met Hélène's friend.

Such an arrangement was, Hélène insisted, absolutely out of the question. She said she couldn't very well ask her friend to compromise himself by meeting a complete stranger. He'd be much more likely to accept the letter, she went on to say, if the whole thing was presented as a personal favour to *her*.

On agreeing to Hélène's suggestion, Anna confided in her about the recipient of the letter. 'Joyce is Lord Haw-Haw,' she said. Then she passed over the envelope.

Before leaving the Tea Rooms, Hélène told Anna that she would phone the following morning to let her know whether the chap at the Romanian Embassy was prepared to help.

36

Late that evening Hélène gave Max the envelope she had been handed by Anna. He carefully extracted a single sheet of paper. Both sides were covered with a typewritten message in code.

All in all, Hélène had enjoyed a highly productive day. She also presented Section B5b with an example of one of a series of Nazi propaganda sheets that Admiral Wolkoff had been encouraging people to type out and then distribute. Under the by-line of 'an English Traveller and Observer', the sheet was headed 'WHAT HITLER ACTUALLY SAID …'

It warned against the supposed Judaeo–Bolshevik plot to create more Communist regimes. Hitler had, it claimed, peaceful intentions. Britain's insistence on pursuing a war against Nazi Germany would, the sheet argued, 'turn the longing for peace and friendship expressed with such deep sincerity in his speeches into bitterness against us'. It proceeded to assert that the world was poised to deliver a damning verdict on Britain, a verdict of 'Suicide while of unsound mind'. And it concluded with a rallying cry to rebellion: 'England! Let us awake!'

When the sheet was forwarded to Section B7, which was supervising Max's investigation, the attached memo declared that the concluding lines came close to exposing Admiral Wolkoff to legal action.

37

Besides meeting Hélène that day – Tuesday 9 April, 1940 – Max fielded an unforeseen report from a member of the secretarial staff at Wormwood Scrubs. Joan Miller, who worked in the Transport Office, notified him of an incident that had taken place the previous evening. Evidently she regarded its security implications as being serious, otherwise she would not have bothered him with it.

The incident occurred in the Russian Tea Rooms. For only the second time, Miller had been dining there. While she was eating by herself, a woman had approached her and initiated a conversation. Miller recognized the woman from MI5's chilly concert hall-turned-canteen, where they both ate their lunch and afternoon tea. About two or three minutes after they started talking, the woman was joined by a friend. The woman then introduced Miller to her friend – Anna Wolkoff.

Miller saw fit to report the incident because she had heard that name in connection with Section B5b's work. Max was sure to be disturbed by her revelation that staff at Wormwood Scrubs were blabbing about his clandestine activities.

38

In what remained of Tuesday evening, Max found time to give the coded letter to one of the Special Branch officers assigned to help him. The officer – something of a veteran – was as obliging as ever. He and Max had worked together a great deal before, notably on Max's brilliant undercover operation against the Communist spy-ring that had penetrated the government munitions factory at Woolwich Arsenal. But Max required assistance of a more straightforward character on this occasion.

He arranged for his Special Branch colleague to have the message duplicated by Scotland Yard's photographic department. The process was soon completed, enabling Max to retrieve the letter, along with the reproductions of it. Now he was in a position to hand the original back to Hélène and to ask the code and cipher specialists at Wormwood Scrubs to examine one of the duplicates.

The letter had been transposed into what was known as a Vigenère cipher. Dating back to the Renaissance, this used a thirteen-letter keyword, placed twice in succession alongside the alphabet. To encipher messages, one had to jump from the appropriate letter in the alphabet to the corresponding letter in the keyword. By reversing the process, the meaning of the constituent message could be exhumed.

Vigenère ciphers were tricky but far from impossible to crack. In this case, the surname of George 'The Russian Lion' Hackenschmidt – a former champion Greco-Roman wrestler who had toured English theatres several decades earlier – was unveiled as the keyword.

Written in a clipped style, the message comprised a long list of comments and suggestions for William Joyce. 'Talks effect splendid but news bulletins less so,' it began. He was counselled to avoid references to the King and instead concentrate on attacking the government. The author of the letter then advised William about the best wavelengths for broadcasting.

'Anti-Semitism spreading like flame everywhere – all classes,' the letter reported before commenting on Churchill's alleged unpopularity and how that could be exploited. 'Stress his conceit and repeated failures.'

The letter went on to praise *Truth*, the newspaper edited by Dolly Newnham's husband. Some assurances about the wellbeing of William's siblings followed. After that, a succession of tips and potential topics for his broadcasts were listed.

'Butter ration doubled because poor can't buy – admitted by *Telegraph* – bacon same,' the message continued. 'Cost living steeply mounting. Shopkeepers suffering. Suits PEP.'

Under the chairmanship of a leading Jewish businessman, PEP stood for Political and Economic Planning, a cross-party research and policy-making organization, responsible for producing detailed assessments of major British industries. Both PEP and its chairman had made regular appearances in Special Branch reports on pre-war Nordic League meetings, at which they'd been portrayed as accomplices in a Judaeo–Bolshevik conspiracy that had supposedly precipitated war with Germany.

Next thing, the letter remarked on the propaganda broadcasts being made from Berlin by William's wife. 'Regret must state Meg's Tuesday talks unpopular with women. Advise alter radically or drop. God bless and salute all Leaguers and CB. Acknowledge this by Carlyle reference radio not Thurs. or Sun. Reply same channel same cipher.'

Max was well enough acquainted with William to recognize the references in this final paragraph. 'Leaguers' referred to members of either the Nordic League or William's own movement, the National Socialist League. 'Carlyle' referred to the nineteenth-century philosopher, Thomas Carlyle, William's favourite writer. And 'CB' presumably referred to the initials of the Nazi agent whose name had featured repeatedly[74] when Max had interrogated William's brother, Quentin, at HM Prison Wandsworth. Once based in London, the agent was a friend of both Quentin and William.

39

Anna received the expected phonecall next morning – Wednesday 10 April, 1940. She had a habit of barking out her home number immediately she picked up the receiver.

Hélène informed her that the necessary arrangements had been made.

Anna asked whether Hélène could retrieve the letter. She explained apologetically that she wanted to add something to it.

But Hélène replied that her friend at the Romanian Embassy might prove difficult to contact. There was certainly no chance of getting hold of him until later that evening. Hélène promised to do her best, though. She told Anna to pop round to her flat at 8.40 a.m. tomorrow.

40

From Max's viewpoint there was nothing remotely perturbing about what Joan Miller had witnessed in the Russian Tea Rooms. The unnamed woman, who had introduced her to Wolkoff, turned out to be none other than Marjorie.

When Max broached the matter with the woman herself, she confirmed Joan's account of what had taken place. Marjorie described how, after Joan's departure from the Tea Rooms, Wolkoff had asked whether Joan was a friend from the Military Censorship Department. To which Marjorie had replied that Joan worked in another part of the building.

Max responded by seeking out Joan. As he discovered, she was a glamorous and well-spoken twenty-two-year-old brunette with full lips and dark, sultry eyes. Max – who enjoyed flirting with women – could not be blamed for finding her attractive.

He asked whether she'd be prepared to assist him. Not with secretarial work, but with something more practical, something very hush-hush. For this sort of informal discussion involving junior staff from headquarters, he favoured the Authors' Club. Jimmy Dickson, his colleague at Section B5b, had introduced him to this snug, inexpensive and reassuringly Edwardian institution, where he could treat his guest to supper.

His club occupied the first floor of a lofty building midway between Victoria Embankment and Whitehall. Overlooking the river, its facilities included a dining room, a bar and a smoking room. Portraits of famous writers stared down at the diners. Among those writers was Sir Arthur Conan Doyle, whose Sherlock Holmes books had taught Max about the need to conduct real-life inquiries in a logical manner. Except for the novelist Graham Greene, who cast a jaundiced eye around him, the club was patronized by few bona fide authors, its habitués mainly comprising journalists, grandees from the publishing world and clergymen with no authorial qualification beyond a self-published booklet.

If Max wanted to show off to Joan and demonstrate his man-of-the-world sophistication, then he had picked the wrong place because the food aroused a drone of complaint from other members. They could count themselves lucky that they weren't faced with the stale ships' biscuits, leaden pancakes and over-ripe meat served aboard HMS *Worcester*. Funny to think that Max's uncle had forked out so much money to send him there.

Persuasive as ever, Max enlisted Joan as an agent, his intention being to deploy her against Wolkoff and friends. Despite the girlish vulnerability of her looks, she shared Hélène de Munck's toughness. And she possessed the advantage of a tenuous connection to Wolkoff. Before the war, she had worked for the West End branch of Elizabeth Arden, the beauty salon that employed one of Wolkoff's wide circle of friends.

Joan was instructed by Max to become a regular at the Tea Rooms, where she could strike up a relationship with Wolkoff. In those situations, he liked his agents to exercise the same caution as when he attempted to befriend an unfamiliar cat. He didn't just march straight up to the creature and start fondling it.

Though he was too self-effacing to succumb to boastfulness, Max was proud of his ability to synchronize the complex work of multiple agents, each striving towards a single objective. Such operations, he reflected with quiet satisfaction, required 'a particular type of mind'.

41

Plenty of dressmaking commissions were coming Anna's way. Laden with cardboard boxes containing new creations, she made recurrent forays across the capital to perform fittings.

First thing on Thursday 11 April, 1940, she took some time off from her tailoring and went round to Hélène's flat. That morning was cold and bright, layers of mist suspended like sheets of pale crêpe de Chine. Newsvendors were selling papers carrying headlines about British troops landing in Norway, which had been occupied by the Germans only three days earlier.

Just as she had arranged, Anna visited Hélène's home at twenty to nine. Hélène presented Anna with a sealed envelope. Anna inspected it.

Hélène remarked that the chap at the Romanian Embassy might want to know what was in it before taking it out of the country.

Opening the envelope and handing the coded letter to Hélène, Anna replied, 'Well, look at it.'

'What's the good of showing that to me? It doesn't mean anything to me.'

Anna said it didn't mean anything to her either. 'But I know what the letter is about …' She gave Hélène a précis of the document, explaining that it contained facts relating to Jewish activities in England. Those facts were, she said, intended for William Joyce to use in his propaganda broadcasts. Her tendency towards self-dramatization leading her to part company from reality, she added that the contents of the letter would have the impact of a bombshell. She asked Hélène whether she could borrow her typewriter, because she wanted to write a postscript to the message.

With Hélène's permission, she used a fresh sheet of paper to type out a couple of sentences in German. She signed off using the initials 'PJ' (Perish Judah), the valedictory salute that was common among British fascists. Alongside she copied the eagle and snake design featured on the Right Club badge. Then she put the letter in a fresh envelope. Once she had sealed this, she handed it back to Hélène, who promised to deliver it to her Romanian friend without delay.

42

At 2 p.m. Hélène gave Max the new envelope. It bore the same address as before. Max opened it and saw that it contained two sheets of paper. Typed on one of these was the coded letter. On the other was Wolkoff's postscript.

Max now had the evidence to prosecute her. By writing the postscript and attempting to send the letter to William Joyce, she'd violated the Official Secrets Act of 1920, which made it illegal to communicate, or even attempt to communicate, with a foreign agent. Under the terms of the Act, 'a foreign agent' didn't – strangely enough – have to be *foreign*, merely someone suspected of committing an act 'prejudicial to the safety or interests of the State'.

Patient as ever, Max didn't activate the legal machinery. Rather than commence proceedings against Wolkoff, he and his colleagues decided to wait. If they bided their time, she might incriminate other people and expose more about the Right Club and its connections. Equipped with sufficient evidence to demonstrate that it was a dangerous Fifth Column organization, Max and co. might be able to persuade the hitherto reluctant Home Secretary to sanction the large-scale round-up of British fascists.

43

Max showed one of his Special Branch colleagues a copy of the postscript Wolkoff had added to the coded letter. The detective-sergeant, who could read German, translated it for him. The postscript urged William Joyce to make more broadcasts focusing on the Jews and freemasons. It also requested that he repeat a specific talk he had given earlier in the year.

As well as getting the postscript translated, Max arranged for the original version of the coded letter to be sent to Berlin. MI5 had a system for these occasions. They'd pass the envelope to Felix Cowgill, head of Section V, MI6's counter-espionage wing. Cowgill would then arrange for the letter to be deposited into a postbox in Holland or Belgium. That way, the envelope would not carry any British postmarks, their absence indicating to its recipient that it must have been smuggled out of Britain.

Over the next couple of days Max's investigation continued to progress as smoothly as one of Bix Beiderbecke's cornet solos. Hélène reported telling Wolkoff that the letter was en route to Germany. 'If this succeeds,' Wolkoff said, 'you will be one of ours, but since you are not a naturalized British subject, you can't join the group. You can only be an associate member. Never mind, you can do just as much work like that.'

44

Still smarting from the pain of her unrequited passion for Lord Cottenham, Anna must have been flattered by the sudden attention she was receiving from someone of Tyler's youth, intelligence, sartorial fastidiousness and dashing looks. But this time she didn't appear to have been left mooning over the object of her desire. Instead, she seemed to have been the focal point of Tyler's skills as a womanizer, a sense of conspiratorial intimacy offering a seedbed for other forms of intimacy. His behaviour towards Anna led her to believe that he was gentle and good-natured. Tellingly, she soon began to use the possessive pronoun in her references to him.

During the daytime on Saturday 13 April, 1940, she went round to his flat to borrow some of the paperwork he'd stolen from the US Embassy. Jock Ramsay had asked her to do this. At odd times in the afternoon or evening when he could get away from his work at the House of Commons, the Right Club leader had taken a cab round to Gloucester Place to look through the documents that Tyler had left for him. Jock wanted Anna to index them and have them photographed.

On the face of it, Churchill's correspondence with Roosevelt showed that Churchill, one of the most vocal opponents of a negotiated peace with Germany, had been scheming behind the Prime Minister's back in an apparent effort to bring America into the conflict. Surely the exposure of these machinations would be sufficient to guarantee Churchill's removal from the War Cabinet and hasten peace? Neither Anna nor Jock realized, however, that Churchill had obtained the Prime Minister's blessing before pursuing the correspondence.

Jock had talked to Anna about these letters. He'd said people wouldn't believe that the British and American leaders were exchanging secret messages, unless he could obtain firm supporting evidence. Anna had assured him that she knew someone who would be prepared to photograph the documents he required.

When she turned up at Tyler's flat, she found the American stooping over a large table as he sorted through a stack of paperwork. For someone as superstitious and swooningly romantic as Anna, the discovery that his flat backed onto her old house on Gloucester Place Mews is unlikely to have passed unremarked. It was such an outrageous coincidence that it lent their relationship an element of destiny.

Among the paperwork Tyler was handling, she caught sight of one of the messages between Roosevelt and Churchill. Pinned to it was another of the telegrams between the two leaders. Though Tyler didn't regard either message as being very significant, she said she was interested in them. She asked whether she could borrow both documents.

Tyler wanted to know whether she was going to show them to Captain Ramsay.

She said she was.

On hearing that, he told her that she was welcome to borrow them.

He also lent her the car he'd bought from her. Driving in the direction of Earl's Court, just under a mile to the west of Roland Gardens, she had to contend with the danger that she might be waved down by the police. Not just the ordinary police, but the traffic police as well. Last Friday, a new campaign had been launched to check that drivers were obeying blackout regulations. Vehicles were only allowed a single low-wattage headlight bulb. Even that had to be blinkered by a little cardboard shield.

Anna hoped to get the stolen documents copied by Nicholas Smirnoff, a photographer who had previously taken pictures for her. She had known him since she was a child. After the Russian Revolution, he had been the secretary to one of the anti-Communist committees on which her father served. Over recent years she and Smirnoff – now in his mid-fifties – had shared many of the same fascist friends. These included Margaret Bothamley, plus Christabel Nicholson and husband.[75]

Now Smirnoff was living with his Belgian wife at 32 Penywern Road, one of numerous shabby streets in the vicinity of Earl's Court Underground Station. Home to a sizeable Russian émigré community, those streets predominantly consisted of large, stucco-clad terraces, divided into boarding houses, flats and hotels, interspersed by shops and small businesses.

Neither of the Smirnoffs was at home when Anna visited their basement flat. She composed a note to Nicholas Smirnoff and slid it through his letterbox. In the message she had written that she wanted to see him urgently.

45

Her message provoked no phonecall or visit. Nor was there a letter from Nicholas via the day's second postal delivery.

Making the most of the car Tyler had lent her, Anna was cruising along Earl's Court Road later in the day. As she passed the fridge and cooker showroom, she spotted Nicholas and his wife out shopping. She hailed them from her vehicle, which she parked at the side of the road. Without getting out of her car, she explained to Nicholas that she was in a great hurry to acquire reproductions of certain documents. She asked whether he would be willing to make those for her.

He said he'd do it that evening.

Anna returned to the Smirnoffs' flat at approximately nine o'clock. In her presence Nicholas started photographing the telegrams, which had been typed on three sides of paper. He used an old-fashioned box camera with a long black bellows mechanism. To line up the telegrams and adjust the focus, he had to peer through a tall viewfinder projecting from the top of the camera's body. He was a perfectionist when it came to photography, though there was, for Anna, nothing new about his working methods. Around ten years earlier – well before her prettiness had begun to deteriorate – he had taken her portrait. In her youth she had possessed haughty self-assurance when faced by the camera's lens. Unlike most photographers, who chivvied their sitters into preconceived poses, Nicholas was content to keep adjusting the set-up while he waited for the subject to relax, waited to capture the desired balance of light and shade. But now there was no such latitude for artistry.

Once Nicholas had finished copying the telegrams, Anna had tea with him and his wife. The negatives were meanwhile hung up to dry. Until that slow process was complete, they couldn't be used to strike prints.

After her chat with the Smirnoffs, Anna left the flat. She took with her the telegrams she had borrowed from Tyler.

46

According to the Gregorian calendar, that day – Saturday 14 April, 1940 – was the first day of the Easter weekend, an important occasion for the Russian émigré community. Like many other exiles, Anna and family supported the Karlovitz Synod, the dissenting wing of the Russian Orthodox Church. This was, in contrast to its rival, administered from Istanbul rather than Communist-controlled Moscow. Denied the opportunity to worship at one of those charming onion-domed churches that were sprinkled across the Motherland, Anna and fellow congregants had to make do with St Philip's Parochial Hall, next to Victoria Coach Station.

Saturday's peal of midnight bells marked the beginning of the main Easter service, orchestrated by a priest who was a friend of Anna's parents. The priest's features were mostly hidden behind a copious grey beard and matching hair, yet his profound anti-Communism was on open display, politics infusing his dealings with worshippers. Under his charming, dynamic leadership, St Philip's had been enjoying a resurgence. So many worshippers were attracted to his Easter services, the police barred traffic from that section of Buckingham Palace Road.

Congregants at St Philip's included Eugène Sabline and wife, together with many of the Wolkoffs' friends. Not just White Russian aristocrats and generals, but also friends from less exalted strata of society. Among those was a middle-aged man who used to work in the kitchen at the Russian Tea Rooms.[76] Insipid though he appeared, he now ran a thriving West End bookshop and lending library, which stocked Russian language novels, gramophone records and pro-Nazi newspapers, the takings from these supplemented by the sale of pornography.

In a symbolic re-enactment of the biblical account of the procession to Christ's tomb, the priest at St Philip's always opened the Easter ceremonies by guiding the congregation around the outside of the church. Each worshipper was supposed to carry a lighted candle, but the blackout regulations forbade that. At least there were no rules against the priest declaiming the ritual verses in Russian, their melodic tones redolent of the era before the Communist revolution. 'Your resurrection, oh Christ our saviour, the angels praise with song in heaven,' he said. 'Grant that we too here on earth may glorify you with a pure heart ...'

When the parade had snaked its way round to the entrance, the priest led his clerical colleagues in the ritual Russian language chorus of 'Christ has risen!'

To which the congregants were required to respond, 'Truly he has risen.'

Everyone then filed into the brightly lit church and took their seats for the marathon service, which didn't usually end until about twenty past three. Afterwards the worshippers, none of whom dared chat while they were inside the church, formed a dense, talkative crowd in the street, where dawn remained a couple of hours away.

Later that Sunday, Tyler would be joining Anna and family at Roland Gardens for their traditional Easter meal. She viewed with chauvinistic pride what she regarded as the incomparable traditions of Russian hospitality, traditions apparent from those memoirs and journals of Imperial Russia that she had read. For confirmation of this largesse, one merely needed to consult a copy of *A Gift to Young Housewives*, the classic nineteenth-century cookbook. It featured a recipe for a form of yeast cake called 'Neighbourly Cake', which required six-dozen egg yolks. Anna and her parents would, in these straitened times, have had trouble paying for that many eggs because shopkeepers were charging as much as three shillings a dozen.

Of the usual Easter delicacies, Anna was especially fond of blinis. Not the kind one found in non-Russian restaurants – the thick and indigestible kind. These were so light that children would compete to see how many they could eat. In Anna's experience, you required only five eggs to make sixty blinis – enough for ten English people but no more than, perhaps, six Russians. Blinis were, she thought, best dished up two at a time, forming a sandwich filled with an impasto of sour cream, hot melted butter, smoked pork, salmon or cod roe and caviar. Sadly, she could not offer Tyler any 'napkin caviar', her favourite variety, which didn't contain any salt or other preservatives. To procure it, one used to send one's servants all the way to Astrakhan where sturgeon spawned. One's servants would squeeze the eggs onto clean napkins, hence the name. Hurriedly folded, these were packed in ice-chips before being transported back across Russia.

While Tyler was with her, Anna had a chance to raise the subject of his accommodation. He'd been formulating vague plans to leave his Gloucester Place flat and rent a house.[77]

Emotionally involved with him to the point where she had started fretting over his wellbeing, Anna was keen for him to move out of his current home, which she had grown to hate. She loathed the idea of Tyler living somewhere so chilly. Her concern for him appears to have led her to suggest that he should rent her uncle Gabriel's house, vacated when her uncle had fled to Switzerland just before war broke out. The house would be most convenient for Tyler. He would only have to stroll across Hyde Park and through Mayfair to get to the embassy. If she could arrange for him to take on the tenancy, she'd be doing both him and her uncle a good turn.

47

On the day of Tyler's latest visit to Roland Gardens, Max received a generous stock of information from Hélène. She reported that Anna Wolkoff had said, 'Hitler is a god … and it would be wonderful if he could govern England.' Hélène also described witnessing an encounter between Wolkoff's friend, Lord Ronald Graham, and James McGuirk Hughes. There was a suspicion among the Right Club set, Hélène remarked, that Hughes was a police infiltrator.

Max knew about him. Less than five days ago, Hughes – who served as Chief of Intelligence for the British Union – had given Anna the coded letter addressed to William Joyce. Hughes had been unflatteringly caricatured in *Crime Cargo*, Max's first novel. Appearing under the guise of the thuggish, pig-faced 'Baldy McGurk', his brief literary existence had – maybe in a moment of wish-fulfilment on Max's part – been painfully extinguished by two soft-nosed bullets, one in the stomach and the other through the lungs.

During the encounter between Hughes and Lord Ronald Graham, witnessed by Hélène, the latter had remarked that he had a pal in the police, who was letting him have inside information. Hélène put Max in the picture about other Right Club contacts as well. She named someone in the government's Air Mail Censorship Department. And she mentioned a contact in the Ministry of Economic Warfare, her reference to whom corroborated a previous report Max had been given by Marjorie.

Until recently, there had, Hélène explained, been a second contact in that particular ministry. The man in question had, however, since been transferred to another branch of government. With each passing report, the threat to security posed by the Right Club assumed more menacing proportions.

48

Anna had already set up a meeting with Hélène for the next afternoon, Monday 15 April, 1940. Their 12.30 appointment had been occasioned by Hélène's revelation that she was travelling to Belgium on Tuesday. She planned to visit her sister, who had been taken ill. Her trip provided Anna with the opportunity to get her to carry out the errand mentioned almost a month ago.

The venue for their rendezvous was the Russian Tea Rooms, still a regular meeting place for the Right Club women. Swelling their number were two recruits who shared an obsession with Nazi Germany, which they had visited numerous times. Those recruits were Mollie Hiscox – who had been at the Manson Mews party – and her forty-four-year-old Lancastrian friend, Norah Briscoe. With minimal prompting, Norah would brandish a pack of photographs of her little boy, show them to people and then announce that she had left him in Germany because she wanted him to be brought up as a German.

She and Mollie were devoting a lot of time to helping the club's propaganda campaign. They staged ostentatiously loud anti-war conversations in pubs. They handed out flyers. They put up stickybacks. And they distributed printed copies of 'Hymn, 1939', an anti-Semitic parody of the national anthem that began with the words, 'Land of dope and Jewry ...'

When Hélène arrived at the Tea Rooms that day, Anna sweet-talked her by saying her name had cropped up in conversation with the Leader. Anna said the Leader was very pleased with her and would like to meet her sometime. Building on this flattery, Anna gave Hélène a sheet of paper on which she had typed some instructions in French. She insisted that Hélène should learn these by heart and then destroy them.

Her instructions related to a couple of her Belgian associates. One of them was her friend, Comtesse Rasseta de Laubespin, who lived in Brussels. Until last year, Rasseta's rather colourless husband, Antoine, had been a senior diplomat at the Belgian Embassy in London. Before their departure from England, they'd mixed with many of the same people as Anna – people such as Francis Hemming, not to mention Captain and Mrs Ramsay. They had also been chummy with the Nazi Ambassador to Britain, Joachim von Ribbentrop and his wife.

49

Though the reason for Hélène's imminent cross-Channel trip was genuine enough, its timing had been orchestrated by Max. His well-baited trap seemed to have worked, otherwise Wolkoff would not have given Hélène those instructions. They were, Hélène said, written in bad French. She presented Max with a translation. Wolkoff's instructions related not just to the Comtesse de Laubespin but also to Guy Miermans – the man whom Wolkoff had talked about when the subject of Hélène travelling to Belgium had first been raised.

Wolkoff wanted Hélène to visit Miermans's home in Brussels. Hélène was told to use Wolkoff's name on arrival at his address. Wolkoff instructed her to ask about the anti-Semitic, anti-Masonic campaign in Belgium, to find out the names of the organizations behind it and to ascertain how many people belonged to them. On top of that, Wolkoff asked Hélène to collect the item of anti-Semitic propaganda mentioned when the two of them had first discussed the possibility of Hélène serving as a courier. Hélène was supposed to enquire whether this document had been translated from Russian into English yet. If it had, she had to pick up the translated version, too.

Her other task entailed visiting the Comtesse de Laubespin, who worked at the Ministry of Foreign Affairs in Brussels. Hélène was supposed to quote Wolkoff's name again, to say that Wolkoff had expected to hear from the Comtesse via the Belgian diplomatic bag and to assure the Comtesse that everything had been going nicely. In addition, Hélène had to remember to express Wolkoff's gratitude for the attachment that had accompanied the Comtesse's recent letter and to offer to pass on any messages for Wolkoff. Hélène also had to enquire about the trustworthiness of Jean Nieuwenhuys, Wolkoff's contact at the Belgian Embassy in London.

50

The waiting was finally over. Just shy of two months after proposing a job swap with someone at the Berlin embassy, Tyler received a reply from Ambassador Alexander Kirk. His response took the form of a brief note. 'Dear Kent,' it began, 'I have delayed answering your letter of 24 February regarding an opening for you in Berlin as I wished to canvass the situation thoroughly.' Ambassador Kirk proceeded to dispense the bad news – that the idea of a job swap no longer appealed to the Code Clerk in Berlin.

So Tyler would not be joining his friend Sylvester A. Huntowski over there. And he would be excluded from the substantial profits on offer from the currency smuggling racket that Huntowski and Donald H. Nichols were launching.[78]

51

Hurried arrangements for Hélène's cross-Channel journey had to be made by Max. Were he to follow protocol, he'd notify Felix Cowgill over at MI6 that the Right Club operation would be straying onto their patch, which nowadays began three miles outside Britain's borders. Max appreciated just how sensitive the two intelligence agencies could be about such matters.

Ten years earlier he had been at the centre of a territorial dispute between the two organizations. Back then, he was still freelancing for his MI6 friend Desmond Morton. At the behest of Desmond, he'd arranged for his team of agents to infiltrate Communist groups across Britain. Efforts had been made to stop MI5 and Special Branch from finding out about the operation because it encroached on their terrain. Yet those efforts had proved futile. With a certain relish, Max told the story of how the Deputy Assistant Commissioner of the Metropolitan Police had accused Desmond of 'exceeding his duties', called him a worm and promised he'd be made to crawl across the carpet at Scotland Yard.

But the passage of time hadn't softened Max's cavalier attitude towards territorial demarcation, his reluctance to liaise with MI6 probably encouraged by Desmond's current glaringly negative view of the organization. Instead of spending time briefing Cowgill about Hélène's trip to Belgium, Max concentrated on some of the practical aspects of Hélène's mission. Foremost among these was the need to secure the cooperation of Section D4d, the MI5 department that dealt with so-called Exit Permits. Max had to obtain just such a permit for Hélène, otherwise she would not be allowed to leave the country.

He'd always banked on the authorities giving him the necessary assistance. Still, he was impressed by the discretion and efficiency with which his request was handled by the appropriate officer at Shoreham Aerodrome in Sussex, from where Hélène would be flying.

In combination with the Exit Permit, Max acquired expensive return tickets for Hélène on the route between Shoreham and Brussels. The outward-bound flight was due to land in Belgium late the following afternoon.

Via MI5's Section D4d, Max also had to ensure that the British Passport Control Officer in Brussels granted Hélène the visa she required for the return journey. To reduce still further the scope for trouble, Max gave Hélène meticulous directions on what she should do when she rolled up at the British Consulate in Brussels, where her visa application would have to be submitted. He told her to inform the consular officials that she was merely visiting Belgium and that she held a Certificate of Employment in Britain. Such an explanation should, he thought, be sufficient to avert any difficulties.

Another potential snag involved the Belgian Customs officers, who were likely to seize whatever documents Hélène received from Guy Miermans. Max therefore arranged for her to place them in a sealed envelope with his London address on it. Before leaving Brussels, she'd then have to hand it to the British Passport Control Officer, who would forward it to Max.

52

Soon Max found himself with the espionage equivalent of an eight-pound trout on the end of his line. His catch took the form of a packed report from Marjorie, who advised him that a man named Smirnoff had been employed by Anna Wolkoff to undertake photographic work. Marjorie also reported that Wolkoff had a very important contact living at 47 Gloucester Place. 'This contact,' Marjorie added, 'claims to be in a position to give Anna confidential information about members of the British intelligence service.'

An application was duly submitted to the Watchers to root out the identity of the contact. No such obvious response to Marjorie's other findings suggested itself. These findings derived from a meeting she had attended the previous Saturday. Hosted by Captain Ramsay at his London home, where Wolkoff was present, the meeting brought together what Ramsay labelled 'the Inner Circle' of the Right Club.

So plausible had Marjorie become in her role as a fascist fanatic that Wolkoff had, she stated, taken to calling her 'the little Storm Trooper' – a reference to the Nazi paramilitary bully boys of that name. Wolkoff even assured Marjorie that she would ride in the same car as the SS chief, Heinrich Himmler, when the Nazis staged their triumphal procession through London.

In recounting what took place last Saturday, Marjorie revealed that Ramsay had said Right Club members should, until they'd assumed control of the government, limit themselves to recruiting from other fascist organizations. New recruits must progress through three ranks, the highest of these entitling them to contribute to anti-war and anti-Semitic propaganda. Occupying the top tier were proven members, such as those present, who could be trusted to operate secretly on behalf of the club.

Ramsay declared that infiltration should be at the heart of their modus operandi, permitting them to have a cell within every fascist movement. Immediately one of those movements seized power, the club would, he said, be in a position to take over from it. By dispersing through other organizations, he reasoned that the government would have more difficulty acting against the club.

After the formal element of the meeting had finished, Marjorie found herself in a group conversation with Captain Ramsay. His policy, he explained, had been never to let the right hand know what the left hand was doing. With misplaced confidence, he identified that as the reason why he'd been able to lead the authorities astray, why neither MI5 nor Scotland Yard knew anything about his activities. Eager recruits, he argued, should be encouraged to apply the same principal by forming independent cells.

He then elaborated on this classic revolutionary tactic. From what Marjorie could recall, he said, 'If you decide to have either loyal shopkeepers or other friends at your address and you think they are of our way of thinking, that is a matter entirely for your own judgement. But I don't want to know anything about it. When you are satisfied that they are ready and can be trusted, *then* you can enlist them as members of the Right Club. They would pay their subscriptions to you, and in due course would be informed – so far as we consider discreet – what to do and who is their head. They, in turn, would go out and do the same thing, but I prefer that it never gets too big an organization.'

Marjorie recounted having a brief one-to-one chat with Ramsay later on. 'He told me that he had had a most interesting man from the United States Embassy to dinner and that this man had told him some interesting things about corruption at the top of his country.'

53

Due to a shortage of paper pulp, caused by the German occupation of most of Norway, the newspapers had become even thinner than ever. Sixteen pages at most. On the morning of Hélène's departure for Belgium – Tuesday 16 April, 1940 – several of these scrawny publications carried stories that were liable to disturb Max. They described the role played by Fifth Columnists in the invasion of Norway, which had, despite continued opposition from British forces, just culminated in the creation of a Nazi puppet government under the collaborator, Vidkun Quisling. Enlarging on a piece that had appeared the previous weekend, the *Daily Telegraph* ran a front-page exposé by an Oslo-based American journalist. He made what would, years later, be unmasked as fanciful claims that the German invasion had succeeded so rapidly thanks to a conspiracy between the Nazis and Norwegian Fifth Columnists.

Press stories such as this were sure to create an additional sense of urgency among Max and colleagues. If a group of dedicated Fifth Columnists could facilitate the conquest of Norway, there was no reason why Anna Wolkoff and her fellow fascists would not be able to pull off the same trick in Britain.

While Max waited to see whether Hélène's mission to Belgium yielded useful results, he was in touch that Tuesday with two of the other agents contributing to his investigation. One of those was Lionel Hirst, who had dined with Wolkoff at the Russian Tea Rooms last week. In the course of their meal she had told Hirst about her friend, Tyler Kent. She'd boasted that Kent had given her all sorts of confidential information. Through him, she claimed to know the details of a meeting between Ambassador Kennedy and Lord Halifax, British Secretary of State for Foreign Affairs. Kennedy and Halifax had, she said, discussed the German invasion of Norway and subsequent problems encountered by the Royal Navy. She told Hirst that the outcome of the battles between the British and German fleets had been grossly distorted by the British government, which needed a propaganda victory to offset news of the recent air attack on the naval base at Scapa Flow.

The other agent who contacted Max that day was Marjorie. She disclosed that Wolkoff planned to go to the Russian Tea Rooms for a chat with Joan Miller on Thursday or Friday evening. Wolkoff had warned Marjorie to be cagey about their activities until they could be certain Joan shared their politics.

'Although I am well aware that B6 are very overworked,' Marjorie admitted to Max, 'do you think it would be possible for us to have some observation on Anna Wolkoff? Recent developments, of which you are aware, give good grounds for thinking that this woman is more deeply involved in pro-German activity than one might at first think.'

Marjorie added that Wolkoff was clearly using her dressmaking as cover for holding meetings with other Nazi agents operating under Captain Ramsay's command. 'It is possible that if the observation was very carefully done we might be able to check up on some new contacts.'

Spurred by Marjorie's recommendations, arrangements were made for the Watchers to shadow Wolkoff one evening.

54

Anna wrote to her uncle Gabriel next day. In her letter, posted to the Swiss hotel where he was living, she mentioned that Tyler's proposed tenancy hadn't worked out as hoped. Tyler had withdrawn from the deal because of the excessive financial demands of the estate agent handling the rental of her uncle's house in Kensington.

Not only did Anna write to her uncle that day, but she also went round to the Smirnoffs' flat. With her, she had a selection of British propaganda leaflets, written in German. She explained to Nicholas Smirnoff that the RAF had been dropping these over Germany. He agreed to her request to copy them for her. Before he set to work, he gave her the prints that she had already asked him to produce. He also handed her the five-by-four-inch glass negatives from which these prints had been struck. The negatives were in an old cardboard box.

Subsequently Anna deposited the box at Tyler's flat, returned the two telegrams she had borrowed and persuaded him to store a parcel for her as well. She said that the parcel contained stickybacks.

Two evenings later, she called round to the Smirnoffs' again and paid Nicholas for his work. He had only photographed eight of the propaganda leaflets, yet she took all the originals away with her. She told him she'd bring them back in a few days' time, so he could finish the job.

55

Max anticipated that Hélène would return from Belgium no later than Saturday 20 April, 1940. Her plane was supposed to land at Shoreham Aerodrome – fifty miles south of London. Alarmingly for Max, though, Saturday had just dawned, but she still hadn't reappeared.

Something could well have gone wrong. However carefully he planned these operations, there was always an element of risk. One could never discount the human factor.

56

Tyler had with him yet more stolen paperwork when he departed from the embassy at the end of his shift. The paperwork comprised top-secret cabled correspondence between Washington and London. It discussed a concept known as 'Lease-Lend', devised to enable President Roosevelt to get round the Neutrality Act, which aimed to ensure that his and other American administrations maintained an isolationist stance.[79] The Act barred him from either selling arms to warring nations or loaning money to help them purchase arms. Previously the Act had served to restrict American aid to the embattled Finns.

Lease-Lend sought to allow Roosevelt to influence the outcome of the current European conflict by providing Britain with vast quantities of war materiel and food. In exchange for these vital supplies, he exacted a punitive price, just one minor component of which entailed handing over all British gold reserves stored in South Africa.

Well-chronicled as the President's grudgingly isolationist stance had been, Tyler – no stranger to political intrigue – knew that the Lease-Lend telegrams were extremely significant. They exposed Roosevelt's double-dealing. If they were made public, there would be important ramifications. Roosevelt, already being touted by the press as a contender for the Presidential election later that year, might forfeit the Democratic Party nomination to a less compromised candidate. Even if he secured his party's endorsement, he would still be hamstrung in his contest with the Republicans, whose traditional isolationist foreign policy meshed with what was then the overwhelming mood of American voters. Roosevelt's removal from the White House would render improbable the Lease-Lend arrangement, without which Britain would in all likelihood be defeated by the Nazis.

As Tyler walked out of the embassy, there was probably little that distinguished him from other well-dressed civilians on the West End streets. Yet he now had in his possession the means to alter the trajectory of the war and consequently the rest of the twentieth century.

Part Five

Keys to the Kingdom

1

The plane touched down at midday or thereabouts on Saturday 20 April, 1940. Hélène was among the passengers disembarking from it.

Within a few hours Max was being briefed on her experiences across the Channel. Despite the assurances he'd received from the British Passport Control Officer in Brussels, she had run into problems obtaining the visa that enabled her to board the flight back to England.

Had everything gone as planned, she would simply have trotted over to the consulate and picked up the document she required. Instead of which, Hélène had been put through a protracted grilling by three or four consular officials – precisely the kind of thing Max had taken such inordinate trouble to avoid. The officials refused to grant her a visa unless she answered their questions. Many of these focused on the names and employment particulars of her Belgian-based relatives.

She had come away with the feeling that the consular staff might start making enquiries that could undermine B5b's entire operation. That was all Max needed – some paper-pusher ruining the best part of a year's patient work.

Why the officials at the consulate had adopted such an obstructive attitude, he couldn't imagine. One thing was for sure, he thought: it demonstrated remarkable stupidity, even allowing for the difficult circumstances no doubt prevailing in Belgium. As he well knew, the consular officials had placed his agent in an awkward spot by behaving like this. If she refused to cooperate, she risked finding herself in a predicament beyond Max's control. Answer the questions candidly, though, and she'd be revealing information that she had no authority to reveal.

He thoroughly approved of her decision to feed her inquisitors a line about being in Belgium to collect some documents on behalf of her employer. No reference was made to MI5 or the British government, she assured Max.

When Hélène had told one of the consular staff that she was expected back in London on Saturday at the latest, the official had asked, 'By whom?'

'By my employer, who gave me a few days' holiday because I wished to see my sister who is not well,' Hélène replied.

To which the consular official said, 'If you are not willing to talk and tell us in detail what is the stuff you are getting, we cannot give you a visa.'

Hélène was then questioned closely about the nature of the items she might be taking with her. She led Max to believe that she hadn't divulged anything further.

Poor Hélène ended up having to pay another visit to the British Consulate before being permitted to leave Belgium. Second time round, she saw the Passport Control Officer. Honouring his earlier commitment to Max, he at last issued her with a visa.

Of course, Hélène didn't just brief Max on her difficulties with the consulate. She also described her arrival in Brussels the previous Tuesday afternoon. As per Wolkoff's instructions, she'd got in touch with the Comtesse de Laubespin. She and the Comtesse had arranged to lunch together. Hélène had then tried to contact Guy Miermans, the other person Wolkoff wanted her to seek out. But Hélène discovered that his telephone number wasn't listed in the directory – something Max found suspicious.

Unable to phone Miermans, Hélène went round to his home address, which she had been given by Wolkoff. It was in a district close to the centre of Brussels. The concierge said Miermans had cleared off some time ago and moved to the seaside. Locating him seemed a hopeless task. Fortunately, Hélène remembered that everyone in Belgium was obliged to register their home address with the police, so she approached the local registration department later that day. She pretended to be Miermans's girlfriend. Her bluff paid off. From the police, she obtained what was supposed to be his current address, yet he turned out not to be there either.

2

The stolen Lease-Lend correspondence left Tyler with several possible courses of action. Were he the pro-isolationist, anti-war zealot he purported to be, the obvious thing was for him to use the American diplomatic pouch to smuggle the appropriate telegrams back to the States. He already knew how easy that would be.

Some two weeks from then, the stolen telegrams would reach the other side of the Atlantic. In the hands of an anti-Roosevelt journalist or politician, they'd have a swift and devastating impact. Matters would have been made even easier by Tyler's friendship with the editor-in-chief at the International News Service, the leading wire service owned by the strongly pro-isolationist press baron, William Randolph Hearst.

Far from acting on his avowed principles, however, Tyler let the stolen Lease-Lend telegrams accumulate in his flat.

3

Max learned from Hélène that she had eventually tracked down Guy Miermans to an address in a small seaside town. By sending a telegram there, she made contact with him. Miermans then phoned her and arranged a meeting in Ostend on the afternoon of Friday 19 April, 1940.

The day before that, she kept her appointment with the Comtesse de Laubespin. While Hélène was there, she was introduced to the Comtesse's husband, Antoine. 'They are not very open in their conversation,' she told Max, 'but it is very clear from what they said that they were closely concerned in pro-German and anti-Jewish activities. I particularly remember one remark made by M. de Laubespin during a conversation on the subject of anti-Jewish propaganda and pro-German connections. He referred to it as "a dangerous game, though it would be a good game and an honourable game if there were any chance of succeeding".'

Hélène got the impression that the Comte and Comtesse had been frightened by the Belgian government's anti-Nazi stance. This had evidently deterred them from embarking on activities of the character being pursued by Wolkoff and her associates. It was transparent, Max concluded, that the Comte and Comtesse, although fundamentally pro-German, were very cowardly.

Obeying Wolkoff's instructions, Hélène quizzed them about whether it was still safe for Wolkoff to send messages from Britain to the Continent through Jean Nieuwenhuys, Second Secretary at the Belgian Embassy in London. 'Yes, of course,' the Comte replied. 'If anything is of sufficient importance we can use the bag as we have done up to now, and you or Anna Wolkoff can use the diplomatic bag through Nieuwenhuys, whom you can trust thoroughly and entirely.'

Wolkoff's instructions also decreed that Hélène should enquire about the availability of new anti-Semitic or anti-Masonic literature. 'On this subject,' Hélène recounted, 'they were evasive and wished to emphasize that in this connection they had not been taking part in any activity. However, after lunch it was clear to me that the Comte did not wish to leave me alone with his wife, and he asked me if he could take me anywhere in his car. In the car I pressed him again on the subject of literature about the Jews and Freemasons. The Comte stopped the car at the Foreign Office, and leaving me in the car, went inside. He came out and gave me a small periodical, which was supposed to contain the names and addresses of Jews and Freemasons in Belgium. At the same time he gave me the addresses of shops at which propaganda of this kind was sometimes available.'

First thing next day Hélène received a phonecall from Guy Miermans, anxious to change their arrangement. Now he wanted to meet her as soon as possible. Complying with his request, she arrived in Ostend around eleven that morning and met him and his wife there. He was, Hélène told Max, a tall, sturdy man in his late thirties. Energetic. Intelligent. Sure of himself without being conceited. Hélène described him as being well dressed and said that his clothes looked as if they'd been made by a good English tailor.

Through talking to Miermans and his wife, Hélène discovered that the couple were quite friendly with some of her relations. But Miermans removed this potential complication by urging Hélène not to tell her relatives about his political work. He said it remained firmly in the past. Max was struck by just how anxious these people were to distance themselves from their previous dealings.

On being asked about the Russian anti-Semitic document Wolkoff was so anxious to obtain, Miermans stated that it wasn't really a *document*. It was, instead, a sizeable book. At present it was in Germany where some Russians, engaged in anti-Semitic propaganda, were translating it. Miermans promised to request the book and send it to England via the diplomatic bag. He and his wife even tried to persuade Hélène that she should stay with them for at least eight days, during which he might be able to retrieve the book. He then arranged to see Hélène again at ten o'clock that evening.

Hélène rendezvoused with him at an address in the centre of Brussels. There, Miermans warned her against dabbling in fascist politics because she'd find herself on the losing side. Like Napoleon before them, he predicted, the Nazis wouldn't be able to defeat Britain because Britain was mistress of the seas. 'You must promise me to give up this anti-Jewish work of which you know nothing,' he pleaded with her. And he asked her to pass on a message: 'Tell Anna to stop this stupidity ...'

Miermans said to Hélène that Europe was getting too dangerous, so he was moving to America. The Belgian authorities were, he added, tapping his phone because they believed he was a German agent.

He had certainly given them cause for suspicion, according to Hélène. During her second meeting with him, Miermans referred not just to a series of lucrative business trips to Germany, but also to an important forthcoming discussion with a group of Germans. Hélène informed Max that Miermans might – provided the Nazis had offered him enough of an incentive – be employed by the enemy.

After her landing at Shoreham Aerodrome, Hélène had gone to see Wolkoff, to whom she had given a carefully edited yet otherwise truthful account of her trip to Belgium. Hélène remembered Wolkoff saying, 'You have dealt with this work very satisfactorily. As I have told you before, an agent needs pluck and initiative.'

Exactly as Miermans had requested, Hélène passed on his plea to Wolkoff to abandon her activities. But Wolkoff made it plain that Miermans could say nothing to dissuade her from pursuing her current plans. Max found her answer enlightening in that it showed just how committed she was.

4

Besotted by Tyler, who had encouraged her feelings for him, Anna was keen to show him off. 'I want you to meet a friend of mine,' she said to him, subsequently announcing that her friend shared her political beliefs.

She ended up taking him round to lunch with Christabel and Admiral Nicholson. Not that Tyler could stay long because he was required at the US Embassy that afternoon. Tyler didn't say anything about the exact nature of his job, yet Christabel seemed to know all about it. She and Anna must have been gossiping.

Like Tyler, Admiral Nicholson had travelled extensively. He could ply his guests with dramatic tales of seafaring life. One of his well-rehearsed recollections harked back to a famous late nineteenth-century incident when he was a young midshipman aboard HMS *Calliope*. His ship had been moored alongside half-a-dozen other warships in a beautiful South Sea island harbour, almost encircled by a coral reef. Surprised by the arrival of a hurricane, the other ships were sunk, but the *Calliope* succeeded in battling her way out of the harbour and into the relative safety of the open sea. News of her miraculous escape had already reached Australia when she docked in

Sydney the following month. Thousands of people flocked there to greet her.

Admiral Nicholson had recently attended a reunion to commemorate the fiftieth anniversary of those events. In a strange coincidence, a senior colleague of Tyler from the embassy was among the guests of honour.

Before Tyler excused himself from the Nicholsons' lunch party, he and Anna behaved in a way that left no doubt that they were more than just friends. Much more.

5

Max was so incensed by the behaviour of the Passport Control Officer and other consular staff in Brussels that he spent part of the day after Hélène's return composing a tetchy account of what had gone wrong with her mission. He sent this to Francis Aiken Sneath's department. 'I shall be most grateful,' he wrote, 'if you can find the time to read the whole report carefully, as I think there is a great deal to learn from it.'

He received further worrying information from Marjorie. She named a couple of the Right Club's government contacts. One of these worked at the Liverpool office of the Air Mail Censorship Department. The other was the previously anonymous fascist within the Ministry of Economic Warfare.

Learning more about the second of these contacts wouldn't be hard for Max. He just had to speak to Desmond Morton, who held the job of Principal Assistant Secretary at the ministry. Desmond could then monitor the man named by Marjorie.

On the same day she had raised the alarm about the Right Club having a contact inside Desmond's organization, Max obtained the results of the surveillance work on Wolkoff. It had led to 47 Gloucester Place being identified as the home address of her associate, Tyler Kent.

6

Summer was approaching, so dusk wasn't due to descend until just past nine – half-an-hour after the blackout curtains had to be drawn. That evening Tyler proceeded towards Piccadilly. Not to the American Club, but to the Ritz Hotel.

There was something Parisian about the vast scale of the Ritz, about its dormer-windowed roofline and the arcade skirting the front of it. One might almost have believed that the entire building had been transplanted from the rue de Rivoli, that fancy shopping street across the river from the Sorbonne, where Tyler had studied Russian.

Since the hotel's main restaurant no longer opened in the evenings, he walked into the arcade and then down the stairway to the basement, where he was due to dine with Anna and a friend.[80] Instead of going to the famous Grill Room, they went to the other basement restaurant, La Popote du Ritz. This had been trading for only a couple of months, yet it had already established itself as London's answer to such New York nightspots as the Empire Room and El Morocco. It had even aroused a disparaging reference from William Joyce on a recent radio show, which Anna had probably deciphered through the static. Joyce had tried to whip up class envy by citing La Popote as somewhere rich Londoners could evade the hardships of rationing.

Lit by an improvised chandelier, the necks of empty wine bottles doubling as candle-filled sconces, the restaurant was always awash with top military officers serving with the Allied nations. Their uniforms were in harmony with the décor, which made customers feel as if they had strayed into a scene from the old movie adaptation of *All Quiet on the Western Front*. Across the wall at the far end someone had painted a panoramic mural depicting a ruined First World War landscape, the trenches and bomb-craters providing an incongruous backdrop to a dance-band. Careful study of the mural revealed lewd graffiti marking the German trenches.

Unlike the upstairs restaurant at the Ritz, there was no dress code. Nor was there a booking system. You merely waited until a table fell vacant. Tyler, Anna and friend were in luck. Presently, they were poised to find out whether the food justi-fied its top-drawer reputation.

In contrast to the overcrowded menus at the hotel where Tyler had stayed when he'd arrived in London a few months before, the Ritz favoured a sparse three-course selection, elegantly typeset in French, which constituted no barrier to either Tyler or Anna. They could, as with any other restaurant, dine there without handing over any ration coupons. But the prices were steep. A meal, a glass of wine and a tip would leave no change from a couple of £1 notes – an appreciable slice of Tyler's weekly salary. Just as well, then, that he could trans-form US government paperwork into Bank of England notes.

7

Fay Taylour was talking about the newsreel she had seen at Studio Two, one of several specialist news cinemas in central London. The film, which received its first screening there on the morning after Anna's trip to the Ritz, devoted most of its running-time to Winston Churchill.

In the eyes of Anna, Fay, Christabel and many other British fascists, Churchill's bellicose posture towards the Nazis made him a bogeyman. Marjorie, who seldom resisted the opportu-nity to deliver sour remarks about him, gave every indication of agreeing with their sentiments. Despite contributing to this shared abhorrence of Churchill, Anna possessed the brand of second-hand connection to him that gives the pronouncements of gossips and namedroppers a flavour of bogus proximity. By a peculiar coincidence, her uncle Gabriel had once met him at a small supper party.

Describing the newsreel screened at Studio Two, Fay said it showed Churchill – in his capacity as First Sea Lord – greeting the survivors of HMS *Hardy*. Their ship had been sunk during the Norwegian campaign, which was still in progress, still hogging the headlines. Before Thursday when the programme at Studio Two would be changing, Fay took the Right Club women to see the Churchill newsreel.

Their destination was next to a vegetarian café on Oxford Street. Until the advent of the blackout, the cinema's tall front elevation had been a West End landmark, its marble cladding adorned by red, white and blue flashing neon letters that spelt out 'Studio One' and 'Studio Two'.

Dedicated to showing foreign language films, Studio One advertised the French comedian, Sacha Guitry, in *Ils Étaient 9 Celibataires (Nine Bachelors)*. But the Right Club women spurned the attractions of those comedic bachelors. Instead, they took the stairs down to Studio Two, a modest, balconied auditorium.

By prior arrangement, they dispersed across the seats bordering the gently sloping, garishly carpeted central aisle. They then settled down to watch the show. Prefaced by a burst of martial music and a sonorous American announcer proclaiming, '*The March of Time* …', it featured a black-and-white propaganda film about Canada's role in the war effort – seventeen minutes of soldiers and generals and factories and speckled footage from the First World War. There was a Disney cartoon as well. The stained-glass radiance of its Technicolor imagery stood out from the rest of the programme, which included the famous Pathé newsreel titles, their crowing cockerel and marching band ushering in a caption that filled a sizeable portion of the screen. 'HMS HARDY'S MEN IN LONDON.'

A long crocodile of uniformed and duffel-coated sailors, filmed in dingy monochrome, replaced the caption. Frequently making furtive eye-contact with the camera, they swaggered past a delighted crowd, many of whom raised their hats and waved handkerchiefs as a mark of respect, the cinema audience supplementing the deep-fat sputter of recorded applause. 'And Hardy's the word for these other heroes of the Royal Navy,' a voice-over declared. 'When their ship went aground, they *len*-ded in Norway as part of an expeditionary force of their own. Now Mr Churchill voices the Empire's congratulations …'

Cut to a shot of Churchill in a dark overcoat and matching homburg. The strapping naval officers and helmeted policemen on either side made him appear diminutive and elderly. His words dispensed in clusters, he began to speak into a microphone. 'We welcome you here ... for yourselves ... and, er, rejoice ... to show you ... how heartily we feel ... towards you ...'

As he said that, the Right Club women started to hiss. In Fay's case, however, the hissing was curtailed by a man in the row behind. He clamped a reproachful hand on her shoulder, precipitating an argument between the two of them that raged while Churchill's speech continued in the background.

'You are *eck*-tually the *ven*-guard ... of the armies ... which ... we and our French allies ... will use ... during this summer ... to purge ... and cleanse ... the soil of the Vikings ... the soil of Norway ... from the ... filthy ... pollution ... of Nazzee tyranny ...'

8

Joan Miller had something important to tell Max. She'd just been taken to dinner by Wolkoff at the Russian Tea Rooms.

Max – who was soon engaged in an adulterous romance with Joan – could congratulate himself on placing another agent within Wolkoff's circle of friends. Now it would be possible to triangulate their activities more precisely. It was the same principle used by the team of three trawlers on which he had served as a Royal Navy Reservist during the Great War. Each ship had been equipped with listening apparatus in the form of Zeppelin-shaped cylinders with microphones inside. These were lowered into the water and towed behind your ship. Unless the sea was really rough, Max recalled, you could use the microphones to obtain a tolerably accurate cross-bearing on enemy submarines.

Over dinner with Joan at the Tea Rooms, Wolkoff had talked a great deal. Much of her conversation was about her close friendship with Lord Cottenham. Several times she remarked on how she hadn't seen him for some time and wondered where he was. Joan expressed the belief that Wolkoff was trying to ascertain whether he still worked for MI5.

After dinner Joan accepted an invitation to go back to the flat where Wolkoff lived with her parents. There, Wolkoff showed her some of the dresses she was making.

Later that evening, Wolkoff – by then parted from Joan – went round to Manson Mews to see Marjorie, who reported that her visitor was in high spirits. Wolkoff told Marjorie about the most marvellous evening she had spent with her American friend at the Ritz. She also spoke about the dinner with Joan, whom she referred to as 'the Child'. Wolkoff added that the Child was quite unsuspecting of her motives. Apparently Wolkoff was planning to make a gift of one of the dresses Joan admired – a gift that would help her to befriend Joan.

Marjorie disclosed that Wolkoff hadn't just talked about Joan. She'd talked about seeing a letter from an officer in British Military Intelligence named 'Liddell'.

The man was plainly Max's boss, Guy Liddell. It transpired that Guy had been in correspondence with J. Edgar Hoover, Director of the FBI, about the possibility of Britain purchasing equipment that could be used to pinpoint German agents making illicit transmissions. The correspondence between Max's boss and J. Edgar Hoover turned out to have been channelled through the US Embassy in Grosvenor Square. Tyler Kent was the obvious source, his link to Wolkoff having previously been revealed. He must have purloined the document and then shown it to her.

Knowledge of this theft raised a disturbing question. What other documents had Kent stolen? In view of the ability of Wolkoff and her Right Club cronies to smuggle material to Germany, there was a strong possibility that Max had found a pipeline through which some of Britain and America's most significant secrets were gushing.

Perhaps he should apply for a warrant to search Kent's flat. But matters were complicated by Kent's status as the holder of a diplomatic passport. Whether a warrant could be served on the home of a member of the US Embassy's staff was a moot point. Before Kent could be prosecuted, the US government would, in any case, have to give its blessing.

Even if a warrant could be served on Kent's flat, there was always the danger that the application might be rejected because Max hadn't sufficient evidence. Other than the reports from Marjorie, what else did Max have?

Were he to obtain a warrant, the situation would still be problematic at best. He might search the place and come up empty-handed. There was, after all, no guarantee that Kent stored the stolen documents at home.

Serving a warrant had other implications, too. It would alert Kent to the fact that he had become the subject of an official inquiry. He'd then modify his behaviour. Once that happened, there wouldn't be a ghost of a chance of discovering anything more about his friends, anything that would enable the scope of Max's investigation to be widened, anything that might transform what already appeared to be a major case into a career-changing intelligence coup.

9

Tyler had patched up things with June Huntley since his bad-tempered departure from Bexhill. Spared for the moment from working night-shifts at the embassy, he spent the evening with the Huntleys at their flat. The three of them chatted and listened to one of the BBC's two radio stations – Home Service and Home Service for the Armed Forces.

Both stations' output was punctuated by news bulletins. These included a version in Gaelic, among the few European languages in which Tyler did not possess some degree of proficiency. An incongruous patchwork of other programmes filled the rest of the schedule – big-band performances, church services, extracts from classical music, comedy shows, lectures and light-hearted ditties of the sort Tyler used to perform with the Princeton Glee Club.

He began sounding off about the BBC, comparing it unfavourably to the latest of its Nazi rivals. 'You should hear the broadcasts from the anti-British radio station,' he said to the Huntleys.

10

Max was kept waiting until Saturday 27 April, 1940. Only then did Section B6 – MI5's surveillance specialists – finally get round to issuing the report he wanted. It was about their latest, disappointingly brief shadowing of Anna Wolkoff, conducted more than a week earlier.

At 5 p.m. on Friday 19 April, the Watchers had assumed their positions outside the Wolkoffs' home. Excluding a couple of cars parked along that stretch of Roland Gardens, the surveillance team saw nothing of interest until 6.20 p.m. when two women departed from the flat, accompanied by a tall, clean-shaven naval officer, aged between thirty and forty. Max suspected that the officer was Lord Ronald Graham. The officer certainly fitted his description.

Facially and in terms of their physique, both women looked similar to one another, the report informed Max. 'Woman A' – whom the Watchers identified as Wolkoff – was dressed in black, the outfit topped by a green French cavalry officers' style peaked cap with a black feather protruding from it. Her counterpart, named in the report as Anne van Lennep, wore a black hat and matching astrakhan coat. She was labelled 'Woman B'.

The naval officer, who came out of the flat with them, got into a car and headed in the direction of Chelsea Embankment. Peaked Cap and Astrakhan Coat went off in another car, which the Watchers followed along Roland Gardens and over to Harrington Road. When they reached the Russian Tea Rooms, Peaked Cap stepped out of the vehicle and said something to Astrakhan Coat, who drove away. The Watchers then tailed Peaked Cap to South Kensington tube station, where she boarded a no. 49 bus to Chelsea. Fifteen minutes after parting from her friend, she entered the Classic Cinema on King's Road.

Emerging into the dusk two hours later, Peaked Cap hiked over to 22 Paradise Walk, took out a key, opened the door and disappeared inside. The Watchers lingered for five minutes before abandoning the surveillance.

From the information Max had already built up, though, it was clear to him that they had tailed the wrong woman – Anne van Lennep instead of Anna Wolkoff. Maintaining his composure, Max sent the surveillance report back to Section B6 with a diplomatically worded memo pointing out that 'some confusion' had arisen.

But the failings of B6 had by then been counterbalanced to some extent by Marjorie's impressive productivity. She'd notified Max about a Right Club propaganda campaign being coordinated by Captain Ramsay. In collaboration with three friends in the agricultural world, all of whom turned out to have MI5 files on them, Ramsay was planning to try to build popular support by spreading his message to farm labourers.

Marjorie also identified another long-term propaganda operation waged by the Right Club, this time coordinated by Wolkoff. Copying the old template created by fascist organizations such as the Nordic League, Right Club members were being encouraged to patronize small shops and, wherever possible, discern the proprietor's attitude towards Jews. Any shopkeepers exhibiting signs of racial prejudice could then be supplied anonymously with anti-Semitic pamphlets and other such material, the objective being that these might one day help to instigate riots against Britain's Jewish population.

11

Not long ago Max had become a member of Surrey County Cricket Club. Members were invited to attend the club's annual general meeting, scheduled for that Thursday. But Max had more weighty questions to consider than the re-election of the club's management committee.

The day before the cricket club's AGM, the British Union had attracted 4,000 people to an open-air rally in the East End of London. And now Max had received a warning from Marjorie about the danger posed by Wolkoff's relationship with her American friend. 'There is no doubt that Tyler Kent is a definite Fifth Column member,' Marjorie asserted. 'He is always reporting to Anna Wolkoff matters which he claims he obtains from confidential sources in the American Embassy and which, to say the least of it, are damaging both to the Allies and America.

'For instance, he recently told Anna Wolkoff that Mr Kennedy had written to President Roosevelt a report saying that things in this country were so bad that serious internal trouble might develop at any time. This report is also alleged to contain information relating to the discussions of the War Cabinet. It is said that the discussion's were most acrimonious, that Mr Churchill was drunk, that Mr Churchill had entirely lost his following in England, due to the appalling losses and muddle in Norway.

'Although this sort of stuff may appear to those in authority to be hardly worth troubling about, it is undoubtedly the sort of verbal propaganda which is very swiftly passed from person to person by word of mouth.'

So far-reaching were the repercussions of the Wolkoff inquiry that Jasper Harker, head of B Division, the section within which Max operated, began to follow its progress. Formerly a high-ranking officer in the Indian colonial police, Harker was a well-groomed, not quite handsome man in his mid-fifties. Within MI5 he had a reputation for being a bit irascible. His interest in the Wolkoff case could not help but exert pressure on Max to bring matters to a successful conclusion. The involvement of someone of such seniority might, on the other hand, enable Max to obtain surveillance and other additional resources more readily.

Max telephoned Section B6 and requested that Anna should be placed under observation from 7 p.m. onwards next evening. Based on the knowledge that she had arranged to visit Marjorie, he mentioned that Wolkoff would be leaving 24 Manson Mews at around 7.15 p.m.

He reminded B6 about the Watchers tailing the wrong person last time. 'Anna Wolkoff is a much shorter and older woman.'

12

Tyler went for a meal at Captain Ramsay's house in Onslow Square on the day of Max's phonecall to Section B6. Delighted that Tyler shared his anti-Semitism, Ramsay afterwards invited the American to join the Right Club. Having accepted, Tyler signed a subscription card and handed over ten shillings. Even though this was sufficient to purchase only the fourth of the club's five ranks of membership, Ramsay rewarded Tyler by appointing him to the second highest of those. He was now a Steward of the Right Club.

In a further display of trust, the Captain deposited a weighty book with him for safekeeping. Bound in deep-red calfskin with the words 'Private Ledger' printed on its spine, the book had a lock. Tyler was nonetheless told about its contents. These comprised the Right Club's membership list.

Among the members were many prominent and influential people. The Captain had promised them that the book would be kept somewhere secure, ensuring their membership remained secret. His ability to fulfil that pledge had been jeopardized by the recent police raid on Molly Stanford's flat and by the news that several fellow fascists had been burgled and their papers ransacked, presumably by MI5. If the same thing happened to the Ramsays' home, the book could end up falling into the clutches of the authorities. Since Tyler not only had access to a safe at the US Embassy but also possessed diplomatic immunity from prosecution in the British courts, he was an ideal guardian for the Captain's precious volume.

13

By the following day Max had netted a couple more reports from Marjorie. She began by letting him know that Captain Ramsay had, in view of likely government action against Fifth Column organizations, decided to suspend a good deal of the

Right Club's work. Ramsay had, however, issued instructions to Wolkoff that attention should still be paid to any contact in a position to supply information regarding government plans.

Through the second of Marjorie's briefings, Max discovered that Ramsay had received a tip-off. It had come from a man named P. G. Taylor, which was one of the favourite aliases used by James McGuirk Hughes, the British Union's Chief of Intelligence. Ramsay had been warned that MI5 was investigating him, Wolkoff and Lord Ronald Graham. He had also been warned that the Security Service had already gathered a lot of material about the three of them.

As well as alerting Max to the tip-off, Marjorie reported on a conversation between her and Wolkoff, who was exasperated because Ramsay had not honoured a promise. This concerned Fifth Column work, which appeared to involve Tyler Kent. Wolkoff said the Captain had sworn not to mention these activities to anyone else. But Wolkoff had discovered that he'd confided in his wife. For the first time Wolkoff seemed really frightened. Though Marjorie regarded her as being neither a coward nor a hysteric, she had started talking about the possibility of being arrested, put on trial and incarcerated in the Tower of London.

Rounding off a commendable haul, Marjorie gave Max a revealing description of a meeting at the Ramsays' house, staged the previous Tuesday. Wolkoff and other members of the Right Club's Inner Circle had attended. When they'd discussed the Norwegian campaign, defeatist comments had peppered the conversation.

Britain's plight was infinitely worse than either the government or press were leading them to believe, Ramsay had assured everyone. 'Personally I should welcome a civil war with shots in the streets,' he'd added.

14

Section B6 granted Max's request to carry out surveillance during the evening of Friday 3 May, 1940. Max had to hope that B6 didn't, like last time, make him wait more than a week before letting him know what the Watchers had seen.

The following day he set down a two-page digest of his findings about Kent, which could be used to satisfy the Head of B Division's sudden interest in the case. Max's summary drew on several of the reports provided by Marjorie, whose identity he continued to protect behind the codename 'M/Y'.

'It is stressed that all information collected by B5b is extremely delicate,' Max warned, the apparent leakage of material about the operation to James McGuirk Hughes surely uppermost in his mind.

That same day Max received a report from B6 on the previous evening's surveillance. Around 6.45 p.m., the lone Watcher – who had participated in the earlier botched operation – had been stationed close to Marjorie's flat in Manson Mews. From that position, the Watcher had seen an Austin 7 Saloon stop briefly outside. Assisted by the government's Vehicle Registration Department, Max discovered that the car belonged to a woman named Enid Riddell.

Inside the vehicle were two women. One of them, known in the report as 'Woman A', got out of the vehicle, which then drove off. She went into the flat. For the next ten minutes or so, the Watcher had nothing to report. Not until a taxicab pulled up in front of Marjorie's place. The cab only stayed long enough for another woman to emerge from it and enter the flat.

Designated as 'Woman B', she had been visible for no more than a moment or two. Even so, the Watcher was still able to provide a passable description of what was believed to be Wolkoff. In fact, the clothes gave away who 'Woman B' really was – Marjorie Amor, *not* Anna Wolkoff.

Twenty minutes later, the car that had dropped off 'Woman A' reappeared. Its driver – 'Woman C' – parked in Manson Mews and disappeared into Marjorie's flat. But the Watcher witnessed no more activity for the next three-quarters of an hour.

At 8 p.m. 'A' and 'C' exited the flat and climbed into the latter's car. Tailed by the Watcher's vehicle, 'C' drove round to the Russian Tea Rooms, where she deposited her companion.

When 'A' entered the Tea Rooms, the Watcher recognized her from previous surveillance. She had since been identified as Anne van Lennep.

The Watcher followed her into the café, where she joined a couple of women. Aged about sixty, the elder of them wore a navy-blue dress and a red straw hat. The younger woman, who looked in her mid-twenties, was dressed in grey. She even had a grey striped scarf. On the basis of the descriptions that came with the report, these women were, in ascending age, Hélène de Munck and Mrs Newnham, wife of the editor of the pro-fascist newspaper, *Truth*.

A couple of the Right Club group left the café at 9.40 p.m. and strolled round to where Anne van Lennep's car was parked. They used the car to drive back to Manson Mews. The remaining woman meanwhile walked there in the company of a fourth woman, who had been working in the Tea Rooms. All of the women went into Marjorie's flat.

Observation persisted on Manson Mews until 10 p.m. The blackout made it impossible for the Watcher to see anything by then. But Max only had to have a discreet word with Marjorie to find out what happened inside the Manson Mews flat.

She reported that Wolkoff had, during the meeting, said the time had come to appoint an understudy. Enid Riddell would be trained for the role currently fulfilled by Wolkoff – the role of aide-de-camp to Captain Ramsay. Wolkoff had also arranged for Enid to attend a dinner party next Thursday. Wolkoff wanted her to dress up to the nines in order to make a favourable impression on someone there. Who that person was remained a tantalizing mystery.

15

Anna had agreed to do Tyler a favour. It entailed going round to Woolworth's. From Tyler's flat, the nearest branch of this department store was towards the Marble Arch end of Edgware Road. Anna could be there in a few minutes if she borrowed the car.

Step through the doors of Woolworth's and one was assailed by a cornucopia of cheap household goods. There was even a seasoning of little luxuries. Perfumed soap. Toys. Boiled sweets. Nothing priced at more than sixpence.

Today Anna made for the key-cutting counter, where she proffered the two Yale keys that Tyler had given her. She asked for duplicates. The great thing about having this done at Woolworth's was that she could always go to the shop's cafeteria and have a quick cup of tea while she waited for them to be cut.

Both keys were from the US Embassy. One of them fitted the door to the File Room and the other opened the Code Room. Tyler wanted them because he was worried that he might be reassigned to a different part of the embassy.

His sudden anxiety had probably been set off by something he'd seen in the files at work. Last autumn, Ambassador Kennedy had sent a scathing message to the State Department regarding their decision to transfer Tyler to the Grosvenor Square Code Room. 'For a clearing house as busy as the London embassy, first-class Code Clerks are essential, not merely clerks in other lines,' Kennedy had written.

If the Ambassador found a replacement for him, Tyler would forfeit his access to the telegrams being sent between Washington, London and other outposts. By obtaining duplicates of the two Yale keys, Anna had just averted that frustrating prospect.

16

Whenever Tyler spoke to Anna on the telephone, she made a point of talking to him in brisk Russian. She hoped that would foil MI5 if they were eavesdropping on calls from her parents' flat.

Lately Tyler had been seeing plenty of Anna and her friends. She introduced him to another staunch fascist, Lord Ronald Graham – Ronnie to pals like Anna. From the US Embassy's fuel allocation, Tyler acquired some petrol for him.

Ronnie ended up inviting Tyler round to his ritzy London pied-à-terre. It consisted of a flat in a sizeable house near to where the Nicholsons lived. His flat was shared on a temporary basis with an ex-Army officer who belonged to the Right Club and British Union. Ronnie's friend openly praised the Nazi regime and criticized the British government's failure to deal with what he portrayed as 'the Jewish menace'. No wonder Anna had started referring to Ronnie's flat as 'the Brown House' – a facetious allusion to the *Braunes Haus*, the Nazi Party's national headquarters in Munich.

Besides being introduced to Ronnie, Tyler had several evenings ago been taken round to the Nicholsons' again. In this instance, however, he hadn't needed to cut short his visit and hurry off to work. Over supper he had the chance to talk expansively about Russia.

So successful was the dinner party, Admiral Nicholson had invited Tyler to lunch at the United Service Club. Known as 'The Senior' by virtue of the senior military men who made up its membership, the club was some two miles from where Tyler lived. It occupied a stone-fronted neoclassical building that resembled the government buildings in Washington, DC.

Both in respect of its setting and clientele, the United Service Club offered a striking contrast to the Barcelona, that unassuming little Spanish restaurant in Soho where Tyler often ate.[81] Through the foyer was a short corridor leading to a huge stairway with a proportionately huge chandelier above it. Off the second-floor landing lay the Quick Luncheon Room, which attracted past and present military men, plus a smattering of Cabinet ministers. Uncommonly for a gentlemen's club, women were permitted to dine there. Food was doled out not through conventional table service but from behind a counter, a strangely unceremonious system for such a grandiose institution.

While Tyler was there, he talked about one of his host's favourite subjects – corruption in high places. By way of illustration, he showed the Admiral samples from his collection of stolen documents. He followed up by asking the Admiral round to his flat to inspect the Churchill–Roosevelt correspondence – or at least a judiciously selected portion of it.

17

Anna's train didn't pull out of Paddington Station until two o'clock on the afternoon of Wednesday 8 May, 1940 – fifteen minutes behind schedule. One simply couldn't place much faith in timetables anymore. There were far fewer trains, too. And those that were available invariably took longer.

Each of the train's carriages was partitioned into six-seat compartments, reached via narrow corridors. Between the headrests and the netting-strung luggage-racks were black-and-white framed photographs of beauty spots such as Lulworth Cove and St Michael's Mount.

The first stage of Anna's journey, which saw her train rattle past a goods yard and under a succession of bridges, grey light pulsing arhythmically through the windows, was scheduled to take an hour and thirty-five minutes. It offered her the chance to relax and maybe even ponder the autobiographical novel she had been writing in her spare time, though there hadn't been much of *that* lately, even at weekends.

Part of the previous weekend had been taken up by a trip to see a family friend – Grand Duchess Xenia. Alongside a Russian Orthodox nun-turned-housekeeper, the Grand Duchess lived at Wilderness House, a mansion given to her by King George V. The house was in the grounds of Hampton Court Palace. Inclined to wistful reminiscences about 'the old Russia', the Grand Duchess shared Anna's hatred of Communism.

Things had been even busier for Anna since the weekend. She'd needed to dash all over the place, carrying out dress-fittings. So much work had been coming her way that she'd started employing a freelance seamstress. What with her dress-making and her Right Club meetings, Anna had had little time for anything else. Catching sight of Francis Hemming and his wife at the Russian Tea Rooms the other day, she had gone up to them and explained that she wouldn't be free to give Francis any more German lessons for a while.

Beyond an encampment of gas-holders was Kensal Rise Cemetery, a couple of vast train sheds and a broad swathe of

308 | Rendezvous at the Russian Tea Rooms

grassland, past which one could see the grim outline of
Wormwood Scrubs Prison, where Marjorie and Joan worked.
As the jail disappeared out of sight, Anna's train began its
gentle chuffing ascent through suburbia, coils of smoke from its
engine inevitably obscuring her view from time to time.
Gradually, London's tight weave of buildings and roads loos-
ened, making way for small fields across which those new
electricity pylons had been crudely stitched.

When Anna alighted on Oxford Station's long northbound
platform, where the subdued light was dimmed still further by
a low canopy, she had almost two hours to kill before her
connection was due. For the second stage of her journey she
boarded a much smaller train to Banbury. Mostly used by shoppers, it took her down a branch-line that spooled through rustic
scenery. She needed to get out at Aynho, a tiny station only
thirty-five minutes away.

Even during daylight hours, it was difficult to know if one had
arrived at one's destination. The majority of station name-boards
had been removed. Others had been replaced with signs featuring letters no more than three inches high, all for the purpose of
giving as little assistance as possible to any German invaders.

From the station, Anna travelled to the village of Barford St
Michael, where the honey-coloured Cotswold stone lent the
buildings a cohesive prettiness. Her goal was Rignell House,
just on the margin of the village. Reached via an avenue of
recently planted horse-chestnut saplings that led through
extensive grounds, encompassing stables and a swimming-pool,
this was an Edwardian hunting lodge with a hilltop setting and
a decidedly forbidding appearance. It served as home to Anna's
friend, Pam Jackson; Pam's husband Derek; and their three
long-haired dachshunds, 'the darling dogs', each of which bore
German names. Derek had filled the place with colourful
modern furniture, set against brightly hued walls. These were
embellished by the sort of figurative paintings that were to
Anna's taste – several Henry Lamb portraits and a large still
life by Augustus John.

Pam's husband derived his substantial inherited wealth
from part-ownership of the *News of the World*, one of Britain's

most popular Sunday papers. A flamboyant, bisexual aristocrat with dark hair and the pinched features of a malign pixie, he embodied the seemingly incompatible roles of amateur jockey and eminent Oxford University research physicist.

His wife was a jovial thirty-three year old with pencilled-in eyebrows, a *retroussé* nose, otherworldly blue eyes and a shrieking laugh. By far the least known of the celebrated Mitford sisters, the children of Lord Redesdale, her siblings included Unity Mitford, a member of the coterie around Hitler. Pam was particularly close to their sister, Diana, wife of Sir Oswald Mosley, who also happened to be a friend of Derek.

Flagrantly pro-Nazi, Derek blamed the British working classes for pushing the country into war with Germany and lamented that the government didn't follow Hitler's lead by crushing them.[82] Both Derek and Pam were, like Anna, impassioned supporters of the British Union, regularly attending meetings at which Sir Oswald spoke. The Jacksons' political outlook was shared by the stream of posh, slightly dim local friends who liked to pop round to Rignell House, where discussion was liable to centre on the military background of so many British Union members and its probable role in helping Sir Oswald overthrow the government.

Like Enid Riddell and Christabel Nicholson, Pam was a client *and* a close friend of Anna, the bonds of friendship tightened by ideological accord. That evening Anna had the chance to tell her about the Right Club's latest activities and those of Captain Ramsay.

Vocal in expressing their opinions, Pam and Derek endorsed Anna's savage anti-Semitism, even going so far as to declare that all Jews in England should be slaughtered. The owners of Rignell House were also in agreement with Anna regarding her belief that Britain ought to make peace with Hitler.

Pam could speak from personal experience when it came to discussing the Führer's motives, intentions and personality. On the first of two pilgrimages she'd made to Nazi Germany, she had visited the party headquarters and met the Führer. Her introduction to him had come through her sister, Unity, who had taken her to meet him at a restaurant in Munich, where they'd dined with his friend, Heinrich Hoffmann, the man responsible for supplying Nazi propaganda to Anna's fascist associates.

During the visit to Rignell House, Pam gave Anna the full story of Unity's recent well-publicized 'accident'. Unity had, Anna was told, developed a powerful infatuation with the Führer, who had given her numerous assurances that a military conflict between Germany and England could be prevented. As soon as war between the two countries had been announced, Unity had evidently suffered some form of brainstorm and shot herself in the head. Pam said the bullet was still lodged in her skull. The doctors were predicting that she would never fully recover. According to Pam, the Führer had paid for all the necessary medical care.

By the time Anna had finished chatting with Pam and also carrying out the scheduled dress-fitting, she'd missed the last train to the Hampshire village where another of the Right Club network lived. Nocturnal railway travel was, in any event, worth avoiding for a number of reasons, not least because the carriages were unheated, the trains were dependably late and the dull, blue-tinted ceiling lights rendered books and newspapers redundant.

18

Anna resumed her journey next morning. If she was in luck, the trip would take a touch over four hours. It involved her catching the train from Aynho back to Oxford, then picking up the mainline connection to Reading, from where she had to transfer to another bucolic branch-line. But she still had to change trains twice more after that.

Irked by just how difficult her journey had been, Anna eventually arrived in the village of Alton. Her ageing friend from the British Union, Muriel Whinfield, was based in a farmhouse just outside the village. Muriel had been with Anna to hear Mosley speak at the Criterion Restaurant the month before last.

A firm believer that a woman's place was in the home, Muriel nonetheless advocated greater female engagement with politics. She set an example by devotedly reading and contributing to the British Union newspaper, *Action*. That week's edition carried a front-page article by Sir Oswald, who was a friend of hers. It laid out his 'Four Points for Peace' with Germany. These provided fertile grounds for conversation between Muriel and Anna. So too did the subject of illicit channels of communication between Britain and the Continent, something about which both women were equipped to discuss knowledgeably.

Muriel had been sending letters to her son, currently imprisoned in Switzerland, where the authorities had arrested him because of his involvement with two Nazi agents. To stop MI5 from censoring or even reading her letters to him, Muriel had employed the services of a fellow British Union stalwart, who smuggled her messages across the Channel. She had recently tried to improve the security of this arrangement by learning how to encode her letters.

19

His self-declared failings as a correspondent notwithstanding, Tyler was keeping in touch with his Russian friends in Moscow. His messages to them could be mailed via Donald H. Nichols, who still worked there.[83] Tyler just had to use the diplomatic pouch if he wanted to send any of his stolen documents to Tanya and her NKVD masters.

These past few weeks, however, Tyler's letter-writing had not extended to even the briefest of notes to his mother. Of late, there had been plenty to distract him from his filial duty.

At that moment on the evening of Thursday 9 May, 1940, he and Anna – fresh from her trip to Hampshire – were waiting in his flat. Enid Riddell was due to call round. He had met Enid a couple of times before, though they'd only talked briefly. They would be dining tonight with Anna and another friend of hers at L'Escargot Bienvenu, a famously high-class French restaurant.

Enid turned up wearing a coat that Anna had made for her. Anna reintroduced the pair of them. Initially, Enid didn't take much notice of Tyler – a novelty for someone accustomed to the flutter of female attention.

The three of them were soon ensconced in Enid's cramped little Austin 7, petrol for which she somehow obtained. She hoarded it in a special auxiliary tank under the bonnet and in a couple of cans that she kept in the car. A fast and skilful driver, she gave Tyler and Anna a lift to the restaurant. It was in Soho, Tyler's old neighbourhood.

Owned by an elderly, white-haired Frenchman, L'Escargot Bienvenu – close to the Nut House Club, where Mira Dimitri and her husband liked to go – had an intimate, authentically French ambience. Here, Tyler's group was swelled by the addition of a short, lean, sallow-complexioned Italian in his early fifties. The man, who dressed with the foppish elan of an American gangster, had close-set eyes, grey hair and dark eyebrows so prominent they looked as if they had been drawn with charcoal. Deeply incised double brackets appeared on either side of his mouth whenever he smiled. His name was Colonel Francisco Marigliano, the Duke del Monte, though Anna addressed him by what Tyler recognized as a silly alias – 'Mr Macaroni'.

She introduced Enid to the Italian. But no such formalities were necessary in the case of Tyler, who already knew him. The Duke del Monte was both a long-time friend of Anna and a neighbour of Tyler's friend, Lady Luba Fletcher. Coming face to face with one another, Tyler and the Duke simply exchanged a casual 'Hullo'.

Del Monte had worked as Assistant Military Attaché at the Italian Embassy since well before the fascists had taken control of his country. He was nonetheless a supporter of both fascism and the Italian dictator, Benito Mussolini. Recently, he had travelled hundreds of miles across Britain searching for a suitably docile pony to present to Mussolini's grand-child, the chosen animal shipped to Italy with an ingratiating note. The Duke's more orthodox duties embraced the harvesting and collation of military information about Britain. And he was required to function as a courier, transporting confidential material back and forward from Italy via the diplomatic pouch. He hadn't long returned from just such a trip to his homeland.

Delicious, vine-fed snails were, as the name implied, L'Escargot Bienvenu's speciality. But Tyler and company weren't in luck, the snail season having ended some weeks earlier. That said, the menu always boasted alternative Gallic delicacies, among them *grenouilles*, *moules marinière* and *tripe à la mode de Caen* – a dish that people tended to love or loathe.

While Tyler and the others were at the restaurant, he spent much time talking to Enid about his days at the US Embassy in Moscow. Reference to this gave rise to her showing more interest in him. For her part, she spoke about her passion for motor racing and about competing in the Le Mans 24-Hour race, as well as the Monte Carlo and Paris-to-St Raphael rallies.

There was also a long conversation across the dinner table about the well-publicized diplomatic row between Britain and Italy. Over two months had passed since the dispute had first erupted. It had been caused by the British government's decision to use its Navy to prevent Germany from exporting coal to Italy by sea. The Italians had consequently submitted a letter of protest to the British Embassy in Rome. Extracts had been quoted in the British press. These warned that Britain's policy would jeopardize relations between the two countries.

Enid – a great admirer of Mussolini's regime – asked the Duke whether he thought his country would enter the war.

He said that he felt Italy would remain neutral. Later in the evening he elaborated on the theme of Italian neutrality. Pulling a series of newspaper cuttings from his pocket, he said the English press was behaving as if Italy were an enemy. He complained that the papers had printed dreadful things about Mussolini, calling him rude names and so forth. His countrymen were, he added, most upset by this.

20

What must have been a hefty bill for their meal at L'Escargot Bienvenu appears to have been settled by Tyler. Brushing aside his evident tiredness, Anna sought to prolong her enjoyment by including him in plans to go dancing.

Enid agreed to drive them to the Embassy Club where the Duke was a member. Anna continued to address him as 'Mr Macaroni', her choice of nickname highlighting not just his nationality but also his dress sense, 'a macaroni' being an archaic synonym for a dandy.

By reputation, the Embassy Club was the world's smartest and most fashionable nightspot. Squeezed between an exclusive jeweller's and a bookshop on Old Bond Street, its discreetly recessed swing-doors concealed a long corridor. Near the end was a counter where the Duke and the rest of the club's predominantly monied customers – actors and actresses, politicians, aristocrats, press barons, and the majority of the royal family's younger representatives – had to flash their membership cards and pay the entrance fee.

The Duke covered the admission price for Anna and the rest of their group, whose visit coincided with the club's weekly Gala Evening when the place was at its busiest. Anna and her party stepped into a spacious yet disproportionately narrow, parquet-floored auditorium with a row of red velvet-upholstered sofas along the far wall. Plentiful mirrors exaggerated the scale of the place and its opulent, bustling sparkle.

Ahead of Anna and friends was a maze of dinner tables with waiters rattling round them like pinballs. To their left was the stage from where Reginald Foresythe and His Orchestra, the famous house band, played thunderously loud swing.

Together with many other West End nightclubs, the Embassy got round Britain's restrictive late-night licensing laws by transforming itself into a so-called 'bottle party club'. Legally speaking, Anna and the others weren't at a nightclub. They were, instead, guests at a private party. As such, it could keep going until the early hours.

Bartenders at the Embassy didn't sell wine and other drinks. They and the waiters just served bottles that members had previously ordered from a local wine merchant. Each of the bottles had a label with the purchaser's name pasted across it.

While you gazed round, chatted and sampled a glass of something, you would frequently catch sight of a trim, sprightly man in evening dress ghosting from table to table. That man – a compatriot of the Duke del Monte – was the club's well-known manager. Loath to intrude, he would pause for no more than a split-second at your table and ask, 'Everything all right?'

A nod or a smile would send him gliding away.

Talk among Anna's party was hamstrung by the volume of the music. Obviously smitten by Enid, the Duke – despite being a married man – monopolized her. The two of them were soon making for the tiny, spotlit dancefloor. Tyler and Anna accompanied them. Anna was now very much in love with her American friend.

She'd been taught to dance when she was at school, where they had practised all sorts of steps. On the tennis court one summer, eight of them had donned sumptuous, high-collared Elizabethan-style gowns and performed a stately pavane.

Conducted by a dapper, rangy black man with a pencil moustache and a demeanour of gentlemanly sophistication, the Embassy Club's band had a repertoire spanning a number of tunes blessed with a propellant rhythm. There was 'Serenade for a Wealthy Widow', one moment as soft and demure as something that a palm-court orchestra might play, the next moment brassy and up-tempo, conjuring an atmosphere at once louche and sexy. There was also the slinky, melancholic 'Garden of Weed', laced with the shimmer of cymbals, the doleful drumbeat. And then there was the jaunty 'Dodging a Divorcée', which evoked Fred Astaire and Ginger Rogers skittering across an elaborate film set.

Endeavouring to perform anything even half as flamboyant as an Astaire and Rogers routine or one of those energetic new dance-steps – say, the Siegfried, the Hitler Kick or the Blackout Stroll, which necessitated the lights being temporarily extinguished – was seldom possible, however, in such a confined space. Regulars had their own style of dancing, their shuffling movements scarcely covering any ground.

Just after midnight Anna, Tyler and the others traded the conviviality of the Embassy Club for the darkness and fresh air outside. So enjoyable had the evening been that they had already spoken about organizing a sequel.

They then groped their way back to Enid's car. With the four of them shoehorned into it, she set off down Piccadilly, round Hyde Park Corner and onto Knightsbridge. Her plan was to drop the Duke off first at his home in Cadogan Square. They were just approaching there when her car suffered a puncture. Bad timing because the rain had started to tap its fingers on the roof.

Instead of stopping the car right away and getting drenched while she installed the spare wheel, Enid was directed round the corner to Shafto Mews where the Duke had a garage.

Safely out of the rain, Anna and her friends began the task of replacing the punctured tyre. The Duke waited until the spare had been fitted before bidding them goodnight. As he walked back to Cadogan Square, the others ducked into the car and set off for Tyler's flat.

21

Anna went round for supper at Tyler's place next evening. Just the pair of them.

Neville Chamberlain meanwhile read out a statement over the radio. 'Earlier this morning, without warning or excuse, Hitler added another to the horrible crimes which already disgrace his name by a sudden attack on Holland, Belgium and Luxembourg,' the Prime Minister said. 'In all history no other man has been responsible for such a hideous total of human suffering and misery as he. He has chosen a moment when, perhaps, it seemed to him that this country was entangled in the throes of a political crisis and he might find it divided against itself. If he has counted upon our internal divisions to help him, he has miscalculated the mind of this people.

'I am not going to make any comments on the debate in the House of Commons which took place on Tuesday and Wednesday, but when it was over I had no doubt in my mind that some new and drastic action must be taken if confidence was to be restored to the House of Commons and the war carried on with the energy and vigour essential to victory. What was that action to be? It was clear that at this critical moment in the war what was needed was the formation of a government which would include members of the Labour and Liberal oppositions and thus present a united front to the enemy.

'What had to be ascertained were the conditions which would be necessary to enable such a united government to be formed, and to this question I devoted myself – with the assistance of some of my colleagues – all yesterday afternoon. In the afternoon of today it was apparent that the essential unity could be secured under another Prime Minister, though not myself.

'In these circumstances my duty was plain. I sought an audience of the King and tendered to him my resignation, which His Majesty has been pleased to accept. His Majesty has now entrusted to my friend and colleague, Mr Winston Churchill, the task of forming a new administration on a national basis.'

The announcement could not fail to enrage Anna.

22

Monday to Friday the following week, Tyler was assigned the 4 p.m. to midnight shift at the embassy, where his recent habit of voicing pro-Nazi opinions had begun to catch people's attention. Prior to his shift-pattern changing, he kept on making the most of his evenings off. Tonight – Saturday 11 May, 1940 he went to dinner in a smart neighbourhood between Kensington Church Street and Holland Park. His busty hostess, whose pregnancy afforded cause for congratulation, was the stepdaughter of a former US Consul-General.

Among the other guests was the elegant, upper-class American wife of a Conservative MP. The woman, still in her twenties, recognized Tyler. She had seen him eating at various West End restaurants. The other coincidence was that she'd socialized with many of the people in Anna's orbit, including Captain and Mrs Ramsay, Jean Nieuwenhuys, plus the Comte and Comtesse de Laubespin. Tyler's latest acquaintance had moreover come with a young English friend, a former debutante who knew Anna, not to mention Barbara Allen.[84]

Dialogue between Tyler and his fellow guests drifted towards events in Europe. Since the German invasion of Holland, Belgium and Luxembourg, it had been revealed that German bombers had attacked several French towns. An announcement had also been made that Britain and France were responding to an appeal from the governments of the three invaded countries. Part of the British Expeditionary Force had, together with French troops, advanced across the Franco–Belgian border.

Tyler was soon regaling his hostess and her other guests with what he presented as an insider's guide to the war. He said that the Germans had been conducting military training in Russia; that French troops were likely to turn tail at the first sign of danger; that Hitler had stationed five Army divisions in Genoa; that Turkey would not intervene in the war; that any German invasion of Romania would be a two-day job at the outside; and that the British were afraid of the Italian Navy.

Another of the guests challenged him by pointing out that every British sailor seemed to express a keen desire to fight their Italian counterparts. Tyler was asked to name a single naval officer who was apprehensive about the prospect of a war against Italy.

With great conviction, he replied, '*The British Admiralty*.' Further resistance against the Germans was useless, he declared. Britain should sue for peace as fast as possible.

23

The May bank holiday had been cancelled, underlining the situation in which Max's country found itself. Monday was now an ordinary working day, yet there were fewer vehicles on the roads than normal. And the pavements near Max's home were a lot less silted up with pedestrians. One could almost believe that London had become trapped in a replay of last autumn. Same beautiful weather. Same rash of Ministry of Information posters. Same gasmasks hanging from people's shoulders. Same feeling of stomach-clenching dread.

Complying with the government's appeal for 'business as usual' on what should have been a bank holiday, Marjorie delivered another report. She informed Max about Wolkoff's dinner the previous week with Tyler Kent, Enid Riddell and an unnamed Italian duke. Precisely where Wolkoff and her companions had dined, Marjorie hadn't managed to find out. The purpose of the dinner had, she believed, been somehow connected to Italian shipping. As to the exact details, she could not be certain. The results of a freshly established series of what were known as 'telephone checks' – phone-taps – were no more helpful in that respect.

24

Much as Jock Ramsay had envisaged, the Right Club circle was continuing its gradual and cautious expansion. Now the coterie at the Russian Tea Rooms incorporated a middle-aged woman who had recently returned from Germany. The woman, jilted by her German fiancé, had been introduced to Anna by Mollie Hiscox. Even though the woman had since been questioned several times by MI5, she had just lined up a job with the Bank of England.[85] For Anna and friends, she offered a potentially rich source of information from within the heart of the British establishment.

On the day she was due to start her new job – Tuesday 14 May, 1940 – the latest in a stream of anti-Semitic, anti-government propaganda emanated from Anna's camp. Produced by Fay Taylour with Jock's help, this took the form of an eight-page newsletter entitled *The Voice of the People and the Home Defence Movement*. Beneath the slogan, 'The language of truth is simple', the newsletter featured a selection of anonymous articles that supported the British Union's 'Stop the War' campaign. These included a paean to the Nazi leader. 'Whether one considers Hitler to be a monster or a saviour, a tyrant or a leader, good or bad,' Fay's newsletter announced, 'one is forced to admit that he has proved himself to be the greatest states-man and general in the entire history of the world.'

Giving vent to familiar Right Club obsessions, the newslet-ter also featured a rant against the Jews, whom it blamed for a cross-section of humanity's woes, even the English Civil War. Other targets for invective were Freemasons and Winston Churchill – 'I venture to prophesy that his career as Prime Minister will be a short and stormy one.'

Ancillary criticism was levelled at William C. Bullitt, one-time American Ambassador in Moscow, now heading the Paris embassy, correspondence from which Tyler had been collecting. Bullitt had done little to win Tyler's loyalty, having several times attempted to sack him when they both worked in Moscow.

Thomas Hosey, another Right Club member who regularly frequented the Tea Rooms, was meanwhile poised to unleash a more subtle form of propaganda. In collaboration with four others, he drafted a series of letters, multiple copies of which were produced on a Roneo duplicating machine. Addressed to 'Dear Mother', 'Dear John' and similar variations, these purported to have been written by a British soldier, hospital-ized in the north of England. The writer explained that he was recuperating from wounds sustained during the Norwegian campaign, which had seen British forces soundly defeated. He proceeded to comment on how poorly equipped he and his comrades had been, and how the Germans had outnumbered them and were far superior. Enlistment in the British armed forces was, he wrote, tantamount to committing suicide. He added that the British government had been lying to its elec-torate about its military predicament and about the intentions of the Nazis, which he described as fair and honourable.

These letters were designed to be crumpled and then dropped in railway carriages and on trams. If everything went according to plan, people would find them, read them and show them to friends and family.

25

Intermittent sunshine next morning lit the gardens and squares around where Max worked. Firework-bursts of purple and red enlivened the otherwise sombre rhododendrons. Little golden flowers cascaded from the laburnums. Pink and white blossom prettified the hawthorn bushes and chestnut trees. Their pollen-heavy, rural aroma made London seem as if it was being invaded by the surrounding countryside.

But one just had to peruse today's edition of *The Times* to lose the associated flush of seasonal optimism. German forces were reported to be continuing their progress through the Low Countries. Magnifying the sense of alarm was a firsthand account of how the invasion of Luxembourg had been abetted by Nazi Fifth Columnists – paratroops costumed in civilian clothes and Germans posing as tourists. The bits about Fifth Columnists and Nazis in civilian clothes – albeit intelligence personnel rather than paratroops – turned out to be accurate.

Still, there was nothing Max could do about the unfolding military debacle, which deepened with the discovery that the Dutch had surrendered. Like a middle-order batsman striving to rescue his team after a flurry of wickets, he could merely concentrate on his own game and hope it facilitated a general recovery.

That day the mysterious Italian who had dined with Wolkoff and the others was identified as the Duke del Monte – an atten-tion-grabbing name. It had cropped up a few months ago in the paperwork for an investigation to which Bill Younger had contributed. The investigation focused on a Hungarian woman, married to a British aristocrat. Not only was the Hungarian suspected of obtaining a British passport under false pretences, but there was also reason to believe that she had been involved in blackmail, spying and arms dealing alongside her Polish lover. While her husband was serving with the RAF in France, she had thrown lavish parties. One of these had been attended by the Duke del Monte.

There was no shortage of information about the Duke on file at the Registry. For several years now he had been the target of sporadic MI5 inquiries, occasioned by his affiliations with Italian fascist organizations such as the London-based *Fascio di Londre*. These inquiries had led to his correspondence being intercepted and his phone tapped. Slightly over four months ago, one of Max's colleagues over at Wormwood Scrubs had produced a memo concluding, 'There is reason to believe that del Monte is connected in espionage matters.'

Compounded by the knowledge that del Monte often functioned as a courier for the Italian government and by the as yet unsubstantiated belief that Mussolini had been funding the British Union, this lent a dismaying aspect to his involvement with Kent and Wolkoff. It suggested that the Duke might be in league with them, offering them an easy route by which they could send all manner of stolen American government documents and sundry top-secret paperwork to Rome and perhaps Berlin, too.

26

Towards the end of last week, a report had arrived at Dolphin Square regarding the enciphered letter to William Joyce. The report provided confirmation that the missive, handed to Wolkoff almost a month ago, had reached Joyce.

More information about Wolkoff had just come Max's way via Marjorie and Joan. His agents had been with Wolkoff at the Manson Mews flat a couple of evenings ago. The three women prepared omelettes, following a recipe that Wolkoff brought back from Sudetenland the previous summer. When Wolkoff and the others eventually sat down to dinner, she treated them to her usual denunciations of Winston Churchill, the Jews and the Freemasons. Mainly, however, she talked about her visit to Sudetenland and her audience with General Karl Hermann

Frank, the Nazi governor's right-hand man. She also mentioned that she'd attended one of the Nuremberg rallies, and that a senior member of the German Foreign Office had floated the possibility of introducing her to Heinrich Himmler, head of the Gestapo.

In passing, she told Marjorie and Joan that she'd been listening to the German radio stations. Britain, she stated, would never be able to stand up to Germany's aerial superiority. With reference to Joan, Marjorie added in a separate report that Wolkoff had said, 'I am sure she suspects nothing. She will be a convert and prove most useful.'

Once Joan had left the flat, Marjorie accompanied Wolkoff to Anne van Lennep's place in Chelsea. Reportedly anxious about something related to Tyler Kent, Wolkoff phoned him from there. By the end of their conversation, she had calmed down.

Then she rang Mrs Ramsay, but nobody answered, so she announced her intention to go round to the Ramsays' house in Onslow Square at breakfast time. Apparently she and Captain Ramsay were planning to pop over to Kent's flat.

27

At 6 p.m. on Wednesday 15 May, 1940 – two hours after Tyler's shift in the Code Room had commenced – a telegram from Winston Churchill to President Roosevelt was sent to Washington, DC, using the Grey Code. The message was accorded the emphatic but repetitive heading, 'SECRET. STRICTLY PERSONAL AND CONFIDENTIAL FOR THE PRESIDENT. MOST SECRET AND PERSONAL.'

Playfully identifying himself as 'Former Naval Person', the erstwhile First Lord of the Admiralty – now Britain's Prime Minister – wrote: 'Although I have changed my office, I am sure you would not wish me to discontinue our intimate, private correspondence. As you are no doubt aware, the scene has darkened swiftly. The enemy have a marked preponderance in the air, and their new technique is making a deep impression upon the French. I think myself the battle on land has only just begun, and I should like to see tanks engaged. Up to the present, Hitler is working with specialised units in tanks and air. The small countries are simply smashed up, one by one, like matchwood. We must expect, though it is not yet certain, that Mussolini will hurry in to share the loot of civilisation. We expect to be attacked here ourselves, both from the air and by parachute and airborne troops in the near future, and we are getting ready for them. If necessary we shall continue the war alone and we are not afraid of that. But I trust you realise, Mr President, that the voice and force of the United States may count for nothing if they are withheld too long. You may have a completely subjugated Nazified Europe established with astonishing swiftness, and the weight may be more than we can bear.'

Churchill then pleaded with Roosevelt to help Britain in every way short of engaging in combat with German forces. 'Immediate needs are: first of all, the loan of forty or fifty of your older destroyers to bridge the gap between what we have now and the large new construction we put in hand at the beginning of the war. This time next year we shall have plenty. But if in the interval Italy comes in against us with another one-hundred submarines, we shall be strained to breaking point. Secondly, we want several hundred of the latest type of aircraft, of which you are now getting delivery. These can be repaid by those now being constructed in the United States for us. Thirdly, anti-aircraft equipment and ammunition, of which again there will be plenty next year, if we are alive to see it. Fourthly, the fact that our ore supply is being compromised from Sweden, from North Africa, and perhaps from Northern Spain, makes it necessary to purchase steel in the United States. This also applies to other materials. We shall go on paying dollars as long as we can, but I should like to feel reasonably sure that when we can pay no more you will give us the stuff all the same. Fifthly, we have many reports of possible German parachute or airborne descents into Ireland…'

'Sixthly,' Churchill added, 'I am looking to you to keep that Japanese dog quiet in the Pacific, using Singapore in any way convenient. The details of the material which we have in mind will be communicated to you separately.'

28

The press was full of stories next morning about the danger of German airborne troops landing in Britain. Volunteers were being encouraged to report to their local police stations where they could enlist in what was nicknamed 'the parashots', an organization dedicated to shooting down enemy parachutists. But Max had already volunteered for the Army's emergency reserve list. In the event of a military crisis, he would have to abandon the Right Club investigation and take on a new role as a soldier. Amid this escalating uncertainty, he was presented with another report by Marjorie. She revealed that Anna's younger sister, Kyra, who lived with Anna and their parents, had talked about befriending a naval officer, said to be part of the intelligence services. 'This man is supposed to have asked Kyra if she was related to Anna Wolkoff and, on being told "Yes", he warned Kyra that Anna must stop her political work or she would be arrested.'

As Marjorie made clear, the anonymous naval officer's warning had gone unheeded. She described how Anna had, by her own account, recently obtained some letters or documents pertaining to negotiations between Britain and the United States. Anna claimed these discussions, involving Churchill, had culminated in a trade agreement giving America privileged status in relation to other neutral countries.[86]

Marjorie also described how Anna had spoken about arranging to have the relevant documents photographed. Knowing that another of the Right Club women had commissioned photographic work from a man named Nicholas Smirnoff, Marjorie suggested that he might have carried out the task. She told Max that the resultant pictures had been passed to the Duke del Monte, who had forwarded them to the Italian government. A subsequent propaganda broadcast from Rome had, she believed, made some form of allusion to the stolen documents.

Part Six

Most Secret and Personal

1

Tyler had been earmarked for the 4 p.m. to midnight shift in the Code Room that day. But he'd since been reassigned to the preceding shift, which began at 8 a.m. Not the best time for a night-owl like him. Another glaring disadvantage of starting work so early was that he would be less likely to find himself alone in the Code Room.

Several hours into Tyler's shift, the President's reply to yesterday's telegram from Churchill chattered through the teletype machine. Tyler set about decoding it.

Labelled 'URGENT', the reply was addressed to Ambassador Kennedy. 'Please transmit the following message from the President to the former naval person,' it read.

'I have just received your message and I am sure it is unnecessary for me to say that I am most happy to continue our private correspondence as we have in the past.

'I am, of course, giving every possible consideration to the suggestions made in your message. I shall take up your specific proposals one by one.'

Yet there was something strange about this message. Ordinarily you could be sure that Roosevelt would be very security conscious. For important telegrams he insisted on employing strip-ciphers. So why had a message of such magnitude been transmitted in the patently redundant Grey Code?

Unlike previous telegrams from Churchill to the President, where a strip-cipher could not be used without compromising the security of that cipher, no obvious reason existed for sending this new message in Grey. Without access to the original plain English text of what the President had written, British cryptographers were denied the chance to break the strip-cipher through careful comparison with the enciphered version. To cable such an important message in Grey Code was therefore irrational. Anyone would have thought the President *wanted* the Germans to read his letter.

But Tyler was unlikely to have known that Roosevelt had, less than five years earlier, used Grey Code against the Italians in just such a manner. Following Italy's invasion of Abyssinia, the President had cabled some sharply worded criticism of Mussolini to the US Embassy in Rome. On Roosevelt's instructions the message had been sent in Grey, enabling the Italians to read it. They could nonetheless register no diplomatic protest without making a public admission that they were intercepting confidential American communications.

Tyler wasn't yet finished with the task of translating the latest batch of Grey Code into plain text. 'First, with regard to the possible loan of forty or fifty of our older destroyers,' the telegram went on. 'As you know a step of that kind could not be taken except with the specific authorization of the Congress and I am not certain that it would be wise for that suggestion to be made to the Congress at this moment. Furthermore, it seems to me doubtful, from the standpoint of our own defence requirements, which must inevitably be linked with the defence requirements of this hemisphere and with our obligations in the Pacific, whether we could dispose even temporarily of these destroyers. Furthermore, even if we could take the steps you suggest, it would be at least six or seven weeks at a minimum, as I see it, before these vessels could undertake active service under the British flag.

'Second. We are now doing everything within our power to make it possible for the Allied governments to obtain the latest types of aircraft in the United States.'

Responding to the third of Churchill's requests, Roosevelt counselled that the Prime Minister should get in touch with Admiral Arthur Purvis, who had taken charge of the British Purchasing Mission in Washington, DC. The President recommended that instructions should be given forthwith to Purvis to discuss the question of ammunition and anti-aircraft equipment with the relevant American government officials. Any of Purvis's requests would, Roosevelt assured the Prime Minister, receive the most favourable consideration.

'Fourth,' Roosevelt replied, 'Mr Purvis has already taken up with the appropriate authorities here the purchase of steel in the United States and I understand that satisfactory arrangements have been made.

'Fifth. I shall give further consideration to your suggestion with regard to the visit of the United States Squadron to Irish ports.

'Sixth. As you know, the American fleet is now concentrated at Hawaii where it will remain at least for the time being. I shall communicate with you again as soon as I feel able to make a final decision with regard to some of the other matters dealt with in your message and I hope you will feel free to communicate with me in this way at any time.

'The best of luck to you.

'Franklin Roosevelt.'

Tyler typed up the decoded version of the message that afternoon. Since his collection of stolen embassy documents included telegrams referring to the mooted Lease-Lend scheme, he would, like as not, have realized that Roosevelt's letter represented nothing more than a tremendously inventive ruse.

By allowing the Nazis to read the message, Roosevelt was warning them of his economic and military support for the British. And by sending the message via Ambassador Kennedy, the President could reassure the strongly isolationist Ambassador that no commitments were being made that would infringe the tenets of American neutrality. The dialogue about Lease-Lend, which must have circumvented Kennedy, could meanwhile carry on unchecked.

Adhering to official procedure, Tyler initialled and numbered the telegram that he had just rendered into plain text. When he departed from the embassy a few hours later, he took with him a copy of the President's message to Churchill.

2

Earlier in the day Max and two of his MI5 colleagues – Sir Vernon Kell and Francis Aiken Sneath – convened a meeting at an address on Victoria Embankment, only a quick cab-ride from Dolphin Square. The scene of their meeting was Scotland Yard, headquarters of the Metropolitan Police.

Visitors to the building were liable to be struck by the nonchalant authority of the plain-clothes officers loitering around the main entrance, smoking and chatting, their accents redolent of the rural provinces. Max and his colleagues had joined the tide of detectives, clerical staff and uniformed officers sluicing the Yard's labyrinthine interior. Bordering its twilit passageways were doors bearing designations such as 'C1' and 'C2', whose significance was perplexing to the uninitiated.

Currently Max and the others were in conference with Commissioner Air Vice-Marshal Sir Philip Game. No longer the RAF deputy-supremo that his title suggested, Sir Philip was London's senior policeman, his eminence rewarded by a capacious first-floor office on the corner of the building. Leather-upholstered armchairs, fit to adorn some exclusive gentlemen's club, furnished the office. For such occasions, he liked to arrange these in a semi-circle around the front of his desk. Despite the formality of the set-up and the ostentatious length of his title, he was known for being calm, softly spoken and down-to-earth. He was in his mid-sixties, short grey hair emphasizing his vintage. Upright though his posture remained, he walked with a pronounced limp whenever he crossed his office.

Max was there to talk to him about the British Union and other potential Fifth Columnists. At the previous day's meeting of the War Cabinet, Sir Philip's political master – Home Secretary, Sir John Anderson – had been installed on a three-man committee entrusted with assessing the threat posed not only by German, Austrian and Italian nationals resident in Britain, but also by British fascists and communists, the Soviet Union still being an ally of Hitler's at that time. Through Sir Philip, Max and his Security Service colleagues were in a position to make an oblique contribution to the committee's findings.

Just over a week ago MI5 had prepared a memo for Sir John Anderson recommending the internment of 500 suspected and prospective Fifth Columnists. The Security Service had long favoured the imprisonment of people who fell into that category, along with a mass round-up of enemy aliens. But Anderson had turned down MI5's advice, which sought to use illiberal methods to save liberal democracy. Anna Wolkoff's links to Tyler Kent, William Joyce and the Duke del Monte gave Max's colleagues reason to urge Sir Philip to get the Home Secretary to reconsider their previous recommendation.

3

For Anna, the rhythm of life in her parents' flat had just altered. Compensating for poor receipts at the Russian Tea Rooms, they'd taken in a lodger. He was a Dutch diplomat whose wife had deserted him and gone to India. The Wolkoffs' lodger had moved into what used to be their spare room, where Anna's mother was doing her best to make him feel comfortable.

At least he wasn't a stranger. He was already a friend of Anna's parents. He had also hobnobbed with the Comte and Comtesse de Laubespin.

Now the Wolkoffs' comparatively small flat was home to five people, Anna couldn't be blamed for wanting to escape from its claustrophobic embrace. Minus Tyler, she and Enid had once again met the Duke del Monte. Second time round they'd gone for an Italian meal at a small hotel in Soho. And tonight Anna had arranged to see Tyler.

When she made her way through the West End, a gentle breeze was ruffling the trees hard enough for their leaves to shimmer like a sequinned dress. One could feel a sense of national emergency on the streets, where roadblocks, observation posts and armed patrols had become a common sight. In the latest edition of the *Evening Standard*, there was a story that discussed the prospect of invasion by German paratroops. But none of this was going to affect Anna's plans for that evening. She would soon be with the man she loved. Unlike Lord Cottenham, he gave ample evidence that he reciprocated her feelings for him.

Tyler had something to show her when she arrived at his flat around 6 p.m. He let her read the telegram from Roosevelt to Churchill that had come through that afternoon. There was nothing improper about the message, yet Anna felt it provided further evidence of the conspiracy between Churchill and Roosevelt, which Tyler had discussed.

Before going out, Tyler insisted on freshening up. While he disappeared into the adjacent bathroom, Anna waited in his bed-sitting room, where she copied down the secret transatlantic telegram he had just shown her.

Approaching an hour went by without Tyler re-emerging. He turned out to have fallen asleep in the bath.

His overwhelming tiredness prompted he and Anna to cancel their arrangement. So she went back to her parents' flat, from where she telephoned Marjorie and asked her to come round. When Marjorie got there, Anna explained that she needed her assistance concerning a message she had dropped through a letterbox in Cadogan Square last Tuesday. Regrettably, her message hadn't reached the person to whom it had been directed. Anna told Marjorie that she suspected the housekeeper of taking it. 'I now want you to tell me a thoroughly dirty story. Then we will type it out and put it in the letterbox,' she added. If the housekeeper really *were* stealing letters, then this would give the woman a nasty surprise.

The Cadogan Square address was, Anna said, the same one to which she'd previously delivered photographs of documents outlining the preferential treatment being given to American companies by the British government. She mentioned that the Italians were charmed by her gift.

4

Anna and Marjorie delayed going round to Cadogan Square until after they had listened to William Joyce's 10.15 p.m. talk on Radio Hamburg. Interference could sometimes render his broadcasts inaudible, but this time Anna and her friend were in luck.

Joyce began with a news bulletin about the invasions of Holland and France. Afterwards Joyce gave another of his crowing lectures, his shrill, punctilious voice endowing his pronouncements with donnish conviction.

'In less than a week,' he said, 'Germany's land and air forces, working in perfect cooperation, have written a new and astonishing chapter in the world's history. Not only have all the calculations of our enemies been nullified but the measure of their success has also transcended our own considerable expectations. The people of England find themselves today cut off from the Baltic states, Scandinavia, Holland and, for all practical purposes, from Belgium ...'

He continued in a similar triumphalist vein for several minutes. 'Perhaps you think that even the most conditional reference to invasion of Britain is out of place,' he added. 'I can claim no special knowledge. I can only look at the map – as you can – and see the array of German power from the north of Norway right down to the Channel. Each hour sees consolidation of German victory in Holland. Life is rapidly returning to normal and civilians are going about their private business as in Copenhagen or Oslo. There is nothing unstable or uncertain in our control of Holland. It is quite established. Now look at the map, if you have one handy. Flushing is less than ninety miles from Dover. Rotterdam is about the same distance from important strategic points on the English coast as London is from Birmingham. The Hague is distant from Harwich only by 120 miles – let us say twenty minutes' journey by a plane whose pilot has no need of hurry. He should comfortably get from Holland to Whitehall before you could get from Richmond to South Kensington or from Earl's Court to Mansion House by underground. This fact might be of less importance if the German armed forces had not proved their incontestable superiority ...'

Once Joyce's fifteen-minute broadcast had finished, Anna typed up a suitably lewd story that Marjorie dictated to her. Anna placed the typescript in an oblong envelope and used a fountain pen to address the envelope, which she slipped into her bag. She told Marjorie that she was sending the letter to the Italian with whom she and Enid Riddell had dined the other night.

Exiting her parents' flat, Anna and Marjorie walked to the junction with Old Brompton Road, a blurred half-moon piercing both the hazy atmosphere and the blackout. Then the two women made a bee-line for the bus-stop almost opposite and boarded a bus. It took them past the Gothic silhouette of the Victoria and Albert Museum, whose ornamentation – cupolas, balustrades, arched windows and spires – appeared calculated to invest it with the antiquarian creepiness of a stately home in a ghost story.

Both Anna and Marjorie got off the bus outside the Brompton Road branch of Woolworth's. Guided by Anna's torch, they crossed over and went down Pont Street. There were small shops on either side, quickly giving way to mansions and blocks of flats. Only a short distance from there, Pont Street flowed into Cadogan Square, a tree-lined park surrounded by large redbrick houses.

When Anna reached the entrance to the cul-de-sac opposite, she came to a halt. Marjorie followed suit.

'It is no. 67 – on the corner,' Anna said as she gave Marjorie the envelope. 'The last house but one. You can't miss it.'

She kept the torch while her Right Club colleague headed towards no. 67, the front door to which was approached via a flight of steps with a portico over them. Anna's friend, the Duke del Monte, had lived there for many years. Until recently, he'd shared the place with his cousin and family. His cousin had at one time held the post of equerry – or aide-de-camp – to the Duke of Gloucester, younger brother of King George VI and husband of one of Anna's old schoolmates.

Anna waited for Marjorie to post the envelope through the letterbox. Subsequently, the pair of them trudged back towards South Kensington. Presupposing that Marjorie had read the name on the envelope, Anna made a facetious remark about the delights of having a name identical to that of a well-known brand of tinned fruit.

5

Marjorie told Max all about it. Her account of both the expedition to Cadogan Square and Wolkoff's links to the Italian government imbued the relationship between Wolkoff and Tyler Kent with even greater menace. The abundant warnings Max had received about that relationship acquired extra credence when he discovered Kent had already played a subsidiary role in an unrelated MI5 investigation of suspected fascist espionage.

It dated back to the closing months of 1939. The main focus was a German Jew named Ludwig Matthias, who had taken Swedish citizenship. His imminent arrival in Britain on a work assignment for a Swedish company had been the subject of a tip-off given to Special Branch by the Stockholm police. Despite his Jewish background, the Swedes had warned the British authorities that Matthias was a Nazi agent.

Responding to the tip-off, Special Branch had deployed plain-clothes officers at King's Cross Station, all set for when Matthias arrived. They tailed him to the Park Lane Hotel on Piccadilly, where he took a room. Special Branch was next morning relieved of its surveillance duties by MI5. The Watchers then followed Matthias around town. Even though Matthias was, it transpired, conducting legitimate business negotiations, there were still strong grounds for suspicion.

Twice he implemented what appeared to be anti-surveillance techniques, giving his MI5 shadows the slip by leaving some offices on Finsbury Circus via the rear exit.[87] And on another occasion he was seen entering the Cumberland Hotel, where he met Tyler Kent in the lounge. Soon afterwards he collected a package from the American's room.

Kent's involvement with an enemy agent would surely enable Max to secure a warrant to search his flat, unless it was protected by his diplomatic status. But there remained the appreciable risk that the ensuing search might not yield any stolen documents. Were that to happen, Max was in danger of being diminished in the eyes of his bosses at MI5. He would moreover forfeit any chance of nosing out additional evidence through monitoring Kent's continued dealings with Wolkoff.

For Max, candid about his dislike of bureaucratic rules and regulations, a tempting alternative presented itself. He could search the American's flat *without* a warrant. Ever since the days when he'd worked for the British Fascisti, Max had, if circumstances required it, been prepared to enter private premises illegally. He was experienced enough to realize that any incriminating material discovered during an illegal search could still be used against Kent. Evidence obtained that way had previously been declared admissible in court.

An illegal search of Kent's home had another conspicuous benefit for Max and possibly the British government. By adopting this illicit approach, they wouldn't be obliged to notify American officials. The possible advantages of that would only make themselves felt if Max's search of the flat dredged up so-called 'true readings' – plain English transcripts – of messages sent from Washington, DC to the US Embassy in London, which acted as the conduit for all diplomatic traffic to and from other American legations across Europe. Paired with the enciphered versions of the messages, routinely collected by the British-run facility through which they were cabled, these plain English transcripts would enable cryptographers from the misleadingly titled Government Code and Cipher School at Bletchley Park to crack the US Navy strip-ciphers that shielded the Americans' most secret communications. Access to enciphered American messages between London and Washington would give British diplomats a crucial edge in their dealings with the Roosevelt administration, which had publicly – though less than wholeheartedly – vowed to prevent America from being drawn into the European war.

6

Christabel Nicholson and husband had just got back from a short holiday in Wales. Anna arranged to meet her next day – Friday 17 May, 1940 – and carry out a fitting for a jacket

Christabel had commissioned. The jacket was part of a substantial list of orders from various customers.

Before proceeding with today's fitting, Anna had to get Tyler's car serviced. Finding decent mechanics nowadays was difficult because so many of them had been conscripted into the armed forces. She was taking the car to a garage on Cranley Mews, which could scarcely be more convenient, as it was just round the back of Roland Gardens. Anna didn't go straight to the garage, though. Instead, she detoured over to pick up Christabel, who was waiting for her in the street.

En route to Cranley Mews, Anna had plenty of things to talk to her friend about, not least the Nicholsons' trip to Wales and the latest instalment of the Churchill–Roosevelt correspondence, shown to her by Tyler. But Christabel disapproved of her relationship with Tyler on the grounds that Anna was cradle-snatching, the American's youthful looks exaggerating the eight-year age gap.

Anna's time with Christabel – sitting in the car, walking from Cranley Mews back to Roland Gardens and carrying out the fitting – also provided a chance for Christabel to voice her conviction that the Germans were sure to invade England, and that they would capture London by Christmas. There had been serious talk among Anna's group that the invasion was scheduled for Sunday 28 July. A Right Club delegation would, they anticipated, then be sent to meet Hitler, who would appoint Captain Ramsay as Britain's leader.

Extra scope for chatter between Anna and friend derived from the previous night's meeting of Information and Policy, another fascist group supported by the Nicholsons. Last night's main speaker had been a Hungarian who delivered a lecture on his country's recent history. Asked about Jewish influence in Hungary, he'd induced a loud round of applause when describing how the Jews had been thrown out of managerial jobs. He'd claimed that his country had nonetheless behaved humanely, to which someone in the audience had said, 'The only way to deal with the Jews is the way Hitler did it.'

On the subject of fascist meetings, Anna's father had received a letter from Mrs Annabel Huth Jackson, an old family friend and customer at the Russian Tea Rooms who invited him to a small gathering at her house on Ladbroke Grove next Wednesday afternoon. What made the occasion so special was that Sir Oswald Mosley planned to deliver a speech to her guests. She had even gone to the trouble of checking with Sir Oswald that it was all right for Anna's father to join them.

7

Max's boss, Guy Liddell, had spoken to the MI6 counter-intelligence specialist, Felix Cowgill, on the day of Wolkoff's trip to Cranley Mews. The venue for their powwow was the Broadway Buildings, MI6 headquarters, near St James's Park tube station. Guy bestowed a dash of New York glamour on the place by calling it 'Broadway'.

While he was there, he had dropped in for a brief chat with the new chief of MI6. From him, Guy learned about the military situation across the Channel the previous day. 'The French were shouting for troops and aircraft and were generally in a frightful flap. Winston had gone over yesterday to calm them down.'

But that wasn't all Max's boss gleaned from the encounter. He had been presented with some inside information about the American President. 'Roosevelt was proposing to give us a hundred destroyers, somewhat out of date but nevertheless useful. He also proposed to give us a portion of his first-line aircraft, provided we could replace them in due course with Spitfires,' the new chief of MI6 revealed. 'There is little doubt that Roosevelt would bring the whole country into the war now if he possibly could.'

8

Gaining access to Kent's home was simple. Max needed to wait until the American had departed for one of his night-shifts at the embassy and his landlady had retired to bed.

Under cover of the blackout, Max could then stroll through the front door, which was kept on the latch. Inside the premises, he just had to saunter confidently up to the first floor and through the unlocked door to Kent's living quarters, an air of confidence vital for deflecting suspicion if he bumped into any of the other tenants.

At first glance, perhaps the most remarkable thing about the contents of Kent's flat, which comprised a large bed-sitting room and a bathroom, was the quantity of clothes. The implications would not have been lost on a man of Max's insight. One: Kent must be a person of no little vanity. Two: he must have plenty of money to indulge that vanity.

In snooping round the flat, Max discovered that Marjorie's references to Kent pilfering documents from the US Embassy were accurate. Max had, however, been told nothing to indicate the disconcerting scale of Kent's thefts. Hundreds and hundreds of stolen US government documents were sitting there, many of which Max examined. These included numerous telegrams between London and Washington regarding plans for the Lease-Lend arrangement.

Max knew how sensitive – not to say important – these were. If they fell into the wrong hands, they could set off a disastrous chain of cause-and-effect, which would begin with Roosevelt being replaced by an isolationist Republican president and climax in Britain losing the war and falling under Nazi occupation.

There was much at stake for Max personally as well. He had probably heard enough from Guy Liddell and Francis Aiken Sneath, both well-versed in the sadistic brutality of Hitler's regime, to realize that his name would feature on the Nazis' blacklist.[88] For anyone in that position, a German victory was bound to have terrible repercussions. Prison cells and concentration camps. Torture. Interrogation. Slow and agonizing death.

9

Despite all the dressmaking commissions Anna needed to fulfil, she set aside her sewing and cutting in favour of a trip to Ashburn Gardens on the morning of Saturday 18 May, 1940. Though she was due to attend Admiral Nicholson's birthday party there in the afternoon, she wasn't prepared to wait that long before seeing his wife. She wanted Christabel to read the copy she had made of Thursday's Roosevelt–Churchill telegram.

As she headed for Ashburn Gardens, the vaporous atmosphere lingering from last night made it look as if one were peering through a dusty window. When Anna got to the Nicholsons' flat, the Admiral wasn't at home, but his wife was. Anna showed the telegram to her.

Christabel was horrified by what she read. Like Anna, she derived from it the erroneous conviction that Churchill had been plotting behind Neville Chamberlain's back.

She used a pencil and a couple of sheets of notepaper to make her own transcription of the message, which she wanted to show her husband and, as she put it, 'some other person of integrity'. Who that should be, she hadn't decided. She considered getting in touch with Chamberlain himself, or perhaps the former Lord Chancellor in Chamberlain's government, or even His Majesty the King.

10

On the Saturday morning of Wolkoff's trip to Ashburn Gardens, Max got together with Guy Liddell to discuss the investigation. They needed to talk through the case because it had reached the stage where they had to decide whether to wrap things up and start applying for warrants.

All such cases, Max appreciated, sooner or later came to a head. Yet he was aware of the consequences of prosecuting Wolkoff, Kent and their associates. In doing so, he'd be sacrificing the services of Marjorie Amor and possibly Hélène de Munck, Lionel Hirst and Joan Miller, all of whom had contributed to the inquiry. One or more of those agents would inevitably have to testify in court on behalf of the Security Service. Their cover would be destroyed, rendering them value-less for future infiltration work.

The decision was nevertheless taken to proceed with the arrests. First, though, Max and Guy would have to raise the matter with the US government, because Kent was not only an American citizen but also the holder of a diplomatic passport, which afforded immunity from arrest.

Neither Max nor his boss was in a hurry to involve Ambassador Kennedy, whose defeatist views had earned him such a dire reputation with the British authorities. Instead, they opted to go through their usual contact at the US Embassy – Guy's friend, Herschel V. Johnson, Kennedy's Number Two.

At 12.30 p.m. Guy phoned Johnson and enquired whether it would be convenient for a colleague from the Security Service to call round to the US Embassy on a delicate matter. Johnson made an appointment for Max to see him at three o'clock that afternoon.

In preparation for the meeting, Max dashed off a short brief-ing paper for the Americans, outlining Kent's dangerous relationship with Wolkoff. Guy read the document and gave it the thumbs-up.

11

Even by her energetic standards, Anna had been enjoying a sociable few weeks. Aside from the evenings with Tyler and others, she'd met the French novelist Louis-Ferdinand Céline during his recent visit to London. Proud of her connection to such a well-known fascist anti-Semite, she had introduced him to her parents and friends, Captain Ramsay among them.

She was now – early on the afternoon of Saturday 18 May, 1940 – sitting next to Tyler in the two-seater Morris convertible she had just had serviced. They were beetling away from London, where the temperature was warm enough to justify Tyler donning his grey flannel summer suit.

Getting out of the capital, if only for a few hours, would do him good. Things had been frantic at Grosvenor Square yesterday. Occasioned by a message from Washington, Tyler's colleagues had issued advice to US citizens resident in Britain that they should return home at the earliest juncture. An attempt had been made to arrange for them to be evacuated to southwestern France, from where they could be transported back to the United States. But this had fallen through. British-based Americans had since been instructed to proceed to the Irish Republic and await rescue. Those remaining in Britain were being told to seek accommodation away from major cities and other likely targets for a German attack.

Machine-gun posts and roadblocks had sprung up on the routes out of London. When these had been negotiated, Anna and Tyler were free to speed through Surrey, across what was then regarded as one of England's most beautiful counties, its green fields rolling towards the horizon, its ancient towns and villages radiating only a vague foretaste of suburban sprawl. The weather grew cloudier as they progressed.

Just beyond Tadworth, a stone crucifix next to the road marked the left-hand turn that Anna and her companion had to take. It ushered them down a narrow driveway, twisted through some woodland and then emerged beside a neo-Georgian, dormer-windowed redbrick mansion, plonked on the far side of an impressive apron of lawn.

12

Max had been to the US Embassy before. At the appointed hour – three o'clock that afternoon – he met Herschel V. Johnson there. The man facing Max was a good deal smaller, older and stockier than him. Johnson had pale, doughy features, a compressed little mouth and narrow, close-set eyes. In defiance of his lugubrious physiognomy, he possessed an air of guarded courtesy, his words pervaded by a melodious Southern accent.

There was something about the idiomatic swagger of American speech that Max loved. Yet he could not retain its rhythms and nuances in his head. Whenever he'd attempted to reproduce them in his novels, the results had been less than satisfactory.[89]

Having got the inevitable formalities out of the way, Max began to explain to Johnson why the meeting had been requested at such short notice. He said his story would be a fairly long one. Information of a most serious nature, he told Johnson, had reached Scotland Yard concerning the activities of Mr Tyler Kent, an American citizen employed by the embassy. Max added that the nature of Mr Kent's duties was unclear, but it was obvious the gentleman in question had access to confidential material.

The authorities had, Max revealed, become suspicious about Kent due to his association with members of an organization called the Right Club. To present a clear-cut picture of all the circumstances, Max announced, it was necessary to know something about the club. He said this was definitely a Fifth Column organization, conducting pro-German activities under the cloak of anti-Jewish propaganda. He then described the club's web of contacts, as well as its use of diplomatic bags to communicate with people in Germany and other foreign countries. Miss Anna Wolkoff was named as the principal agent involved with this activity. Loath to mention MI5 – the existence of which wasn't in those days officially acknowledged – Max told Johnson that Scotland Yard had, for some time, been aware that Wolkoff attached considerable importance to Kent.

Passing mention was made of how Kent had first come to the notice of the authorities. Max said it went back to October last year when Scotland Yard was tipped-off about a chap named Ludwig Matthias, a suspected Gestapo agent visiting London. Naturally, Max continued, he had been placed under surveillance. Matthias had spent several hours with Kent, during which Matthias was handed a bulky envelope.

346 | Rendezvous at the Russian Tea Rooms

Johnson's response to Max's disclosures was swift. He told Max that, in his opinion, it was most regrettable that Scotland Yard had not informed them of these occurrences at the time. Regardless of whether anything incriminating was unearthed about either Kent or Matthias, he said, they wouldn't have allowed Kent to carry on working in the embassy's Code Room.

There was nothing Max could say to placate Johnson, though Max managed to appear remorseful over the decision not to tell the embassy about Kent's rendezvous with an alleged German agent. Max mustered only a half-hearted excuse in defence of himself and his colleagues. He said the decision had been taken because Scotland Yard had been unable to link Matthias to any espionage activities while he was in town.

Kent had, Max explained, next caught the eye of the authorities in February this year when an absolutely reliable source had alerted them to the fact that Wolkoff regarded Kent as a valuable contact. Max talked about how their source had, a month later or thereabouts, notified them of Kent's close relationship with Wolkoff, his pro-German outlook and his practice of feeding her confidential diplomatic material.

In citing further examples of the Code Clerk's treachery, Max referred to reports that Kent had made derogatory and libellous remarks about Winston Churchill's behaviour at a supposedly confidential session of the War Cabinet; that he had leaked the contents of correspondence between the US Embassy and the British government about radio equipment; that he had told Wolkoff about private discussions between Ambassador Kennedy and a member of the War Cabinet; and that he had given her information about the recent naval engagements off the Norwegian coast. Max also mentioned that one of his sources believed that Kent was using the American diplomatic bag to communicate with Right Club contacts in the United States.

At this point Max gave Johnson a copy of the briefing paper drafted earlier that afternoon. Johnson started reading the document. When he finished, he said he considered there were sound reasons for thinking a serious leakage of information from the embassy had taken place. The references to the material given by Kent to Wolkoff had, he admitted, more than a substantial basis of truth. His government would, he assured Max, treat the whole affair with extreme seriousness.

Johnson said he'd phone Ambassador Kennedy straight away. The Ambassador was, you see, out-of-town for the weekend.

Max told Johnson that the authorities were planning to arrest Wolkoff on Monday morning. Obviously, he added, if the question of diplomatic immunity did not arise, they'd like to arrange a simultaneous search of Kent's living quarters.

That would be perfectly acceptable, Johnson replied.

13

Kingswood Court was a hotel-cum-nursing home that had a marble-floored hall and a grand, elegantly curved staircase. Anna and Tyler, who had just driven there, were having tea with Enid Riddell.

Their friend was spending a rare few days with one of the residents – her dressing-gowned, partially sighted grandmother and custodian of the family trust fund. Enid loved to portray herself as a martyr to the needs of her octogenarian granny, whose health she described as 'awfully touch-and-go'.

Anna and Tyler didn't have time to linger. They were soon motoring back to the capital, where they were both expected at Admiral Nicholson's birthday celebration. Tyler had other things to do before the party, so Anna turned up at the Ashburn Gardens flat by herself. As a gift to her host and his wife, she was clutching a bunch of gardenias, filched from a table display at the Russian Tea Rooms.

When Tyler joined her later that afternoon, he carried a portfolio. Anna was worried by how weary he looked, weariness shading into something more significant. Recently she had been brooding a great deal about his health. He was quite fragile really, she'd decided. And, with a pang of guilt, she sensed that his condition wasn't helped by all the time he had been spending with her when he should have been catching up on his sleep between shifts in the Code Room. Even Tyler himself had been candid enough to remark that he might have to check into somewhere like Kingswood Court. Going all the way back to the burst appendix he'd suffered during his junior year at Princeton, he had been dogged by periods of poor health.

At the Nicholsons' party Tyler got into conversation with his hosts about politics. Christabel and her husband told him about their pre-war trip to Germany and talked enthusiastically about their meeting with Hitler.

In the portfolio, which Tyler had brought round, were upwards of a dozen carbon copies of the stolen US Embassy telegrams that Captain Ramsay had seen already. Tyler intended to show these to the Nicholsons, but he didn't have much time to spare, because he had arranged to go to dinner with a friend.

14

Over at the US Embassy, Herschel V. Johnson agreed to delay until Monday morning any measures that might arouse Kent's suspicions and alert other people implicated in his activities. Johnson also pledged the embassy's fullest cooperation.

Max phoned Dolphin Square and asked a colleague to send the appropriate form to the Home Office, requesting a detention order against Wolkoff under Regulation 18b of the Emergency Defence Regulations. His colleague rang the admirably efficient Private Secretary to Sir John Anderson first. She said there was nothing to worry about. The detention order would be signed by Sir John either that evening or during the course of tomorrow.

Before leaving the US Embassy, Max assured Johnson that he'd be in touch next day: Sunday 19 May, 1940. On that note, he set off for Scotland Yard, a one-and-a-half-mile journey across town. He was heading over to the offices of Special

Branch. These could be accessed by driving through the arched gateway on the Embankment, connecting the Yard to its huge as yet unfinished extension, work on which had been suspended since the beginning of the war.

Special Branch was entered via a door to the left of the gateway. Max spoke to the Superintendent on duty and made the necessary arrangements for Wolkoff's arrest. Throughout his investigation Max had been impressed by how cooperative the police were being.

15

A cool wind undercut the balminess of the sunshine next day. Max had an appointment at an address on Cromwell Road. Herschel V. Johnson's flat was in the basement of that address, which was across the road from the Natural History Museum.

Max got there at 2.30 p.m. and briefed him on the current position regarding the operation. In response, Johnson stressed that the American government would take as firm action as possible against Kent. Johnson also mentioned that Ambassador Kennedy was seriously considering the possibility of cabling Washington to call for the suspension of Kent's diplomatic status. Without that suspension, Johnson noted, the British police would not be permitted by law to search Kent's flat.

Though Johnson told Max that he'd proceed with great caution in order to ensure that Kent did not learn about any of this, he admitted to having already made enquiries at the embassy. Johnson said he'd heard that Kent had been attracting attention due to his emphatically pro-German views.

Later that afternoon Johnson was planning to drive out to see Ambassador Kennedy, who was weekending in Windsor. Johnson would be discussing the case with his boss. He promised to contact Max in the evening and reveal the outcome of those discussions.

16

Max discovered that Kent was involved with a Mrs Irene Danischewsky, who made frequent visits to 47 Gloucester Place, which the Watchers were keeping under observation. While MI5's Registry didn't have a file on her, they did have files on her husband, his father and his uncle. Mrs Danischewsky's Russian émigré husband was one of the directors of the White Sea and Baltic Trading Company, part of a clutch of interconnected firms belonging to his family. Based near London docks, their company owned coalmines, tugs and barges. It also specialized in the import and export of coal, turpentine and paraffin as well as lubricating oil. For almost a quarter of a century, it had been scrutinized by the British secret services.

More than a hundred pages of letters, reports and memos detailed a series of allegations against Mrs Danischewsky's father-in-law, her husband's uncle and fellow directors of the company, said to have ties to the Soviet government and intelligence apparatus. In tandem with the Tyler Kent connection, these allegations offered good reason to place Mrs Danischewsky under surveillance and obtain permission to tap the telephone at her marital home in Bayswater.

17

Word came through that German armoured units had pierced Allied defences in Belgium and France. But Max didn't have time that evening to dwell on the mortal danger facing himself and his country. Soon he received the promised phonecall from Herschel V. Johnson. Rather than discuss the Kent/Wolkoff case over the phone, where they might be overheard by one of the operators at the local telephone exchange, Max went back to Johnson's basement flat.

When Max got there, Johnson broke the good news about the meeting with Ambassador Kennedy. The Ambassador, who thought the whole business was 'most extraordinary', had waived any diplomatic privilege to which Kent might be entitled. Legal advice obtained by Johnson confirmed the Ambassador's right to take this decision.

Now that the potential impediment of diplomatic privilege had been removed, Max told Johnson that the police were going to raid Kent's flat next morning. Wolkoff would be arrested simultaneously.

18

A little before midnight Tyler walked into the Code Room at the US Embassy, where he was scheduled to be on duty until 8 a.m. Unusually for a night shift when all but a skeleton crew manned the building, he found himself working alongside another Code Clerk, a twenty-two-year-old fellow Southerner who had just been posted there. About an hour-and-three-quarters after their shift had begun, the embassy's cockney-accented doorman ventured into the Code Room. He presented Tyler with an envelope addressed to Herschel V. Johnson. Tyler would have known that there was a fair chance it contained another of the messages from Churchill, which had often come by way of Johnson.

Disregarding protocol, Tyler tore open the envelope. Inside he found a letter from the British Prime Minister's Private Secretary. Enclosed with it was a message written by Churchill to Roosevelt, ready for transmission in Grey Code. Marked 'SECRET AND PERSONAL FOR THE PRESIDENT FROM FORMER NAVAL PERSON', the message referred to recent discussions Roosevelt had conducted with Lord Lothian, Britain's Ambassador to the United States.

Pencil in hand, Tyler started hastily copying Churchill's entire message. 'Lothian has reported his conversation with you,' Tyler wrote. 'I understand your difficulties but I am very sorry about the destroyers. If they were here in six weeks they would play an invaluable part. The battle in France is full of danger to both sides. Though we have taken heavy toll of enemy in the air and are clawing down two or three-to-one of their planes, they still have a formidable numerical superiority. Our most vital need is therefore the delivery at the earliest possible date of the largest possible number of Curtis P-40 fighters now in course of delivery to your army.

'With regard to the closing part of your talk with Lothian, our intention is, whatever happens, to fight on to the end in this island and provided we can get the help for which we ask, we hope to run them very close in the air battle in view of individual superiority. Members of the present administration would likely go down during this process should it result adversely, but in no conceivable circumstances will we consent to surrender.'

Since Tyler had access to all the telegrams between London and Washington, he would have known that Roosevelt was planning to fulfil the British Prime Minister's request for ships and aircraft. That being the case, Churchill's latest message was nothing but another brilliantly plausible instalment in the campaign of disinformation, aimed at the Germans. Its main objective appears to have been to deter the enemy from persisting with the war by convincing them of Britain's unwillingness to surrender, of the exorbitant military cost of vanquishing her.

'If members of the present administration were finished and others came in to parlay amid the ruins,' Churchill's message resumed, 'you must not be blind to the fact that the sole remaining bargaining counter with Germany would be the fleet, and if this country was left by the United States to its fate no one would have the right to blame those responsible if they made the best terms they could for the surviving inhabitants. Excuse me, Mr President, for putting this nightmare bluntly. Evidently I could not answer for my successors who in utter despair and helplessness might well have to accommodate themselves to the German will. However, there is happily no need at present to dwell upon such ideas. Once more thanking you for your goodwill.'

The minute Tyler had finished copying the message, he went and showed the original document to the Vice-Consul, who was at that moment the most senior officer on duty. Tyler then commenced the task of encoding the message. But he had worked his way through only about a couple of lines before his immediate boss, Rudy Schoenfeld – whose steeply accented eyebrows contributed to an expression hovering between perpetual concern and perplexity – came into the Code Room.

Rudy studied the letter from Churchill's Private Secretary, along with the attached message. As he reached the end of the message from Churchill, the phone rang.

It was a call from a British officer who said he worked for the Admiralty.[90] He referred to the letter from Churchill to the President. This mustn't be sent, he told Rudy. He added that the Prime Minister wished to have it returned to him by six in the morning. So the officer from the Admiralty suggested dropping round to the embassy to collect it.

Of course, Rudy replied. He told the man from the Admiralty that he'd be happy to receive him.

Promptly scooping up the letter and the partially coded version of it, Rudy exited the room. Tyler was given no explanation as to what was going on.[91]

19

For the second consecutive morning a mist, gradually dispersed by a crisp breeze, hung over central London. On the off-chance Tyler Kent didn't go straight home from the embassy after his shift ended at 8 a.m., a surveillance team had been posted to keep track of him when he walked out of the building. Max – for whom today promised to match the high tempo of hot jazz – was meanwhile passing one of the new sandbagged machine-gun nests protecting both ends of Whitehall. Motorists had to have their security passes checked before they were allowed through the barriers.

Emphasizing the air of crisis, of Fifth Columnists skulking everywhere, of imminent invasion, each of the elephantine government buildings on either side was encircled by coils of barbed wire. And soldiers with fixed bayonets were stationed outside the entrances to those buildings, verifying people's credentials.

In recent months one had sometimes encountered sentries guarding significant locations, yet there had been something lacklustre about the way they had shouted, 'Halt!' Now they really meant it.

Max was bound for a huge, elongated grey stone edifice. To enter the Home Office, one of five government departments located within that building, he needed to go through an arched doorway opposite the Cenotaph, where men traditionally doffed their hats in silent tribute to the First World War dead.

Nowhere near as comfortless and austere as it used to be, the interior of the Home Office nevertheless possessed an inhospitable, vaguely ecclesiastical Victorian loftiness, footsteps and smudged voices reverberating between its vaulted ceilings and assorted hard surfaces. Max was there to see Sir John Anderson's Private Secretary and pick up the detention order made out against Anna Wolkoff.

The order would normally have been despatched straight to Scotland Yard. In this case, though, Max was anxious to make sure as few people as possible were aware of Wolkoff's impending arrest. Were the detention order to go through the usual channels, there was always a risk that one of the Right Club's contacts within the Metropolitan Police might see it. Then Wolkoff might receive a warning. Then she might, in turn, alert Tyler Kent, mucking up the entire operation. Kent and Wolkoff might destroy the evidence against them and perhaps even go to ground.

Both Sir John Anderson and his Private Secretary were based on the first floor, just beyond the Schools Inspectorate. Thankfully, no bureaucratic obstacles had sprung up overnight, so Max was able to collect the three-page detention order.

Mission accomplished, he left the Home Office and passed the paperwork to one of his staff at Dolphin Square. Responsibility for organizing a raiding party that could be sent round to the Wolkoffs' flat was delegated to Max's friend, Jimmy Dickson. Max regarded him as a safe pair of hands.

From his days as a fraud investigator, Jimmy had plenty of experience of working with the police.

20

As he emerged into Grosvenor Square, Tyler had with him a copy of the Prime Minister's message to President Roosevelt. Tyler could have done with some rest, but he had a full day ahead of him.

Irene Danischewsky was due to visit his flat that morning. And in the afternoon they were planning to take advantage of the fine weather by going to the botanical gardens at Kew. Tyler's evening would be spent with Anna Wolkoff, Enid Riddell and the Duke del Monte. The four of them had arranged to eat at La Coquille, a fish restaurant near Trafalgar Square, popular with eminent people from big business and government. After dinner, he and the others were planning to go dancing at the Embassy Club again.

21

From the Home Office, Max went to Scotland Yard for a meeting with Sir Norman Kendal, the ageing ACC – Assistant Commissioner/Crime. The pair of them had abundant scope for preliminary small-talk. Being an obsessive ornithologist, Max might not have been expected to approve of Sir Norman's passion for grouse-shooting, but Max was accustomed to mixing with people who loved hunting. His first wife used to run a hotel that catered for a shooting and fishing clientele.[92]

Joining Max and Sir Norman at their morning conclave was Ambassador Kennedy, plus one of his subordinates. The Ambassador had a breezily forthright manner and a voice to match.

Max double-checked with Sir Norman about the legality of the planned raid on Kent's flat. Through his willingness to use illegal searches as an investigative tool, Max had demonstrated contempt for legal process, yet he appears to have been astute enough not to expose this.

Sir Norman was an Oxford-educated former barrister. In the years he'd served at the Yard, he had proven adept at gauging whether one had assembled evidence of sufficient quality to secure a guilty verdict. Based on what he'd been told, he concluded that Kent had probably passed American secrets to the Nazis via Wolkoff. Accordingly, he rubber-stamped Max's plans and set about procuring the necessary search warrants.

Kennedy confessed to feeling very strongly that Kent shouldn't be permitted to remain at liberty for a moment longer. If it turned out that the British authorities were unable for one reason or another to launch a prosecution, then Kent would, the Ambassador predicted, be indicted in America.

22

Yesterday Anna had been knocking back vodka and chatting with a friend in the Hungarian Csárda, a little Soho restaurant just a few doors down from the Royalty Theatre. Who knows how long she would have to wait until she got another chance to speak to her friend or enjoy the alcoholic tang of vodka? Not something that Russian ladies of her pedigree were brought up to consume in public. Ample punishment for this breach of etiquette had been dispensed in the shape of a man from MI5 and three police officers who had turned up at her parents' flat this morning.[93] Monday 20 May, 1940. The officers comprised a sergeant, an inspector and a Woman Police Constable.

Anna's father wasn't at home, but her mother and sister, Kyra, were present to lend moral support. Their uninvited visitors ordered them to show their Identity Cards. Once these had been inspected, the search warrant was read to Anna and family. So too was the detention order.

'I am satisfied that with a view to preventing Anna Wolkoff, 18a Roland Gardens, London SW7 acting in any manner prejudicial to the public safety or the defence of the realm it is necessary to make this order.'

While the document was being read to her, Anna had time to contemplate the irony that she had, less than three months ago, sent Sir Vernon Kell a newspaper article urging the internment of so-called enemy aliens, German Jewish refugees rather than White Russians like herself. 'Now, therefore, I, in pursuance of the power conferred on me by Regulation 18b of the Defence Regulations, 1939,' the voice continued, 'hereby make the following Order. I direct that the above mentioned, Anna Wolkoff, be detained.'

Whenever Anna was the target of accusations of any kind, she assumed a posture of supercilious decorum. Offered the chance to respond to the reading of the detention order, she remained mute. Nor did she say anything when the consequences of the order were explained to her.

She was told she had the right to appeal to an Advisory Committee to have the order revoked. Facilities for such an appeal and for making representations to the Secretary of State would, she was informed, be provided at the place of detention. She didn't respond to that either.

Next, she suffered the indignity of having her bedroom subjected to a thorough search. With the exception of what used to be her sister Alice's room but had since been taken over by her parents' lodger – who was not present – the search extended to the rest of the flat.

Among the items discovered by the intruders were a four-page account of Anna's trip to the Continent last year, a wodge of anti-Semitic stickybacks and a blue leather wallet with a swastika on it. Piles of her correspondence and general paperwork were loaded into a suitcase that the MI5 officer commandeered. The correspondence included a letter she'd recently received from her friend, the novelist Louis-Ferdinand Céline. His message, left inside a red exercise book, thanked Anna for the hospitality she had shown him. 'How are the British rebels – Captain Ramsay and the other plotters?' he enquired.

Soon the search was completed. Next, the Woman Police Constable went through Anna's pockets. These contained twelve shillings in silver coins, which Anna was permitted to keep.

Under the vigilant gaze of the policewoman, Anna packed her overnight things into a suitcase. She took it with her as she was hustled out of the flat. Much to her lingering distress, she didn't have the chance to say goodbye to her beloved father, who had not yet returned home.

23

At about 7.15 a.m. that morning a black police car pulled up outside the US Embassy. Max was sitting in the vehicle. With him were a trio of tall plain-clothes officers – Detective Inspector Joseph Pearson and two Detective Sergeants.

Franklin C. Gowen, the forty-four-year-old Second Secretary at the embassy, his jowly features transmitting an impression of stolid middle-age, climbed into the police car, where Max and the others were ensconced. Gowen had just been given instructions by Ambassador Kennedy. Should Kent claim that they had no business searching his rooms due to his diplomatic status, Gowen had been ordered to tell Kent to raise the matter with the Ambassador.

Like an owl swooping on its oblivious prey, the police car soon accelerated out of Grosvenor Square. Kent's flat was less than a mile away. Well clear of the rush-hour, Max and the others were spared any significant hold-ups. They arrived only a few minutes later.

In his capacity as a Security Service officer, Max was unable to carry out arrests or raids on suspects' homes, so he had to let burly Detective Inspector Pearson take the lead. Pearson went straight up to the entrance to 47 Gloucester Place and rang the bell.

A maid opened the door.

Pearson asked to see Mr Tyler Kent. Correct procedure dictated that Pearson also flourished his police identification card.

Hearing Kent's name, the maid said she'd have to go down-stairs and have a word with her employer. As she retreated to the basement, Max, Gowen and the three detectives advanced into the house. One of the Detective Sergeants trailed behind the maid while the other men sprinted up to the first floor.

When they reached the landing, they encountered a woman who turned out to be Kent's landlady. The two detectives, accom-panying Max and Gowen, showed their police identification cards to her, along with the warrant to search her house. Asked whether Kent was at home, she pointed towards the closed door adjacent to the landing. She said *that* was Mr Kent's room.

Pearson reached for the handle and tried to open the door, but it was locked. So he rapped on it. There was no answer, provoking him to knock again.

Somewhere on the other side of the door, a man shouted, 'Don't come in!' The voice bore an American accent. Not the type of accent Max was used to hearing in the gangster films he loved, the sort that transformed 'shirts' into 'shoits'. Much more refined than that.

Max's colleague gave the door another knock. The same voice repeated, 'Don't come in!'

All patience exhausted, Pearson shoulder-charged the door.

24

Pearson's weight against the door generated enough impact to produce a splintering noise. One of the door panels split and the bolt, previously holding the door shut, was ripped free.

Together with Gowen and the Detective Sergeant, Max followed Pearson into the bed-sitting room, where they were confronted by Tyler Kent. He was standing beside his bed, wearing only pyjama bottoms.

So *this* was Wolkoff's American friend, who had been in Max's sights for the past twelve weeks. Max immediately explained that the house was being raided by the police. His personal effects would all have to be searched, Max told him.

Pearson then identified himself as a police officer and announced that the search had been authorized by warrant. The strange thing was, Kent appeared quite calm, his composure seemingly indicative of someone who believed that his powerful friends would protect him.

That self-possession vanished when he saw a police officer marching towards the closed door nearby. 'You can't go in there!' he yelled. Without further ado, Kent added, 'There is a lady …' He let his sentence trail off as the detective opened what turned out to be the door to his bathroom.

Lurking on the other side was a shapely and attractive redhead. She was naked apart from the top half of a pair of men's pyjamas. Embarrassing though the circumstances were, she seemed as unruffled as her companion. She identified herself as Mrs Irene Danischewsky.

Both Kent and his lady friend were ordered to get dressed. They did so under police supervision. Kent had plenty of clothes from which to choose. Numerous shirts and ties. A tweed jacket. Five suits. Two sets of evening dress. A couple of hats. Three overcoats. And a leather jacket.

He ended up swapping his pyjamas for a suit. Fully clothed as well, Mrs Danischewsky was led away for questioning by Pearson in another part of the building.

Kent now received the obligatory police caution. 'You are not obliged to say anything unless you wish to do so, but what you say will be taken down in writing and may be given in evidence against you.'

Only then could Kent be questioned. Max asked him whether he had any documents – stored in the house or elsewhere – pertaining to the American government and, more particularly, to the US Embassy in London.

'I have nothing belonging to the American government,' Kent replied with brazen confidence. 'I don't know what you mean.'

Whereupon Max asked Kent whether he was acquainted with any of the following people. Max reeled off a list of names, many of which sounded foreign, Anna Wolkoff's among them. In most cases, Kent said 'No'.

Having worked through the list, Max quizzed him about the

allegiances of those people. Were they, Max wanted to know, loyal to Great Britain or to their countries of origin?

Kent replied that he couldn't say. After a momentary silence, he turned to Franklin C. Gowen and said, 'Do you think I should answer these questions?'

'By all means,' Gowen replied. 'Answer everything.'

When Max enquired whether Anna Wolkoff was a loyal British subject, Kent tried to dodge the question, but Max would not allow him to escape so easily. In the face of Max's extended probing, Kent wouldn't give anything resembling what Max considered a straight answer.

Ultimately, the American relented. He said Anna regarded herself as loyal, only *that* was a matter of opinion.

25

Mrs Danischewsky's interrogation had finished. Max told her she was free to leave. She then walked out of the building.

There was nothing to fear from Mrs Danischewsky, Max explained to Gowen. Her entanglement with Kent was, Max stressed, nothing more than a case of infatuation. Max admitted to knowing this because the telephone at her home had been tapped and she was under observation. He said she was frightened by the prospect of her husband learning about her liaison with Kent. Detaining her made no sense, he assured Gowen.

Max – who was already familiar with Kent's flat and some of its contents – then helped Pearson and the two other officers search the place. But his Special Branch colleagues could not devote their full attention to the task because they had to keep an eye on the American.

Despite the advice received from Sir Norman Kendal, the Assistant Commissioner/Crime at Scotland Yard, Max still harboured doubts as to the legality of what they were doing, yet he pressed ahead with the search. Opposite the entrance to the flat was a cupboard in which he discovered an import-ant-looking ledger, bound in red leather. Its contents could not be examined, though, as it was clamped shut by a small brass lock. Max forced it open, exposing pages criss-crossed by pre-printed lines and columns, intended for double-entry bookkeeping.

At the front of the ledger were well over 200 handwritten names, arranged in alphabetical order. Clearly this was the Right Club's membership list.[94] Next to the names were details of each person's status within the club and the subscriptions they had paid. The list included people whose activities had been monitored by Max's division of MI5. Lord Sempill, the Japanese agent, fell into that category. As did Anne van Lennep's friend, the German baroness and suspected Nazi spy who had fled Britain just before the outbreak of war. Many people cited in MI5 paperwork about the Nordic League, the British Union and sundry fascist groups were also on the list.

Another name liable to catch Max's eye – partly on the grounds of it being so unusual – was that of William Brinsley Le Poer Trench, a penniless bank clerk who had recently got engaged to the young stepdaughter of Max's friend, Dennis Wheatley. In the light of Le Poer Trench's membership of the Right Club, there was an element of good fortune about the fact that the stepdaughter had lasted just five weeks in her role as a filing clerk at MI5 before, much to Dennis's annoyance with her, being sacked for various minor transgressions.[95]

Max just had to flick through the ledger to find the names of all manner of big fish. The Duke of Wellington. Francis Yeats-Brown, a retired Army officer who had penned the bestselling adventure novel, *The Lives of a Bengal Lancer*. Baron Redesdale, father of the famous Mitford sisters. Sir Alexander Walker, chairman of Johnnie Walker, the whisky distillers. Colonel Harold Mitchell, MP, Vice-Chairman of the Conservative Party. Sir Ernest Bennett, Labour Party MP and supporter of the Nordic League. Lord Carnegie, who was married to Princess Maud, Queen Victoria's grand-daughter. Commander Peter Agnew, another Conservative MP. In all, there were sixteen parliamentarians, half-a-dozen from the House of Lords and ten from the House of Commons, representing the three main parties.

Sensitive to the political ramifications of his work, Max would have comprehended the ledger's power as a source of scandal. Here, after all, were numerous establishment figures with links to a Fifth Column organization. All right, the presence of their names on the list didn't prove they had supported let alone participated in the activities of Anna Wolkoff and their leader, Captain Ramsay, but their inclusion within the ledger was still very suspicious.

Tucked between its pages were a couple of loose sheets of paper. One of these, carrying the embossed House of Commons letterhead, featured anti-Semitic verses written in the same sharply tilted copybook handwriting with which the membership list had been compiled. The other loose sheet of paper was a letter from William Joyce to Captain Ramsay. Dated 1 July 1939, it referred to Joyce's successful application to join the Right Club, for which he had enclosed a five-shilling enrolment fee.

Elsewhere in the cupboard where the club's membership book was kept, Max found a black briefcase and two suitcases. Inside were piles of paperwork, which mostly turned out to be US Embassy documents, some of them originals, others copies.

Persisting with the search, Max came across an envelope lying on a nearby desk. The envelope, which bore Kent's name, contained a letter headed 'Kelly Castle, Arbroath' and signed 'Jock Ramsay'.

Alongside the desk was another cupboard, the contents of which Max inspected. He found a cardboard box holding three postcard-sized glass photographic negatives. These reproduced typewritten pages. He knew enough about photography to discern that the negatives were not the work of an amateur.

From the same cupboard Max fished a voluminous light-brown leather suitcase. On opening this, he found stacks of documents and torn-up telegrams, a blank manila envelope and half-a-dozen folders with more paperwork inside them. Completing the collection were some packages stuffed with telegrams.

When Max skimmed through the stolen documents, two carbon copies caught his attention. Each of them had an identical printed letterhead. 'Box 500, Parliament Street, London SW.' The letterhead was unmistakable to Max because it was used by MI5, Box 500 being the Security Service's main postal address. Dating back to Thursday 19 October and Tuesday 7 November last year, both of these letters had been sent to the US Embassy by Guy Liddell.

Several other noteworthy items were also found during the search. There were two pairs of Yale keys. But neither of these fitted the locks in Kent's flat, the implication being that they were keys from the embassy. There were also more than a thousand stickyback labels. A proportion of them bore messages such as 'War destroys workers not Hitlers.' Most of the labels were, however, emblazoned with anti-Semitic slogans. Doggerel expressing comparable sentiments appeared on a couple of sets of printed flyers, likewise stored in Kent's rooms.

Besides all that, there was a substantial sum of cash. Equivalent to more than two months of Kent's after-tax salary, this included a rare £50 note, though Max did not spot it at first. Kent had a brace of ten-shilling notes as well, plus six £5 notes that had been slipped inside a jotter. Written on the £5 notes were the addresses of five people, two of whom had Germanic names – names that rendered the money suspicious.

Without pausing to compile an inventory of everything in the flat, Max prepared to transport the confiscated items back to the US Embassy. He rang for a taxi and presented Gowen with what appeared to be American government property. This consisted of the letters, the Yale keys and the photographic negatives. Plus there were the documents inside the briefcase and three suitcases. These were made up of more letters, not to mention coded messages and transcripts of telegrams between Washington and various American embassies. Large numbers of the documents had been grouped in folders with subject labels. 'Chamberlain', 'American and European Affairs', 'Churchill', 'Jews', 'Germany', 'Russia' and the like.

At length Pearson and the two other detectives heaved the cases down from the first floor and loaded them into the waiting taxi. It still had room for Max and Gowen, who ordered Kent to go with the police officers. Kent and those three detectives would be using the squad car.

Sometime before parting from Kent, Max revealed that he knew about the meeting between Kent and Ludwig Matthias at the Cumberland Hotel last October. The revelation was perhaps calculated to unsettle the American and make him easier to interrogate that afternoon.

Pearson and the two Detective Sergeants escorted Kent downstairs. The detectives got into the car with Kent. Both the police car and the taxi then set off for Grosvenor Square.

26

Two of the detectives marched Kent into the US Embassy and through to Room 119, where they locked themselves in and stood guard over him. While they did that, Max and Gowen lugged the confiscated ledger and document-filled cases up to Ambassador Kennedy's spacious second-floor office. Reached through an anteroom hung with nineteenth-century photographs, the office had tall windows overlooking Grosvenor Square. The room's pale-blue silk wallpaper seemed incongruously feminine next to its sombre mahogany furnishings.

Facing Max was a portrait of an Edwardian predecessor of Kennedy, an urbane gentleman who eyed the office's current occupants with what could be interpreted as patrician disdain. Upper-class urbanity wasn't a trait one would associate with the present Ambassador. Gowen began by speaking to him about how best to conceal news of Kent's arrest from other staff at the embassy.

Kennedy endorsed the idea that colleagues should, if they asked about the errant Code Clerk, be informed that Kent was busy. Any visitors wanting to see Kent should be directed to Room 115, where they'd be invited to wait until he was free. Phonecalls for him should be transferred to the anteroom, through which Max and Gowen had carried the confiscated items.

With Kennedy's permission, Gowen was going to attempt to impersonate Kent and perhaps that way gain extra information about his contacts. But Gowen was under no illusion as to the difference between his voice and that of Kent. To get round this problem, he'd tell callers he needed to speak quietly because there were so many people around. And he'd keep pecking at the keys of a nearby typewriter as a means of lending verisimilitude to his story.

Before Gowen had a chance to put into practice his deception scheme, he was notified that a woman had just phoned, asking for Kent. She'd told one of his colleagues, 'Mr Kent's house has been raided by the police this morning' – or words to that effect.

Referring to the clutter now lining the office where Max and the others had gathered, Kennedy said, 'Let's look at the evidence, then.'

The ensuing inspection offered sobering proof of the magnitude of the Code Clerk's betrayal. When the Ambassador hurriedly leafed through the folder marked 'Churchill', he found a copy of the telegram from Churchill to Roosevelt, pleading for the loan of aircraft, ammunition, anti-aircraft guns, as well as forty or fifty destroyers.

Filed next to this was one of Kennedy's own memoranda, which exposed his potentially embarrassing anti-British, isolationist opinions. The memo advised the President to refuse Churchill's request. 'If we have to fight to protect our lives, we would do better fighting in our own backyard,' Kennedy had written.

Such copious evidence of the embassy's deficient security enraged the Ambassador, whose anger had a tendency to turn his face as red as his remaining hair. Kennedy's rage was only intensified by Max's ensuing admission that Kent had been under surveillance since October the previous year when he'd staged a meeting with a suspected Nazi agent. It was a self-serving revelation designed to mislead, to imply that Max had been in control of the affair all along. Glowering at him across the desk, Kennedy said, 'Send the traitorous bastard in!'

27

Max, Gowen and Kennedy were joined in the second-floor office by Herschel V. Johnson and one of the Detective Sergeants who had searched Kent's flat. With them was another of the embassy's senior staff.

Ready to transcribe the interrogation, a secretary also entered the Ambassador's office. She could apparently be trusted to be discreet about what she heard.

Inspector Pearson escorted Kent into the room moments later. Kent remained strangely calm.

'This is quite a serious situation you have got your country involved in,' Kennedy said to Kent. 'From the kind of family you come from – people who have fought for the United States – one would not expect you to let us down.'

'In what way?'

'You don't think you *have*?' Kennedy's tone was incredulous. 'What do you think you were doing with our codes and telegrams?'

'It was only for my own information.'

'Why did you have to have them?'

'Because I thought them very interesting.'

Exasperated by such disingenuous replies, Kennedy halted the interrogation and went outside for a private discussion with Max.

28

At Kennedy's behest, Max took over the questioning when the two of them walked back into the room. It was an important moment for Max.

'I am talking to you now by invitation of your Ambassador and not in any way in connection with matters which concern only Great Britain at the moment,' Max explained to Kent with the pugnacious exactitude of a barrister at a trial. 'The situation as I see it is this ... I think it is just as well you should know you can be proved to have been associating with this woman, Anna Wolkoff.'

'I don't deny that,' Kent replied, insolence diffusing from those four words.

So experienced was Max in questioning uncooperative subjects that he didn't let this fluster him. 'I am in a position to prove that she has a channel of communication with Germany, that she has used that channel, that she is involved in pro-German propaganda, to say the least,' he calmly informed Kent. 'As your Ambassador has just said, you have been found with documents in your private rooms to which he considers you have no proper title. You would be a very silly man if you do not realize that certain conclusions might be drawn from that situation, and it is for *you* to offer the explanation, not *us*.' There was no response from Kent, so Max focused on the ledger found in the Gloucester Place flat and said, 'What is this?'

'I don't know what it is.'

'Who gave it to you?'

'I haven't any idea.'

Max brushed aside Kent's attempt at stonewalling. 'By whom was it given to you?'

'It was given to me by Captain Ramsay.' Kent lied to Max by saying, 'What it contains, I don't know.'

'Why did Captain Ramsay give it to you?'

'He asked me to keep it.'

'When did he give it to you?'

'About three weeks ago,' Kent said. 'I don't know exactly.'

'He simply asked you to keep it for him? Where did he hand it over to you?'

'I think he brought it to me.'

'He brought it to *your* place?'

'Yes.'

'Was Anna Wolkoff there when he gave it to you?'

'I don't think so. I'm not positive.'

'And you claim to have no knowledge of what is in this book?'

'Positively none.'

Shrewd and observant when it came to psychology, human or otherwise, Max followed this with a sharp blow aimed at Kent's vanity, so evident in his extensive wardrobe. 'Don't you think it strange that a Member of Parliament should come to you – a minor official in an embassy – and give you a locked book to take care of for him?' Max enquired. In boxing parlance, his intention was clearly to goad Kent into an exchange of blows that could leave a pugilist vulnerable to a knockout punch. But Kent's granite-jawed self-regard remained untouched.

The attempt at provocation having failed, Max switched to a tone of man-to-man frankness. 'Now, seriously,' he said, 'doesn't it strike you as odd that a Member of Parliament should bring you a locked ledger and ask you to take care of it for him?'

'I don't know.'

'You are adopting a sort of naive attitude which doesn't deceive me for a moment. You are either hiding something or ...'

'Well, the fact remains that I don't know what is in that thing, and I haven't seen it open. He simply requested that I keep it for him.'

'That is not answering my question,' Max snapped. 'I have asked you whether you did not think it curious that a man in Captain Ramsay's position should bring it to you – a young and obscure man – a book to which he apparently attaches some importance, and ask you to keep it for him. Did you know that Captain Ramsay was associated with Anna Wolkoff?'

'Yes, if by "associated", you mean he knows her ...'

'There is no time to go into all these details here. There will probably be further opportunity on future occasions.' Max produced a letter bearing Kent's handwriting. 'Here is a letter that you wrote to Anna Wolkoff on 21 March 1940.'

'May I see that?

'Certainly.' Handing him the letter, Max referred to a section in which Kent had written that he hoped to see her when he returned from his trip to Bexhill. Max also quoted a sentence about how Kent wanted to make the acquaintance of more of her 'interesting friends'. 'Now, who *are* the "interesting friends"?' Max asked.

'I think that was with regard to meeting Captain Ramsay,' Kent said. 'I think I had that in mind. Then I *did* meet him and found him rather interesting.'

'In what way?'

'In conversation. We had sort of common views ... to a certain extent.'

But Max didn't pursue that line. 'The first time that you came to my attention,' he said, 'was in February 1940 when your friend, Anna Wolkoff, was telling people that she had made an extremely useful contact with a young man at the American Embassy. I am going to speak to you now extremely bluntly. I am afraid I must take the view that you are either a fool or a rogue because you cannot possibly be in a position except that of a man who has either been made use of, or who knows all these people. I propose to show you.' Max then set about demonstrating his knowledge of Kent's links. 'Now on 16 April 1940 it was reported to me that Anna Wolkoff was telling some of her close associates in the Right Club ... I presume you know what the Right Club is?'

'I *have* heard of it,' Kent replied with fake innocence.

'She was telling her associates,' Max persisted, glancing at Kennedy as he spoke, 'a story which purported to be based on an interview you, Mr Ambassador, had with Lord Halifax. And it concerned the landing of the Germans in Norway and the difficulties that had been encountered by the British Navy in connection with that. I believe I am right in saying that this is only a small indication but it has some of the truth. I don't know how you are prepared to explain that Anna Wolkoff should know *that*, even if you claim that you didn't tell her.'

'I don't remember what I said in conversation in April 1940.'

'You have a very good memory for what you have *not* said but not a very good memory for what you *have* said,' Max retorted. 'I talked to you this morning about this man Matthias. Now you were in a restaurant with Matthias on 8 October 1939. He then went and paid a short visit to your room at the Cumberland. On leaving, Matthias was carrying a packet approximately ten by six inches which he was *not* carrying when he went into the hotel.'

'I certainly don't remember that incident at all. I am guilty of one thing and that is smuggling a box of cigars through the British Customs, which I subsequently lost. And that was the object of the visit to my room.'

Without challenging Kent's account of the meeting at the Cumberland, Max said he planned to examine Wolkoff's behaviour on 16 April in more detail later. He went on to say, 'I believe you had dinner with Anna Wolkoff at the Russian Tea Rooms on 12 April.'

'I had dinner there two or three times. I don't remember the dates.'

'In the conversation you had with her on that occasion, she claims that you gave her confidential information regarding the North Sea battles – the success had been greatly exaggerated and that it was British propaganda designed to cover heavy British losses sustained in the air attack on Scapa Flow.' Max set out the version of events given to Ambassador Kennedy and then leaked by Kent. 'On 21 April,' Max continued, 'Anna Wolkoff visited you at your rooms and, just after she came out of there, she was in possession of some information about correspondence which had been going on between officials in the British government and officials in the American Embassy on the subject of the purchase of certain technical radio apparatus.'

'There may be something on that in some of those papers,' Kent responded. But he said that he didn't know to what Max was referring.

'Have you ever tried to send any communications to America via the diplomatic bag?'

'Just one or two personal letters to my family.'

'I mean to anyone else?'

'No.'

'Has Anna Wolkoff ever spoken to you about the broadcasts from a man who is known as "Lord Haw-Haw"?'

'I think so.'

'Do you know who he is? Do you know his name?'

'No. I have heard from various sources that he's supposed to be an Irishman.'

Max changed tack. He remembered that Wolkoff's sister, Kyra, had earlier on phoned Kent's flat, presumably with the intention of warning him about Anna's arrest. 'Did you expect Kyra Wolkoff to ring you up this morning?'

'No, I don't know her well at all.'

Left with little alternative but to switch direction again, Max motioned towards the ledger and said, 'You definitely state that to the best of your knowledge and belief you had no knowledge of what the contents of this book are?'

'No. It was given to me and I made no attempt to open it.'

'And you still cannot offer any explanation as to why he should give to you a book for safekeeping?'

'I haven't thought about it much, to tell the truth.'

Once more, Max expressed amazement that Kent didn't find it odd that Captain Ramsay had entrusted him with the book.

'Well, I suppose it does seem a bit odd.'

As soon as he had wrung this concession from Kent, Max shifted the focus of the interrogation to the stolen US Embassy paperwork. 'It is not for me to discuss the question of your position with regard to these documents belonging to your government, because that is not my affair at all. But your explanation about this appears to me to be extremely unconvincing, and your explanations of every point raised are unconvincing.'

Kent told Max he would try to be a little clearer second time round. He asked whether Max wanted to know why he'd taken the documents.

The Ambassador butted in and said *that* was what interested him. 'You don't expect me to believe you for a minute that you had them for your own entertainment?'

'I didn't say "entertainment". I said "interest".'

Max put it to Kent that he felt he was entitled to have them, so he could refresh his memory about their confidential contents.

'I think in the future it would have been very interesting,' Kent said.

'You know you are in an extremely ...' Max paused while he adjusted the trajectory of what he was saying. 'If you were

English,' he resumed, 'you would be in a very difficult position. You don't impress me by your cocky manner.'

'I haven't been making any attempt to be cocky or to impress you, but I say that the reason is just what I stated.'

'You thought they would be *useful* to you in the future?' Max said, misquoting Kent, disbelief colouring his speech. 'What did you mean, they would be "useful"?'

'I hadn't any definite plan as to what use I'd make of them. But they were doubtless of importance as historical documents and throw an interesting light on what we are going through.'

Kennedy said, 'You know of course that it is against the law for you to have these documents?'

'I am not aware of that.'

'Well, let me assure you that it *is*,' the Ambassador said in reply to Kent's latest display of implausible naivety. 'You were not by any chance going to take them with you to Germany when you asked for a transfer there without our knowledge?'

'No, I couldn't have got them out,' Kent replied, though he knew it was perfectly possible to smuggle large quantities of documents out of Britain using the diplomatic pouch. He shied away from any reference to this, preferring to back up his statement by telling Kennedy that he was not in a job that gave him exemption from luggage searches by Customs officials.

Max assured him that many countries *would* offer him exemption.

Kent said that was very far from his thoughts.

Then Max tried a different approach. 'I just want to ask you once again about Anna Wolkoff. I asked you this morning whether you considered whether Anna Wolkoff was a loyal British subject. It seemed a perfectly fair question to put to you or any other witness, but you could not – or would not – give me a straight answer. The best I could get from you was that she considered that she was, but that *that* might be a matter of opinion.'

'Well, if you mean that she holds some views that are apparently at variance with some of the ideas ... possibly of the

British government, that is quite true. But it doesn't mean that she is not a loyal British subject.'

'Does a loyal British subject communicate secretly …?'

Without waiting for Max to finish his sentence, Kent replied, 'No, but I have absolutely no knowledge of that.' Kent's premature denial afforded Max an inadvertent hint that he already knew about the messages Anna was sending to Germany. The hint swelled into something more explicit when Kent added, 'That is the first I have heard of it. If you say that she is in communication with the enemy, why of course she is not a loyal British subject. But when you put the question to me this morning, I didn't know that.'

'But this morning you wouldn't say yes or no. A person is either loyal or disloyal.'

'If you think that everybody that doesn't approve of what is being done by the country is disloyal that would …'

'Now you are merely trying to talk like a parlour politician, but we are dealing with fundamentals.'

'As far as fundamentals are concerned, I have no knowledge of Anna Wolkoff …'

Kennedy interrupted, saying to Max, 'If you prove that she is in contact with them, she is more or less a spy. If the United States government decides to waive any rights they may have, do I understand that that might very well make Kent part and parcel of that?'

'Subject to the production of evidence under law, yes,' Max replied. He was satisfied with the outcome of the questioning, which had, he believed, demonstrated that Kent wasn't telling the truth. It had also shown that Kent had something to hide and was implicated in the activities of the Right Club. 'I think honestly that at this stage nothing very useful is to be got by carrying on this conversation,' Max said to the Ambassador.

Kent was escorted out of the room by Detective Inspector Pearson. Max's Special Branch colleague would be transporting Kent to Cannon Row Police Station, where Sir Norman Kendal had arranged for him to be held.

Most Secret and Personal | 375

29

Following her arrest, Anna was taken through the morning traffic to Rochester Row Police Station, not far from the Russian Orthodox Church where she worshipped. Much later that day, the Woman Police Constable and another of the officers who had participated in the raid on her parents' flat accompanied her across London. The customary mode of transport for prisoners was a police van, where she would have been locked in a booth even smaller than a toilet cubicle. But the approaching blackout made the rest of her journey impracticable by road.

Euston Station granted the obvious alternative. Standing sentry in front of its forecourt, where police vans could deposit their prisoners, was a vast, soot-blackened cousin of the Arc de Triomphe. On the station concourse a medley of noises typically competed: the echoing voice of the tannoy announcer, the clatter of carriage doors being slammed, the hissing, sighing and rhythmic sh-sh-shing of steam trains. Such familiar sounds invited Anna to grieve over how much her circumstances had changed since she had last set foot in a mainline station.

For a woman so preoccupied by social status, the experience of being marched down the platform and onto the Manchester train by a police escort must have been mortifying. To passers-by, Anna would have appeared nothing more than a common criminal.

As her train rattled out of London and into the green spring countryside, she had plenty of time to contemplate what awaited her. Potential guidance was offered by her Right Club colleague Fay Taylour's prison experiences four years earlier. Instead of paying a fine for contravening the newly introduced speed limit on British roads, Fay had spent a few days in jail.

On arrival at HM Prison Manchester, Anna passed into the custody of the Governor, the jail's senior official. She was then presented with a copy of her detention order, signed by the Home Secretary.

Whether or not they had been convicted, new inmates were always taken to the prison's unwelcoming Reception Area, where they had to remove their clothes and have a bath. After their height and weight had been measured, they were fingerprinted and subjected to a medical examination. The reception process also entailed answering numerous questions fired at them by the officer in charge. Are you single or married? What's your religion? Where were you born? What's your trade? And so on.

Once the new arrival had responded to these, she was given her first unappetizing taste of prison food. This was far removed from the cuisine at L'Escargot Bienvenu, where Anna had dined only a few evenings ago.

Despite the seriousness of the charges against her, the warders treated Anna with considerable kindness, yet that could not assuage her misery. Still, at least her status as a prisoner under the Emergency Defence Regulations spared her the final ignominy of being forced to swap her clothes for one of those ill-fitting uniforms worn by the ordinary inmates. Nor did she have her pyjamas, cigarettes and other possessions confiscated. But she wasn't permitted to keep her cigarette lighter. Fortunately she had some matches. She would, however, have to be careful she didn't use up her supply.

Her metamorphosis from Miss Anna de Wolkoff into Prisoner 352 completed, she was led away to her cell. Usually no bigger than about seven feet by thirteen feet, jail cells were standardized in their contents and layout. They all had whitewashed brick walls. As the studded wooden door opened and you walked into your cell, you faced a double-barred window, placed inaccessibly high. Except for a small mirror and a card that had the prison regulations printed on it, the cell's whitewashed walls were devoid of adornment. Its furnishings were limited to a wooden table and stool, along with an uncomfortable bed-board. This had to be propped against the wall when not in use, some bedding draped over it. Balanced on a shelf in the corner of your cell were a bar of soap, a jar of salt, some lavatory paper, a pint pot, a slate and a piece of chalk. The remaining contents of your new home comprised a chamber pot, plus an enamel water jug, basin and plate.

Locked in these spartan surroundings, Anna had nothing but her cigarettes to soothe her, the smell of tobacco, the taste of smoke and the warm surge of nicotine purveying a tangible link to the world she had left behind. Without her cigarettes, she was certain she would not have been able to cope.

Overnight she kept recalling things she needed to tell her parents. But when she sat down to compose a letter to them next morning on prison notepaper, which looked so ugly in comparison to the monogrammed paper she normally used, she was too upset to remember what she had been intending to write.

30

After Kent had been taken away yesterday, Ambassador Kennedy told Max something disturbing. The Ambassador mentioned the need to cable Washington regarding Kent's diplomatic status. Contradicting what Herschel V. Johnson, Kennedy's second-in-command, had previously said to Max, it became apparent that Kent's diplomatic immunity had *not* been revoked. Further interrogation of the Code Clerk might be ruled illegal for that reason. Max's case would then be thrown into disarray. So Kennedy had assured Max that he'd get in touch with the State Department and request Kent's dismissal from US government service.

On the morning of Tuesday 21 May, 1940, Max was due to find out the current state of play. When he rolled up at Grosvenor Square, Kennedy presented him with a pile of paper-work found in Kent's flat. These documents weren't, Kennedy explained, the property of the American government.

During their conversation, Max said he was hoping to interview Kent again that day.

Kennedy asked Max to deliver a note to Kent.

The Ambassador showed Max the typewritten message.

'Sir,' the message began. 'The Department of State in a cable received today notified me, and you will accept this notice, that you are dismissed from government service as of 20 May 1940. Yours truly, Joseph P. Kennedy.'

If possible, Kent should be persuaded to provide a receipt for the message, Kennedy said to Max. Kennedy added that his colleagues at the embassy had now had time to examine the material recovered from Kent's flat. The importance of those documents to both the United States and the Allied cause could not, he said, be exaggerated. Max was told to let his superiors know that, if any senior British government official doubted the gravity of this matter, they should phone Kennedy.

31

Already pining for conversation with those she loved, Anna finally knuckled down to the task of writing to her parents. In the four-page letter she penned from prison, she feigned bewilderment at the dramatic twist her life had taken. Her letter was filled with requests, most of them directed at her mother. Self-pity seeping from the paper, Anna wanted Mme Wolkoff to ask their Russian Orthodox priest to say prayers for her. Mme Wolkoff was also urged to send Anna a nightgown as well as some food, and to run a series of errands related to her dressmaking business. Anna used the letter to ask her parents to relay messages to friends such as Admiral and Christabel Nicholson, soliciting cigarettes and matches. Tyler was the target for another of Anna's messages. Her parents were instructed to pass on her thanks to him for being so caring towards her.

The letter concluded with a reference to a phonecall she had received before her arrest. Lord Cottenham, known to her as Cotty, was the caller. Probably aware that Max and colleagues were monitoring her, Cotty – who had been working for MI5 – had told her to let him know if she was ever in a tight spot. He'd pledged eternal friendship and promised assistance should she ever require it.

Memory of his phonecall encouraged Anna to direct her parents to ask Enid Riddell to visit Lord Cottenham right away and get him to fulfil his promise. She assumed it would be simple for him to obtain permission to visit her and arrange for them to talk in private. If anyone could help her wriggle out of her present predicament, it was him. Yet her letter made it clear that her priority was for her parents to convey her message to Tyler.

32

Rigged out in smart civilian clothes, Max arrived at Cannon Row Police Station not long before lunch that day. Tuesday 21 May 1940. Max was brought face to face with Kent, who had been escorted through from one of the cells. The American wore the same suit he'd worn the previous day.

When Max presented him with the letter from Ambassador Kennedy, he was at first reluctant to sign a receipt for it. But Max talked him into obliging. Mindful that nothing should be said that might prejudice any future legal proceedings, Max went on to ask Kent to explain why he had abstracted the documents from the embassy files.

Kent maintained his previous claim about wanting them because of their historical interest.

It was an explanation Max found no more credible than when he'd heard it yesterday. He kept challenging Kent to make a clean breast of the real motive for the thefts. Kent wouldn't, however, elaborate.

Here, Max's relentlessness seemed to pay dividends.

'I took these documents,' Kent abruptly declared, 'because I consider they show a dishonest discrepancy between news which was given to the public and the actual trend of political affairs as was known in diplomatic circles. I considered it was my duty to make these facts known.'

Max enquired when he intended to do this.

Kent was unable to offer anything resembling what Max construed as a satisfactory answer.

Then Max questioned him about how he had been planning to make those facts public.

'At the moment I have no definite idea as to the procedure I shall adopt,' Kent said, his choice of tense implying that his confinement in a prison cell was no more than a temporary inconvenience.

Perhaps he was planning to write a book, Max ventured.

'Of course not,' Kent retorted. Expert in the art of deception, he was swiftly acquiring a facade of self-righteous indignation that befitted his new role as a principled opponent of the underhand dealings of politicians.

Moving on to another subject, Max asked why photographic negatives of sensitive embassy documents were found in his possession.

He replied that he'd been trying out a camera, which he had contemplated buying from a friend. Quizzed as to the identity of that friend, Kent named his Jewish colleague from the US Embassy's Code Room.

Next came a question about the two sets of Yale keys unearthed in Kent's flat, keys that fitted the doors to the embassy's File and Code Rooms.

These had, Kent admitted, been cut so that he could have access to confidential government documents even if he was transferred to a different post within the building.

An array of questions about his involvement with Anna Wolkoff and Captain Ramsay followed.

The interrogation was, Max realized, close to the point where it might, in the likely event of charges being brought against Kent, be viewed as improper. So Max, anxious not to undermine the case that he had put together with such diligence, wrapped up the interview and arranged for Kent to be taken back to his cell.

33

Kent's story about borrowing a camera from a friend could be checked without much trouble. The colleague who had supposedly lent him the camera turned out to have been posted to the US Embassy in Madrid two or three weeks ago. Kent must have hoped that Max had neither the facility nor desire to contact the man. As Max discovered, the story about the camera was yet another lie.

He also appears to have briefed Sir Norman Kendal – Scotland Yard's Assistant Commissioner/Crime – on his latest interview with the duplicitous Code Clerk. A swift decision was duly reached to press charges against the American if possible.

Now Kent had been dismissed from his job at the embassy, proceedings under British law could be initiated because he no longer had diplomatic immunity. Permission was nevertheless sought from the American government before setting in motion the legal process. Within a few hours of Max's visit to Cannon Row Police Station, news came through via the US Ambassador that the Roosevelt administration had no objection to Kent being prosecuted by the British authorities.

34

Even though Kent and Wolkoff had been arrested, Max's agents continued to work on the case, their cover intact. Soon after his second interview with Kent, Max received a report from Marjorie about a visit she'd paid Mrs Ramsay that evening. The intention of the visit had been to enable Marjorie to discuss Wolkoff's detention. On her way out of the Ramsays' Onslow Square home, Marjorie had suddenly been asked by Mrs Ramsay if she would do her a favour. Mrs Ramsay – whose telephone wasn't working – said she'd like Marjorie to ring Christabel Nicholson before nine o'clock next morning and give her a message. The message was that Mrs Ramsay wanted to see her.

Marjorie informed Max that she'd done just as Mrs Ramsay had requested. Finding that Mrs Nicholson wasn't at home, Marjorie had tracked her down to a department store on Brompton Road. Mrs Nicholson was there, collecting money in aid of National Lifeboat Day.

The women adjourned for lunch in a nearby branch of the Kardomah café chain, where Mrs Nicholson vented her fury with Wolkoff. She even declared that Wolkoff deserved to be shot.

Mrs Nicholson confided in Marjorie about copies she herself had made of documents stolen by Kent – documents which, she claimed, were sufficient to prove that Churchill and other high-ranking people were guilty of corruption. She spoke about how the copies needed to be photographed and how she had kept them in her house overnight. But there was some confusion in Marjorie's report as to where they were now.

For the moment, though, action was not taken against Mrs Nicholson. If Max waited and kept her under surveillance, she might implicate and expose hitherto unknown Right Club associates. And he might end up being able to place more of them behind bars.

35

By seven o'clock that evening Max had arrived at the Home Office. Alongside Sir Vernon Kell and Guy Liddell, he was there for a meeting with the Home Secretary, Sir John Anderson. Nicknamed 'God's butler', Anderson was a horse-faced, charmless man in his late fifties, who sounded like the snootiest of gentlemen's gentlemen. Hence the nickname, its aptness underlined by his habit of wearing old-fashioned high collars.

Also in attendance at the meeting was the senior civil servant at the Home Office. He had a couple of Whitehall colleagues in tow.

Sir John kicked off the meeting by referring to the memo MI5 had submitted earlier that month. Dwelling upon the danger to national security posed by Fifth Columnists, specifically the British Union, this recommended the use of much larger scale internment than had previously been attempted. Circumspect and austere in manner, his pronouncements customarily delivered with succinct self-assurance that brooked no dissent, Sir John rebuffed MI5's proposal and challenged Max and colleagues to provide detailed support for the allegations made in it.

Max's voice attained a hushed intensity as he gave an adroit summary of all the pertinent material. His summary endeavoured to bolster MI5's argument that the British Union was a Fifth Column organization, 20 to 30 per cent of whose members would be 'willing, if ordered, to go to any lengths' on behalf of Germany. Secret discussions were, according to MI5, being staged between the fascist groups in preparation for the anticipated German occupation, the secrecy of those discussions accounting for the regrettable dearth of evidence. Once the invasion had commenced, the fascists would either align themselves with the enemy or seize control and make peace with Germany. MI5 therefore implored the government to take prompt measures against the fascists, many of whom had strong links to the Nazis.

Such was the force of Max's calculatedly perturbing speech that Guy Liddell seldom felt the need to enlarge upon what was being said. While the number of probable British Union collaborators represented little more than educated guesswork, other aspects of Max's speech were constructed on sturdier foundations.

There was, for instance, no question that German intelligence had been targeting the British Union and similar fascist organizations in an attempt to recruit spies. Nor was there any doubt as to the readiness of those groups to make peace with Germany, the British Union's 'Stop the War' campaign attesting to that.

Likewise, Max's allegations about meetings between Mosley and leaders of the various fascist movements were undeniable. MI5 had also accumulated details of references by Ramsay, Mosley and others to both the British Union and Right Club seizing power – references that would turn out to be driven less by realism than bravado. And there had been suggestions that, in the event of an invasion, Mosley and Ramsay would be installed as puppet leaders, British equivalents to Vidkun Quisling in Norway.

In response to Max's speech about the threat embodied by British fascists, the Home Secretary said he found it difficult to believe that Mosley's followers would try to help the enemy. He buttressed that line of argument by citing recent issues of *Action*, within which the British Union leader had appealed to the patriotism of his supporters.

These allusions to patriotism were, Max countered, an example of Mosley's insincerity. Phrases like that were, he said, nothing more than figures of speech to him and his supporters. Max described some of the underground activities being conducted by the British Union. He also talked about the recent investigation that had exposed links between Tyler Kent and Captain Ramsay.

While Anderson conceded that the case against Ramsay was rather serious, he said it did not seem to involve the British Union.

His comment led Max to exaggerate the truth by explaining that Ramsay and Mosley were in constant touch with one another. Max emphasized the connection between the two fascist leaders by remarking that many Right Club members belonged to the British Union, too. The nucleus of the Right Club adherents still gathering at the Russian Tea Rooms certainly contained a preponderance of members or former members of Mosley's movement. Bringing to a close his response to the Home Secretary, Max spoke about certain British Union supporters who appeared to be stockpiling weapons.

Palpably shaken by what Max had just told him, Anderson nevertheless insisted that he needed to be reasonably convinced that the British Union might turn against the government. Unless he was presented with evidence as to their likely treachery, he said he thought it would be a mistake to go ahead and jail Mosley and his supporters. Were he to sanction their imprisonment, he added, they'd be exceptionally bitter after the war when democracy would no doubt be going through a testing time.

Guy Liddell responded with impassioned vehemence, stressing the urgency of the matter. Rather than debate the fine points of individual cases, he said, surely it was possible to make up their minds about whether the British Union was assisting the enemy? And, if they reached that conclusion, wasn't it possible to find some means of *dealing* with Mosley's organization?

But Anderson didn't really answer these questions. Instead, he reaffirmed his aversion to locking up British citizens unless the case against them was absolutely cast-iron. He mentioned that tomorrow the War Cabinet would be debating whether there should be a clampdown on the British Union. Preparatory to that meeting, Anderson requested further evidence from Max and his MI5 colleagues about the disloyal propensities of the Mosleyites.

At 8.45 p.m., just over half-an-hour before the blackout was due to descend, the meeting broke up. Guy was infuriated by what he perceived as Anderson's obstinacy. He speculated on whether Anderson was either a very calm and cool-headed person or, perhaps, he hadn't the least idea of just how dangerous the current situation was. 'I longed to say that if somebody did not get a move on there would be no democracy, no England and no Empire,' Guy admitted.

36

Since the War Cabinet was scheduled to discuss the British Union at half past ten the following morning, there wasn't much time available for writing the briefing document requested by the Home Secretary. In the absence of fresh material about the collaborationist potential of the British Union, the decision was taken to focus on the Right Club, implicating Mosley by association with Ramsay.

Max's pivotal role in the Right Club investigation made him the obvious person for the late-night chore of report writing.

'This note is written primarily for the information of higher authority,' he began. 'It is not intended in any way to be a full report. It merely gives the essential facts regarding the treasonable activities of Anna Wolkoff and Tyler Kent, and the implication of these activities with regard to other members of Captain A. Maule Ramsay's Right Club ...'

Over the ensuing half-dozen pages, Max encapsulated the demonstrable security threat posed by Wolkoff, Kent and Ramsay. Based on the well-documented meetings between Ramsay and Mosley, along with the overlapping membership of their organizations, he also made the contentious yet not unreasonable allegation that the British Union represented a similar threat to the nation's security.

As an insurance policy lest his report didn't do the trick, he could always try to influence the War Cabinet by lobbying the Prime Minister. Max could do this through an old friend, who had proven a fruitful contact in the past. That friend was Desmond Morton. Five days earlier he'd left his job at the Ministry of Economic Warfare and been appointed as one of Churchill's two Personal Assistants. No great surprise, because Desmond had over recent years enjoyed an increasingly close friendship with Churchill, his neighbour in rural Kent.

Guy Liddell spoke to Sir Vernon Kell about the idea of petitioning the Prime Minister. Though their boss approved of the concept, he decided to approach Churchill via a different route. Not through Desmond but through the government's Chief Diplomatic Advisor, Sir Robert Vansittart, on whom Guy had bestowed the affectionate nickname 'Van'. That evening Van was sent a copy of Max's report. Another copy – presumably because Sir Vernon could get no response from Van – ended up being passed over to Desmond a little later.

Where discretion was required, Desmond used the United Service Club for meetings. It had been there that he had first recruited Max into MI6.

Practically a decade older than Max, Desmond was a tall, vigorous ex-Army officer, who concealed his wary character behind a mask of brash chumminess. But the idea of employing him as an intermediary between MI5 and Churchill soon hit a snag in that the Prime Minister wouldn't be attending the crucial session of the War Cabinet. First thing next day, Churchill was scheduled to fly across the Channel for talks with the embattled French government, whose armies were being swept aside by the Germans as they advanced towards the Channel coast. His place at the War Cabinet meeting would be taken by his predecessor, Neville Chamberlain. Arrangements were, however, made to enable Churchill to read the report before he set off for France. He could then pass it on to Chamberlain.

Max, Guy and their MI5 colleagues now had a nervous wait for the Cabinet's verdict.

37

A communiqué from Downing Street was unlikely to be forthcoming until after lunch next day. Between now and then, Max had plenty to keep him busy – *so* busy that something significant appears to have slipped his mind.

Earlier he'd been informed that Francis Hemming, who worked for the War Cabinet Secretariat, was an alleged Right Club sympathizer and close friend of Wolkoff. Barring illness or absence, Hemming would be taking minutes at the vital Cabinet meeting, yet seemingly Max didn't try to prevent him from carrying out that function. It gave Hemming privileged access to confidential information that could be leaked to the Right Club and, from there, to the British Union.

While the War Cabinet met, Max went about his duties. These involved a visit to Scotland Yard. In the offices of Special Branch, he received a phonecall around lunchtime. The call was from Detective Inspector Pearson, who had just served a search warrant on Enid Riddell's flat in Knightsbridge. Apart from a postcard from a lady friend, which made it clear that both Riddell and friend were acquainted with Captain Ramsay, the search had yielded nothing of consequence.

Pearson had already questioned Riddell concerning her association with Kent and Wolkoff. According to the detective,

Riddell had been stubborn in her refusal to admit that she knew the couple well. But she had eventually conceded that she'd been a friend of Wolkoff for many years and had known Kent for a few months. She said he and Wolkoff were engaged in some kind of joint project, the nature of which she didn't really understand. From what she could gather, she explained, 'it was anti-Communistic and anti-Semitic'.

Max told Pearson to bring Riddell over to Scotland Yard. There, he set about quizzing her. She proved a tough customer, much tougher than her petite blonde looks suggested.

With predatory intent, Max circled around the subject of the messages she had left for Kent yesterday at the US Embassy and his flat. These concerned their dinner engagement on the evening of his arrest. Under Max's tenacious questioning Riddell grudgingly admitted that she had arranged to meet Kent, Wolkoff and the Duke del Monte at a restaurant on St Martin's Lane.

Her uncooperative attitude persuaded Max that she knew a great deal more than she was prepared to acknowledge. Emerging from the interview, he made up his mind to speak to Sir Norman Kendal at the first opportunity and request an immediate detention order against her.

38

By Thursday 23 May, 1940, three days after the arrest of Wolkoff and Kent, MI5 learned that the tactic of petitioning Churchill had, as Guy Liddell put it, been 'to some degree successful'. Taking into account the document Max had submitted, the War Cabinet had decided to intern Ramsay, Mosley and a selection of fifty-seven other fascists. Substantial numbers of enemy aliens, resident in Britain, would be detained as well, though the Cabinet had baulked at MI5's desire to incarcerate them all.

The government had also drafted an amendment to Regulation 18b of the Emergency Defence Regulations. It was an amendment that provided for the future detention of additional British-based fascists, not to mention Communist Party activists, whose Soviet leadership was still allied to the Nazis. Rushed through Parliament that afternoon, the modified clauses of Regulation 18b conferred on the authorities the power to detain without trial anyone 'likely to endanger' public safety, the defence of the realm, public order or the prosecution of the war.

In the wake of that afternoon's meeting of the War Cabinet, Francis Hemming had confessed to the Cabinet Secretary that he and his wife knew Anna Wolkoff. Max was the obvious person to interrogate Hemming about this.

Not surprisingly, Hemming tried to distance himself and his wife from Wolkoff. 'She never attempted to ask me about my work,' he insisted, 'and I, of course, had never said a word on this subject in conversation with her. Nevertheless, with the war becoming more embittered, my wife and I, after talking the matter over together, came to the conclusion that we did not want to know people who held the views which she seemed to hold or to have held before the war started.' Challenging the limits of plausibility, Hemming even claimed that his sudden desire for German lessons had nothing to do with the threat of invasion. He said he'd employed Wolkoff as a tutor purely because knowledge of the language would assist his natural history studies.

39

Four or five plain-clothes detectives were next day loitering at the back of Hood House, the wing of Dolphin Square where Max worked. They were waiting for Mosley to drive into the residents' car park, their sense of anticipation perceptible in their silence. Today – Friday 24 May, 1940 – was when the round-up of British fascists was scheduled to begin.

Yet Mosley hadn't shown his face. By the look of it, he must have discovered that he was about to be arrested.

Earlier on, Detective Inspector Pearson, again entrusted with a starring role, had enjoyed more success with Captain Ramsay, who had just returned from his Scottish estate. At half past eight Pearson and a colleague had approached him outside his home in Onslow Square.

Going by Pearson's account of what happened, Ramsay did not seem remotely taken aback by their presence. 'He said "Are you police officers?"' Pearson recounted. 'I replied "Yes, sir," and he said, "Have you come to arrest me?" He then admitted us to the house where I served upon him a detention order made by the Home Secretary under Defence Regulation 18b.'

40

The seventh-floor landing at Hood House was only yards from Section B5b's offices. Max may have been one of the two men, both in civilian clothes, who were standing there. The landing was flanked by the lift door and a large window, offering a view every bit as vertiginous as that from the yard-arms of HMS *Worcester*, where Max and his schoolmates used to balance like a team of acrobats, canvas stretched across the deck below in lieu of a safety net.

When the lift door opened, Mosley stepped onto the landing. He was accompanied by several detectives and his wife, Diana, whose father, Lord Redesdale, featured in the Right Club membership book, which Max had examined.

Everyone trooped into one of the two adjoining flats rented by Mosley. He delayed until that point before asking to see their arrest warrant. They showed him the Regulation 18b detention order and explained that he'd be taken to HM Prison Brixton, though his wife would not be permitted to visit him until tomorrow. At which the couple said their farewells. Then the detectives escorted Mosley back to the lift.

For Max, the other significant development that day concerned Home Secretary Sir John Anderson, who had reversed the previous decision to prosecute Kent in the British courts. Anderson had now ratified a deportation order against the former Code Clerk.

But Max carried on pursuing leads stemming from the case. He could now call upon extra manpower in the form of the staff he'd recruited earlier in the year and then sent to MI5 headquarters for training. Among those four recruits, hired to examine hundreds of letters making what turned out to be largely groundless allegations of Fifth Column activity, Max fostered an atmosphere of loyalty and jovial efficiency. In a humorous play on words, representative of the atmosphere at his Dolphin Square base, one of those recruits nicknamed the group 'Knight's Black Agents'. The prevalent light-heartedness couldn't, however, disguise the significance of the work being undertaken by Max and his brood.

Hélène de Munck had lately been directed to go to the Russian Tea Rooms and try to engage Mme Wolkoff in conversation about her imprisoned daughter. On the day of Ramsay's arrest, Hélène gave details of her most recent visit. She revealed that Mme Wolkoff, who didn't appear to know what had become of Kent, had expressed hope that the authorities would remain ignorant of Anna's relationship with him. Mme Wolkoff was upset that Anna had placed her family's wellbeing in jeopardy through her 'foolishness'.

41

At ten o'clock the following morning Max had an appointment with Ambassador Kennedy and Herschel V. Johnson. He was meeting them at the US Embassy for a chat about developments in the Kent/Wolkoff case, on which he had now been working for nearly a year.

To sustain Marjorie Amor's fascist credentials and deflect any suspicion among Wolkoff's friends that she might have been involved in the operation against them, arrangements had been made for her to be arrested under Regulation 18b later that day.

Within the next few days, Hélène de Munck was also earmarked for detention, along with nine more of Wolkoff's coterie. They included Enid Riddell, Anne van Lennep and Fay Taylour, all of whom were going to be sent to HM Prison Holloway. From inside the jail, Marjorie and Hélène could continue gathering information, which Max would be able to deploy against Wolkoff, Kent and the rest of the Right Club's membership.

Muriel Whinfield and several other British Union supporters with whom Wolkoff had dined at the Criterion almost three months previously were on the internment list as well. But there appears to have been insufficient evidence against Francis Hemming to justify a warrant against him. Lord Ronald Graham, Mrs Ramsay, Lord Sempill, the Duke of Wellington, Lord Redesdale and sundry Right Club members were meanwhile allowed to retain their freedom – leniency that reeked of aristocratic privilege.[96] Yet the bulk of Britain's highborn fascists, many of whom appeared to fit the criteria for detention without trial, found themselves under MI5 surveillance. In a tacit warning, some of them had their movements restricted as well.

Just before setting off for the US Embassy, Max received a visit from Detective Inspector Pearson. The Special Branch officer handed him a blue-grey envelope, which had already been torn open. It had been forwarded to Scotland Yard by the Duty Sergeant at a west London police station. How it had come to be handed to him around three thirty yesterday afternoon by a middle-aged woman named Mrs Welberry was a long and peculiar tale.

As Mrs Welberry told the Duty Sergeant, she worked two hours each morning for Admiral and Mrs Nicholson at their flat in Ashburn Gardens. They employed her as a cook and cleaner. Her story began with her being waylaid in the kitchen by Mrs Nicholson, who was brandishing a sealed envelope. Mrs Nicholson slipped this into Mrs Welberry's handbag, which had been left hanging from the door-handle. Mrs Welberry was instructed by her to take the envelope home and bury it in the garden or hide it behind the cistern or in some other safe place.

Back home that evening Mrs Welberry heard a news item on the radio about Captain Ramsay's arrest. Remembering that Mrs Nicholson had in the past spoken about having Ramsay to dinner, she asked her husband whether she should take the envelope to the police. Her husband advised her to wait until the morning and see how Mrs Nicholson behaved.

Next day Mrs Welberry was a bit late getting to the Nicholsons' flat. When she eventually arrived there, Mrs Nicholson said, 'You made me sweat, Kitty.'

To which Mrs Welberry asked why.

Mrs Nicholson explained that she thought Mrs Welberry had been arrested and caught with the papers in the envelope. 'For goodness sake either stick them in your corsets or bury them in the garden,' she urged her.

At home that afternoon, Mrs Welberry related the incident to her husband, who demanded that she open the envelope. Its contents meant nothing to her, but the sight of a reference to the British fleet led her to hand it to the police. This accounted for why Max was now studying two sheets of notepaper covered by pencil-written scrawl. He recognized the writing as a copy of a telegram from Churchill to Roosevelt, appealing for covert military assistance from America. So Max got in touch with Guy Liddell. Max told him about Mrs Welberry and the envelope.

Guy gave Max permission to visit the Nicholsons' flat. Max was also granted leave to apply for an order against Mrs Nicholson under Regulation 80a of the Defence Regulations, compelling her to answer his questions or else risk prosecution.

Only about thirty minutes after Pearson had shown him the envelope, Max had his scheduled meeting at the US Embassy, where he outlined MI5's position regarding the case against Kent. From a practical standpoint, he explained to Kennedy and Johnson, they would probably achieve the best results if Kent's deportation were delayed. Before being sent back to America to face trial, Kent could be subjected to rigorous inter-rogation with the goal of acquiring testimony incriminating Ramsay and Wolkoff.

Kennedy said to Max that this arrangement would probably be most satisfactory, because the State Department was exceedingly anxious about the whole affair. Naturally, he added, they wished to avoid undue publicity. No sooner had Max been given permission to carry out another interview with Kent than the Ambassador left the room.

42

Two mornings had passed since Anna heard the terrible news. She'd been informed that she would be locked up for the remainder of the war.

Neville Chamberlain had not so long ago predicted the conflict would go on until 1943 at the earliest. His forecast prominent in her thoughts, Anna braced herself for the prospect of spending year upon year stuck in a prison cell. Was it any wonder she was currently afflicted by such unutterable depression?

At least the prison authorities were still treating her with surprising benevolence, even going so far as to waive some of the rules. Being a detainee held under Regulation 18b, she should have been restricted to a single visitor each week. She should also have been limited to a weekly quota of two incoming and two outgoing letters. Yet the warders permitted her to exchange any amount of correspondence and see however many visitors she wanted. She could even ask her mother to send her twice-weekly consignments of the Russian food she craved.

Last Thursday Anna, spine aching from the hard bed on which she'd slept, had written to the Advisory Committee set up to decide whether the evidence justified the detention of each of the prisoners arrested under the Emergency Defence Regulations. Pleading her innocence, Anna's letter was candid about her anti-Semitism but disingenuous in its claim that she had never been part of any political group. It stated that she could get numerous well-known and respected current or former government employees – Francis Hemming probably among them – to submit character references attesting to her honesty.

She followed her appeal to the Advisory Committee with another rambling missive to her parents. In her letter she fretted over Tyler's health and asked them to tell him that she was thinking of him. She went on to remind them to get Enid Riddell to go round and speak to Lord Cottenham, who hadn't so far been in touch with her. Adamant that Cotty was a staunch friend and that he'd honour his pledge to assist her should her hour of need ever arrive, she decided she should drop him a line as well.

43

Guy Liddell had heard from Sir Vernon Kell that the Kent/ Wolkoff case had proved decisive in persuading the Prime Minister to support the policy of interning British fascists. One of Wolkoff's Right Club friends who had not so far been detained was Mrs Christabel Nicholson.

On Saturday 25 May, 1940, Max's case against her was stiffened by the results of tapping the Wolkoffs' phone. The MI5 monitor provided a transcript of a highly suspicious conversation between Mme Wolkoff and Mrs Nicholson. It began with Mme Wolkoff inviting Mrs Nicholson to read the letters Anna had written from prison in Manchester. These had, Mme Wolkoff said, contained messages for Mrs Nicholson.

'Is it wise to send me messages?' Mrs Nicholson replied.

'She doesn't call you by your right name.'

Mrs Nicholson asked whether Anna was at Strangeways Prison.

Anna had been taken to a prison in Manchester itself, Mme Wolkoff explained.

There was, Mrs Nicholson said, a rumour that Mosley was being sent there. Mrs Nicholson, who had once worked as a Prison Visitor for the Home Office, assured Mme Wolkoff that she'd write to the prison doctor about Anna. 'She is a dear thing,' Mrs Nicholson concluded, 'but she may talk too much ...'

44

The air had become pleasantly warm by half past nine next morning when Max arrived at 8 Ashburn Gardens. With him were Detective Inspector Pearson and a Woman Police Constable from Special Branch.

Presently, Admiral Nicholson ushered the three of them into the ground-floor flat. Max found him somewhat vague. His wife turned out not to have dressed or breakfasted yet. When Mrs Nicholson eventually deigned to join them, Max introduced himself as Captain King from the Military Intelligence Department. He was struck by how much younger she was than her husband. Twenty years or so. Max introduced her to Pearson and the Woman Police Constable as well. They were, he explained, looking into certain matters with which they thought she could help. He said they'd like to ask her a few questions. He added that he had no objection to her husband being present. 'In fact I would prefer it ...' Before posing the first of his questions, Max ran through the standard police caution. This formality out of the way, he asked whether she knew Anna Wolkoff.

'Yes, very well.'

Then he enquired if she was also acquainted with Tyler Gatewood Kent.

Again the answer was, 'Yes.'

He responded by asking whether she had any idea where Mr Kent worked.

'Yes, I know where he is employed.' She said his job had been at the US Embassy. Her use of the pluperfect tense implied that she was aware that Kent no longer worked there, and probably that he had been arrested. 'He came to tea once on my husband's birthday,' she continued. 'I had heard of him from Anna Wolkoff. I know they were on very friendly terms.' As a footnote to what she had just said, Mrs Nicholson mentioned that she thought they were having an affair.

In an abrupt change of course, Max pulled out a Right Club membership card, discovered during a search of Captain

Ramsay's home. Handwritten on the card was the name, 'Christabel Nicholson'. Max enquired whether the handwriting was hers.

'Oh, yes, rather.'

Now was the moment when Max confronted her with the two sheets of notepaper that had been in the envelope she'd urged Mrs Welberry to hide. He invited her to provide an explanation.

But she said she could give none.

Elaborating on his previous question, he asked whether her handwriting was on the notepaper.

She admitted it was.

Under what circumstances, Max asked, had she written the document?

'That was something I copied from something I saw, and I thought it was very important. I was asked, "What do you think of this?" I copied it without reference to anyone. I think it was about 6 May.'

Why, Max asked, did she remember the date?

'It may have been on 18 May – on my husband's birthday. I am not very good on dates, but perhaps that is when I first saw the papers ...'

Max probed her about who had shown her the papers from which she'd made her copy.

'I'm afraid I won't say. It was shown to me by someone very patriotic, who thought my husband might have access to someone in authority to whom he could show it.'

What was the reason for transcribing that particular document, Max wanted to know.

'My friend considered it showed evidence of corruption in high places,' she said. 'I thought so too, and made a copy with the intention of showing it to some absolutely honourable person in high quarters.' Talk of trustworthiness in the upper echelons of government prompted Mrs Nicholson to embark on a sprawling monologue about politics and Jewish intrigue.

At the end of this florid display of paranoia, Max enquired whether it was Anna Wolkoff who had shown her the document.

'No, definitely not,' she snapped. Yet she rendered her denial redundant by adding, 'I am very fond of Anna and I will not say anything about her that will implicate her.'

Max pressed Mrs Nicholson to name the source of the document but she persisted in refusing to cooperate. He could tell she was becoming decidedly upset, her palpable anguish causing her husband to appear ill at ease. Even Max found the conversation distressing. Now was not, however, the time for him to show compassion. He pushed home his advantage by announcing that a Regulation 80a order had been issued against her, placing her under legal obligation to furnish the requested information. As a method of spotlighting the gravity of the circumstances into which she had got herself, he permitted her to read the order.

Ever more indignant, she reiterated her refusal to name her friend. 'I think it would be most disloyal to my friend,' she said. 'You are trying to intimidate me and get my friend shot.'

Turning to Admiral Nicholson, Max appealed for confirmation that he hadn't intimidated her. He had, on the contrary, behaved with what he regarded as the utmost patience and civility.

Admiral Nicholson accepted that the interview had been conducted in a perfectly courteous and proper manner. He said to his wife, 'It appears to be a very serious business and you *must* tell the officers.'

Vague though the Admiral was, Max felt grateful to him for being so helpful.

'Can I have a few minutes alone with my husband?' Mrs Nicholson asked.

Max agreed on condition that the Woman Police Constable remained with them, just out of earshot.

After less than five minutes, the Admiral called Max and Pearson back inside. Once they had returned, Mrs Nicholson – grief infusing her voice – said, 'It was Anna Wolkoff who showed me the document.'

Without bothering to question her further, Max went into another room and used the Nicholsons' telephone to ring Scotland Yard. In describing to Sir Norman Kendal what had just taken place, Max expressed the belief that Mrs Nicholson had broken the law.

Sir Norman assured him that she was, indeed, liable to prosecution. Orders were consequently issued for Pearson to arrest Mrs Nicholson. Arrangements were also made for an additional officer to be sent round to search the premises.

Leaving the police to their task, Max soon afterwards walked out of the Nicholsons' flat. He stepped into a bright spring day, precisely the sort of day on which he might, during those far off pre-war days, have been striding across the Doone Valley on Exmoor, the air vibrating with the high-voltage hum of insects, the distant speck of a sparrowhawk wheeling high above on the thermals.

45

Letters and parcels, delivered to Anna by the prison's Lady Deputy-Governor, brought news from the outside world, together with little treats from her mother. These included the morale-boosting gift of a soft pillow, which the prison authorities allowed her to keep. It had done a great deal to alleviate her backache.

Of late, Anna had slipped into the routine of counting down the hours until the post was due to arrive, time flowing as unwillingly as cold béchamel sauce. Perhaps there would be something for her today. Perhaps the Lady Deputy-Governor would hand her another package. Or perhaps she could dare to hope that there might be a response to the letter she'd written to Lord Cottenham, her potential saviour. Weeks had passed since then, weeks in which the bulk of the British Army had retreated across Belgium and France, then been evacuated from the beaches of Dunkirk.

Anna's mother had recently done her a favour by telephoning Cotty, whose butler had answered. The butler had told Mme Wolkoff that His Lordship had been called away on urgent business at eight o'clock that morning and might not be back for about a fortnight. Mme Wolkoff had asked whether a letter could be forwarded to Lord Cottenham. 'His movements are so uncertain I don't know where he is myself,' the butler had replied. 'There is a possible chance I might hear from him, but anyway if you write he will get it when he returns.'

Neither this message nor its predecessors had, however, shamed Cotty into responding to Anna. Bitter though she was about so many aspects of her life, she didn't permit those feelings to corrode her treasured memories of their friendship. She wanted to avoid that at all costs. A surge of disappointment nonetheless flooded over the emotional defences she had erected. There was, she thought, nothing like a crisis for revealing who were your genuine allies. She was convinced Tyler – her good-natured, lovely Anatoly – belonged to that steadfast band. News of his imprisonment having reached her, she pondered ways in which he could be helped. Only she was powerless to do much except worry about him and moon over the past and wait until she was freed by the government or by the Nazi invasion that appeared imminent.

Five years and four months later ...

US Customs officials have detained Tyler for well over an hour now. He is being kept aboard the SS *Silveroak*, a British freighter that berthed in Hoboken, New Jersey earlier this morning. Tuesday 4 December 1945. Right from the start he has had that kind of journey. His departure from England, where he'd been in jail since his arrest, was delayed two months on account of a dock strike.

Prior to embarkation, his mother sent him letters and telegrams urging caution because she suspects the US government might try to assassinate him en route home. She thinks they want to prevent him from making public the secret correspondence between Roosevelt and Churchill, which she calls 'the greatest intrigue of all time'. But here he is, alive and well and poised to go ashore.

A cold wind blows across the deck, exacerbating the winter chill. From the gangway, Tyler steps onto the pier. He is ushered towards the wooden shed that runs all the way back to the pierhead. As he enters the shed, a slight smile animates his features. Someone on the periphery of his vision simultaneously takes aim. That someone is, however, a press photographer, not the predicted assassin.

Waiting for him in the Superintendent's Office are his elderly mother and her friend. They are accompanied by two broad-shouldered men from the Shields Detective Agency. Both former lieutenants with the New York Police Department, they have been employed by Tyler's mother to protect him from the imaginary killers she warned him about.

Dressed in a smart yet slightly old-fashioned get-up, rimless pince-nez emphasizing that impression, his mother is a matronly woman whose grey hair has been styled in a chignon. It is topped by a skewed black hat with a cluster of feathers sprouting from the brim. For all the exasperation she arouses in Tyler, the sight of her causes his smile to expand into a delighted grin. He hasn't clapped eyes on her since he was last in town near the start of 1939 – more than seven months before his fateful posting to London. Fateful not just for him but also for Anna, whom he succeeded in deceiving until they were in the dock together at the Central Criminal Court.

He goes straight up to his mother, puts one arm round her and pecks her cheek. She reciprocates his undemonstrative show of affection with a pat on the back and a demure kiss – so demure you would not guess how devoted she is to him.

Speaking in a crisply enunciated accent that has grown more British than American, he says, 'Darling, how are you?'

'I'm fine. It's nice to see you.'

His mother and her three companions are not the only people ready to greet him. Completing an ill-matched quintet is a representative from the press tycoon William Randolph Hearst's stable of newspapers. These are eager to secure exclusive rights to the Tyler G. Kent story. Or, at least, to *his* side of the story, which he and his mother have been striving to transform from a tale of treachery into the tale of a patriotic whistleblower who has fallen victim to a US government conspiracy.

In the Customs area, a group of uniformed officials behind a decrepit counter examine Tyler's luggage. He has with him a trunk, a Gladstone bag, a couple of suitcases and a large tin box. While he waits for the officials to wave him through, his ruminative expression is frozen in the glare of a news photographer's flashbulb.

When he and his retinue re-emerge onto the pier, he has to contend with more than twenty other press photographers, not to mention newsreel cameramen and reporters. There are representatives from the New York dailies, from the BBC, from the British press, from American radio networks, from the leading wire services, as well as magazines such as *Time*, *Newsweek* and *Life*.

Unable to rein in his vanity, Tyler confronts the expectant journalists with the same determination with which his venerated antecedent, Davy Crockett, once stood on the ramparts of the Alamo as the Mexican Army advanced. Tyler blames pressure from the American authorities for the years he has spent in jail. He adds that he does not think the British, left to their own devices, had any intention of bringing charges against him. By now warming to the flatteringly heroic role in which he has cast himself, he says, 'I did take certain documents from the embassy to my flat, but it was for the purpose of turning them over to the United States Senate. I considered that those documents contained information which the Senate and the people of the United States should know about, relating to foreign relations. I considered I had a moral right to handle the documents.'

One of the reporters enquires how he planned to show those documents to the Senate.

'That is a method I had not worked out.'

He is asked to explain why duplicate keys to the US Embassy in London were found in his possession.

'The keys I had were issued to me quite legally and officially,' he replies, a tone of wounded rectitude masking the deceitfulness of what he has said. He goes on to announce his preparedness to testify before the Senate committee set up to examine the unprovoked Japanese attack on Pearl Harbor, which dragged the United States into the Second World War. His testimony, he admits, will not strictly concern Pearl Harbor. It will be about the other reasons behind America's entry into the conflict. But he doesn't elaborate. Instead, he declares, 'I'm very glad to be back in the United States. I think in the near future I will have something to say of interest to the people of this country.'

His final teasing commitment only seconds old, Tyler brings his improvised press briefing to a premature close. Many of the assembled journalists are left frustrated. Without elaborating on what happened in London, Tyler and his entourage walk off the pier. Its wire-fenced exit beckons them onto the main waterfront thoroughfare, where the long line of saloons and rundown hotels and boarding houses offers Tyler a glimpse into his future, into a life as turbulent as the life he has forsaken.

Epilogue

A Game of Consequences

1

The presence of almost fifty journalists at Tyler Kent's December 1945 homecoming provided confirmation that his case had, between then and the raid on his flat, become a cause célèbre. In ostensible endorsement of his quayside allegations about being the victim of a conspiracy, five-and-a-half years earlier the American and British governments had tried to stop the press from covering his arrest. However, the *New York Herald Tribune* had soon got wind of it. The result was a brief item published on Saturday 25 May, 1940. It reported the detention by the British authorities of an unnamed employee at the US Embassy in London. But another ten days would pass before the case received additional coverage. Initiated by a Home Office press release, a flood of newspaper articles was unleashed on both sides of the Atlantic. Only then did the authorities unveil the identity of the American employee who was being detained. So far, there had been no reference to either Anna Wolkoff or Mrs Nicholson.

Against a backdrop of escalating military threat, of the fall of France, the evacuation of part of the British Expeditionary Force from the beaches of Dunkirk and the start of the air war in the skies above southern England, Max Knight and his fellow investigators continued the process of collecting evidence, studying confiscated items and exploring fresh leads.[97] Through the early weeks of the summer of 1940, his agents[98] carried on frequenting the Russian Tea Rooms and helped to secure the internment of Admiral Wolkoff, said to be impatient for the German occupation of Britain 'when he could spit in the faces of the English'.

Knight's agents also filed reports on Mrs Ramsay, who confided in Hélène de Munck about her jailed husband's prospects. A victim of wishful-thinking, Mrs Ramsay believed that armed British Union members were likely to help him escape from prison. Failing that, she pinned her hopes on a revolution or a German take-over, which would culminate in Home Office staff hanging from lamp-posts.

Further questioning of Kent contributed to the evidence-gathering process. Three more times during the week after Mrs Nicholson's arrest, Knight interrogated the American. Kent remained adamant that there was no 'specific object in mind' when he purloined the documents from the embassy.

Given his fierce anti-Communism, his ties to British fascists, his complicity in leaking confidential material to the Duke del Monte and his meeting with a Swedish spy allegedly employed by the Nazis, the obvious assumption was that Kent had been working for the fascist powers. Yet MI5's enquiries began to cast doubt on that. Kent's former boss, Ambassador William C. Bullitt, said the young man 'came from a very good family, but was a complete rotter and always had been'. Bullitt added that Kent had been foisted on him against his wishes. 'At the end of three months he was discovered to be in the pay of the Soviets.'

Why Kent hadn't been prosecuted and dismissed from government service, the surviving fragment from Bullitt's statement fails to elucidate. The most probable reason is that the troublesome Code Clerk had a powerful sponsor in the form of Secretary of State Cordell Hull, a family friend who occupied the position immediately above Bullitt in the hierarchy.

Kent's affair with Irene Danischewsky was an aspect of the case that came under MI5 scrutiny as well. Their relationship had potential significance due to her being the wife of one of the directors of a company long suspected of links to Soviet espionage. Mrs Danischewsky therefore found herself subject to prolonged questioning. Sensitive to her tricky domestic situation, Knight and his Special Branch colleagues arranged for her marital home to be searched while her husband was not there. Nothing emerged to suggest that her clandestine entanglement with Kent extended beyond the sweaty precincts of adultery.

Consideration was also given to the substantial amount of British currency discovered in Kent's possession at the time of his arrest. None of the names written on the paper money, two of them suspiciously Germanic, yielded anything worthwhile. Another intriguing though fruitless development concerned the discovery that three of his £5 notes emanated from a bank account operated by MI6. When the homes of Kent's Right Club associates were raided, a fourth note was disinterred. It had previously been paid to an MI6 agent working in Italy – just one of many tantalizing dead-ends.

Kent's stash of British currency did, however, provide conclusive evidence of his participation in illicit activities. He claimed that the money originated from his employers, who paid him in British currency, but staff at the US Embassy confirmed that he was lying. Its employees didn't receive their salaries in pounds. The nature of the transaction between Kent and his unnamed paymaster took on an even more dubious shade once the authorities realized that at least three of his £5 notes had been handed over at the same time. Apparently those notes, which represented a sizeable payment, had passed through several hands yet still displayed consecutive serial numbers.

For the British authorities, perhaps the most unsettling aspect of this phase of the investigation was the failure to locate any of the photographic prints made for Wolkoff by Nicholas Smirnoff. Equally elusive were some papers belonging to Mrs Nicholson, papers assumed to contain transcriptions of US Embassy documents or possibly summaries of their contents. Deposited in a sealed envelope with her solicitor, these had since vanished from the company's files.

What promised to be a crucial piece of evidence against Kent did not emerge until much later that summer when two detectives from the American Foreign Service visited the US Embassy in Moscow. Most likely encouraged by allegations that Kent had been storing items in the safe at the Grosvenor Square embassy, the detectives searched its Russian counterpart. They found the briefcase Kent had left behind when he had been transferred from Moscow to London.

As the detectives opened the briefcase, which was not locked, they must have suspected it would be packed with another batch of stolen US government paperwork. They were, instead, confronted by an unexpected array of items. These included a Colt .38 revolver, a pocket edition of *Lyall's Languages of Europe* and an eighteenth-century French pornographic novel. Also among the bric-a-brac were four nude photos, one of them depicting an anonymous man and a woman. Two of the others portrayed Kent's former girlfriend, Tatyana Alexandrovna Ilovaiskaya. The remaining picture featured a woman identified by embassy staff as an actress from a small Moscow theatre.

High on the list of valuable evidence unearthed that summer was a document forwarded to MI5 by the BBC Monitoring Service. This consisted of the script of an anti-French talk transmitted on Saturday 27 April, 1940 by the New British Broadcasting Service, one of the Nazi propaganda stations. Entitled 'Britons Despise Froggies', the talk featured the pre-arranged codeword used to acknowledge that William Joyce had received the letter that Wolkoff had handed to one of Knight's agents. Near the beginning of a characteristically long and verbose speech, calculated to make British listeners feel resentful towards their French allies, the broadcaster said, 'To the average Englishman, they are just "Froggies", despised for centuries. Ever since the time of Henry II we have been at war with them.' Much later the speaker deployed the prearranged codeword, 'Carlyle', surname of William Joyce's favourite philosopher, Thomas Carlyle. 'We thank the French for nothing,' he said. 'Where is their Shakespeare? Who is their Carlyle?'[99]

Employing a similar principle, Wolkoff incorporated hidden messages within her letters from HM Prison Manchester. At the insistence of the Home Office, there was a tightening up of the benign and indulgent regime under which she had been living. One cannot, however, imagine either the new or old prison regimes allowing her to listen to the radio programmes featuring her old friend and Right Club colleague, Margaret Bothamley, who had moved to Germany just before the war. From July 1940, Bothamley made anonymous twice-weekly Nazi propaganda broadcasts on the English language section of the German radio service, where she worked alongside William Joyce.

Unlike Wolkoff, Tyler Kent – now almost 200 miles away in Brixton jail – continued to experience a more agreeable environment. Permitted to mix with other prisoners, he struck up a friendship with a con-man. The pair of them turned out to have a friend in common, Gerald Hamilton, a bewigged homosexual rogue whose pear-shaped body attested to his gourmandizing gluttony. Sometimes he and Kent had dined together in wartime Soho. Widely acknowledged as the model for the title character in Christopher Isherwood's celebrated novel, *Mr Norris Changes Trains*, Hamilton may have first met Kent in 1936 during a trip to Moscow. Despite expressing vocal disdain for the working class and lending his support to the British Union's 'Stop the War' campaign, Hamilton had for many years been a Soviet agent. He'd reported to a leading Soviet spymaster, with whom he had fallen out prior to meeting Kent in London.

Kent's prison routine was also enlivened by frequent visits from Irene Danischewsky. Within a week of his incarceration, Kent had been presented with a deportation order, which raised the prospect of him standing trial on the other side of the Atlantic. The scale of his thefts meant that he faced as long as 19,290 years in an American prison. So positive was he that no such trial would take place, he didn't even bother obtaining legal advice.

His complacent attitude was rooted in his awareness of the political ramifications of the documents he had stolen or copied. Those ramifications seemed all too obvious to Assistant Secretary of State Breckinridge Long, one of President Roosevelt's key allies. On seeing the list of documents, the contents of which were assumed to have been leaked to the Nazis, he wrote in his diary, 'It is a terrible blow – almost a major catastrophe.' He predicted that the Germans would use the documents to publish a book, 'which will have as its purpose the defeat of Roosevelt and the election of [...] an appeasement ticket – an administration to succeed ours which will play ball with Germany or surrender America'.

Most of the political dynamite within the paperwork obtained by Kent was packed into the documents related to the concept of Lease-Lend, confusingly dubbed 'Lend-Lease' by the British. Were Kent to be charged in an American court, the Roosevelt–Churchill telegrams would have to be used as evidence, their subject matter exposed to press scrutiny. Coverage of the

Lease-Lend messages had the capacity to alter the political future of his country and, by extension, the rest of the world.

If the contents of those telegrams were divulged in the press, Roosevelt's chances of remaining in office after the imminent elections would have been severely diminished. The electoral power of the messages did not lie in any damage that could be inflicted on Roosevelt by confirming he wanted to provide material aid to Britain. Roosevelt's desire to help the British had already been made clear to the American public in early June 1940. Recent Gallup Polls had moreover revealed that 73 per cent of Americans favoured supplying all possible assistance to Britain, short of direct military engagement.

Where the telegrams possessed devastating electoral potency was in the news that Roosevelt had employed devious tactics to circumvent the laws preserving his country's neutral status. If those methods were made public, he could have been sufficiently compromised to lose the nomination as the Democratic Party's Presidential candidate. Even if he secured the nomination, having such a blemish against his name would mean that he risked losing to a Republican candidate vigorously opposed to aiding the British war effort.

As a nightmarish corollary, the Lease-Lend arrangement, which involved the provision of ships, tanks, aircraft, food and other supplies to America's beleaguered ally, would never have come to fruition. Divested of this vital material support, officially sanctioned in March 1941, Britain would have succumbed to military defeat, relinquishing its vast empire and global pre-eminence to the Nazis. Without Lease-Lend, which was later extended to the Soviet Union, by then at war with Germany, the Nazis would, as Stalin grudgingly conceded, also have been victorious in eastern Europe.

Wolkoff and Nicholson's understanding of the politics behind the Lease-Lend correspondence led them to mirror Kent's complacent attitude towards the prospect of being put on trial. Both women were confident that the British government would be no happier than the Roosevelt administration to have any of the numerous stolen telegrams read in court.

Sure enough, the British authorities *did* have qualms about pressing criminal charges against Wolkoff, Kent and Nicholson. Yet those doubts were overridden by the Director of Public Prosecutions's yearning to stage a trial that 'would serve as an effective warning to other persons who are engaged or contemplating being engaged in subversive activities such as those of the Right Club'.

Whitehall colleagues of the Director of Public Prosecutions nevertheless had misgivings about this brand of deterence. Holding the trials of Kent and the others behind closed doors offered an enticing alternative. For reasons of political pragmatism the arrangement suited not just the Americans but the British, too. By shielding certain of the documents from public scrutiny, the British authorities could avoid damaging the Presidential candidacy of a sympathetic and potentially crucial ally.

Even if the court proceedings were conducted in camera, the State Department remained fretful about information seeping into the press. Nothing the British could say would persuade them to allow some of the key prosecution documents to be deployed as courtroom exhibits. Hamstrung by this lack of cooperation, the British authorities nonetheless initiated legal proceedings.

During early August 1940, Kent and Wolkoff appeared at the first in a sequence of preliminary hearings at Bow Street Magistrates Court, London. Kent faced five charges under the Official Secrets Act, accompanied by two counts of larceny. The indictments against Wolkoff concerned breaches of the Official Secrets Act, plus an even more serious infringement of the Defence Regulations, a charge arising from her documented attempt to communicate with William Joyce.

After four hearings, Kent and Wolkoff were jointly committed for trial at the Central Criminal Court, better known as the Old Bailey. Fearful that the trial would hinder Roosevelt's re-election by exposing the closeness of his dealings with Britain, Churchill pledged to arrange for it to be delayed until after the Presidential contest that November. But no such delay was forthcoming.

In the run-up to the trial, Mme Wolkoff, who had become convinced that her daughter's boyfriend had been spying for the Soviets, was reported as having had tea with the Duchess of Kent, sister-in-law of the reigning British monarch. The Duchess – a friend of Princess Mira Dimitri – had apparently promised to assist Anna Wolkoff 'to the full extent of her power'.

2

By Wednesday 23 October, 1940 when Kent and Wolkoff stepped into the dock at the Old Bailey, Hitler had indefinitely postponed his planned invasion of Britain and had instead launched the long-expected aerial assault on London. Roosevelt and Wendell Wilkie, the President's Republican challenger, had meanwhile activated their election campaigns. For Roosevelt, this had been jump-started by the announcement that he'd agreed to deliver fifty destroyers to the Royal Navy. The agreement, which complied with Churchill's earlier request for assistance, involved America acquiring ninety-nine-year leases on eight British naval bases in Newfoundland and the Caribbean.

Previously an enthusiastic advocate of military aid for Britain, Wilkie had lately pledged that, 'Our boys will stay out of European wars.' Under the strain of Wilkie's relentless portrayal of him as a warmonger, the President's once ample lead in the polls dwindled. His opponent's success with this tactic emphasized the latent political power residing in the documents at the centre of the case Knight had investigated.

The trial of Kent and Wolkoff began with the heavily guarded court being cleared of everyone bar the judge, the jury, the defendants, their legal counsel, their prison escorts, as well as a few court officials and a number of observers. These included Max Knight, the American Consul-General and the writer Malcolm Muggeridge, who was representing MI6. Some journalists were there, too, but they were only permitted to attend part of the proceedings. In return, they had agreed to allow their accounts of the trial to be censored.

Following protracted legal argument, it was decided to hold separate hearings for the two defendants, both of whom pleaded 'Not guilty'. Clasping the neck of her voluminous fur cape, worn over a stylish grey suit, Wolkoff vacated the dock and left her American friend to endure the first of these trials. It would last four days, the ebb and flow of statement and cross-examination interrupted by air-raid sirens that would send everyone scurrying down to the cellars to await the 'All clear'.

Kent's sojourn at the Old Bailey was also punctuated by another visit from Irene Danischewsky, who believed that he had acted with the best interests of Britain and America at heart. In the building's murky basement, she declared to him that she would love him all her life.

When the moment came for him to take his place in the dock and defend himself, he persisted with his belated portrayal of himself as a patriotic whistleblower, anxious to use the stolen documents to warn his countrymen about the duplicity of their government. As justification for his behaviour, this would do nothing to fend off the larceny charges, but it boosted his otherwise negligible chances of fighting off the indictments under the Official Secrets Act.

His explanation for his actions was hopelessly flawed, though. Were it anything more than a desperate ruse, he would have long since employed the American diplomatic pouch to send pertinent samples from the Roosevelt–Churchill correspondence across the Atlantic. These could easily have been despatched to one of the many pro-isolationist newspapers or politicians, or to his friend at the International News Service, owned by the strongly pro-isolationist press tycoon, William Randolph Hearst.

A mere twenty-five minutes of deliberations by the jurors at the Old Bailey presaged guilty verdicts against Kent on six of the indictments, the exception being a larceny charge that had been dismissed by the judge because of a legal technicality. Sentencing was, however, deferred until Wolkoff's trial ended.

Her ordeal commenced that day. Again, the hearing was broken by air-raid sirens. And again it was staged in camera, with police standing guard outside the courtroom's locked doors, the glass panels of which were covered by thick brown paper. Part of the reason for this secrecy was to protect the identities of Hélène de Munck and Marjorie Amor, who testified against Wolkoff. Hearing apparent friends and allies such as de Munck and Amor contribute to the prosecution case was bound to deepen the defendant's sense of paranoia, disillusionment and loss.

In court, de Munck withstood particularly vicious grilling about her personal life, aimed at discrediting her. The cross-examination presumably centred on rumours that she was a drug addict. Wolkoff went on to spend three days in the witness box, proffering a string of sometimes risibly far-fetched excuses for her behaviour. She refused to acknowledge that there was anything irregular about the substantial archive of US government documents stored at Kent's flat. She said he was planning to write a book about the war – something he had already rejected during interrogation by Knight. Wolkoff even claimed that she'd only obtained photographic copies of the Roosevelt–Churchill telegrams because Kent needed to use them as reproductions in his book. The prints and negatives of these had, she explained, been delivered by her to Kent's flat, yet she declined to summon Kent as a witness to corroborate what she had said and to tell the jury why the prints were not there when the police had searched the place.

Challenged regarding her role in delivering the letter to William Joyce, she admitted that she had been given an envelope addressed to him. Though she denied communicating with Germany, she conceded that she had sent letters to the Continent via the Belgian diplomatic pouch. Her insistence that she remained entirely loyal to her adoptive country encouraged the prosecution to ask why, immediately after she'd been handed the letter by James McGuirk Hughes, she hadn't taken it to the police or Sir Vernon Kell or Captain King, alias Max Knight. She could only offer a nebulous, wholly implausible and occasionally unintelligible response. At some future date, she said, she intended to ensnare Hughes and de Munck, then hand them over to MI5.

Enid Riddell, Captain Ramsay, Sir Oswald Mosley and other fascists appeared on her behalf as defence witnesses. But neither their testimony nor the promised help from the British monarch's sister-in-law could prevent the jury from finding her guilty on all charges.

Dapper as always, Kent was ushered back into the dock, ready to be sentenced alongside Wolkoff. They were fortunate that the death penalty for espionage offences had not come into force until a week after they'd been arrested. Wolkoff spurned the judge's invitation to say anything further in her defence. Kent on the other hand seized the chance to insist that no criminal motives underlay his theft of the US Embassy paperwork. Despite his protestations of innocence, he was given a seven-year prison sentence. The judge now turned to Wolkoff, who lowered her gaze as he addressed her.

'You, a Russian subject – who, in 1935, became a naturalized British subject – at a time when this country was fighting for her very life and existence sent a document to a traitor who broadcasts from Germany for the purpose of weakening the war effort of this country,' he said. 'It is difficult to imagine a more serious offence, but I take into consideration in your favour that this document did not contain information relating to naval or military movements. You have said you did not know what was in the document. If that be true, it makes the offence more serious. For all you knew it might have contained information of a vital nature.

'I also take into consideration the fact that you undoubtedly have been led to do this by the anti-Jewish obsession on your part – a virus which has entered into your system and destroyed your mental and moral fibre. To some extent that may be some excuse. The only useful sentence I can pass as a warning to others, lest there be others so minded, is one of ten years' penal servitude.'

Chin held high, Wolkoff said nothing as she followed a female prison warder down the steps into the basement.

3

A couple of days earlier, Roosevelt had been re-elected and the opportunity for the Right Club to influence the outcome of the Second World War had passed. While Kent and Wolkoff embarked on their prison sentences, the British and American press carried a flurry of censored stories related to the case, branded 'the biggest spy trial of the war'. Adding to the sequence of betrayals Wolkoff had suffered – by Mrs Nicholson, Hélène de Munck and Marjorie Amor – her beloved uncle Gabriel, still resident in Switzerland, disowned her through the medium of the personal column of *The Times*. 'I, Gabriel Wolkoff,' the item announced, 'wish to place on record my severe condemnation and complete disavowal of the activities of my niece, Anna Wolkoff, resulting in her sentence.'

It was a gesture that sparked a declaration of allegiance by her sister, Kyra, which acknowledged Anna's guilt. 'Anna has done a very wrong thing,' Kyra conceded, 'but she is still my sister.'

The ensuing month brought another setback for the family. Anna Wolkoff's father, who had already been interned, was forced into bankruptcy and the Russian Tea Rooms closed down. Obliged to find an alternative means of earning a living, Anna's elderly mother took a job as manageress of a canteen. Even the indolent Kyra had to contribute to the household, which she did by becoming a barmaid.

Initially detained at HM Prison Holloway in north London, Anna was soon transferred to the prison in Aylesbury. There she joined numerous other female prisoners detained under Regulation 18b, her friend Dolly Newnham among them.[100] Before long, Mollie Hiscox and Norah Briscoe, two more of the Tea Rooms clique, would be added to their number.

Kent was in the meantime held at Wandsworth jail, from where he had launched an appeal against the outcome of his trial. The chances of him succeeding were reduced when he dismissed his legal counsel and, with typical over-confidence, started representing himself. In protest against the eventual rejection of his appeal, he launched what would become a five-day hunger strike. At the end of that, he was moved to HM Prison Camp Hill on the Isle of Wight, a low-security establishment for long-term first offenders, who were treated with enlightened compassion, periodic theatre shows and discussion groups invigorating their routine.

Swiftly recovering from his hunger strike, Kent began work on the prison farm, his spirits lifted by fresh air, satisfying employment, good food and plenty of engaging things to read. The prison authorities also permitted him to send and receive letters, many of them from Irene Danischewsky who enclosed French- and Russian-language books. In the absence of her husband, now on military service with the British Army, her passion for Kent swelled. Endearments such as 'Darling Tyler' prefacing her letters, their surface dabbed with perfume, she wrote about life in London during the blitz. Her tone was romantic and demonstrative. 'Well, darling,' one of her messages concluded, 'I am overcome with a wish to sleep and I must leave you in this letter – the better to dream of you, my love.'

By contrast Kent's replies were only sporadic, their language stern, noncommittal, chiding and sometimes downright insulting. Another recipient of his occasional letters was his mother who, back in the United States, had launched a campaign to secure his release.

His mother's efforts ran in parallel to another campaign, the objectives of which were altogether different. Precipitated by an FBI investigation that highlighted probable Communist penetration of the US Embassy in Moscow, the bureau's director, J. Edgar Hoover, had ordered what would be the first of many probes into Kent's past.

4

Over the summer of 1941 two of the people whom Kent had met through Wolkoff made court appearances. The first of them was Mrs Nicholson, who faced what the Director of Public

Prosecutions regarded as a watertight case. At her trial she admitted to copying a telegram from Roosevelt to Churchill, but she still pleaded her innocence, 'muddled thinking' and a catalogue of flagrant lies being her defence against multiple charges. She even tried to persuade the jury that she'd only become a Right Club member because she liked the uniform Wolkoff had designed. Much to the surprise of the authorities Mrs Nicholson ended up being acquitted of all charges, a verdict abetted by the American government's refusal to allow the relevant Roosevelt–Churchill telegram to be deployed as evidence.[101]

Unlike the others, he wasn't being tried for breaches of the Official Secrets Act. Presumably because the Director of Public Prosecutions felt that legal action wouldn't succeed, no charges had been levelled against him concerning his dealings with Kent.

Ramsay's trip to the High Court stemmed not from the stolen documents but from an article in the *New York Times*, which had appeared while Kent and Wolkoff were awaiting trial. The piece alleged that Captain Ramsay was a Fifth Columnist, that he had been pro-Hitler and that he had supplied the German Embassy in Dublin with US government documents given to him by Kent. Ramsay had duly instigated libel proceedings against the *New York Times*, its parent company and its distributor.

On the question of whether he had been defamed by being labelled a Fifth Columnist and a supporter of Hitler, the judge ruled against him, declaring that Hitler would call him a friend and that he 'was disloyal in heart and soul to our King and government'. Where the judge came down in his favour was on the claim that he had passed documents to the German Embassy in Dublin, a false allegation deriving from some imaginative and overzealous sub-editing. But the Right Club leader's victory mutated into defeat when the judge awarded damages of a farthing – the most trifling component of Britain's coinage – against each of the three defendants.

Still in prison, Ramsay shrugged off requests for him to resign his parliamentary seat. From jail, he began to submit written questions to the House of Commons, his anti-Semitic mania and anger at internment serving as dominant themes. Exquisite irony lay in the fact that he and other fascist prisoners were victims of detention without trial, hallmark of the totalitarianism they admired. Compounding the irony was their eagerness to solicit help from the parliamentarians they despised.

Retrospective justification for the use of internment would be supplied by various post-war discoveries, not least the revelation that the British Union had, just as MI5 suspected, been in receipt of funds from the Nazis during the run-up to war. Hitler had, what's more, envisaged Mosley playing a key role in helping to run Britain after a successful invasion. Mosley's fellow British fascists had also been identified by the Germans as providing a source of assistance. Utilizing the inside knowledge of the leader of the Central London branch of the Nazi Party, who had moved in the same circles as the Wolkoffs, a register of individuals likely to be willing collaborators had even been drafted by Britain's would-be conquerors. That list, known as the White List, featured Captain Ramsay, Anna Wolkoff and eight other Right Club members.[102]

The readiness of some British fascists to assist the Nazis was nowhere more apparent than in their defection from their country's armed forces to the so-called British Free Corps, a tiny unit within the SS. Another vivid enactment of these collaborationist tendencies can be seen in the way that British fascists, one of whom belonged to the Right Club, systematically harboured SS troops fleeing from British prisoner-of-war camps.[103]

Similar proclivities were on display within an MI5 undercover operation that began around the time that Kent and Wolkoff were jailed. At its heart was a London bank clerk named Eric Roberts, whose talents had been recommended by Knight. Employing the alias of 'Jack King', which echoed Knight's alternative identity as Captain King, Roberts made contact with a web of British fascists, who volunteered their services to the Nazis and tried to pass significant government secrets to them.[104] His investigation spotlights an undeniable pattern of treachery that conflicts with today's accepted wisdom about wartime Britain, about the threat from British-based fascists being nothing but a risible myth, nurtured by government skulduggery and newspaper scare stories. Yet this pattern of treachery can be misleading. Its tacit implication that supporters of home-grown fascist movements would automatically affiliate themselves with the Nazis was contradicted by the willingness of large numbers of them to fight for their country against the Germans.

5

Via a question posed on Tuesday 11 November, 1941 in the House of Commons by a pro-fascist Labour MP, who launched an attack on Churchill's dealings with Roosevelt, the secret correspondence between the two leaders flickered into prominence again. Despite the Home Secretary's refusal to answer the question, it triggered a story in the *Washington Times-Herald*, speculating on whether Roosevelt had made covert commitments to aid the British war effort. Such speculation appeared to fizzle into irrelevance less than a month later when the Japanese provoked America's entry into the war by attacking the US fleet moored at Pearl Harbor.

Kent's mother remained determined, however, to use the circumstances of his arrest to pressurize the American government into arranging for his release. Refused entry to Britain, she sent a couple of emissaries to visit Kent and harvest information for her. The second of these trips was undertaken by a Baltimore radio reporter named Ian Ross MacFarlane. His journey back to Washington during late 1942 spawned perhaps the oddest episode in the entire saga.

Grounded in Nova Scotia by bad weather, he bought several cups of coffee for a fellow passenger named John Bryan Owen, son of an eminent figure in the Democratic Party. Meteorological

conditions over that area didn't improve while they were waiting, so MacFarlane, Owen and the other passengers had to
complete their transatlantic journey by sea. Aboard their ship
MacFarlane gave Owen a detailed account of the lead-up to
Kent's imprisonment. Owen – who had himself been deported
from Britain under Regulation 18b – proved receptive to the
notion that Kent was a martyr to the political machinations of
the President. 'I am going to make my life's work the exposure
of the Kent case,' Owen is said to have announced.

True to his word, he started campaigning on Kent's behalf
from his New York City flat. In the early hours of Sunday 3
January, 1943, a neighbour phoned the police to report a suspiciously loud thud that had emanated from Owen's home. His
corpse was discovered lying on the floor. While the medical
examiner attributed his death to natural causes, the *New York
Journal-American* would, quoting police sources, allege that he
had taken his own life by overdosing on prescription medicine.
This discrepancy encouraged Kent's mother to make wild allegations about Owen having been murdered as part of a
conspiracy to protect Roosevelt. Embraced by a fascist-leaning
broadcaster on the NBC network, her allegations fuelled a
rumour that has now found enthusiastic believers among the
raging paranoiacs of the digital age.

Nearly eighteen months after Owen's death, the plight of
Kent attracted renewed interest through a debate in the House
of Commons about the prolonged detention of Ramsay and other
Regulation 18b prisoners. Claims were made during the debate
that Ramsay and Kent had only been imprisoned because they
knew about secret negotiations between Roosevelt and Churchill.
These claims caught the attention of anti-Roosevelt politicians
on the other side of the Atlantic, who raised the matter in both
the Senate and House of Representatives.

Grabbing the chance to feed the controversy, Mrs Kent
compiled the unambiguously titled, 'A Petition for Justice on
Behalf of a Loyal American Against Whom Injustice Continues'.
With financial assistance from a gullible fascist anti-Semite
who had inherited a vast fortune, she distributed thousands of
copies of her leaflet. These helped her win the backing of a

smattering of obscure anti-Semitic and fascist publications, which hailed her son as a hero.

By then fearful that Kent was in danger of befalling the same fate as John Bryan Owen, she cabled him instructions to 'Observe caution for your personal safety.' Far from being stalked by assassins, Kent was living a safe and relatively contented existence at HM Prison Camp Hill, where he immersed himself in the novels of Marcel Proust and Stendhal. Despite his supercilious attitude towards most of the other inmates, he had been put in charge of the library and allowed to teach evening classes in various foreign languages. His routine was interspersed by monthly visits from Irene Danischewsky.

Lovelorn and unwavering in her devotion to him, she refused to believe stories told to her by the police that he had betrayed her with at least three other women. Her naivety may also have encompassed another aspect of her life. In letters to Kent she referred to her friendship with a London-based Russian named Ludmilla. Nothing out of the ordinary there, except that her friend was employed by the Soviet Embassy, for which employment and spying were synonymous. Kent's former NKVD contacts could well have asked Ludmilla to befriend Irene as a means of keeping tabs on him.

The recent publicity about his case compelled the State Department in September 1944 to issue a lengthy press release clarifying his crimes, arrest and trial. Inevitably, the official statement provoked another spate of newspaper stories on both sides of the Atlantic.

Mrs Kent followed up the news coverage by petitioning Congress and filing a motion with the United States Supreme Court. Her motion requested that the President should be ordered to negotiate her son's release and safe passage home. Yet neither of these manoeuvres had the desired effect. Like his White Russian accomplice, Kent remained in prison.

Healthy and cheerful, Wolkoff had established an industrious regime. She passed her days reading, sewing, tending the prison vegetable garden, growing bulbs in the greenhouse and teaching dressmaking to other prisoners. One Christmas she had even found time to direct the prison nativity play. Tellingly, she cast herself as the Virgin Mary. Reflecting their subsidiary roles in the Right Club, Mollie Hiscox and Norah Briscoe had played angels fluttering behind her. Fabric for the costumes had been supplied by her mother, who had since died. The refusal of the authorities to grant permission for Wolkoff to attend the funeral can have done little to alleviate the sense of simmering grievance that had driven her towards political extremism.

Wolkoff's father and most of her fascist friends, held under Regulation 18b, were no longer in custody by the autumn of 1944, the government's Advisory Committee having rejected MI5's pleas for their continued detention. Sensible though the internment of fascists had been and humanely though they had, in general, been treated, Churchill became embarrassed by the whole episode, which saw two of his cousins-by-marriage interned. He ruefully acknowledged that imprisonment without trial was 'in the highest degree odious ... the foundation of all totalitarian government, whether Nazi or Communist'.

6

Max Knight's successful investigation of Wolkoff and her associates came at a cost. His earlier decision to arrange for Hélène de Munck to travel to Belgium and meet Wolkoff's fascist contacts tarnished that success by placing his boss, Guy Liddell, in an embarrassing situation. After MI6 heard about the mission,[105] a row erupted between them and MI5. It concluded with Liddell making an apology to MI6 for straying onto their territory without permission.

Even so, the Kent/Wolkoff investigation yielded positive consequences for Knight, which temporarily stretched into his private life. By bringing him together with Joan Miller, the attractive young MI5 secretary who had assisted him, Knight's unhappy second marriage ended up being shunted towards its inevitable demise.

He wasted little time in employing Miller as a secretarial assistant in Section B5b's Dolphin Square offices, the two of them becoming embroiled in what appears to have been an unconsummated romance. When Knight's second wife, Lois, decamped to Oxford to take up a wartime job at the headquarters of the local police force during the autumn of 1940, he and Miller started living together. But their relationship only lasted until around the beginning of 1943.

So acrimonious was his parting from Miller that she would, years after his death, portray him with sly malice in her memoir, *One Girl's War*. Taking her cue from the disparaging remarks he sometimes made about homosexuals, remarks that were common in mid-twentieth-century Britain, she claimed that he had been leading a furtive double-life as the lover of his recently acquired chauffeur and other young men. People who knew him have typically dismissed this aspect of her portraiture, though it has been gleefully propagated by writers focusing on the history of MI5. Its trustworthiness is further diminished by the unreliability of much of her book. Confident perhaps that MI5 would never expose the fabricated aspects of her memoir by declassifying the paperwork documenting the Right Club case, she claimed some of the credit for Knight's work. She did so through falsely depicting herself as one of the principal undercover agents toiling on the investigation.

Within the Security Service, the Right Club inquiry had boosted Max's standing to the point where he even appears to have been sheltered from the repercussions of a subsequent undercover operation that ended disastrously. The focus of this investigation was Ben Greene, cousin of the novelist Graham Greene. A fervent pacifist and parliamentary candidate for the Labour Party, the lesser-known Greene was a fascist fellow traveller whose internment had been secured on the basis of evidence from Harald Kurtz, one of Knight's agents. Through a series of legal challenges by Greene, Kurtz had been exposed as having given false statements to Knight. Freed from prison in 1942, Greene launched an abortive legal action against the government for libel and false imprisonment.

Just when it would have been prudent to curry favour with Guy Liddell, who was still his commanding officer at MI5, Knight embarrassed Liddell by installing another young secretary as Joan Miller's successor. His stock within MI5 nonetheless remained high enough for him to be recommended for an OBE in the King's 1943 birthday honours list. The justification for the award was concealed by the fiction that he was 'Major Knight', prized for his services as a 'Civil Assistant' at the War Office.

More good news arrived in the form of Knight's latest girlfriend agreeing to become his third wife. During March 1945 – by which time they were living in the Surrey town of Camberley,[106] yet to feel the hot breath of London's expanding suburbs – he was drawn back into the Right Club case by Irene Danischewsky. She approached him on behalf of Kent. A couple of meetings between Knight and Danischewsky followed, the second of these over cocktails at the Hyde Park Hotel, scene of the New Year's Eve ball where her romance with Kent had begun.

From HM Prison Camp Hill, Knight received a letter written by Kent, who was seeking an interview with him. Receptive to this request because he continued to brood over what he perceived as 'various loose ends which are still untied', Knight set about obtaining permission to visit the American.

Their meeting was scheduled for Friday 11 May, 1945, only three days after the war with Germany had finished. When Knight spoke to Kent, he discovered that the former Code Clerk's purpose in soliciting an interview had not been to volunteer fresh information. Kent merely wanted to discuss what was going to happen following his imminent release from prison, his original sentence having been trimmed as a reward for good behaviour. More specifically, he wanted to find out whether the British government would press ahead with the deportation order due to be served against him once he was freed. Alert to the danger that he would be put on trial again if he returned to the United States, he was weighing up the possibility of moving to Argentina or the Republic of Ireland instead.

Knight could not resist initiating a discussion with Kent about events leading to his arrest five years earlier. The American managed to hoodwink Knight – usually so sceptical

– into believing that he had been transformed by his spell in jail, his earlier surliness, aggression and political fanaticism replaced by stoic calmness. It was an impression counter to the experiences of the prison staff, yet Knight came to the conclusion that Kent was responding to questions with newfound sincerity. In a sign of failing judgement, already exhibited in his disastrous dealings with Harald Kurtz, he drafted a report on the encounter, which backed Kent's story about having no idea that Wolkoff would send any of the collection of stolen documents out of the country.

'I feel forced to record that I am now prepared to believe Kent,' the MI5 officer wrote. 'I consider that Kent's weakness is his incredible ingenuousness. He is even more naïve than most Americans regarding diplomatic matters and intelligence work. I think that, although Kent was bereft of all sense of honour with regard to his actions while employed by the United States government, the espionage angle simply never occurred to him. I have no doubt that his inexperience was cleverly exploited by flattery, both by del Monte and Wolkoff.'

Yet such a change of heart could not be squared with Knight's rueful acknowledgement of the inherent fragility of this line of argument. He conceded in his report that Kent had still offered no satisfactory explanation for the hoard of British currency found at 47 Gloucester Place.

After the meeting with the imprisoned American, Knight spoke to Irene Danischewsky and 'promised to help as far as he could, within his province'. But that didn't appear to embrace the Home Office, which set into motion plans to deport Danischewsky's lover. Urged on by State Department concerns that Kent might attempt to stow away on a ship bound for some destination beyond their jurisdiction, the Home Office made arrangements to detain him until he could be sent back to America.

Two-and-a-half months later, he was taken in a prison van to Newport on the Isle of Wight, from where he would be catching the ferry to the mainland. Loitering on the quayside was Danischewsky. She had been hoping to catch a glimpse of him, but she somehow missed him.

Back on the mainland, Kent was transported to London and held at HM Prison Brixton, where he received welcome news that the US Justice Department did not intend to prosecute him. While he waited for the British to issue a deportation order, the trial of William Joyce opened a few miles away at the Old Bailey.

Curiously, Joyce – who had been charged with treason – never testified in his own defence, and no mention was made of his salaried work for MI5. Nor were there any references to the tip-off he had received from Knight, or the coded letter he had been sent, his reticence probably secured thanks to a deal with the Security Service. In return for not speaking in his own defence and exposing the awkward truth that the British government had been paying him while he'd been spouting anti-British propaganda from Berlin, Joyce appears to have arranged for his wife, Meg, to be spared any criminal charges. Like him, she had been guilty of broadcasting on behalf of the Germans, yet she avoided even the lenient one-year prison sentence meted out to Margaret Bothamley and other Nazi propagandists. The apparent bargain between Joyce and MI5 may have extended to an understanding that the anticipated guilty verdict would be followed by a successful legal appeal, which would result in him dodging a trip to the gallows.

An arrangement of that nature explains Joyce's otherwise inexplicable confidence that the Court of Appeal would grant a last-ditch reprieve. His optimism was, however, misplaced. Whatever arrangement he might have struck with MI5 did not save him from a fatal encounter with the hangman.

Joyce's doomed legal challenge had already been dismissed by Tuesday 20 November, 1945 when Kent was taken under police escort to the flat in Bayswater where his girlfriend lived. She had recently arranged for Kent's possessions, kept in storage by his solicitor, to be delivered there. These comprised luggage, various indexed papers and his collection of pornographic photos, as well as a stack of clothes, some of which she had repaired for him. He and Danischewsky, who already suspected her romance was 'an entirely one-sided experience for me alone', had very little time together before he was whisked off to the port of Tilbury, midway between London and Southend. The two lovers appear never to have seen each other again.[107]

Snubbing Kent's high-handed demand that his employment contract with the State Department obliged them to provide first-class travel back to America, the police escorted him onto a British freighter bound for New Jersey. His departure had been postponed by almost two months due to a dockworkers' strike. The impromptu, headline-snagging waterfront press conference when he disembarked on the other side of the Atlantic represented the next phase of what would be a partially successful campaign to rebrand himself as a victim rather than a traitor. Despite trumpeting that he would 'in the near future … have something to say of interest to the people of this country' and that he would be willing to assist with the ongoing US government inquiry into the Japanese attack on Pearl Harbor, Kent honoured neither commitment. Invited to testify at the inquiry, he declined the offer, admitting that he had nothing relevant to contribute.

Between his return to New York City and June 1946, he lived at his mother's rooming house in Washington, DC, subsidized by the wealthy anti-Semite who had helped to campaign for his release. Through one of his mother's contacts, he struck a deal with the Consolidated Features Syndicate, a company that supplied articles for newspapers across America. His contract, which netted a handsome $1,000 advance, required him to write a series of pieces about his experiences since 1934. But he soon began to worry that his reminiscences might goad the US government into changing its mind about not prosecuting him. Afraid he would be indicted under the Yardley Act, which he had violated by showing confidential telegrams to Ramsay and Wolkoff, Kent sought formal assurances from the State Department that they did not object to him fulfilling his journalistic commission. No such assurances were forthcoming, so he backed out of his contract, a less risky source of income having by then presented itself.

At a party in Washington during January 1946, he met Clara Hyatt, the dowdy forty-eight-year-old ex-wife of a former

American diplomat.[108] In the eyes of the ruthlessly self-centred Kent, who manifested a psychopathic disdain for other people's feelings, she could offer him a lot more than the glamorous and devoted Irene Danischewsky. What Clara, thirteen years his senior, lacked in youth or physical allure, she made up for with her compliant personality and huge inherited fortune. Less than six months after their encounter in Washington, he married her at a ceremony in New Mexico, moved onto her large dairy farm in Maryland and set about squandering her money, a privilege for which he charged her a gigantic annual management fee. Their marriage ensured that he would never have to work again. It also bankrolled his taste for luxury and social status, not to mention his compulsive womanizing.

7

Wolkoff was still being held at Aylesbury Prison, where the authorities had assessed her as 'crafty and not to be trusted'. Another report described her as 'a very clever woman who succeeded in conveying a completely false impression of herself to most people with whom she came in contact'.

Enid Riddell, Bertie Mills and Admiral Wolkoff, all long since released from detention,[109] brightened her remaining period of imprisonment by making pilgrimages to see her. She also received supervised visits from Barbara Allen.

Though the authorities feared that she was 'still likely to be a danger to the community', Wolkoff was released from prison in June 1947, prior to which she had been stripped of both her British citizenship and capacity for speaking Russian fluently, the latter denuded by infrequent use. Her experiences over recent years had done nothing to dampen her anti-Semitism. This prompted her to inform people that she'd been the victim of a Jewish juror who had engineered her wrongful conviction.

Penniless when she emerged from prison, she did not even have the option of moving back in with her widowed father, his tenancy of the Roland Gardens flat having ended long ago.

Admiral Wolkoff was now lodging in a farmhouse in Wales, where he had a job cutting fabric for bedspreads. His old friend, the Russian Orthodox priest at St Philip's Church, came to Anna Wolkoff's rescue, persuading Vladimir and Ellinor Baratchevsky, loyal friends of her family, to let her stay with them. Politically speaking, it was an almost perfect match. In his free time, Wolkoff's host worked for a Belgrade-based anti-Communist, anti-Semitic émigré organization called the Russian National Labour Union of the New Generation, his extra-curricular activities embracing the supply of bogus information to the Soviet Embassy.

For around the next eighteen months, broken by trips to see her elderly father, Wolkoff lived with the Baratchevskys, who had a small, inter-war semi-detached house in the north London suburb of Cricklewood. There, she welcomed a stream of fellow fascists. Her associates included her friend and one-time landlord, Bobby Gordon-Canning, former British Union linkman between Mosley and Hitler.

Unashamed of his Nazism, post-war revelations about the Holocaust having rendered it even more abhorrent, Gordon-Canning's home was adorned by a granite bust of the Nazi leader. Wolkoff's friend belonged to a faction whose vitriolic anti-Semitism found an outlet in support for the Arabs against Jewish refugees fleeing to Palestine. Within that faction were Enid Riddell and Captain Ramsay, who had lost his parliamentary seat by then. Ramsay's final noteworthy act in the House of Commons had been to table a motion for the reinstatement of the Statute of Jewry, medieval legislation that institutionalized anti-Semitic discrimination and required Jews to wear identification badges of the type brought in by the Nazis.

As a counter-measure against any MI5 monitoring, letters and packages for Wolkoff were not addressed to her lodgings in Cricklewood. They were, instead, sent to a West End bookshop run by her landlord. Further secrecy was ensured by having her post addressed to 'Miss Orthos', an instructive choice of pseudonym, Orthos being a two-headed monster in Greek mythology.

Obliging though her hosts were, life with them had one substantial drawback. Wolkoff, who was reliant on them for her meals, found herself compelled to adhere to the strict, nutritionally inadequate diet imposed on the household by her cranky landlady. When an old friend of her parents discovered that Ellinor Baratchevsky was not feeding her properly, he arranged for Irene Katchourin, the teenage daughter of a neighbour, to supply her with regular meals.

Just before moving out of the house in Cricklewood, Wolkoff was asked by Katchourin's father to make his daughter a dress as a thank-you present. But Wolkoff refused, saying, 'My dresses are far too good for Irene.'

Supported by her skills as a designer and seamstress, Wolkoff found accommodation in South Kensington. To escape the lingering taint of her criminal conviction, she applied to the authorities to change her surname. MI5 had no objections, yet the Home Office turned her down on the grounds that 'members of the public [were] unlikely to be so ready to report upon her if they did not know her as "the notorious Anna Wolkoff"'.

That notoriety gained further substance during the mid-1950s when Marjorie Amor's claims about Wolkoff leaking confidential material to the Italians were verified. Newly released documents showed that the entire text of Roosevelt's 15 May 1940 telegram to Churchill about ways of assisting the British war effort had reached Rome. From Wolkoff's friend, the Duke del Monte, this had made its way to Hans Georg von Mackensen, the German Ambassador in wartime Rome. Mackensen had forwarded a summary of the text to Berlin and promised to send 'the documentary evidence ... by the next reliable opportunity'.[110] His evidence clearly consisted of one of the photos taken by Smirnoff and then handed to the Duke del Monte by Wolkoff.

8

While Wolkoff was eking out a comparatively shabby existence in post-war London, Kent was enjoying a prosperous and self-indulgent way of life. Together with his wife, Clara, he ushered in the new decade with a year-long yachting cruise. Like other people before her, she was finding that physical proximity didn't coax him into exposing much about himself, great tracts of his life remaining mysterious.

On their return to America, he received some unwelcome news – the FBI wanted to interview him. Ever since the earlier announcement that the US Justice Department would not be prosecuting him, Kent appeared to have nothing more to fret about from that quarter. Both the FBI and MI5 had, however, been adding to their files on him over the past decade.

In August 1950, MI5 had identified what seemed to be a connection between him and Kurt Jahnke, head of a leading Nazi espionage agency. The connection derived from an interview with Jahnke's former assistant. Codenamed 'Dictionary', the assistant told the MI5 interrogator that Kent had been enlisted by Jahnke as an agent in Switzerland during 1938. It was a story that meshed with a previous statement by an erstwhile colleague of Kent at the US Embassy in Moscow, who had alleged that Kent had been spying for the Germans since 1938 and had tried to recruit him. But Dictionary's story featured too many discrepancies for MI5 to regard it as convincing. Normally reliable, he appeared to be feeding them what they wanted to hear.

Only two months after Dictionary's interrogation, the FBI had edged towards the assumption that Kent may have been employed by the Soviets, not the Nazis. Their suspicion was nourished by a meticulous statistical analysis of the stolen paperwork found in Kent's London home. It betrayed certain biases. Most of the documents emanated from London, Berlin, Washington or Rome. Down in tenth place on the list was Moscow. 'Hard to imagine anyone working for and believing in the Nazis would have neglected the Soviet Union,' the accompanying evaluation observed. What was also noted was the worthlessness of much of the material to the Germans and its immense value to the Soviets.

Ludwig Matthias, the German-born Jew who met Kent at least once in London, had provided the obvious conduit for some of the stolen documents. On the evening of Sunday 8 October, 1939, when he was under surveillance by MI5, he certainly received a fat, document-sized envelope from Kent.

Though the surveillance had been triggered by a tip-off from the Stockholm Police that Matthias was a German agent, his name does not feature in the extensive records of the German intelligence-gathering organizations. Being Jewish and a self-declared anti-Nazi, he was much more likely to have been acting for the Soviets. Kent all but confirmed the illicit nature of that Sunday evening transaction by giving Knight contradictory accounts of it, which ignored the telltale envelope. He even went so far as to deny that the rendezvous had ever occurred.

In the aftermath of Matthias's departure from London, the role of intermediary between Kent and the Soviets appears to have been taken by Eugène Sabline, who held regular meetings with both Kent and staff from the Soviet Embassy. Sabline's behaviour in the wake of Kent's arrest only emphasizes his probable role as a go-between. Outwardly unprompted, Sabline wrote a letter to the British authorities in which he endeavoured to distance himself from Kent. With fake candour, Sabline admitted that he had met Kent, yet he claimed the two of them had rapidly lost touch, which was of course far from the truth.

Had there been any liaison between the FBI and James Angleton, one of the counter-intelligence specialists at the recently founded Central Intelligence Agency, then the FBI's suspicions about Kent working for the Soviets would have been reinforced. The fount of Angleton's information was Walter Krivitsky, a senior NKVD officer who had defected to America not long before the war. During the months between his defection and subsequent murder in a Washington hotel room by Soviet assassins, Krivitsky had helped the authorities to apprehend a series of NKVD agents operating within the British and American governments. Interviewed by an American journalist, Krivitsky – his trustworthiness amply demonstrated – had also gone a long way towards substantiating Ambassador Bullitt's claim that Kent had, as early as 1934, been a Soviet employee. Krivitsky revealed that an unnamed member of the team travelling with Bullitt to Moscow that year worked for the NKVD. Through the treachery of an American member of staff, Krivitsky said the NKVD had been 'aware of everything that went on at the Embassy, including the contents of the major communications between Washington and Ambassador Bullitt'.

Of the original team that had accompanied Bullitt to Moscow in 1934, Kent's friend, Henry W. Antheil, was the other plausible candidate for the role of NKVD mole.[111] Ever since Antheil's death in strange circumstances shortly after his transfer from the Moscow embassy in 1940, rumours have circulated that he was spying for the Soviets. But those persistent rumours ignore the fact that he was exonerated by successive FBI and State Department investigations.[112]

Assuming Kent had, as Krivitsky suggests, been recruited before his departure for the Soviet Union, then that would account for the way he behaved when Bullitt started hiring staff for the Moscow embassy. Logic dictated that Kent should have persisted with his studies at Georgetown University's School of Foreign Service and waited until the State Department lifted its temporary freeze on employment within its diplomatic section. Yet Kent, whose educational trajectory had been directed towards a career as a diplomat, suddenly abandoned his studies and launched an all-out campaign to land a job as a Junior Clerk at the Moscow embassy. It was a job for which he was ridiculously over-qualified, a job that did not merit feverish string-pulling with such an array of prominent American establishment figures, a job that brought with it little prospect of advancement to some more appropriate and congenial level of employment. While Kent may have been desperate for a job, his parents being at that point anything but prosperous, he could have used his family's considerable influence more productively.

Guy Burgess, the MI5 officer and Russian spy who defected from London to Moscow in 1951, would later enrich and possibly distort our understanding of Kent's Soviet links. These two men already had connections in that they were both friends of Gerald Hamilton, the former Soviet agent with whom Kent remained in contact after the war. Burgess talked about having been notified of Kent's activities by their Russian paymasters. And he proceeded to allege that the Soviets had asked him to feed information on Kent to MI5. He said that the Soviets – allied to the Germans at that stage – were seeking to boost Burgess's standing within MI5 and embarrass the transatlantic allies.

By March 1951 the FBI was exploring the feasibility of bringing espionage charges against Kent. There was also a desire to put Kent in front of a Federal Grand Jury. On three occasions between then and September 1951, FBI agents questioned him, but he demonstrated himself a shrewd interviewee, capable of disclosing little that had not already appeared in the transcript of his trial. Without either fresh evidence about his activities in London and Moscow, or proof that he had been engaged in espionage or subversion since his return from Europe, the FBI's plans for a Federal Grand Jury were thwarted. The bureau soon afterwards closed its investigation of him.

In a manoeuvre that mocked the notion that he had ever spied for the Soviets, Kent cultivated a friendship with George Deatherage, leader of the Knights of the White Camellia, a fascist organization that made the Ku Klux Klan appear moderate. Kent joined the group and solidified their friendship by providing Deatherage with accommodation on the seventy-five acre waterfront estate that he and his wife had just bought in Florida. There, Kent built what he called 'Hermit's Cove', a huge faux-English manor house with its own landing stage and boathouse for his forty-six-foot-long cruiser.

His next major acquisition, which took place in 1959, was a newspaper called the *Putnam County Weekly Sun*, published in the nearby town of Palatka. Under his proprietorship, most of the usual local news coverage ended up being axed in favour of pieces arguing that 'an Invisible Government' controlled the United States. Other articles praised the Ku Klux Klan, as well as attacking Jews, African-Americans and Franklin D. Roosevelt, who had died more than a decade earlier. When John F. Kennedy – son of Kent's former boss at the London embassy – was installed in the White House in 1961, Kent greeted his election with the absurd headline, 'Kennedy Proclaimed First Communist President of America!'

Kent's recasting of himself as a fascist spokesman would have dramatic ramifications. His publication quickly caught the attention of the FBI, the Attorney General, the Justice Department and, most significantly of all, the *Miami Herald*, Florida's leading liberal newspaper. Delving into Kent's past, the *Herald* ran a story that would be picked up by the wire services and carried all over the world. The story, which featured an interview with ex-Ambassador Joseph P. Kennedy, bore the headline, 'He Helped Nazis, Now Peddles Hate in Florida Newspaper'.

The attendant withdrawal of advertising from the *Putnam County Weekly Sun* forced Kent to shut down the paper. Unable to find a buyer, his wife sustained considerable losses. Yet the same intellectual arrogance that had seen him represent himself in Britain's Court of Appeal lured him into risking even more of her money by filing libel suits against Joseph P. Kennedy, the *Miami Herald* and the *St Petersburg Times*, its sister paper, which had also run the exposé. Two years later the suits ended in defeat, leaving Kent with an even more tainted reputation and his wife with a much-reduced fortune.

9

Since the interview with Kent at HM Prison Camp Hill eighteen years ago, Knight's life had taken a similarly unpredictable path. He had remained with his third wife, but his MI5 career had been in the doldrums, not helped by his unfashionable conviction that post-war relations between Britain and the Soviet Union would speedily deteriorate, and that the Security Service was paying insufficient attention to the Communist threat. His fears would be proved correct by the onset of the Cold War and by the discovery that the Soviets had penetrated British intelligence. But the dismaying scale of that penetration still hadn't emerged by the time Knight left MI5 and threw himself into a moderately well-paid new career as a freelance writer and broadcaster specializing in natural history.

It was a career he had first sampled in 1947 while still employed by the Security Service. That February saw his debut as a guest on a BBC radio programme called *The Naturalist*, his warm voice and tangible love of his subject ultimately earning him the job of compèring the show. Within a few years he was making frequent appearances on a range of other radio programmes, including *Woman's Hour* and *Country Questions*. He had even featured in two short wildlife films, distributed through cinemas by Columbia Pictures.[113] And he was appearing on television, often alongside Wendy, his pet mongoose, which he classified as 'the most amusing, affectionate and interesting mammal' he had ever kept. Her ear-nuzzling behaviour contrasted with the marmoset who bit him during a live television broadcast.

As early as 1960, he was using *The Naturalist* as a forum for the nascent debate about man's negative impact on the environment, be it the spread of toxic chemicals or the retreating Arctic ice cap. From his position on the governing council of the Zoological Society, he went on to champion the conservation value of Regent's Park Zoo and equivalent institutions. By then, he had completed his improbable metamorphosis from being a denizen of the secret world into a minor celebrity, asked to bestow his fame on equally minor events such as the Kensington Kitten and Neuter Cat Club's annual show.

He had also been signed by the prestigious A .P. Watt literary agency. Exploiting his renown as a broadcaster, the agency helped him carve out a thriving sideline as a writer of natural history books. For the remainder of his life he would produce these at the rate of at least one a year. Many of them, such as the wonderfully titled *How to Keep a Gorilla*, were manuals offering guidance on caring for exotic animals and birds, comical reminiscences buttressing the advice. Parrots provided a topic that recurred in book after book, among them *Talking Birds*, which carried illustrations by another former MI5 officer – David Cornwell, soon to find literary stardom using the pseudonym John le Carré.

Always good with youngsters, Knight was pressed into service during the early 1960s as a regular on 'Nature Parliament', part of the BBC's popular *Children's Hour* radio slot. He appeared on the programme under the suitably reassuring guise of 'Uncle Max', the nickname given to him more than three decades earlier by Dennis and Joan Wheatley.

His health declining with the onset of angina, he made his final broadcast on Monday 28 June, 1965 when he was the celebrity guest on *Desert Island Discs*. American hot jazz records by Jelly Roll Morton and others dominated his selections. Punctuating these were charming, espionage-free reminiscences, which incorporated a story about how he had gone backstage after the jazz musician, Sidney Bechet, had played in London during the 1950s. 'The first thing he said was, "You were the fellow I sold a bass clarinet to, and you want to sell it back to me",' Knight told the listeners.

Just two-and-a-half years on from this broadcast, Knight died at the age of sixty-eight. He was rewarded with an obituary in *The Times*, which referred to him as 'the well-known naturalist and writer'. But, appropriately for someone who had lived such a rigorously compartmentalized existence, there was no reference to his other life as one of MI5's most brilliant case-officers.

In honour of his passing, World Wildlife – precursor of the World Wildlife Fund – launched a memorial appeal that led to the creation of the Maxwell Knight Young Naturalists' Library within the Natural History Museum in London. One person unlikely to have contributed to the appeal was Anna Wolkoff.

Embittered, overweight, wracked by superstition and still prone to strident monologues about Jews and Communists, she earned a paltry living by making clothes for a few customers. Through the kindness of a friend, who seems to have charged only a nominal rent, she had, however, found sanctuary in the ramshackle grandeur of pre-gentrification Chelsea. Her new home was 52 Tite Street, where her bohemian benefactor Felix Hope Nicholson – an eccentric homosexual aesthete straight out of the 1890s – lived with his elderly mother. Wolkoff, who had started calling herself 'Baroness Wolkoff', joined one of a shifting yet close-knit community of lodgers, often more than a dozen at a time, inhabiting this five-storey maze of dark, creaky-floored rooms and corridors. Dotted with portraits, antiques and other dusty relics of the Hope Nicholson family's past, the house possessed a *fin de siècle* patina that made it desirable as a film location.

The lodgers were all friends or friends-of-friends of Hope Nicholson, so Wolkoff and the others socialized with their landlord. His regular soirées attracted guests such as his sister Marie-Jaqueline and the dandy Brian Howard, partial model for the character of Anthony Blanche in Evelyn Waugh's novel, *Brideshead Revisited*. Had Wolkoff known that both of these guests were former MI5 employees, she might have been less sanguine about her latest domestic arrangements.

She'd been given a small room near the top of the house, from where she had to walk downstairs to use one of the shared bathrooms or the coin-operated phone. In the initial absence of her own cooking facilities, she would regularly dine on boiled eggs, cooked in her electric kettle.

Amid the clutter of her accumulated possessions, she enjoyed a quiet life. When she wasn't busy with her dressmaking, she painted, wrote letters, decorated Easter eggs that were sold in aid of the Russian Orthodox Church and produced an unpublished biography of her ancestor, the nineteenth-century explorer, Admiral Lazareff. Other than trips to the British Library and holidays with the Liechtenstein royal family in their castle at Vaduz, she seldom went out, though she struck up a friendship with a woman who lived a couple of doors away. Wolkoff validated the prison authorities' assessment of her deviousness by leading her new friend to believe that she'd been wrongly convicted of espionage and had since received a royal pardon.

Compared with Kent and Knight, Wolkoff's post-war life was uneventful. Even their latterday antics, however, paled next to the gloriously strange adventures of her erstwhile friend, Johnny Coast, whose days as a Russian Tea Rooms regular had been curtailed by his wartime posting to Singapore, where he had joined the British Army garrison. In a savage twist of fate, his Right Club colleague, Lord Sempill, had provided the Japanese with the technology and know-how that would enable them to launch successful aircraft-carrier-based assaults on Singapore and Pearl Harbor. The attack on

Singapore was only the prelude to its capture. Along with thousands of other servicemen, Johnny Coast had been taken prisoner and forced to work as a slave labourer, building the infamous Burma Railway.

From a Javanese dancer, who toiled alongside him, Coast acquired a life-transforming passion for southeast Asian culture, dance especially. After the war, Coast settled in that part of the world and formed a Balinese dance troupe that later toured America, where he mixed with the likes of Bob Hope, Olivia de Havilland, Bing Crosby and other Hollywood stars.[114] Reinventing himself again, he then became a showbusiness manager and impresario, his client-list spanning artistes as varied as Bob Dylan, Luciano Pavarotti, Mario Lanza and Mary 'The Singing Nun' O'Hara. He also worked as a television presenter and collaborated with David Attenborough on several BBC programmes about Bali.

Whether Coast was among the seventy faithful friends and relatives who attended Wolkoff's seventieth birthday party in October, 1972, there is no indication. A belated birthday present came in the shape of a publishing deal, not for a book but for a magazine feature. Commissioned by *Harper's & Queen*, Wolkoff's article was a eulogy to the rich delicacies served as part of the traditional Russian Easter celebrations. Naturally, she rounded it off with a selection of recipes.

The summer after becoming a septuagenarian, Wolkoff went over to the southern Spanish province of Malaga to visit Enid Riddell, who remained among her staunchest allies. Riddell operated a fashionable restaurant there called Rascascio. Housed in a converted farmhouse on a bougainvillaea-swathed hillside outside the town of Estapona, it had a celebrated surf-and-turf grill, tended by Riddell.

On Thursday 2 August 1973 Riddell – still an aficionado of fast cars – was driving Wolkoff along the main coast road. Several months later, Wolkoff's friend and Chelsea neighbour, Joyce Mendoza, would claim that Wolkoff had experienced a premonition of what happened next. At a junction on the edge of the town of San Pedro de Alcántara, the car collided with a vehicle driven by a young Spaniard. Exhibiting the same lack of caution that had been her undoing more than thirty years earlier, Wolkoff wasn't wearing a seatbelt. Both Riddell and the Spanish driver survived the impact, but Wolkoff was hurled fatally across the road. Her violent death possessed the type of casual, parenthetical brutality with which the great Russian émigré novelist Vladimir Nabokov might, had she been one of his characters, have wrapped up her story.

10

Long before Wolkoff – fashion designer, painter, spy – enacted her final role as a human cannonball, Tyler Kent had commenced his own much slower descent. As a result of his failed litigation, he had been forced to sell his boat and put Hermit's Cove on the market.

In the mid-1960s he and his wife, their marriage overshadowed by his protracted silences and belligerent outbursts, moved to a remote corner of Arizona. But he still could not escape his past. He was traced by a security officer from the State Department, who conducted another interview with him about his activities at the Moscow embassy.

With his wife's fortune ebbing, her continued position on the Board of Trustees of the Metropolitan Museum of Art in New York offering a reminder of better days, the pair of them swapped Arizona for a flat in the Mexican town of Jocotepec, near Guadalajara. To avoid being recognized, he began calling himself Tyler Patrick, the surname borrowed from his late mother's maiden name. Using his wife's money, he tried to recover lost financial ground through currency speculation, but the collapse of the peso ensured that his gamble left them largely dependent on the small income from her remaining wealth locked in trust funds. Supplementing this were donations from rich members of the far right, who had come to regard Kent as a martyr to a conspiracy by the liberal establishment.

A key staging-post in his slide from affluence to penury occurred during 1982 when he and his wife left Mexico and took up residence on a trailer park. His once lean, muscular physique nothing but a distant memory, he was now a potbellied, wheezing asthmatic with a white goatee, an air of fastidious condescension and a piping, indisputably Southern-accented voice, any sign of his earlier anglicized tones banished.

Not long after moving to the trailer park on the outskirts of the bleak, windswept Texan town of Mission, he was tracked down by Robert Harris, a British journalist yet to establish himself as a writer of bestselling thrillers. When Harris talked to him about the Right Club case and filmed their conversation for a BBC news programme, Kent once again seized the chance to depict himself as an innocent victim of political chicanery.

He would go on to reprise this role many times, repetition lending spurious authority to what he was saying. 'I thought Roosevelt's policy contrary to the best interests of the United States,' he told another researcher. 'Alarmed by what I read in the despatches passing through my hands, I began making copies.' Brushing off questions of disloyalty to the US government, he declared, 'I had a higher loyalty to the people of the United States. I intended to show the documents to the US Senate.'

Kent's ploy of casting himself as a whistleblower, as a morally upright victim of injustice, has met with enduring success. Nowhere is this more evident than in the preparedness of latterday political commentators to cite him as the first in a series of martyrs to the cause of freedom of information, as a precursor to Bradley Manning, Edward Snowden and Julian Assange.

The credibility of Kent's self-justifying portrayal of himself has been fed by some right-wing historians. For them, Kent was a pawn in an MI5 plot to justify action against Mosley and the British Union, portrayed as true patriots who would never have collaborated with the Germans. Historians of that ilk have also come to see Wolkoff as a convenient patsy in a Machiavellian game. Crucial to their conspiracy theory is the letter to William Joyce, which James McGuirk Hughes handed Wolkoff. Unsubstantiated rumour congealing into supposed historical fact, they have painted Hughes as an MI5 agent, integral to an entrapment operation, the whole tangled conspiracy incorporating the fabrication of evidence.[115]

Right-wing apologists for Kent and Wolkoff have found support from their opposite numbers on the left, whose criticism has been directed at the wartime British government's use of detention without trial and MI5's complicity in the denial of civil liberties. However well-merited, such concerns ignore not only the dire situation in which Britain found itself, but also the genuine threat posed by many of the internees, who were unequivocal supporters of Nazism – a fact the Germans planned to exploit.

Within only a few months of his interview with Robert Harris, Kent and his wife – now in her nineties – had transplanted themselves yet again, this time to a trailer park on the periphery of Ingram, a small Texan town around fifty-five miles northwest of San Antonio. Their new home was large enough for Kent to have his own bedroom. He even had a small study, most of the space taken up by filing cabinets, bookshelves and a wardrobe, bulging with suits and jackets that attested to his lingering vanity. There he nurtured plans to revisit Britain, a country he had claimed to detest. As ever, there was a telling discontinuity between his words and actions. Leaving aside questions of finance, this last transatlantic trip was destined to remain a pipedream, due to his inability to secure permission from the British government to return to the country.

Despite the attritional nature of her marriage, Clara Kent remained jovial and energetic. But her husband's health went into steep decline as he approached his seventy-eighth birthday. Diagnosed with cancer of the colon, he was admitted to Sid Peterson Memorial Hospital in nearby Kerrville on Friday 11 November, 1988. He died nine days later, a world away from the privileged milieu into which he had been born, from the yachts and expensive houses of his recent past, from the febrile glamour of wartime London's restaurants, nightclubs and cocktail parties where he had cut such a debonair figure.

Sources

Rendezvous at the Russian Tea Rooms derives from around a million words of notes, amassed over a period in excess of ten years. These notes have been culled from more than thirty archival collections across the world and from a wide range of other sources, many of them previously untapped and in some cases very difficult to locate until the advent of the digital age. Film and audio footage, as well as long interviews with people linked to the key participants, has augmented the printed sources.

When I set about marshalling the colossal array of material at my disposal, I already knew that I didn't want to produce an orthodox history book. I wanted to assemble the material in a way that is better suited to communicating the nuances of character and environment, which lie at the heart of my chosen story. Though the finished book possesses the shape and texture of a novel, it is not an exercise in so-called 'faction'. It remains a work of non-fiction. Gaps in the evidence haven't been straddled by creative embellishment or fabrication. Ostensibly dubious dialogue and details about everything from the insides of buildings to the prevalent fashions during a specific week all come from archival sources. Even descriptions of the British weather originate from the National Meteorological Archive, which offers astonishingly precise data. References to the thoughts, opinions and memories of the protagonists, each of whom would seem barely credible within a novel, have been taken from their letters and other autobiographical documents. Had I produced a page-by-page set of source notes, it could easily have been as long as the book itself. A summary of my sources is, instead, listed over the following pages. For a more detailed list of specific sources, you should visit www.paulwillets.uk, which also includes additional footnotes.

Archival sources

Architectural Association, UK; Authors' Club Archives, UK; BBC Sound Archive, UK; BBC Written Archives, Caversham, UK (Maxwell Knight files, BBC news transcripts); Board of Deputies of British Jews, UK; British Film Institute, UK; British Pathé News, UK; British Postal Museum and Archive,

UK; BT Group Archives, UK; City of Westminster Archives
Centre, UK (2518/1–5; 2518/19; 2518/20); Collection of Denis
Wyte, UK; Collection of Peter Rient, USA (unpublished
'Autobiography of Mrs Gertrude Mansfield'); Earl Gregg Swem
Library, the College of William and Mary, Williamsburg, USA;
Federal Bureau of Investigation, USA; Foreign Affairs Oral
History Collection, Association for Diplomatic Studies and
Training, USA; Franklin D. Roosevelt Presidential Library and
Museum, USA (Kent, Tyler, Small Collections, Containers
1–7); Hoboken Historical Museum, USA; Howard Gotlieb
Archival Research Center, Boston University, USA; Imperial
War Museum, Duxford, UK (daily digests of foreign broadcasts,
transcripts of broadcasts, 1939–40); Imperial War Museum,
London, UK (Papers Relating to the London Auxiliary Fire
Service, 1939–40); Leeds Russian Archive, UK (MS1285/63–72;
MS1285/573; MS1285/1722; MS1285/2608); London
Metropolitan Archives, UK (Electoral Registers; LMA
ACC3527/377(1); ACC/3527/577; A/KE/517; A/KE/539 (14);
GLC/AR/BR/06/075760/01; GLC/AR/BR/07/0067; GLC/AR/
BR/17/035372; GLC/AR/BR/19/0538; GLC/AR/BR/19/4359;
GLC/AR/BR/23/063688; LCC/CE/WAR/01/2; PDO/0583/01);
London Transport Museum, UK (bus routes and timetables);
Marine Society Archives, UK (HMS *Worcester* school records);
Met Office National Meteorological Archive, UK; Metropolitan
Police Historical Collection, UK; National Archives, UK (CAB
65/13; FO 371/24251; HO 45/23774; HO 45/24895/22; HO
45/25391; HO 45/25728; HO 45/25741; HO 144/2181/234; HO
144/2181; HO 144/2181; HO 144/2181; HO 144/2181; HO
144/2181; HO 144/2181; HO 144/21381; HO 144/21933; HO
144/21933; HO 144/22454; HO 144/22454; KV 2/227; KV 2/245;
KV2/345; KV 2/543-5; KV 2/677; KV 2/696; KV 2/755; KV 2/839-
43; KV 2/884; KV 2/902; KV 2/965; KV 2/1117; KV 2/1212; KV
2/1275; KV 2/1343; KV 2/1363; KV 2/1382-4; KV 2/1651; KV
2/1698; KV 2/2143; KV 2/2256-8; KV 2/25692; KV 2/25728; KV
2/2780; KV 2/2819-20; KV 2/2869; KV 2/2894; KV 2/2899; KV
2/3800; KV 3/12; KV 4/28; KV 4/185-6; KV 4/227; KV 6/120-3;
LCO 2/1454; MEPO 2/3442); National Archives, USA (Box 480-
1); National Monuments Record, UK; National Portrait Gallery,

UK; National Railway Museum, UK (timetables and routes); Ritz Hotel, UK; Royal Institute of British Architects, UK; Wellcome Library, UK (WA/HMM/CM/Col/44: Box 363); Wheaton College Archive and Special Collections, Illinois, USA (SC/004, Box I.B.2:54); Yale University Library, Manuscripts and Archives, USA (Tyler Gatewood Kent Papers [MS. 310]).

Image section credits
The author and publisher would like to thank the following copyright-holders for permission to reproduce their material. While every effort has been made to trace the owners of copyright images reproduced in this book, the publishers would like to apologize for any omissions and will be pleased to incorporate missing acknowledgments in future editions.

Critical Past.com: 4, 5, 13, 25.

Crown Copyright: 3, 15, 28, 32, 33.

Franklin D. Roosevelt Presidential Library and Museum: 6, 11, 30, 37.

Getty Images: 22, 34.

Hearst Publications: 1, 9, 10, 12.

Ian S.L. Fraser and the Giltsoff family: 23.

Imperial War Museum: 29.

Kerry Taylor Auctions: 14.

National Portrait Gallery: 2, 18.

© Norman Parkinson Ltd/Courtesy the Norman Parkinson Archive: 21.

Peter Rient: 7.

RIBA Library Photographs Collection: 16, 24.

Surrey Heath Museum: 35, 36.

Selected bibliography

Andrew, Christopher, *The Defence of the Realm: The Authorized History of MI5* (Allen Lane, 2009).

Antheil, George, *Bad Boy of Music* (Hurst & Blackett, 1947).

Baird, Alice (compiled by), *I Was There: St James's, West Malvern* (Littlebury & Co., 1956).

Baker, Phil, *The Devil Is a Gentleman* (Dedalus, 2009).

Barnes, James J. and Patience P. Barnes, *Nazis in Pre-War London, 1930–1939* (Sussex Academic Press, 2005).

Bearse, Ray and Anthony Read, *Conspirator: The Untold Story of Churchill, Roosevelt and Tyler Kent* (Macmillan, 1991).

Bennett, Gill, *Churchill's Man of Mystery* (Routledge, 2007).

Benney, Mark, *Jail Delivery* (Longmans, 1948).

Black, Alastair, Dave Muddiman and Helen Plant, *The Early Information Society: Information Management in Britain Before the Computer* (Ashgate, 2007).

Bohlen, Charles E., *Witness To History: 1929–1969* (W. W. Norton, 1973).

Briscoe, Paul (with Michael McMahon), *My Friend the Enemy: An English Boy in Nazi Germany* (Aurum, 2007).

Cabell, Craig, *Dennis Wheatley: Churchill's Storyteller* (Spellmount, 2006).

Clough, Bryan, *State Secrets: The Kent–Wolkoff Affair* (Hideaway Publications, 2005).

Costello, John, *Ten Days to Destiny* (William Morrow, 1991).

Curry, Jack, *The Security Service, 1908–1945: The Official History* (Public Record Office, 1999).

Demarne, Cyril, *Our Girls: A Story of the Nation's Firewomen* (Pentland Press, 1995).

Doherty, Martin, *Nazi Wireless Propaganda* (Edinburgh University Press, 2000).

Dorril, Stephen, *Blackshirt: Sir Oswald Mosley and British Fascism* (Viking Penguin, 2006).

Farndale, Nigel, *Haw-Haw: The Tragedy of William and Margaret Joyce* (Macmillan, 2005).

Fritsche, Peter, *Life and Death in the Third Reich* (Belknap, 2008).

Gardiner, Juliet, *The Thirties: An Intimate History* (HarperCollins, 2010).

——, *Wartime: Britain, 1939–45* (Headline, 2004).

Gillman, Peter and Leni, *Collar the Lot! How Britain Interned and Expelled Its Wartime Refugees* (Quartet Books, 1980).

Gottlieb, Julie V., *Feminine Fascism: Women in Britain's Fascist Movement* (I. B. Tauris, 2000).

Griffiths, Richard, *Patriotism Perverted: Captain Ramsay, the Right Club and British Anti-Semitism, 1939–40* (Constable, 1998).

A Guide to the City of Moscow (Cooperative Publishing Society of Foreign Workers in the USSR, 1937).

Hinsley, Francis Harry and C. A. G. Simkins, *British Intelligence in the Second World War: Volume 4* (HMSO, 1994).

Jeffrey, Keith, *MI6: The History of the Secret Intelligence Service, 1909–1949* (Bloomsbury, 2010).

Jeffreys-Jones, Rhodri and Andrew Lownie, *North American Spies: New Revisionist Essays* (Edinburgh University Press, 1991).

Jowitt, Earl, *Some Were Spies* (Hodder and Stoughton, 1954).

Kahn, David, *The Codebreakers* (Scribner, 1996).

Knight, Maxwell, *Animals and Ourselves* (Hodder & Stoughton, 1962).

——, *Be a Nature Detective* (Frederick Warne & Co, 1968).

——, *Birds as Living Things: An Introduction to the Study of Birds* (Collins, 1964).

——, *Crime Cargo* (Philip Alan, 1934).

——, *Gunmen's Holiday* (Philip Alan, 1936).

——, *Keeping Pets* (Brockhampton, 1971).

——, *My Pet Friends* (Frederick Warne, 1964).

——, *Some of My Animals* (G. Bell & Sons, 1954).

——, *Talking Birds* (G. Bell & Sons, 1961).

——, *Taming and Handling Animals* (G. Bell & Sons, 1959).

Martland, Peter, *Lord Haw-Haw: The English Voice of Nazi Germany* (National Archives, 2003).

Masters, Anthony, *The Man Who Was 'M'* (Blackwell, 1984).

Miller, Joan, *One Girl's War: Personal Exploits in MI5's Most Secret Station* (Brandon Books, new edition, 1987).

Morgan, Captain W. A., *The Thames Nautical Training College H.M.S. Worcester, 1862–1919* (Charles Griffin, 1929).

Nasaw, David, *The Patriarch: The Remarkable Life and Turbulent Times of Joseph P. Kennedy* (Penguin, 2013).

Panter-Downes, Mollie, *London War Notes, 1939–45* (Longman, 1972).

Pugh, Martin, *Hurrah for the Blackshirts! Fascists and Fascism in Britain Between the Wars* (Jonathan Cape, 2005).

Quinlan, Kevin, 'Human Intelligence, Tradecraft and MI5 Operations in Britain, 1919–1940' (PhD thesis, Cambridge University Faculty of History, June 2008).

Rand, Peter, *A Conspiracy of One* (Globe Pequot Press, 2013).

Saikia, Robin (ed.), *The Red Book: The Membership List of the Right Club* (Foxley Books, 2010).

Seton-Williams, M. V., *The Road to El Aguzein* (Routledge & Kegan Paul, 1988).

Simpson, A. W. Brian, *In the Highest Degree Odious: Detention Without Trial in Wartime Britain* (Clarendon Press, 1992).

Smith, Jean Edward, *FDR* (Random House, 2007).

Stafford, David, *Churchill and Secret Service* (John Murray, 1997).

Stafford, Frederick H., *The History of the Worcester* (Frederick Warne, 1929).

Stephan, John J., *The Russian Fascists: Tragedy and Farce in Exile, 1925–1945* (Hamish Hamilton, 1978).

Swift, Will, *The Kennedys Amidst the Gathering Storm: A Thousand Days in London, 1938–1940* (J. R. Books, 2008).

Thurlow, Richard C., *Fascism in Modern Britain* (Sutton Publishing, 2000).

Turner, E. S., *The Phoney War on the Home Front* (Michael Joseph, 1961).

Wheatley, Dennis, *Drink and Ink* (Hutchinson, 1979).

——, *Stranger than Fiction* (Hutchinson, 1959).

Wolkoff-Mouromtzoff, Alexander, *Memoirs of Alexander Wolkoff-Mouromtzoff (A. N. Rousoff)* (John Murray, 1928).

Zakharov, Vasili, *No Snow on Their Boots: About the First Russian Emigration to Britain* (Basileus Press, 2004).

Ziegler, Philip, *London at War, 1939–1945* (Sinclair-Stevenson, 1995).

Articles

In portraying not only Tyler Kent, Anna Wolkoff and Max Knight, but also the minutiae of the world they inhabited – anything from London roadworks or the prevalent fashions on a specific day – I have made use of countless magazines and newspapers. Most of these date from the 1930s and 1940s. They include publications as varied as the *Washington Times-Herald*, the *Sunday Pictorial*, the *Daily Worker*, the *Straits Times*, the *United Empire*, *Vogue*, *Action* and the *Bystander*. Here are a few articles that I found particularly useful:

Batavis, Raymond J., 'The Strange Wartime Odyssey of Louis C. Beck', *World War II Quarterly* (1 September 2008).

Documents on German Foreign Policy, 1918–45, Series D, Vol. IX (1956).

Farson, Eve, 'Censors in Jail', *London Calling*, BBC Publications (1940).

Hayes, Nicholas, 'Kazem-Bek and the Young Russians' Revolution', *Slavic Review*, 39:2 (1980).

Johnson, Eric A. and Anna Hermann, 'The Last Flight From Talinn', *Foreign Service Journal* (May 2007).

Leutze, James, 'The Secret of the Churchill–Roosevelt Correspondence', *Journal of Contemporary History*, 10 (1975).

Levine, Isaac Don, interview with Walter Krivitsky, *Plain Talk* (October 1948).

Pryce-Jones, David, profile of Anna Wolkoff, *Harper's & Queen* (April 1974).

Wolkoff, Anna, Russian Easter cuisine, *Harper's & Queen* (April 1974).

Film, radio, television and oral history sources

'A woman looks at art objects …' (CriticalPast.com, c.1937).

Fanny S. Chipman, oral history interview (Foreign Affairs Oral History Collection, Association for Diplomatic Studies and Training, 1987).

Paul C. Daniels, oral history interview (Harry Truman Library and Museum, 1974).

The First Days (GPO Film Unit, 1939, directed by Humphrey Jennings, Pat Jackson and Harry Watt).

Max Knight, *Desert Island Discs* (BBC Radio 4, 1965).

'M' Is for Maxwell Knight (BBC Radio 4, 2009).

Newsnight, interview with Tyler Kent (BBC TV, 1982).

Edward R. Pierce, oral history interview (Foreign Affairs Oral History Collection, Association for Diplomatic Studies and Training, 1997).

Edward J. Thrasher, 'The Well-Tempered Diplomat: Reminiscences of the United States Foreign Service, 1938–1967' (Foreign Affairs Oral History Collection, Association for Diplomatic Studies and Training, 1994).

'White Russian Anna de Wolkoff at work in her haute couture boutique …' (CriticalPast.com, c.1937).

Interviews and correspondence

I was fortunate enough to have the chance to interview and correspond with many people whose lives overlapped with those of the book's three central participants. These generous people include Page Huidekoper Wilson, surely the last surviving member of staff who served with Tyler Kent at the US Embassy in London. Among my other exceptionally patient and helpful interviewees were Kyril Zinovieff and the late Mme Elena de Villaine, whose vivid memories of the Wolkoff family stretch back to the interwar period. Further invaluable material was very kindly supplied by Len Deighton, Andrew Barrow, Irene Katchourin, Neil Rutledge, the late Alex Vale, the late Peter Vansittart, the late Joan Wyndham, not to mention Peter Rient, son of Mrs Gertrude Ganghadaran, who worked with Tyler Kent at the US Embassy in Moscow. I also received contributions from a number of people – including former MI5 employees – who insisted on remaining anonymous.

Acknowledgements
Books generally appear under the name of a single person, yet numerous people help to coax them towards their final shape and texture. This is particularly true of non-fiction. And *Rendezvous at the Russian Tea Rooms* is no exception.

I'm extremely grateful to my friend and agent Matthew Hamilton at Aitken Alexander Associates not only for his inspired suggestions – editorial and otherwise – but also for his calm support and steadfast belief in this book. He's really earned his commission. Both Andreas Campomar, my ever-enthusiastic editor at Constable, and Howard Watson, his copy-editor, have dispensed superlative advice, which has further improved this book. Other tremendously valuable editorial guidance came from Joel Rickett, Peter Krämer, Virginia Ironside, David Willetts, Gillian Stern and Jo Willingham, the latter of whom must have felt as if she's been sharing our house with Tyler Kent, Anna Wolkoff and Max Knight.

Enormous gratitude is also due to the people – many of them very elderly or now deceased – who spoke to me or corresponded with me regarding aspects of the story. Their first-hand familiarity with its main participants helped to give my research a frisson of immediacy.

Romany Reagan, who assisted me with my American research, is someone else to whom I'm indebted. Another weighty consignment of thanks is en route to Paul King, friend and fellow Wolkoff/Kent obsessive, who patiently trawled through enormous stacks of archive material on my behalf. Thanks are owed to Andrew Lownie and the late Peter Carson, too, for providing all sorts of invaluable material and connections. Without Peter's generosity, for instance, I would probably never have had the privilege of talking to Kyril Zinoviev and the late Mme Elena de Villaine.

Support of all kinds, be it encouragement, practical help or answers to specific questions, has come from various friends: Marc-Henri Glendening, David Collard, Keiron Pim, Andrew Lycett, Denis Wyte, Robert Hastings, Dave Fogarty, Cathi Unsworth, Mike Meekin, Gretchen Ladish, Marc Fireman, Jem

Bailey, Andrew Smith, Guy Myhill, Andi Sapey, Branka Viker-Young and Richard Austen. Several of those steadfast friends also played much-appreciated roles in the creation of the images that appear on this book's dustjacket. Other valuable contributions came from Theodora Burrow, Duncan Spilling, Natasha Burrow, and Liv Smith, plus my friends Dickie Leggett, Virginia Ironside, Emma Bown, Callum Coates, Emmeline Prior and Jon Glover (aka 'Mr Cholmondley-Warner').

In addition I'd like to thank numerous other immensely kind people who took the trouble to assist me, often donating considerable time and specialist knowledge to my research. They comprise Vsevelod Korbin Scott-Campbell; Lars and Jan-Olof Wolinder; Nigel West; David Pryce-Jones; Mike Pentelow; Sandra Brownjohn; Glyn Cowans; Robin Muir; Stephen Walton, Curator of the Documents and Sound Department at the Imperial War Museum, Duxford; Andrew Baptista of the GB–Russia Society; Matthew C. Hanson, Archivist at the Franklin D. Roosevelt Presidential Library and Museum; Amber Aldred and Georgina Bissenden at the Ritz Hotel; Ross Macfarlane, Research Officer at the Wellcome Library in London; Oriole Cullen, Curator of Early Twentieth-Century Dress at the Victoria and Albert Museum, London; Edward Bottoms, Archivist at the Architectural Association; Barbara Irvine at the Russian Refugee Society; Stefan Dickers, Library and Archives Manager at the Bishopsgate Institute, London; Nemonie Craven Roderick at the Jonathan Clowes Literary Agency; Mark Beswick, Archive Information Officer at the Met Office National Meteorological Archive, Exeter; Keith Call, Special Collections Assistant at Wheaton College Archives, USA; Richard Davies at the Leeds Russian Archive; Julian Porter, the Curator of Bexhill Museum; Bill Gordon, the Archivist at Surrey County Cricket Club; the staff at Kerry Taylor Auctions; Chris Schuler, Chairman of the Authors' Club, London; Barry Attoe at the British Postal Museum and Archive; Michael Palmer, Archivist and Deputy Librarian at the Zoological Society of London; Dorota Walker, Reference Services, Asian and African Studies, the British Library; Mark Jackson, Book Service Manager at the Marine Society; Mary

Lambert at the People's Pledge; Paul Bickerdyke and the National Railway Museum's 'In Reach' team; David Ades of the Robert Farnon Society; Jessica Hogg and Louise North at the BBC Written Archives Centre; Tony Shrimplin at the Museum of Soho; the staff at the Opulence Hotel, 47 Gloucester Place, London; Ray Pallett of the popular music website, www.memorylane.org.uk; Ben Bromley, Public Services Archives Specialist at Earl Gregg Swem Library, the College of William and Mary, Williamsburg, Virginia, USA; Geoff Levy of the *Daily Mail*; Katherine Mirren; Bette Epstein and Joanne M. Nestor at the New Jersey State Archives, USA; David Webster at Hoboken Museum, USA; Keith Lovell at the BT Group Archives; Donna Roberts, Syndication Library Management Coordinator at Hearst Magazines UK; the staff in the Serials Room at the National Library of Spain; Brian Polley, Caroline Warhurst and Helen Grove at the London Transport Museum, London; Dan Collins at Hastings Reference Library; Georgina Salmon, Heritage Assistant at Surrey Heath Museum; Steve Condie, former Development Lead at BBC History; Adele and Alice Ridgeward; Rose Alexander at Keystone Law, as well as David Wall, classic car expert and proprietor of David Wall Cars, a shrine to the era of elegant motoring. Lastly, I would like to thank David Higham Associates and Penguin Books for granting permission for me to quote an extract from Graham Greene's *The Confidential Agent*.

Notes
Part One: Gospel of Hate

1   A. K. Chesterton's long involvement with British fascism led to his founding of the National Front in 1967.

2   Mrs Gertrude 'Truda' Ganghadaran (née Rient) worked in the Military Attaché's office at the US Embassy in Moscow. She had met Tyler Kent at a party thrown by a colleague named Jack Marsalka, whom the FBI came to suspect of involvement in Soviet espionage, their suspicions nurtured by his post-war vice-presidency of a Soviet front organization based in America.

3   Tyler Kent was also related to the Patton family, of which General George S. Patton – among the most celebrated Second World War commanders – was a member.

4   Gene Pressly was the ex-husband of the novelist Katherine Ann Porter. In Paris they had been tenants of Ford Madox Ford, whose memoir, *It Was the Nightingale* (1934), he translated into French. Later Pressly would be portrayed unflatteringly by Porter as 'David Scott' in the novel *Ship of Fools* (1962).

5   As the Soviet spymaster Alexander Feklisov has confirmed, the NKVD made a habit of recruiting junior staff from Moscow's foreign embassies, resentment and frustrated ambition offering motivation for treachery. It's a template common to William Marshall and John Vassall, two British Embassy employees subsequently convicted of passing information to the Soviets.

6   Takuidi Egushi's freelance work for a Japanese general, along with repeated visits to the Japanese Embassy and the home of its Military Attaché, lent further credence to MI5's suspicions.

7   In 1942 Valya Scott became the secretary and girlfriend of Ralph Parker, a British Communist serving in Moscow as the *Daily Worker*'s Russian correspondent. Parker had earlier been the subject of an MI5 investigation by Max Knight. Both she and Parker were subject to protracted monitoring by British intelligence.

8   Mikhail Bulgakov was among the guests at one of these parties in 1935. He used it as the basis for the famous Satanic Ball sequence in *The Master and Margarita* (1966).

9   Tyler Kent would later inform the FBI that Calligos had tried yet failed to recruit him as an NKVD spy. The credibility of his story is not helped by his failure to report the incident to his superiors at the US Embassy.

10   The venue was the Crofton Hotel at 13–15 Queen's Gate, proba-
      bly chosen because it was next door to the home of Joyce Tregear,
      one of Anna Wolkoff's fascist friends. Dark-haired and glamor-
      ous, Tregear was a prominent figure in London high society and
      worked as secretary to Norman Hay, co-founder of Information
      and Policy, an anti-Semitic, pro-Nazi offshoot of the Link.

11   During late 1940, the officer – Lieutenant Thomas Willes – noti-
      fied the British authorities of several incriminating conversations
      with Princess Mira Dimitri. The first of these was while they
      were in Austria together in 1936. He told Max Knight that
      Dimitri had drunkenly confessed that she and Anna Wolkoff
      were spying for the Italian government. 'She referred to the
      dangers of such a life, and said there was no escape from this
      kind of work ... She would have liked to have thrown it all up
      but Anna Wolkoff would not let her.' Knight was unable to find
      any evidence to justify detaining Mira Dimitri. She nevertheless
      remained under suspicion until she emigrated to America in
      1944.

Part Two: The Devil Rides In

12   His host was Charles Birkin, a young socialite and writer of
      macabre horror stories first collected in *Devil's Spawn* (1936).
      Birkin lived at 15 Portman Square.

13   Max Knight's novels were *Crime Cargo* (1934) and *Gunmen's
      Holiday* (1935).

14   Karl Hermann Frank would bear ultimate responsibility for the
      massed deportation of Czechs to concentration and forced labour
      camps. He also organized the destruction of the village of Lidice
      and other reprisals against the Czech population.

15   The Ramsays' Scottish home – a fortified so-called 'tower house'
      located near the town of Arbroath – should not be confused with
      its near-namesake, Kellie Castle, now owned by the National
      Trust for Scotland.

16   Max Knight had also known William Joyce's first wife, Hazel
      (née Barr). In the mid-1920s Knight, who was teaching at a
      private school in Putney, had met her on a bus and briefly
      courted her.

17   One of the building's other tenants was David Lloyd George,
      Liberal Party MP, former Prime Minister and long-standing
      admirer of Hitler.

18   She had been staying at Sigray Castle, the recently modernized eighteenth-century ancestral home of Count Antal Sigray, patriarch of one of Hungary's wealthiest families. Ever since his youth, he had spent a lot of time in London, where he had visited Anna Wolkoff earlier that year.

19   Anna Wolkoff had designed an eighteenth-century-style evening-gown inspired by François Boucher's portrait of the Marquise de Pompadour. The dress was for her friend Pam Jackson (née Mitford) to wear to a masked ball at the Austrian Embassy in January 1935.

20   Her neighbours' child was Len Deighton. He would go on to study at the Royal College of Art before writing spy thrillers such as *The Ipcress File* (1962) and *Funeral in Berlin* (1964). 'I was to meet many people who were spies of one sort or another,' he revealed, 'but the enigmatic Anna [Wolkoff] was at the root of my interest in espionage.'

21   Mary Allen had set up the Women's Reserve in 1932. By providing its recruits with tuition in skills that ranged from shooting to pilot-training, she envisaged her organization being 'useful in a national emergency'.

22   On hearing about her grandfather's plans for a new career, the Pre-Raphaelite artist Sir Lawrence Alma-Tadema expressed disbelief: 'Poor Wolkoff – his troubles have weakened his brain. Isn't every capital strewn with men who have tried to live by painting and failed? And men who started as boys. Wolkoff must be over thirty-five.' Two years later, Alma-Tadema was invited to an exhibition of Wolkoff's paintings, exhibited under the pseudonym of A. N. Roussoff. 'Not only was every single thing first-rate,' Alma-Tadema noted, 'but everything was *sold*. In all my life I have never known of such an instance.'

23   Before her marriage, she was known as Marjorie Firminger. She had written a lesbian novel, published in France yet banned in Britain. Under the name of 'Val Ritter', Wyndham Lewis had portrayed her scathingly in his novel, *The Snooty Baronet* (1932).

24   J. G. 'Jimmy' Dickson had published five novels by then. The second of these, *Gun Business*, had drawn effusive praise from Dylan Thomas, who wasn't alone in rating Dickson highly. The *Sunday Dispatch* acclaimed him as 'one of our best young thriller writers'. Dennis Wheatley, who had probably met him through Max Knight, puffed his work repeatedly in the press.

25 In Jimmy Dickson's 1936 novel, *Traitors' Market*, Louis Vernier
    – a spymaster who masterminds an international trade in state
    secrets – is described as having 'a great fondness for children
    and animals and all defenceless things'.

26 While still a student, Bill Younger had published an acclaimed
    volume of poetry entitled *The Inconstant Conqueror* (1935).
    After the Second World War, he became a bestselling crime
    novelist using the pseudonym 'William Mole', the surname
    surely chosen as an MI5 in-joke.

27 Bill Younger was asked to investigate Manci Gertler, the beau-
    tiful wife of Lord Howard of Effingham.

28 Anthony J. Barrett's post had since been filled by Ed Thrasher,
    who recalled being given some last-minute advice before leaving
    Washington: 'The man you are replacing, had to leave Moscow
    under mysterious circumstances. I can't tell you the story. Just
    do your work, don't meddle in things that aren't your business,
    and you'll be all right.' Curious about the reason for Barrett's
    sudden departure, Thrasher tried to find out more from Tyler
    Kent, who said he had been sworn to secrecy and that nothing
    would be served by revealing the full story.

29 Max Knight's artist friend was Philip Rickman, whose work still
    enjoys a keen following.

30 Those colleagues were Roger Hollis and Dick White, both of
    whom would rise to the rank of Director-General of the Security
    Service.

31 Tyler Kent met either Margaret Annie or Marie-Claire Johnson,
    both in their mid-twenties. They were the daughters of Axel
    Axelson Johnson, President of the Johnson Shipping Company,
    which went on to play a significant role in assisting the German
    war effort.

32 Tyler Kent had been awarded a half-share of the Oliver Bishop
    Harriman Foreign Service Scholarship, for which the children of
    employees in US embassies and consulates were eligible.

Part Three: Stop, Look, Listen

33 William Joyce was still in receipt of a sizeable weekly payment
    from the British government. The payment could have been an
    inadvertent leftover from his days as an MI5 agent but, quite
    possibly, he was still working for the Security Service.

34 Tyler Kent used Peter Larsson & Son, a tailoring business located above a firm of shipbuilders at 36 Great Pulteney Street. In May 1940, he owed the equivalent of around £1,800 in 2015 currency.

35 Anna Wolkoff's studio-flat, located at 17 Queensberry Mews West, had been taken over by a young, yet-to-be-successful painter named Francis Bacon.

36 Kyra Wolkoff had rejoined them after a short spell in Berlin, where she had struck up a friendship with the leading German movie actor, Gustav Fröhlich, one of the stars of *Metropolis* (1927). His girlfriend, Lida Baarova, was the mistress of Josef Goebbels, the Nazi propaganda chief.

37 Thirty-three years old and blessed with vampish good looks, Alexandra 'Alice' Wolkoff had earlier resigned from her job at the Victoria and Albert Museum in a failed attempt to become a film actress. The handsome actor, Michael Wilding, later to marry the movie star, Elizabeth Taylor, was among the show-business friends she'd acquired. She had since left London and, with money from a wealthy boyfriend, rented a cottage in the Oxfordshire village of Brill. To earn a living, she had opened the cottage first as a café and then a boarding house. She had simultaneously embarked on a lesbian relationship with her landlady, Muriel Halliday – a friend of Anna Wolkoff. That autumn, Halliday had been arrested and fined for the unauthorized possession of confidential documents.

38 Among Admiral Wolkoff's conquests was Nathalie Brassoff, the attractive widow of Tsar Nicholas II's brother.

39 As well as travelling extensively, Mrs Straker worked for a range of charities. Besides helping refugees in Greece and elsewhere, she was involved with the Fairbridge Farm Schools, a scheme for giving children from English slums a fresh start in Australia, Canada or New Zealand.

40 Truda Ganghadaran eventually obtained an American passport. After the German invasion of Russia in June 1941, the Soviets were anxious to endear themselves to the US government, so they granted her an exit visa. She and her infant son left Moscow a month later and travelled to America.

41 Typecast as officious Establishment figures, Raymond Huntley went on to appear in films as varied as *Our Man in Havana*

(1959), *Room at the Top* (1959) and *The Great St Trinian's Train Robbery* (1966).

42 Tyler Kent may have further shielded the two agents by neglecting to cable the message to the FBI. Alternatively, he may have delayed sending the telegram until the Soviets could alert the agents, who were experts in sending and receiving illicit radio transmissions.

43 The Wolkoffs' friend – a close associate of Sir Oswald Mosley – was Mrs Annabel Hugh Jackson, who had lived at 22 Brompton Square.

44 His name was Anthony Ludovici. Among the founder members of a fascist organization called the English Array, he had once been secretary to the French sculptor, Auguste Rodin. He had since devoted himself to breeding Siamese cats, propagating the Judaeo–Bolshevik conspiracy theory and expounding his feline-influenced views on eugenics – the science of improving the hereditary traits of the human race. His belief that society was being eroded by racial interbreeding encouraged him to support the policies of discrimination, repression and sterilization being pursued in Nazi Germany.

45 'Source U.35' was Jona 'Klop' Ustinov, father of the actor, Peter Ustinov, whose screen credits include *Spartacus* (1960) and *Lola Montès* (1955).

46 Tyler Kent had possibly acquired his taste for Spanish cuisine while he was a student at one of the University of Madrid's summer schools, held at the castle in Santander. During his time in London he took to dining regularly at another of Soho's Spanish restaurants, the Majorca, where the cuisine was more elaborate.

47 As a qualified medical practitioner, she was entitled to be called Dr Christabel Nicholson, but she was usually referred to as Mrs Christabel Nicholson.

48 This was Anthony Ludovici, the Right Club member to whom Mrs Ramsay's previous comments had alluded.

49 The party took place at 84 Gloucester Place, where his hosts were Countess Benckendorff and her daughter, Katherine, a debutante who was a close friend of the novelist Evelyn Waugh's second wife, Laura.

50 Born Lubov Schaposchnikoff, she had been married to Captain William Hicks who had during 1918 taken part alongside the

British Consul-General, Robert Bruce Lockart, in an attempt to overthrow the Soviet government. Lockhart's lover, Baroness Moura Budberg, remained part of Lady Fletcher's latterday clique. A long-standing Soviet spy, Budberg lived in London with the writer H. G. Wells.

51   Tyler Kent came into contact with at least one member of this set – Dr Oreste Sinanide, a Greek beautician with a shop promoted under the slogan, 'Beauty is a social necessity, not a luxury'. Sinanide specialized in a quack electro-therapy, marketed as 'The Art of Rejuvenation'. He was an associate of Gino Gario, a suspected fascist agent who wrote for *L'Italia Nostra*, official newspaper of Mussolini's British-based followers. The opium-addicted Chilean diplomat, Tony Gandarillas (lover and patron of the English painter Christopher Wood) was also integral to the Dimitris' clique. He possessed a disparate range of friends encompassing the ballet impresario Sergei Diaghilev and the Duke of Westminster, alleged backer of the Right Club.

52   MI5 later discovered that the Duke of Kent paid Mira Dimitri an allowance, used to fund the schooling of her daughter, probably fathered by the Duke. When he died in a plane crash during August 1942, his wife stoked these suspicions by abruptly cancelling the allowance.

53   Mrs Mary Hope, wife of the Hon. Henry Hope, second son of Lord and Lady Rankeillour.

54   Monja Danischewsky later scripted a string of films, including the Hollywood crime story, *Topkapi* (1964), co-starring Peter Ustinov, whose father made a minor contribution to the Kent/ Wolkoff investigation.

55   Olga and Irene are the aunts of the actress, Helen Mirren, whose surname is an anglicized version of 'Mironoff', their family name. Olga was involved in a long-running relationship with George Dawson, a cockney jailbird and onetime scrap-metal dealer. Between 1945 and 1951 he became a multimillionaire from the sale of surplus military equipment. He was investigated by the US House of Representatives and the French government on charges of illegal arms-dealing. Eventually he and Olga married but their union came to an acrimonious end in 1954 when allegations of mutual adultery, domestic violence, fraud and intimidation were aired in the courts.

56 The soldier-turned-stockbroker was Captain Neville Gladstone. He had a fondness for fly-fishing that probably facilitated his relationship with Max Knight. He was married to a debutante-turned-interior designer, who would, in June 1940, also be recruited as a case-officer at Section B5b.

57 The son of a Brigadier-General, Captain Tony Gillson had married a wealthy American who inhabited the Monte Carlo and New York set. He and his wife owned a string of racehorses and an Oxfordshire estate.

58 Captain Henry Brocklehurst was praised by Max Knight for his 'most amazing number of personal contacts, which ranged literally from personal friendship with the Royal Family to cockney coffee-house keepers in the East End of London'. Previous accounts of the Kent/Wolkoff investigation have sometimes confused Henry Brocklehurst with a member of the Right Club named Philip Brocklehurst.

59 John Bingham, later to become the Seventh Baron Clanmorris of Newbrook, would remain in MI5 until his retirement, inspiring elements of the character of George Smiley, the astute and imperturbable spymaster in John le Carré's novels. Bingham was also a thriller writer whose books would form the basis for episodes in *The Alfred Hitchcock Hour* (1962–65) television series.

60 If Tyler Kent could pull off the hoped-for transfer, he would also be reunited with Phillip H. Fahrenholz, another of the Moscow crowd. Already stationed in Berlin with Ambassador Alexander Kirk, his long-standing lover, Fahrenholz was suspected by the State Department of supplying narcotics to Kirk and of being embroiled in Sylvester A. Huntowski's illicit activities.

Part Four: No Turning Back

61 Max Knight's boss, Guy Liddell, had already warned the Americans about a leak in the London embassy. During early February 1940, Liddell heard from MI6 that the Nazis had, since at least the start of September 1939, been obtaining material from the telegrams between Ambassador Kennedy and President Roosevelt. The material had found its way to Kurt Jahnke, who ran the Jahnke Büro, a German intelligence agency. Tyler Kent cannot have been responsible for these leaks because they started before he was posted to London. On

Wednesday 14 February, 1940, Liddell wrote in his diary that Jahnke's informant had also been handing over MI6 reports, adding that the unnamed culprit was 'said to be in the F.O. [Foreign Office] and to be either a clerk or the wife of a clerk'. Perhaps conceived as a subtle ruse to persuade the Americans to tighten their lax security, Liddell told Herschel V. Johnson – running the US Embassy in Kennedy's absence – that the Germans had concealed their informant's identity behind a codename, 'the Doctor', and hinted that he was based at the embassy. While Johnson launched a fruitless search for the fictitious infiltrator, MI5 appears to have identified Jahnke's real informant: Harold Fletcher, a Liaison Officer at the Government Code and Cipher School at Bletchley Park, nominally part of the Foreign Office. He had access to the Kennedy–Roosevelt telegrams, which the British decoded at Bletchley. According to written testimony by Gula Pfeffer, a German internee who had acted as a recruiter for Jahnke, she had been blackmailing Fletcher. In May 1935 he had travelled to Berlin to meet Jahnke. Though there was insufficient evidence against Fletcher to launch a prosecution, MI5 continued to keep tabs on him.

62   Letters written in Russian were sent for translation by the Postal and Telegraph Censorship Department's Uncommon Languages section, based at the Prudential Building on Holborn. Veronica Seton-Williams, Anna Wolkoff's former acquaintance from the Watch Room at Sub-Station V, had coincidentally been posted there. Seton-Williams remembered Wolkoff's letters passing through the system.

63   The venue may have been chosen because one of the Right Club's members, Miss C. L. Edmonstone, had rooms at the neighbouring St Ermin's Hotel.

64   Officials at the Foreign Office filed records of these pronouncements under the label 'Kennediana'. The hostility of Kennedy's stance has led to plausible claims that he was being monitored by MI5, yet no evidence has been put forward to validate these. Evidence has, however, surfaced about the existence of Section X, a branch of MI6 that cooperated closely with MI5 in tapping the phones of London-based embassies. Whether the US Embassy was among these remains unconfirmed.

65   The soldier was Anna Wolkoff's friend, Johnny Coast.

66 Max Knight's occasional habit of signing himself as 'M' has led to repeated claims that he's the model for the character of that name in Ian Fleming's James Bond novels. According to Andrew Lycett, biographer of Ian Fleming, there is no evidence to support this seductive assertion.

67 A good example of this is provided by Alexander Kazem-Bek, one-time leader of the Young Russia movement and would-be Führer of the émigré radical right. His fascist credentials notwithstanding, Kazem-Bek would eventually be unmasked as a Soviet spy. Like Tyler Kent, he was a close associate of Eugène Sabline.

68 Anatoly Baikaloff was a well-educated fifty-six-year-old journalist whose Primrose Hill phone number soon found its way into Tyler's address book. A professional revolutionary in his youth, he and Stalin had been colleagues. Since moving to London in 1919 as part of a Soviet trade delegation, Baikaloff had rejected Communism.

69 Wilfrid Duncan Smith was destined to become a celebrated Spitfire pilot and the father of Iain Duncan Smith, future leader of the Conservative Party.

70 The manageress of the Digby House Hotel would later provide the *Sunday Dispatch* with a sensationalized version of Tyler Kent's weekend in Bexhill. Her account stated that June Huntley had tried to obtain sensitive information about the RAF from the local airmen whom she and Kent had befriended. Rightly aggrieved, Huntley forced the newspaper to print an apology the following month.

71 Tyler Kent's new friend was Catherine Georgievsky, forty-two-year-old daughter of a Russian academic-turned-politician whose status had earned her a niche within émigré high society. In her role as manuscripts expert at the Wellcome Medical Museum on Wigmore Street, she had been on a pre-war collecting trip to Nazi-occupied Czechoslovakia with her brother, John. He had not only helped her to purchase items for the museum, but also to work out ways of circumventing Czech export regulations. These entailed assuming fake names.

72 This was Ferdinand Mayer-Horckel, a twenty-three-year-old German Jewish refugee, working as one of Max Knight's agents. Using the stage name 'Ferdy Mayne', he would go on to enjoy a prolific career in film and television, often as a purveyor of suave

deceit. His diverse and extensive credits include *Barry Lyndon* (1975) and *Dynasty* (1981).

73   The Right Club member was Boris Toporkoff, a former soldier in the Tsarist Army, whose hatred of Britain flavoured his conversation.

74   The agent was Christian Bauer, who had been based in Britain until November 1937, ostensibly as a foreign correspondent. After a trip abroad, he was prevented from re-entering the country.

75   Nicholas Smirnoff had first met Mrs Nicholson at the home of Lady Hardinge, wife of Sir Alexander Hardinge, Private Secretary to King Edward VIII and King George VI.

76   This was Vladimir Baratchevsky, whom Anna Wolkoff nick-named 'Bara'. As the final section to this book shows, he would later play a significant role in her life.

77   Tyler Kent planned to rent somewhere with a friend from the Code Room at the US Embassy. The friend could have been either Hyman Goldstein or Tevis Wilson. Posted to the London embassy in late October 1939, Wilson was pro-German and anti-British in his utterances. He had a liking for disreputable company that soon embraced not just Tyler Kent, but also a former British Army captain with a drink problem and a stash of illegal firearms.

78   Those profits were so substantial that Huntowski, still just a lowly Navy Department employee, could afford to move into a luxurious Berlin flat previously occupied by a Swedish aristocrat.

79   According to the official version of history, the concept was not formulated until many months later.

Part Five: Keys to the Kingdom

80   Their companion was probably Barbara Allen's Bentley-driving brother-in-law, Geoffrey Allen, who was accustomed to holiday-ing in St Moritz and socializing with celebrities such as the Hollywood mogul, Sam Goldwyn.

81   The Barcelona's upstairs dining room had latterly been colo-nized by a rowdy discussion-group of artists and writers including Dylan Thomas, Humphrey Jennings, Lee Miller, Henry Moore and Lucian Freud.

82   In the summer of 1940, Derek Jackson joined the RAF, where he
      was authorized to develop military applications for his work as
      a research scientist. David Pryce-Jones, author of *Unity Mitford:
      A Quest* (1976), recalled interviewing the pilot of the large
      bomber used as Jackson's mobile laboratory: 'The pilot was a
      man named Ken Davidson. When they were over Germany,
      Jackson would start singing Nazi songs and saying, "We're
      bombing the wrong country. We should be bombing Britain."
      One of Ken's jobs was to make sure the rest of the crew didn't
      attack Jackson.'

83   In the letters Tyler Kent despatched to Moscow, he probably
      heard that Donald H. Nichols's Russian girlfriend – such an
      integral member of their clique – had vanished. Enquiries by
      Nichols revealed that she had been sent to a prison camp in
      Siberia. Nichols had since started dating Kent's former girl-
      friend, Tanya.

84   The American guest was Mrs Rosemary Bull, wife of Bartle
      Bull, MP, who was serving in the Coldstream Guards. She had
      been accompanied to the party by Patricia Dalglish, who had
      other connections to Tyler Kent's current milieu. As well as
      socializing with the Duke del Monte, Dalglish was close to one of
      the Duke's erstwhile colleagues at the Italian Embassy.

85   The new recruit was Barbara Kelly. Since returning from
      Germany, Kelly had been sharing a house with Mabel
      Constanduros, the creator and star of *The Buggins Family*
      (1928–48), the BBC's first radio soap opera.

86   Evidently, Anna Wolkoff was referring to the three-and-a-half-
      month-old telegram in which Churchill had informed Roosevelt
      that American ships, unlike vessels belonging to other neutral
      countries, would not be forced into port and searched.

Part Six: Most Secret and Personal

87   Ludwig Matthias also appears to have inadvertently given his
      MI5 shadows the slip one night after dining at the Trocadero
      Restaurant on Shaftesbury Avenue. They tailed him from there
      to Green Park Underground Station, where he was seen to
      inspect the loitering prostitutes. He engaged one of them in
      conversation, then hustled her into a taxi, which disappeared
      into the blackout before the Watchers could follow.

88   In May 1940, the senior officer at the Reich Security Head Office compiled a list of 2,700 enemies of the Nazi regime. Max Knight – under his favoured alias of 'Captain King', resident of Hood House, Dolphin Square – featured on that list.

89   His novel, *Crime Cargo*, offers plentiful evidence of both his love of American idiom and his painful inability to reproduce it. 'Jumpin' beans!' exclaims one of his characters. 'You Britishers are a swell lot!'

90   In one of the myriad interconnections between the cast of the Kent/Wolkoff saga, that officer was Group Captain Bill Elliott, a close friend of Pamela Jackson, Right Club member and friend of Anna Wolkoff.

91   In fact, Churchill was having second thoughts about the wording of the message to Roosevelt.

92   The hotel was the Royal Oak at Withypool, where the writer, R. D. Blackmore, had written part of his bestselling novel, *Lorna Doone* (1869).

93   The novelist, Len Deighton, who lived next-door to Anna Wolkoff's previous Gloucester Place Mews home as a child, remembers seeing the police arrest her. 'One night I was awakened by the sounds of cars and voices. My mother and father were in their dressing gowns standing at the window. I leaned out of the window and I could see two Wolseley police cars and half-a-dozen men. I vividly remember the curious way the cars were diagonally parked. Anna was put into a car and they drove away.' Given that Wolkoff was no longer living next-door to him in May 1940, the young Deighton must have witnessed a previous arrest, most likely in connection with her activities on behalf of the Nordic League and British Union.

94   One of the more obscure names belonged to Dr James Mellotte, an associate of Captain Ramsay, later suspected of trying to assist a Nazi invasion of Britain from the Irish Republic.

95   William Brinsley Le Poer Trench mixed with Joachim von Ribbentrop, the Comte de Laubespin and prominent members of both the Nordic League and the Link. Dennis Wheatley's stepdaughter, Diana, later married him but the marriage did not last long. After the war, Le Poer Trench edited the *Flying Saucer Review* and set up the International Unidentified Flying Object Observer Corps. Through an improbable sequence of bereavements, he inherited the titles of 8th Earl of Clancarty,

Viscount Dunlo, Baron Trench, Viscount Clancarty and Marquess of Huesden.

96 Lord Sempill, who worked for the Royal Navy Air Service, was doubly fortunate in that he would also avoid being prosecuted for carrying out espionage on behalf of the Japanese military.

Epilogue: A Game of Consequences

97 When he sifted through Anna Wolkoff's papers, Max Knight spotted a Right Club application form completed by someone named Muriel Wright. Two of his Section B5b colleagues were sent round to her address to interview her. Knight was alarmed to discover that she no longer lived there, having found a job with the Government Code and Cipher School at Bletchley Park, where she worked for MI6. 'It is important to note that this discovery considerably strengthens the case against Anna Wolkoff and also the possible conspiracy charges against Captain Ramsay,' he wrote. Though MI6 shared his fears, the Muriel Wright line of inquiry seems to have petered out.

She was the woman whom Wolkoff had bumped into after the Nordic League meeting at Caxton Hall in May 1939. Despite getting Wright to fill out a membership form for the Right Club, Wolkoff appears to have decided against involving her, which explains her absence from the club's membership book.

98 One of those agents, codenamed M/G, was a young, left-wing Austrian refugee named Friedl Gaertner. She would go on to contribute to the famous D-Day deception scheme. Max Knight had earlier persuaded Dennis Wheatley to provide Gaertner with cover-employment as a research assistant. Under instruction from Knight, who wanted her to infiltrate the London branch of the Nazi Party, she posed as a fascist sympathizer.

99 The BBC did not identify William Joyce as the speaker, though there was evidence that he had been appearing on the New British Broadcasting Service. 'Reports concerning the nationality of the announcer are conflicting,' noted a BBC monitoring bulletin several weeks earlier. 'Some of the monitors maintain that the accent is Irish, others that it is English. Another listener [...] thought he detected a resemblance to one of the Bremen announcers.' Joyce was, of course, not only a frequent broadcaster on Radio Bremen but also an Irishman with a hard-to-place accent.

100 MI5's case against Dolly Newnham made use of a report that quoted her as saying, 'I am so impatient [for a German invasion] and wish Hitler was already here – I can hardly wait.'

101 The verdict did not prevent the government from using Regulation 18b to keep Mrs Nicholson in detention. She remained there until late 1941 when a hearing of the Home Office Advisory Committee led to her release. Enduringly fascinated by the supernatural, she went on to become Honorary Secretary of the Ghost Club, whose members included Dennis Wheatley and the comedian Peter Sellers.

102 Dr Gottfried Roesel, leader of the Central London branch of the Nazi Party, also ran a Nazi propaganda organization called the Anglo–German Information Service. Before the war, he had worked closely with the British Union as well as the Link, the fascist organization run by his next-door neighbour, Admiral Sir Barry Domvile, who was a friend of Anna Wolkoff's parents. Domvile inevitably features on the White List of potential collaborators. The other Right Club members on the list are the Duke of Wellington, Francis Yeats-Brown, Sir Ernest Bennett, A. K. Chesterton, Peter and Dorothy Eckersley, Arnold Leese and Lord Sempill.

103 In 1947 Arnold Leese, veteran fascist and Right Club member, was one of eight British fascists who were prosecuted and imprisoned for this. They appear to have been part of a larger network whose activities were monitored by MI5 telephone taps.

104 One of those fascists was 'Mrs Gallagher', probably Mrs Myra Gallagher, against whom MI5 already had firm evidence. An Austrian with British nationality through marriage, Myra Gallagher had been a client at Anna Wolkoff's shop, where she ran up a huge unpaid bill.

105 MI6's discovery appears to have occurred sometime before the end of May 1940. There is evidence to suggest that the organization responded by breaching the rules, too. One of their agents, Sir Paul Dukes, hero of a daredevil mission during the Russian Revolution, proceeded to establish himself as a regular at the Russian Tea Rooms. Being someone who loathed the Nazis just as much as he loathed the Communists, he was unlikely to have patronized the place for any reason other than work.

106 They lived at The Homestead, 47 Park Road, Camberley, Surrey, where Max Knight and his menagerie would remain for many years.

107 Irene Danischewsky resumed her marriage when her husband, Alex, returned from fighting for the British Army in Burma. She told the historian, John Costello, who tracked her down in 1982, that she had eventually confessed to her late husband about the affair and that they had gone on to enjoy a happy marriage. In Costello's notes on the conversation, he observed that she was 'very alarmed and upset' by his call because her family was unaware that she and a convicted spy had enjoyed an adulterous wartime romance. She added that she was 'quite alone' and that 'publicity would mean exposure and make life not worth living'. Her niece, Katherine, sister of the actress Helen Mirren, has confirmed that Irene 'cut herself off from the rest of the family'.

108 Clara Hyatt's ex-husband, A. Dana Hodgson had, curiously enough, travelled with Tyler Kent from America to Eastern Europe in 1934 as part of the same group of State Department employees. Hodgson – another womanizer – had been posted to the US Consulate in the Finnish capital.

109 Admiral Wolkoff was freed in January 1944. Three years before that, Mme Wolkoff had persuaded her friend, Grand Duchess Xenia, to spend part of a Christmas visit to Balmoral lobbying King George VI to help secure her husband's release. Remembering 'the kindnesses which King George [had] shown her husband' in the past, Mme Wolkoff had been optimistic about this strategy. The long delay between then and Admiral Wolkoff's release suggests that her optimism was not justified.

110 Hans Georg von Mackensen's telegram to Berlin was found among a cache of German Foreign Ministry records, preserved by a former employee.

111 Neither Sylvester A. Huntowski nor Jack Marsalka, both of whom would have been viable candidates, were part of Bullitt's initial team.

112 A few weeks after Kent left Moscow, Henry W. Antheil was transferred to Helsinki. In June 1940, he took a commercial flight to the Estonian capital on official business. The airliner vanished before it got there. Matters might have been clarified

by the ensuing inquiry, but this was stymied by the Soviet invasion of Estonia the following weekend. The mystery of Antheil's death had to wait over seventy-five years for a solution. His plane turned out to have been shot down by Soviet aircraft imposing the aerial blockade of Estonia.

When his possessions were gathered together, a colleague found cards with the combination of the Code Room safe written on them. Further inspection of Antheil's wardrobe revealed a folder containing government cables that had been amended. Grounds for even greater suspicion were provided by the discovery that he had been leaking sections of the reports sent from the Moscow embassy to Washington, DC. Fishy though these revelations appeared, an inquiry by the State Department unearthed explanations that had nothing to do with espionage.

Antheil's falsification of messages was motivated by a desire to foil State Department attempts to transfer him to another embassy. His desire to remain in Helsinki originated from his having recently acquired a Finnish fiancée, whom he feared wouldn't be allowed to accompany him abroad. Even the leaks were unrelated to espionage. He had been sending the extracts to his brother, a vigorous opponent of totalitarianism, who was writing articles for *Esquire* magazine. The information was used to publicize both the conflict brewing in Europe and the brutality of Stalin's regime.

During the mid-1950s, rumours surfaced that Antheil had been a Russian agent. These appear to have sprung from an insider who had heard about the earlier State Department probe. The FBI then conducted its own investigation, which exonerated Antheil. Rumours about him being a spy have nonetheless lingered along with claims that he was an agent of the NKVD spymaster, Alexander Feklisov, alias Alexander Fomin. Yet Feklisov was not involved in espionage until after Antheil had left the Soviet Union. And when Antheil was based in Helsinki, Feklisov was working in Washington, DC.

113 The first of these films comprised a general portrait of his menagerie. The second film was about an orphaned cuckoo named 'Goo', which he had painstakingly reared and then trained, ready for its release back into the wild.

114 In the immediate post-war years, Fay Taylour also found her way to Hollywood. She raced cars and worked as a saleswoman

for a Beverly Hills-based dealership specializing in Rolls-Royces, Jaguars and other luxury British cars.

115 The conjectural nature of this was highlighted by Kevin Quinlan in his PhD thesis, 'Human Intelligence, Tradecraft and MI5 Operations in Britain'. Quinlan's overall analysis of the Kent/Wolkoff case is supported by Christopher Andrew, author of the definitive history of MI5, which draws on otherwise closed Security Service files.

Index

478 | Index